Behavioral Interventions in Cognitive Behavior Therapy

Behavioral Interventions in Cognitive Behavior Therapy

PRACTICAL GUIDANCE FOR PUTTING THEORY INTO ACTION

SECOND EDITION

Richard F. Farmer
Alexander L. Chapman

AMERICAN PSYCHOLOGICAL ASSOCIATION
WASHINGTON, DC

Published by
American Psychological Association
750 First Street, NE
Washington, DC 20002
www.apa.org

To order
APA Order Department
P.O. Box 92984
Washington, DC 20090-2984
Tel: (800) 374-2721; Direct: (202) 336-5510
Fax: (202) 336-5502; TDD/TTY: (202) 336-6123
Online: www.apa.org/pubs/books
E-mail: order@apa.org

In the U.K., Europe, Africa, and the Middle East, copies may be ordered from
American Psychological Association
3 Henrietta Street
Covent Garden, London
WC2E 8LU England

Typeset in Goudy by Circle Graphics, Inc., Columbia, MD

Printer: Bang Printing, Brainerd, MN
Cover Designer: Berg Design, Albany, NY

The opinions and statements published are the responsibility of the authors, and such opinions and statements do not necessarily represent the policies of the American Psychological Association.

Library of Congress Cataloging-in-Publication Data

Farmer, Richard F. (Psychology professor)
  Behavioral interventions in cognitive behavior therapy : practical guidance for putting theory into action / by Richard F. Farmer and Alexander L. Chapman. — Second edition.
    pages cm
  Includes bibliographical references and index.
  ISBN 978-1-4338-2035-9 — ISBN 1-4338-2035-8 1. Cognitive therapy—Methodology.
I. Chapman, Alexander L. (Alexander Lawrence) II. American Psychological Association.
III. Title.
  RC489.C63F37 2016
  616.89'1425—dc23
                                        2015005749

British Library Cataloguing-in-Publication Data

A CIP record is available from the British Library.

Printed in the United States of America
Second Edition

http://dx.doi.org/10.1037/14691-000

CONTENTS

Behavioral Interventions in Cognitive Behavior Therapy

1

OVERVIEW

Cognitive behavior therapy (CBT) has emerged as a widely used and efficacious treatment approach for a variety of psychological conditions (Dobson & Khatri, 2000; Hofmann, Asnaani, Vonk, Sawyer, & Fang, 2012; Tolin, 2010), including depression, anxiety disorders, personality disorders, substance abuse disorders, eating disorders, and couple's distress. CBT is, however, a broad and heterogeneous concept that represents a variety of therapeutic approaches that emphasize, to varying degrees, cognitive, behavioral, emotional, physiological, and environmental factors in relation to psychological disorders (Forman & Herbert, 2009). There are at least 10 schools that can be identified under the umbrella of CBT (David & Szentagotai, 2006). One of these is represented by the influential cognitive approach to understanding and treating psychological disorders advanced by Aaron T. Beck (1963, 1976; A. T. Beck, Freeman, & Associates, 1990) and his daughter, Judith S. Beck (2005, 2011). A primary assumption of their model is that

http://dx.doi.org/10.1037/14691-001
Behavioral Interventions in Cognitive Behavior Therapy: Practical Guidance for Putting Theory Into Action,
Second Edition, by R. F. Farmer and A. L. Chapman

distorted and dysfunctional thinking influences mood and behavior and that such biased forms of thinking are common to all psychological disorders. Associated theory additionally holds that each specific form of psychological disorder is defined by a unique set of thought distortions and underlying core beliefs unique to that condition. An implication of this model is that therapeutic activities should be geared toward the promotion of realistic, accurate, and balanced thinking and that the modification of thinking will, in turn, produce associated changes in mood and behavior. An additional assumption of this model is that the modification of underlying beliefs, or schemas, is required to bring about lasting therapeutic change (J. S. Beck, 2011).

Cognitive perspectives that have informed developments in CBT vary in the degree to which the environment is viewed as a determinant of thinking, emotion, and action. Some cognitive theories, for example, emphasize a cognitively constructed environment over the physical environment as the primary determinant of emotion and behavior (e.g., Mahoney, 1991). Other models highlight the role of concepts such as schemas, which are regarded as cognitive structures central to the evaluation and interpretation of experiences that, in some instances, also predispose persons to emotional and behavioral disorders (e.g., J. E. Young, Rygh, Weinberger, & Beck, 2014). Other cognitive-oriented theories place the environment on equal footing with perceptions of the self or environment as determinants of behavior and emotion (e.g., Bandura, 1986).

In contrast to models that emphasize the predisposing or causal properties of cognitive constructs, behavior theory and therapy generally avoid ascribing mental concepts a causal role in behavior and instead place primary emphasis on the physical environment (Baum, 2005). From a behavioral perspective, thinking and emotional responding are examples of behavior and are subject to many of the same influences as more observable behaviors. Later in this chapter, we highlight several primary determinants of behavior from a behavioral perspective (which are further elaborated in detail in Chapter 2) as well as the various origins of cognitive and behavior therapies. Perhaps because of their different origins and frequently conflicting theories regarding the determinants of behavior, there has occasionally been an uneasy marriage between these two psychotherapy traditions. Indeed, the term *cognitive behavior therapy* incorporates several points of view that can, at times, be contradictory or even incompatible.

Many excellent resources describe cognitive-oriented therapeutic interventions geared toward the modification of evaluations, attitudes, underlying beliefs, and schemas (e.g., A. T. Beck, Rush, Shaw, & Emery, 1979; J. S. Beck, 2011; Burns, 1980; Dobson, 2010; Leahy, 2003; J. E. Young et al., 2014). Although we touch on cognitive therapy and cognitive change techniques throughout this book, we primarily highlight and emphasize the theory, rationale, and application of behavioral interventions within CBT. Even though cognitive and behavioral interventions can occasionally be at odds in relation to therapeutic assumptions and goals, we also strive to highlight areas of compatibility and instances in which integration is desirable or possible.

BEHAVIORAL INTERVENTIONS IN CBT: UNDERLYING ASSUMPTIONS AND COMMON FEATURES

In this section, we provide an overview of behavioral perspectives on abnormality and psychological disorders. We also briefly review several of the core underlying assumptions associated with behavior therapy and behavioral interventions. We then discuss some of the primary features that differentiate behavior therapies from other approaches.

Behavioral Views on Abnormality

Within psychology and psychiatry, "deviant" or "defect" models of abnormality predominate (Farmer & Nelson-Gray, 2005; Martell, Addis, & Jacobson, 2001). That is, individuals who have psychological disorders or who display problematic behaviors are often regarded as deviant or abnormal, principally on the basis of what he or she presumably has. Within cognitive therapy, for example, those with psychological disorders are often regarded as having maladaptive schemas that serve as psychological nuclei of behavioral and emotional disorders (A. T. Beck et al., 1990; J. E. Young et al., 2014). Within medical model approaches, diseases or dysfunctional biological processes are often presumed to underlie psychiatric syndromes (Charney, Sklar, Buxbaum, & Nestler, 2013). Within psychodynamic models, the quality, integration, and differentiation of internalized self and other mental representations and the relative maturity of inner defensive coping mechanisms are viewed as etiologically relevant for psychological disorders (Kernberg, Selzer, Koenigsberg, Carr, & Appelbaum, 1989). In each instance, the presumed internal defect that the person has (e.g., maladaptive schemas, aberrant neurochemistry, malevolent internalized self and object relations) is targeted for therapy; it is assumed that this internal anomaly must be changed, removed, or altered in some way if the person is to no longer be deviant or disordered.

Behavior theory and therapy have a different view. Within behavioral traditions, the search for internal causes of behavior is largely avoided. Although it is acknowledged that genetic endowments might predispose individuals to respond in certain ways when relevant situational features are present (Skinner, 1971, 1989), the behavioral tradition is primarily concerned with what one does and the contexts within which behavior occurs (R. O. Nelson & Hayes, 1986b; Nelson-Gray & Farmer, 1999). Furthermore, from the behavioral perspective, notions of what constitutes normality and abnormality are found in cultural norms, values, and practices. Culture provides the context for referencing which behaviors are acceptable or valued and which are deviant (Baum, 2005). Notions of what are normal or abnormal behaviors occasionally shift as cultural values and practices change over time. In the mid-1800s in the United States, for example, the Louisiana Medical Association produced a report that proposed a mental disease unique to Black slaves called *drapetomania*, or a mania to seek freedom, which caused slaves to run away from their masters (Zimbardo & Gerrig, 1996). Similarly, before the mid-1970s, both the American Psychiatric Association and the American Psychological Association regarded homosexuality as a form of mental disorder (Morin & Rothblum, 1991).

From a behavioral perspective, the determinants of what might be regarded as abnormal behavior are no different from the determinants that shape and maintain normal behavior. What is regarded as "psychopathology" in some quarters is often viewed from a behavioral perspective as a "problem in living," or a justifiable response to dysfunctional or stressful environments, which may be further exacerbated by inadequate behavioral repertoires for responding to or coping with life's problems. Indeed, evidence suggests that the emergence of at least one episode of a major mental disorder by the end of early adulthood is the rule rather than the exception for persons in the general population (Farmer, Seeley, Kosty, Olino, & Lewinsohn, 2013; Moffitt et al., 2010). Consistent with such data, the behavioral perspective assumes that there is nothing inherently defective or deviant about persons who report emotional or behavioral problems.

Behavioral Interventions Within CBT: Description and Application

Some people have unpleasant reactions to terms such as *behavior therapy*, *behavior modification*, or *behaviorism*. As noted by Martell et al. (2001), such terms tend "to call up associations with rats, mazes, M&Ms, and an obsession with predicting and controlling people's actions" (p. xxv). Although sometimes it is easy to understand how these reactions might have come about, it is also true that these reactions are often the result of a profound misunderstanding of behavior theory and behavioral approaches to therapy (Todd & Morris, 1983). Just like Martell and colleagues (2001), we ask that if you have any preconceptions about behavior theory and therapy, you suspend these for the time being because contemporary behavior theory and therapy might not be what you think it is.

A Focus on Behavior and Its Context

Behavioral perspectives are associated with a number of assumptions about the individual, the context within which he or she lives, and the factors that influence his or her behavior. As suggested earlier, psychological disorders from a behavioral perspective are defined by behavior, occurring both within the individual (sometimes called *covert behavior*) and as overt actions that can be observed by others (or *overt behavior*). Behavioral perspectives on psychological disorders are further concerned with the functional relationships that exist between the behavior of a person and the environment that establishes the context for such behavior. Within some forms of behavior theory, the *three-term contingency* represents the basic unit of analysis (Skinner, 1969). When applied to behavior therapy, the three-term contingency concept refers to the interaction of the person with his or her environment and includes three elements: the occasion within which behavior occurs, the behavior itself, and the consequences that follow behavior. When behavior therapists attempt to develop hypotheses about behavior, this framework is often used.

The first of these three elements, the *antecedents of behavior*, includes conditions or stimuli that set the occasion for behavior to occur. Antecedent conditions or stimuli can include specific persons, places, objects, or events. Among the factors that influence whether a person will engage in a particular form of behavior in a given setting is the person's learning history for such behavior under similar conditions. That is, if a certain form of behavior was performed in similar situations before, and if such behavior resulted in reinforcing outcomes, then the behavior is more likely to occur in comparable future environments.

The second of these three elements, *behavior*, refers to anything a person does. This includes not only behavior that other people can potentially observe another person do, such as speak or perform some other physical movement, but also covert behaviors. Covert behaviors are those behaviors that occur "within the skin" or on the inside, and are at least observable or noticeable by the person within which they occur. Such covert behaviors would include thoughts, emotions, and physical sensations.

The last element of the three-term contingency, *consequences*, refers to the effect that behavior produces. Technically speaking, behavior is reinforced if the consequences that follow behavior increase the likelihood of that behavior again occurring on future occasions. Conversely, a behavior is punished if the consequences that follow decrease the likelihood of that behavior again occurring in similar future situations.

A Focus on Why People Act the Way They Do

When behaviorally oriented clinicians talk about the function of behavior, they are basically talking about *why* people behave the way they do.

Functionalism is based on Darwinian evolutionary principles (Farmer & Nelson-Gray, 2005; Rachlin, 1976). In Darwinian evolutionary theory, the physical structure of a particular species is determined by its associated function. Natural selection involves the selection of the most adaptive physical structures on the basis of functional properties associated with that structure—namely, those associated with the enhancement of gene fitness. In behavior theory, the behavior of an individual that is functional in particular environmental contexts (i.e., produces reinforcing consequences) is selected or made more likely, whereas behavior that is not functional (i.e., does not produce reinforcing consequences) is not selected or, over time, becomes extinguished.

Within functional or selectionist accounts of human behavior, behavior is largely, if not exclusively, determined (Hull, Langman, & Glenn, 2001). For selection to occur, there must be variation along some dimension because the absence of variation precludes the possibility of differential selection. In behavior theory, forms of behavior produced by an individual vary, and some units of behavior are selected because they prove more successful than others (Baum, 2005). Similarly, the selection of cultural replicators (e.g., customs, rules, values) involves the process of selection acting on variations and the transmission of selected practices from one member of a group to another through behavior transfer processes such as imitation, modeling, reinforcement for rule following, and arrangement of social contingencies (Baum, 2005; Schneider, 2012). Those cultural practices that prove to be the most beneficial or enhance fitness tend to be retained by a culture over time. *Environmental determinism* is the overarching process associated with the selection of variations in an individual's behavior during his or her lifetime and in cultural practices over successive generations (Skinner, 1981).

Behavioral accounts are also often associated with the concept of *contextualism*. Contextual approaches to the study of behavior emphasize how events and behavior are organized and linked together in meaningful ways (i.e., "the act in context"). Contextualism, then, is primarily concerned with the context within which behavior is embedded or the contextual flow in which behavior occurs (Hayes, Hayes, Reese, & Sarbin, 1993).

Common Features Among Behavioral Assessments

The focus of contemporary therapies varies in accordance with underlying theory and presumed mechanisms of behavior change. Interpersonal therapies, for example, tend to focus on social behavior and relations with others. Cognitive therapies focus on automatic thoughts, underlying assumptions, and schemas. Humanistic therapies tend to emphasize immediate experiences, emotions, and the provision of validation by the therapist for these experiences and emotions. Psychodynamic therapies emphasize historical material, mental representations of self and other, and the use of particular defense mechanisms. Biological therapies generally emphasize neurochemical functions and neurocircuit activity. Each form of therapy targets what is understood through associated theory to be the most central determinant or cause of problematic behavior. Consequently, the types of interventions used and the means through which they are delivered vary considerably across these general classes of therapies.

Contemporary behavior therapies are primarily concerned about the contexts within which a client's problematic behavior occurs. This is because behavior therapists place emphasis on potentially modifiable antecedents and consequences associated with the maintenance of problematic behavior (Follette, Naugle, & Linnerooth, 2000). Behavior therapists are also concerned with the client's behavioral repertoire on the basis of the idea that some clients display problematic behaviors because they have not yet learned alternative and more adaptive forms of action. In the case of behavioral deficits, for example, a behaviorally oriented therapist might seek to teach new behaviors that can replace or substitute for problematic behaviors. Behavior therapists also assess a client's motivation for change. Generally, a behavior therapist thinks about the concept of motivation somewhat differently than do therapists from other orientations. Rather than viewing motivation as an inner drive or some other inner force that causes people to act, behavior therapists are more inclined to view motivation as a state or condition resulting from environmental events (an idea we develop more fully in the next chapter when describing establishing operations and rules). When viewed in this way, motivation is modifiable, something that can be increased or decreased as a result of environmental manipulations.

In the behavioral assessment of clients, several features associated with the functional context of behavior are assessed and evaluated (Farmer & Nelson-Gray, 2005; Hayes, Strosahl, Bunting, Twohig, & Wilson, 2004). Among these are the following areas:

- *The antecedents of problematic behavior.* Are there situations in which problematic behaviors frequently occur? Are there common internal antecedents that immediately precede such behavior? What environmental cues have been previously associated with reinforcement for behavior and accordingly occasion behavior when present in current situations? Are there verbal rules that govern problematic behavior (e.g., "If I make myself vomit afterward, I can eat this ice cream and not gain any weight.")? Are there establishing operations that increase the reinforcing value of certain behaviors (e.g., engagement in overly restrictive dieting practices as an establishing operation for subsequent binge-eating episodes)?

- *The consequences of problematic behavior.* What are the consequences that follow problematic behavior? Are the short-term consequences similar to or different from the longer term consequences? Are positive reinforcing (rewarding) consequences instrumental in the maintenance of behavior, or are negative reinforcing (relieving) consequences more likely influencing behavior?
- *The client's learning history as it relates to current problematic behaviors.* What factors in the client's past shaped and established the behaviors that the client seeks to change? Are these factors of any influence today?
- *The client's current behavioral repertoire.* A comprehensive assessment of the client's behavioral repertoire would cover four response domains: overt motor behaviors, thoughts and mental images, emotions, and physiological sensations.
  - *Overt behaviors.* What forms do the client's problem behaviors take? Does the client display effective coping, social, and problem-solving skills? Is the person's behavioral repertoire sufficiently large to allow for the possibility of responding flexibly in common situations? Do avoidance coping repertoires predominate? Are there behavioral excesses that are problematic (e.g., substance abuse, gambling, risky sexual behavior)?
  - *Thoughts.* Is the person plagued by negative evaluations of self, world, or future? Does the person confuse evaluations of events and objects with the actual events and objects ("I am a bad person," versus "I am having the evaluation that I am a bad person, but thinking this doesn't necessarily make it so.")? Are experiences such as emotions and evaluative thoughts about those experiences fused (e.g., "Anxiety is bad and must be avoided.")? Is the client preoccupied with the past or anticipated future possibilities? Is the client able to be fully in the present moment and respond as effectively as possible to what is occurring?
  - *Emotions.* Does the client excessively experience negative emotions? Are the client's expressed emotional experiences appropriate in situations in which they are displayed (e.g., are they restricted, exaggerated, intense, or excessive)? Is the client highly emotionally reactive or flat in his or her emotional responsiveness?
  - *Physiological sensations or responses.* Do certain physiological responses define part of a larger response pattern (e.g., flushing or sweating while also experiencing anxiety-related

emotions)? Does the client associate normal physiological activity with catastrophic outcomes (e.g., an increased heart rate is associated with an impending heart attack, shortness of breath is associated with smothering, feelings of fullness after a meal are associated with becoming fat)?

- *The client's motivation for change.* Does the client indicate a willingness or motivation to change his or her behavior? Can the client articulate personal values or goals? Is the client's current behavior consistent with his or her values or goals? Is the client aware of likely outcomes associated with unhealthy patterns of behavior and, if so, does this affect the client's behavior?

Decisions as to which behavioral interventions are appropriate are decided individually for each client given the outcomes associated with assessments of these areas. That is, behavior theory and therapy suggest that the factors that influence behavior vary across individuals. Even though two people may have similar problematic behavior patterns, it is recognized that factors accounting for these behavior problems likely differ. Several typologies of alcoholism, for example, suggest at least two distinct subtypes. One type is characterized by persons who display anxious-dependent traits, binge drinking versus continuous episodes, and avoidant coping styles, and the other type is exemplified by an early age of onset, continuous versus episodic binge drinking, and engagement in aggressive or criminal behavior when intoxicated (Wulfert, Greenway, & Dougher, 1996). Whereas the form of problematic behavior might appear to be the same among members of both groups (e.g., excessive drinking), the hypothesized maintaining factors associated with each subtype—negative reinforcement processes in the former and positive reinforcement processes in the latter—suggest different functional properties associated with the same behavior across individuals.

Common Features Among Behavioral Interventions

In Chapters 4 through 10, we discuss specific behavioral interventions in greater detail. There are a number of general characteristics of behavioral interventions (Farmer & Nelson-Gray, 2005; O'Leary & Wilson, 1987; Spiegler & Guevremont, 2010), some of which other schools of therapy share, including the following:

- *An empirical orientation,* as reflected in its grounding in the basic behavioral sciences, use of empirically supported intervention strategies, and use of ongoing assessments of the client's behaviors targeted for therapeutic change.
- *Therapist–client collaboration,* in which the client is an active participant in the therapeutic process and the client and therapist

work together to develop a formulation of the client's problem areas and a plan for therapy based on this formulation.

- An *active orientation*, in which clients are actively encouraged to do something about their problem areas rather than only talk about them.
- A *flexible approach*, in which hypotheses concerning the client's problem areas undergo continuous testing and evaluation, with the overall client formulation and corresponding therapeutic activities modified and adjusted as warranted by new information or observations.
- An *emphasis on environment–behavior relations*, with clients described in terms of what they do; that is, the actions they perform and the thoughts, emotions, and physical sensations they experience. These actions are further conceptualized with reference to the situational contexts within which they occur.
- A *time-limited and present focus*, in which the time allotted for therapy varies in accordance with the nature and severity of the problem areas addressed in therapy, with emphasis placed on one's current situation rather than the past.
- A *problem and learning focus*, in which solutions to problematic behaviors are sought, with these solutions often geared toward teaching new or adaptive behaviors, changing aspects of dysfunctional environments, or providing relevant information about behaviors of interest.
- An *emphasis on both change and acceptance processes*, in which interventions that promote therapeutic change are undertaken in a context that conveys valuation of the client and encourages the development of client self-validation and the adoption of a nonjudgmental approach to the experience of thoughts, feelings, and bodily sensations as they occur.

AN OVERVIEW OF THE HISTORY OF BEHAVIOR THERAPY AND BEHAVIORAL INTERVENTIONS WITHIN CBT

A review of the history of the behavior therapy movement establishes a context for understanding the foundational role of behavioral interventions in CBT. The next sections offer a brief overview of the history of the movement. More detailed accounts are provided elsewhere (Dobson & Dozois, 2001; Farmer & Nelson-Gray, 2005; Hayes, 2004a; Kazdin, 1978; O'Donohue, 1998).

Basic Theories of Learning

The theoretical roots of contemporary behavioral interventions are found in the foundations of modern learning theories. In the late 1800s and early 1900s, Russian physiologists such as Ivan Sechenov, Vladimir Bechterev, and Ivan Pavlov investigated reflexive and conditioning processes. This body of research eventuated into the learning paradigm referred to as *respondent* or *classical conditioning*. The basic idea behind classical conditioning is that some environmental stimuli, when presented in a particular way, yield a reflexive, innate (or unlearned) response. For example, when a rubber hammer is struck right below the kneecap (*unconditioned stimulus*, or UCS), a reflexive knee-jerk response follows (which in this case would be an *unconditioned response*, or UCR). The knee-jerk is an unlearned, innate response to the type of stimulation that a rubber hammer strike against the knee produces.

In the case of classical conditioning, Pavlov (1927) and colleagues demonstrated that a neutral object or event, when repeatedly paired or associated with the UCS, will come to acquire certain stimulus properties over time (i.e., this previously neutral stimulus will become a *conditioned stimulus*, or CS). This CS, in turn, will come to elicit a response (i.e., a *conditioned response*, or CR) under some circumstances that appears quite similar to the UCR produced by the UCS. Pavlov and colleagues further demonstrated that CRs often occurred in the presence of stimuli that resembled or were similar to the CS in some way, a process called *generalization*. Additionally, Pavlov found that if the CS was repeatedly presented without the UCS, the CR would eventually disappear. This process was referred to as *extinction*.

In clinical contexts, classical conditioning processes are perhaps most evident in the conditioned emotional responses that some clients have acquired to stimulus events that, on the surface, seem quite neutral. This is perhaps most strikingly apparent in the case of emotional reactions to trauma-related stimulus cues. What becomes a traumatic event for an individual can often be thought of as a UCS that, at the time of the original trauma, elicits a number of reflexive or unlearned responses (UCR), such as fear. By definition, persons with posttraumatic stress disorder have strong emotional reactions, or CRs, to events or objects (CSs) that are in some way similar to those that were present at the time the original traumatic event occurred. Even though these CSs, or trauma-related cues, are no longer directly associated with the original UCS, they nonetheless continue to elicit CRs that look and feel like the original UCRs. Classical conditioning processes have similarly been suggested in the acquisition of some phobias (Merckelbach, Arntz, & deJong, 1991).

During the late 1800s and early 1900s in the United States, experimental investigations into learning processes were also beginning to take place, starting with Edward Thorndike's (1898) doctoral research. In his research with hungry cats, Thorndike demonstrated that the time latencies for displaying escape behaviors that allow access to food (e.g., pulling on a wire loop to open a door) decreased gradually and steadily over successive trials. In accounting for his observations, Thorndike proposed that it was the consequences associated with the cats' actions that determined whether such actions would be strengthened. If a response typically resulted in reward—in this case, access to food—then it would be strengthened. Those actions, however, that did not result in reward would, over time, become weakened. In Thorndike's theory, referred to as the *law of effect*, the learning process and associated behaviors are influenced by the consequences that follow behavior.

B. F. Skinner further developed and refined Thorndike's theory of instrumental behavior, which resulted in an *operant theory of behavior*. An operant was defined by Skinner (1938) as a unit of behavior that operates on the environment by producing consequences. Whereas in classical conditioning a stimulus (S) event elicits a response (R), or S → R, in operant conditioning, the concept of selection by consequence (C) was emphasized, or R → C. That is, Skinner suggested that much of the behavior that people display is selected and shaped over the course of a lifetime by the consequences that such behavior produces. Skinner regarded selection by consequence as a form of ontogenetic selection. In addition to ontogenetic selection processes, Skinner (1981) proposed that human behavior is also the result of phylogenetic selection processes (or Darwinian or natural selection) and cultural selection processes (or the selection of cultural practices based on their associated consequences). A common core element associated with each form of selection (phylogenetic, ontogenetic, and cultural) is evolutionary theory. As suggested by Skinner (1981), human behavior is

> the joint product of (i) the contingencies of survival responsible for the natural selection of the species and (ii) the contingencies of reinforcement responsible for the repertoires acquired by its members, including (iii) the special contingencies maintained by an evolved social environment. (Ultimately, of course, it is all a matter of natural selection, since operant conditioning is an evolved process, of which cultural practices are special applications). (p. 213)

When applied to accounts of human behavior, the theory of selection by consequences suggests that the effects produced by behavior directly influence future behavior (see also Biglan, 2003). Several of the behavioral interventions described in this book are based on this basic principle.

Early Applications of Learning Theories to Behavior Change

Although the first empirical observations that eventuated into modern learning theory go back to the late 1800s and early 1900s, it was not until the early 1960s that therapeutic interventions based on behavioral principles began to have widespread influence. There were, however, some early efforts to apply learning theory to behavior change. Examples include the work of Mary Cover Jones (1924), who demonstrated that a child's fear of an animal could be decreased through counterconditioning methods, in which the feared stimulus (in this case, a rabbit) is paired with a positive stimulus (in this case, the child's favorite food). The bell and pad method for treating enuresis developed by Mowrer and Mowrer (1938) is another example, as is Andrew Salter's (1949) book-length treatise on therapy methods grounded in Pavlovian conditioning. These early efforts to translate behavioral principles and modern learning theory into behavior change techniques, however, did not result in an immediate impact on clinical research and practice.

The Emergence of Behavior Therapy

More than 50 years elapsed between the first experimental studies on basic learning processes and the formal beginnings of the behavior therapy movement. In the late 1950s, important simultaneous developments took place in three countries, the aggregate of which heralded the beginnings of behavior therapy (Kazdin, 1978). In 1958, Joseph Wolpe, a psychiatrist working in South Africa, published the first manualized treatment protocol. The treatment was based on the behavior-change principle that he termed *reciprocal inhibition*, which, in turn, was grounded in Pavlovian and Hullian behavior theory. Wolpe suggested that anxiety or neurotic states could be reduced or eliminated by pairing the experience of anxiety with an incompatible feeling state, such as relaxation. The publication of the treatment procedure allowed clinicians and researchers worldwide to evaluate the efficacy of this approach and its associated underlying theory.

Hans Eysenck (1959), a psychologist in England, published a paper that introduced the term *behavior therapy* to a broad audience. (Although Lindsley, Skinner, & Solomon [1953] as well as Lazarus [1958] published works before Eysenck that used the term behavior therapy, the dissemination of these works was more restricted.) This was followed in 1960 with the publication of an edited book that described a number of treatment methods, such as desensitization, negative practice, and aversion therapy (Eysenck, 1960). Evident among these treatment techniques was the influence of Pavlovian learning theory, most notably notions of classical conditioning and extinction. This book was the first to bring together diverse treatment applications under the name of behavior therapy. In 1963, Eysenck established the journal *Behaviour Research and Therapy*, the first professional journal of its type.

In the United States during the late 1950s and early 1960s, behavioral techniques based on Skinnerian principles of operant conditioning were being developed and evaluated. Operant learning principles and methods were applied to the behavior of children (Bijou & Baer, 1966), persons with developmental disabilities (Lovaas, Freitag, Gold, & Kassorla, 1965), and those with psychosis (Ayllon & Michael, 1959). By the mid-1960s, the term *behavior modification* became widely applied to the practice of applying learning principles to producing behavior change (e.g., Krasner & Ullmann, 1965; Ullmann & Krasner, 1965). The 1970s also witnessed an emergence of behavioral assessment technologies to complement behavior modification approaches (Ciminero, Calhoun, & Adams, 1977; Goldfried & Kent, 1972; R. O. Nelson, 1977).

The Emergence of CBT

Although early manifestations of cognitive therapy can be found in the work of George Kelly (1955), Albert Ellis (1957), and Aaron T. Beck (1963), it was not until the 1970s and 1980s that contemporary CBT became firmly established and gained considerable momentum. Bandura's (1977) *social learning theory*, later termed *social cognitive theory* (Bandura, 1986), elevated symbolic cognitive processes to determinants of behavior. In his theory of reciprocal determinism, for example, behavior, cognitive factors, and environmental influences reciprocally and continuously interact and influence one another. For his concept of self-efficacy, Bandura proposed that an individual's beliefs about his or her personal efficacy, or ability to successfully perform coping behavior, were determinants of whether such behavior will be demonstrated. The social learning theory movement was influenced not only by fundamental learning principles but also by principles derived from basic research in experimental and social psychology (O'Donohue, 1998). At this time, the "cognitive revolution" was well underway within academic psychology, and clinicians and researchers sought to incorporate cognitive mediators of learning into their models of abnormal behavior. In so doing, greater use was made of unobservable, hypothetical constructs to explain behavior. Although this was already a feature of some learning theories (e.g., Wolpe, Eysenck), the use of nonobservable or nonmanipulable constructs or processes to explain behavior was generally avoided by those from an operant learning perspective (e.g., Skinner).

Beginning around the late 1970s, interest in behavior therapies began to wane. One factor that contributed to this was the cognitive revolution, now firmly established and highly influential within academic psychology. Another was the publication of several groundbreaking scholarly works that described new and innovative therapies largely consisting of cognitive restructuring interventions (see Dobson & Dozois, 2001, for a review), including A. T. Beck and colleagues' (1979) treatment manual titled *Cognitive Therapy of Depression*. Similarly, around this time, a number of influential books on CBT were beginning to be published (e.g., Mahoney, 1974; Meichenbaum, 1977).

A defining feature of cognitive therapies, both historically and currently, is the strong emphasis on the cognitive mediation of behavior—specifically, how individuals interpret their world, view themselves, or think about the future (A. T. Beck et al., 1979). Central cognitive concepts such as automatic thoughts, processing biases, core beliefs, and schemas are often used to explain variations in emotion and behavior and are central treatment targets in many cognitive therapies. From a cognitive therapy perspective, primary therapeutic tasks involve assisting clients by identifying their idiosyncratic way of thinking and modifying thought processes through rational examination and logic (e.g., examining the evidence for or against a thought, evaluating the meaning one associates to a particular thought, hypothesis testing the validity of certain thoughts, replacing illogical or biased thoughts with more accurate ways of thinking).

Toward the Next Generation of Cognitive and Behavior Therapies

The past two decades has witnessed the emergence of a new generation of cognitive and behavior therapies (Hayes, 2004b). This latest generation represents a marked theoretical evolution over previous generations and has been applied to phenomena that received comparatively little emphasis in previous iterations of CBT. For instance, many new-generation approaches such as acceptance and commitment therapy (ACT; Hayes, Strosahl, & Wilson, 2012) and dialectical behavior therapy (DBT; Linehan, 1993a, 2015) emphasize factors such as emotion and language. ACT, DBT, and other recent CBTs also incorporate mindfulness and acceptance principles, techniques, and practices into the framework of therapy (Hayes, Follette, & Linehan, 2004; Segal, Williams, & Teasdale, 2002). Emphasis on values identification and clarification in ACT and on interpersonal relations in DBT, functional analytic psychotherapy (Kohlenberg & Tsai, 1991), and integrative behavioral couples therapy (Jacobson & Christensen, 1996) also represent new additions to the traditional CBT frameworks.

Similarly, behaviorally oriented researchers and clinicians have incorporated into their models the important symbolic function of language. Among other functions, language provides persons with emotional experiences without exposure to actual physical events or objects represented by words (Forsyth & Eifert, 1998). For example, the phrase "big, hairy tarantula" is often enough to produce some emotional discomfort in a person with a spider phobia. Emotions in humans are closely tied to language (Forsyth & Eifert, 1998), as exemplified by the frequent pairing of the emotional experience (anxiety) with the evaluation of that experience ("it's bad"), such that the two become functionally equivalent ("anxiety is bad"). New behaviorally oriented theories of cognition and language have emerged in recent years (e.g., Hayes, Barnes-Holmes, & Roche, 2001), as have therapies tied to this emerging perspective (Hayes et al., 2012).

Another key feature that distinguishes this most recent generation of approaches from previous generations is their collective focus on the context, broadly defined, in which behavior occurs (e.g., Biglan & Hayes, 1996; Martell et al., 2001). That is, comparatively less emphasis is placed on the modification of the physical environment to alter behavior or on the modification of the content of particular behaviors, thoughts, and emotions to promote therapeutic change. Rather, in these newer forms of CBT, a greater emphasis is placed on the modification of contexts in which these responses are experienced. For instance, mindfulness-based approaches encourage clients to experience their thoughts from a context within which thoughts are regarded simply as thoughts, not literal truths or unqualified representations of reality. Similarly, acceptance-based interventions are geared toward altering the context from one in which unwanted thoughts and emotions must be changed or eliminated to one in which such experiences are accepted, valued, and used adaptively. Taken together, this latest generation of CBTs more broadly deals with the range of human experience and, in so doing, delves into areas and change principles not previously acknowledged or systematically addressed in more traditional behavioral and cognitive therapies.

LOOKING AHEAD

This book is intended to serve as a general reference, and our primary goal is to offer an informative and easy-to-understand presentation on the basic theory and essential applications of behavioral interventions within the CBT framework. In the course of our presentation, we provide a description of the theory and practice of behavior therapy for adults that we hope is both useful and accessible to students and clinicians with varying degrees of behavioral training. We aim to provide some insight into how therapists with a behavioral perspective think about a client, his or her problem areas, and the therapeutic process. Finally, our hope is that readers will find the behavioral interventions described in this book to be useful additions to their therapeutic armamentarium.

Chapters 2 and 3 of this volume deal with behavioral assessment, case formulation, and treatment planning. Within these chapters, we outline the principles, goals, and structure of the initial assessment sessions. In so doing, we delineate the objectives, processes, and applications of behavioral assessment approaches used in the development of a case formulation and explain how data from these assessments inform treatment selection and the evaluation of therapy outcome. We also summarize the primary elements of a behavioral case formulation of the client's problem areas and outline the procedures and considerations associated with developing and exploring the formulation with the client.

Chapters 4 through 10 detail specific behavioral interventions including indications for their application, steps associated with their implementation, and markers of resultant therapeutic change. Chapter 4, for example, describes several strategies used in behavior therapy to increase or decrease clinically relevant behaviors by changing the environment. Procedures discussed in this chapter primarily involve the altering of the antecedents or consequences that occasion clinically relevant behaviors.

In Chapter 5, we describe examples of behavioral intervention strategies for altering thinking patterns. Within the chapter, emphasis is placed on the functional properties of detrimental modes of thinking rather than the modification of distorted or inaccurate thought content. Chapter 6 describes a set of interventions designed to help clients learn how to engage in particular behaviors in an effective and flexible manner to attain goals or enhance quality of life. The emphasis here is on *changing* behaviors by building skills. Several contemporary CBT-oriented treatments include skills training as a key component of the overall treatment approach given that skills-based interventions have demonstrated effectiveness for a variety of clinical problems. Chapter 7 builds on this earlier chapter by emphasizing skill-based interventions commonly used to enhance interpersonal effectiveness.

The next three chapters primarily highlight interventions for problems with mood and emotions. In Chapter 8, we describe a behavioral approach to the therapy of depression that is gaining broader empirical support as an effective therapy for an array of clinical problems, behavioral activation. In this chapter, we not only describe behavioral activation as a therapeutic technique but also use this as an opportunity to illustrate several behavioral perspectives on psychological disorders. Chapter 9 describes an intervention framework for reducing unjustified and maladaptive emotional responding and corresponding behavioral tendencies. Exposure-based interventions involve exposing the client to stimuli that elicit an emotional response and blocking action tendencies that are consistent with the unwanted or undesirable emotional response. Although exposure interventions are most commonly used and perhaps most effective for clinical problems related to anxiety and fear, they are also increasingly applied to other clinical problems and emotional experiences. In chapter 10, we describe emotion regulation interventions for assisting clients in tolerating or coping with uncomfortable emotions.

Chapter 11 describes techniques and interventions for navigating therapeutic challenges that are commonly encountered. Within that chapter, we develop a behavioral framework for thinking about and responding to behavior that interferes with treatment in the therapeutic context. Finally, in Chapter 12, we discuss considerations and approaches for bringing therapy to a close, emphasizing the importance of addressing termination issues periodically throughout therapy and as early as the treatment planning stage. We also describe the potential benefits of adding a continuation phase and booster sessions after the conclusion of the acute phase of therapy as a means for reducing the likelihood of relapse and problem recurrence, respectively. In the course of this discussion, we also describe several intervention strategies for relapse prevention.

SUMMARY

CBT is increasingly regarded as the treatment of choice for a wide variety of psychological conditions and psychiatric disorders. Theoretical elements that distinguish behavior therapy approaches from those of other schools of therapy include the following:

- Whereas most schools of therapy emphasize internal causes of behavior, behavior theory and therapy place emphasis on the environment as the primary determinant of behavior.
- Behavior theory and therapy are based on principles of determinism and functionalism, in which behavior that is functional (i.e., produces reinforcing consequences) is selected or becomes more probable over time, whereas behavior that is not functional (i.e., fails to produce reinforcing outcomes) is not selected.
- In behavior therapy, the three-term contingency (i.e., the antecedents of behavior, the behavior itself, and the consequences that behavior produces) often constitutes the basic level of analysis and serves as a guide for intervention selection, application, and evaluation.

2

PRINCIPLES, GOALS, AND STRUCTURE OF INITIAL ASSESSMENT SESSIONS

Behavioral assessment is an approach for assessing persons, what they do, and the circumstances under which they are most likely to engage in behaviors of clinical interest (R. O. Nelson & Hayes, 1986a). When viewed from this perspective, behavioral assessment is not defined by a set of techniques. Rather, the behavioral assessment approach is primarily guided by the theoretical principles on which it is based. One key principle is that behavior varies in relation to the antecedent conditions that occasion behavior and the consequences that behavior produces. Together, these constitute the context of behavior. A primary goal associated with behavioral assessments is the identification of potentially modifiable contextual features associated with maintenance of problematic behavior (Follette, Naugle, & Linnerooth, 2000). Knowledge of the common contexts for behavior can suggest hypotheses about why a person does what he or she

http://dx.doi.org/10.1037/14691-002
Behavioral Interventions in Cognitive Behavior Therapy: Practical Guidance for Putting Theory Into Action,
Second Edition, by R. F. Farmer and A. L. Chapman

does. This knowledge, in turn, can be used in the selection of intervention approaches that specifically alter the contextual landscape within which problematic behavior occurs, thus affecting the frequency, intensity, or duration of those behaviors over time.

In this chapter, we provide an overview of the principles, structure, and goals of the initial assessment sessions. We begin with a description of the central distinguishing features of behavioral assessments. We then discuss the importance of therapist–client relationship factors in recognition that these are important features of all therapies, including cognitive behavior therapy (CBT). Much of the remainder of the chapter focuses on the goals, processes, and applications of behavioral assessment approaches used in the development of a case formulation that, in turn, informs treatment selection and the evaluation of treatment outcome. Included within these sections are descriptions of techniques that can aid in the identification of the client's primary problem areas, methods for evaluating both the form and function of potential target behaviors, and strategies for evaluating impairments in functioning and coping resources. We conclude this chapter by describing some considerations associated with bringing initial assessment sessions to closure.

CORE FEATURES OF BEHAVIORAL ASSESSMENTS

A therapist who works within a CBT framework and approaches the assessment of a client's problem areas from a behavioral perspective recognizes the uniqueness of the individual and his or her context. Behavioral assessments are idiographic, or person centered, which is often in contrast to other approaches that are largely centered on the assessment of variables or constructs. One of the more common variable-centered approaches is the medical model approach in which the goal is to evaluate the presence of behavioral and physiological markers indicative of a disease and make a positive diagnosis when enough key markers are evident. This practice is most apparent in the use of psychiatric diagnoses in categorizing individuals. If a person displays a threshold number of markers or symptoms, a positive diagnosis is made, and a treatment is selected on the basis of the diagnosis. The focus of treatment, then, is on the diagnosis, specifically the symptoms that define the diagnostic concept, and not the whole person in interaction with his or her environment.

Behavioral approaches to assessment are distinguished from medical model and other approaches by a unique set of goals and features. These distinguishing aspects of behavioral assessment are delineated in the following section.

Goals of Behavioral Assessments

In clinical behavioral assessment, the primary emphasis is on the person, the clinically relevant behaviors he or she displays, and the environmental variables that select, influence, and maintain those behaviors (Sturmey, 2008). Given this emphasis, there are at least five general goals associated with behavioral assessment (R. O. Nelson & Hayes, 1986b). These include the following:

- a clarification of the nature of the client's problems, and identification of associated target behaviors;
- an evaluation of the extent to which the client's problems impair his or her functioning (e.g., in the areas of family life, social and occupational functioning, personal distress);
- the identification of factors that support and maintain problem areas;
- the collaborative development of a formulation of the client's problems, and development of a therapeutic intervention plan based on this formulation; and
- an ongoing evaluation of the effectiveness of the treatment strategy.

In this chapter, we are primarily concerned with the first three goals; in Chapter 3, we discuss the two remaining goals.

Distinguishing Features of Behavioral Assessments and Therapy

Several specific features distinguish behavioral assessment approaches from more traditional approaches (R. P. Hawkins, 1986; R. O. Nelson & Hayes, 1986b). Among the more important are the following:

- The level of analysis in behavioral assessment is the act in context, or the whole person in interaction with the environment.
- There is recognition that each person lives in a unique context and has a unique learning history and genetic endowment, with behavioral assessment and treatment approaches tailored to the client's uniqueness and individual needs.
- Behavior is viewed as situationally specific rather than cross-situationally general, which highlights the importance of external influences on behavior.
- Limited inference is used in behavioral assessment; construct or diagnostic labels are generally avoided as explanations for behavior, and behavior itself is the focus of therapy.

- The client's problem areas are clearly defined in behavioral terms.
- The emphasis in therapy is on the development of effective behavior and competencies.

These features, and how they are manifested within behavioral assessment and treatment approaches, are elaborated in the next section and in several of the chapters that follow.

CLIENT–THERAPIST RELATIONSHIP FACTORS

Initial contacts with the client are perhaps among the most important because the risk for dropping out of therapy is especially high within the first few sessions (Fiester & Rudestam, 1975). Clients often come to therapy with a good deal of ambivalence and fear, and perhaps some degree of guilt or shame associated with their behavior. They may also have somewhat unrealistic expectations about what therapy can offer and disappointed to learn that there is no "magic bullet" that can resolve long-standing problems within a session or two. For these and other reasons, an important therapeutic goal within the first few sessions is to establish a warm and collaborative therapeutic relationship and clarify for the client what he or she can expect as the therapeutic process unfolds. This would include orienting the client as to what will happen at each stage and providing a realistic therapy timeline. In so doing, the therapist must be aware that correcting misunderstandings about what therapy can accomplish might contribute to client disappointment and hopelessness. When providing clients with reasonable and realistic expectations for therapy, it is important that therapists instill hope and confidence concerning its potential effectiveness.

Establishing Rapport With the Client

A number of perspectives converge on the idea that the therapy process is enhanced when the therapist demonstrates genuineness, respect, warmth, acceptance, validation, and accurate empathy (Morganstern & Tevlin, 1981). These characteristics help the therapist establish rapport with the client and set the foundation for the development of a trusting relationship. Other important therapist behaviors include appropriate demeanor (e.g., relaxed, interested, sympathetic, engaged), facial expressions (e.g., smiles, nods), and eye contact (neither too much nor too little), along with a style of communicating that is easily understandable and relatively free of technical language (Livesley, 2001; Morrison, 1995).

Ideally, the therapist and client work together to develop and maintain a therapeutic context in which relationship issues can be constructively addressed as they emerge (Linehan, 1993a; Livesley, 2001). This includes an understanding between both parties that behaviors displayed by either the client or therapist that interfere with therapy (e.g., lateness, failures to keep agreements, noncompletion of between-session activities) are open for constructive discussion (Linehan, 1993a).

A therapist might keep in mind, too, that the therapeutic relationship is itself a context that can facilitate behavior change. Clients who have weak social skills, for example, can benefit from a therapeutic relationship that strengthens appropriate social behavior through natural social reinforcement (Kohlenberg & Tsai, 1991). Similarly, a therapist can discourage problematic interpersonal behaviors when a client displays them and suggest more adaptive alternatives. If, for example, a client's problem area includes excessive demands on others, a therapist might elect not to reinforce demands when the client states them. A therapist might instead attempt to evoke other behaviors inconsistent with excessive demandingness or dependency but that have similar functions (e.g., the assertive expression of needs, the making of appropriate requests). A therapist might alternatively try to facilitate behaviors that are the opposite of problematic ones. In the case of excessive dependency, for example, the therapist might elect to naturally reinforce occasions when the client demonstrates autonomous action.

Developing a Collaborative Therapist–Client Relationship

CBT is an action-oriented approach to therapy; therefore, it is important for the client to be an active participant in the therapeutic process and to share responsibility in carrying out the therapy. To this end, the client might be encouraged to be actively involved in all aspects of therapy, including the development of a formulation of his or her problem areas and any decisions concerning how to best approach these areas therapeutically. Stylistically, the therapist can facilitate the development of a collaborative relationship by frequently checking in with the client with questions such as, "Do you have anything you would like to add?" or "Is it alright if we now turn attention to your drinking habits?" Other stylistic approaches for enhancing the therapeutic relationship include taking the client's agenda seriously, assessing and highlighting the importance of the client's goals and values, using "we" statements, and conveying that the therapist and client are a "team" working together toward the same goals.

CONDUCTING INITIAL ASSESSMENTS: CLARIFYING THE CLIENT'S PROBLEMS AND IDENTIFYING TARGET BEHAVIORS

How a therapist conducts initial sessions will often vary in accordance with his or her theoretical orientation. This is particularly evident in the types of information a therapist attends to during initial meetings with the client and in the selection of areas or concepts to assess that have relevance for the subsequent development of a *case formulation*. As defined by Eells (1997), a case formulation is "a hypothesis about the causes, precipitants, and maintaining influences of a person's psychological, interpersonal, and behavioral problems" (p. 1). Therapists working from various perspectives will frequently generate case formulations that emphasize hypothesized causes of behavior suggested by their theoretical frame of reference. Their therapeutic activities, in turn, will often be directed at influencing theoretically prescribed determinants of behavior to bring about positive therapeutic change. In this section, we highlight both general procedures for identifying problem areas that would be of subsequent focus in therapy and assessment approaches specific to the development of a behavioral case formulation of the client's presenting complaints. The process of generating a behavioral case formulation from assessment information is more fully described in Chapter 3.

Presenting Problem or Complaint

When clients initially discuss their problem areas, it is often useful for the therapist simply to listen for a reasonable period of time (e.g., up to 10 minutes in an hour-long session; Morrison, 1995) without interrupting or probing. Doing so allows the client the opportunity to freely describe his or her reasons for coming to therapy, and the nature of his or her problems. Such an approach also conveys to the client a genuine interest in what he or she has to say as well as a willingness to work collaboratively. This approach also provides the therapist with an opportunity to informally evaluate how the client organizes his or her thoughts and explains the events of his or her life. Therapists can also generate hypotheses concerning mood and interpersonal style during this period.

After the period of *free speech* (Morrison, 1995), the therapist might make several inquiries to clarify and assess the problem area. When clients express current problems, descriptions are often somewhat vague. Examples might include, "My relationship with my wife isn't so hot," "I have problems with my nerves," "I've really been bummed out these past few months," or "I just want to die." In such instances, the therapist needs to probe further and identify manifestations of the problem (e.g., the behaviors, thoughts, and emotions involved), the current contexts within which they typically emerge, and the consequences that follow instances of the problem. It is also useful for the therapist to clarify the history and severity of the problem (e.g., when it first emerged, how long it has been going on, whether it is experienced as continuous or intermittent, the types of contexts that it reliably occurs within).

Assessing Response Classes on the Basis of Correlated or Descriptive Features

Behavioral assessors will often collect information about the kinds of behavior clients display. Responses to assessment measures about the types of behavior frequently displayed constitute one method for sampling behavior and might also suggest possible target behaviors for therapy. Such assessment methods are primarily concerned with *how* people behave (R. O. Nelson & Hayes, 1986b), with individuals classified according to the forms of behavior they exhibit. Such information can be useful in the behavioral assessment of a person's problem areas, particularly in instances where multiple problem areas are evident (Nelson-Gray & Farmer, 1999). Sole emphasis, however, on behavior descriptions and response–response relations has limited value from a behavioral perspective, particularly when it comes to altering behavior patterns (Naugle & Follette, 1998). That is, behavioral summaries captured by diagnostic or construct labels do not provide guidance as to how behavior came about or what factors might be influential in the maintenance of behavior, or *why* people behave the way they do.

Diagnostic Assessments

Shortly before the publication of the third edition of the *Diagnostic and Statistical Manual of Mental Disorders, Third Edition* (DSM–III; American Psychiatric Association, 1980), semistructured *diagnostic interviews* such as the Schedule for Affective Disorders and Schizophrenia (SADS; Endicott & Spitzer, 1978) were beginning to appear. These were largely used by researchers who were primarily concerned with identifying groups of persons who were similar based on symptom presentation. Before interviews like the SADS, research in the area of depression, for example, was difficult to integrate and synthesize because studies operationalized and assessed the depression construct differently. What defined a depressed person in one study might have differed from what defined a depressed person in another study.

Since the publication of *DSM–III*, numerous diagnostic interviews have been developed that assess single disorders (e.g., posttraumatic stress disorder), a group of related disorders (e.g., the personality disorders), or several distinct classes of psychiatric disorders (e.g., the full range of Axis I disorders described in *DSM*). Although still widely used in research, diagnostic interviews are now being used more frequently in general clinical practice, particularly in practices that specialize in the provision of therapies for a limited number of conditions.

The principle use of psychiatric diagnosis from a behavioral perspective is found in its classification and communication function. Because diagnostic concepts are largely defined in terms of behavioral acts, diagnoses may also suggest target behaviors for intervention. Many evidence-based therapies have been evaluated with reference to persons with particular diagnoses (Barlow, 2014), and thus knowledge of an individual's diagnosis might also suggest an effective treatment approach.

Questionnaire, Checklist, and Rating Scale Assessments

Similar to diagnostic categories, psychological constructs are also often defined in terms of groupings of behaviors that are endorsed by or evident for an individual. We might conclude, for example, that a person is experiencing excessive levels of anxiety if he or she endorses several moderately or highly intercorrelated items on questionnaires related to the anxiety construct.

Over the past few decades there has been a surge of published *self-report measures* that are easy to complete, relatively brief, and highly focused on particular problem areas. Questionnaire assessments are usually geared toward understanding the client's experience relative to other persons. To this end, a client's score on a questionnaire is usually referenced to those from a larger normative sample, and the client's position within the general population is inferred on the basis of the number of standard deviation units his or her score is from the normative mean. Sometimes cut scores are used to denote a threshold of extremity. These scores are then used to make inferences about the client in certain situations.

Checklists and *rating scales* are often completed by someone familiar with the client and typically consist of sets of behavioral acts to which the respondent indicates how frequently, if at all, the behavior occurs. Examples of such measures include the parent and teacher rating scales of the Child Behavior Checklist (Achenbach & Rescorla, 2001) and the Conners' Rating Scales (Conners, 2008). Checklist data are often useful in behavioral assessment because they not only indicate the severity or frequency of behavioral problems but also frequently suggest specific behavioral targets.

Identifying Behavioral Repertoires and Skills Deficits

During the first stages of assessment, it is often useful initially to categorize problematic behaviors within one of two broad categories: behavioral excesses and behavioral deficits. *Behavioral excesses* may take several forms.

By definition, they are apparent when a person displays particular forms of behavior that are excessive in terms of frequency, intensity, or duration. The behaviors also occur to an extent that they become associated with distress or impairment in functioning.

The associated functions that behavioral excesses have for an individual need to be determined on a person-by-person basis. Several behavioral excesses are maintained, at least in part, by positive reinforcers such as pleasant tactile stimulation (e.g., promiscuous sex), intermittent generalized reinforcers (e.g., compulsive gambling), or notice from the social environment (e.g., disruptive attention-seeking behavior). Frequent displays of anger, aggression, or coercive behaviors are often maintained by both positive reinforcers (e.g., physical intimidation that results in others' compliance with requests) and negative reinforcers (e.g., displays of anger that result in others' withdrawing or retreating). Other forms of behavioral excess are maintained by negative reinforcers and are most evident among persons who display strong avoidance and escape behavioral repertoires. The act of avoidance or escape generally results in the termination or cessation of contexts experienced as unpleasant and aversive. When behavioral excesses are examined, there often is some type of associated reinforcement process.

Behavioral deficits are apparent when persons do not demonstrate an adequate range of behavior in a variety of contexts or do not display adequate flexibility when adjusting behaviors in accordance with shifting circumstances. When behavioral deficits are evident, there are generally two reasons. One is that past environments did not adequately model, shape, or reinforce such behaviors. Another possibility is that absent behaviors have been learned at one time and are part of the person's repertoire. They appear absent or deficient, however, because they either have been subjected to punishing contingencies or have been extinguished. Individuals who have significant behavioral deficits in important areas tend to be less skillful in the behavior they display and less successful in obtaining reinforcement from the environment for their behavior.

Evaluating Coping Behaviors

Coping behaviors are often important to assess because such behaviors reflect how a person responds to adversity. Many of the types of problem behaviors with which clients seek help in therapy are, paradoxically, often the product of coping efforts that worked in the short term but pose long-term problems (e.g., Hayes, Strosahl, & Wilson, 2012; Linehan, 1993a; Martell, Addis, & Jacobson, 2001). When effective and nonharmful coping behaviors are deficient, as is often the case among persons with long-standing problems, CBT-oriented therapists will often assist clients in developing or strengthening alternative and adaptive coping skills. Problem-solving skills, social skills, self-regulation skills, mindfulness skills, and acceptance skills are examples of coping skills that are often targeted for strengthening within CBT.

- *Problem-solving skills* are particularly useful for assisting the client to find effective solutions to problems that arise. Clients who are vulnerable to feeling helpless, or who repeatedly engage in coping responses that also have a number of associated maladaptive qualities, are often deficient in their ability to generate novel or alternative ways of responding to problems.
- *Social skills* are requisite for developing and maintaining social and intimate relationships and for obtaining reinforcement from others. Individuals who have deficit social skills frequently also have deficits in coping because they are less successful in accessing or mobilizing the social environment and less likely to receive support, aid, advice, or direction from others.
- Self-regulation has been defined as any efforts a person uses to alter inner states or responses (Vohs & Baumeister, 2004). *Self-regulation skills*, therefore, are skills a person may or may not have developed for exercising self-control in areas as diverse as emotions, thoughts, impulses, attention, and bodily sensations.
- *Mindfulness skills* refer to several skills or abilities that have in common the fostering of a full awareness in the moment. Component skills include attention, awareness, observation, discrimination, nonjudging, and the maintenance of a present or here-and-now focus. Behavior patterns that are antithetical to mindfulness include rumination, worry, and dissociation.
- Many people who come to therapy have had the experience of growing up in an invalidating environment (e.g., Linehan, 1993a). As a consequence, many clients struggle with issues of self-worth, value as a person, and acceptance of themselves and their experiences. *Acceptance, self-validation, and tolerance skills* are often helpful for clients who are overly reactive, highly sensitive, and impulsive (Robins, Schmidt, & Linehan, 2004). Acceptance as a skill involves the ability to focus on the current moment, and accurately perceive without distortion or judgment. Part of acceptance, then, involves a type of openness to and acknowledgment of one's experience, devoid of accompanying evaluations or distortions.

A number of behavioral interventions in CBT seek to develop, strengthen, and maintain effective coping behavior. Examples of behavioral interventions designed to foster these skills are reviewed in Chapters 4 through 10.

Assessing Impairments in Functioning

There are several reasons for evaluating the degree of functional impairment associated with the client's problems. First, the degree and pervasiveness of impairment indicate the severity of the problem (Morrison, 1995). When significant impairment is observed in several domains of functioning, the problem likely requires more intensive forms of intervention. When impairments are more focal and limited, therapy might emphasize functioning in the few contexts in which impairment is most pronounced. When a client reports no impairment, time might be taken to clarify why he or she came to therapy.

Second, the level or nature of impairment can have relevance for the choice, course, or emphasis of therapy modalities and interventions. Moderately severe to severe impairments, as indicated by an inability to maintain personal hygiene, suicidal preoccupation, or the influence of hallucinations or delusions on behavior, might suggest more intensive therapeutic modalities such as inpatient psychiatric care or day hospital programs. When impairments are pervasive, long-standing, and affect several areas of functioning, as is sometimes observed among persons with severe personality disorders, long-term therapy might be contemplated. Depending on the client's areas of strength and impairment, therapy might also be offered in multiple modalities (e.g., individual therapy, group skills training, telephone consultations, pharmacotherapy). Because of risks or safety issues associated with some forms of impairment, the emphasis of therapy might also be prioritized according to the potential for harm. Suicidal preoccupation or behavior, when present, would likely take precedence over impairments with less potential for lethality, such as those related to quality of life (Linehan, 1993a). In Chapter 3, we provide detailed guidelines for prioritizing client problem areas.

Third, psychological disorders are often defined, in part, by the presence of behavioral patterns associated with subjective distress or impairment in occupational or social functioning. The inclusion of the term *impairment* in the definition of psychological disorders, which is the case for the vast majority of DSM-defined disorders, represents an effort to lessen the influence that cultural beliefs, values, mores, and norms have on the judgments about the person. Although it is recognized that concepts of harm or loss of benefit are judged with reference to the standards of a person's culture, the inclusion of the impairment criterion decreases the likelihood that certain behavior patterns will arbitrarily be labeled as abnormal by external observers.

In the following sections, we touch on a number of domains in which impairments are likely to be revealed. In addition, we introduce some issues within each area that might be important for a behavioral assessor to consider.

Personal Functioning

In the evaluation of one's personal functioning, it is useful to compare how the person is currently functioning with how well he or she has functioned in the past. This information not only suggests a level of impairment but also might clarify what behavioral skills or coping resources already exist in the person's behavioral repertoire. Examples of questions for evaluating this area include the following:

- "What difficulties has this problem caused you?"
- "Does this problem cause you any discomfort or distress?"
- "Has this problem had an impact on things that you enjoy or have enjoyed in the past?"
- "For the time that this problem has been going on, have you experienced any difficulties taking care of yourself?"
- "Have you had difficulty sleeping? Any changes in your weight or appetite? How about energy level?"
- "Since you have had this problem, have there been times when you felt out of control?"
- "Has this problem resulted in your avoiding situations or activities that you would not have avoided before?"
- "Have you previously sought help for this problem?"

Family and Social Relations

Solid family or social relationships might protect against the development of many forms of psychological disorder and can enhance physical and psychological health (Moak & Agrawal, 2010). Impairments in these areas might not only increase one's vulnerability to psychological disorders but also exacerbate any problems that may already exist (Lewinsohn & Gotlib, 1995). When assessing family and social relations, it is important to distinguish whether current problems in these areas are due to avoidance tendencies (e.g., withdrawal from interpersonal relationships), deficits in social skills (e.g., relevant social behaviors have not been learned), suppression of social behavior by the environment (e.g., social behaviors have been learned but are punished when displayed), or a low rate of positive reinforcement for social behavior (e.g., the individual lives within a context that does not positively support social behavior).

- "Since this problem emerged, have you noticed any changes in your relationships with family? Your spouse or partner? Friends? Coworkers?"
- "Have you had any recent difficulties or conflicts with people?"
- "How would you characterize your current relationships with family and friends?"

- "Is there someone in your life now that you would feel comfortable going to if you had a problem or needed help? Do you see this person often?"

Occupational and School Functioning

For many individuals, the first signs of impairment often emerge in response to the demands of day-to-day living. Work or school life is often filled with daily demands for performance, with the added pressure that performance is constantly evaluated (e.g., by supervisors or teachers).

- "Has this problem had any effect on your work (or studies)?"
- "Have you missed any days from work (or school)?"
- "Have you been reprimanded at work (or school) because of this problem?"
- "In the past, have you had many jobs? If so, what were the circumstances that prompted you to leave your jobs?"

Legal Difficulties or Proceedings

Legal difficulties are more likely when a person's history includes substance abuse, bipolar disorder, and antisocial behaviors (Morrison, 1995). A review of the person's legal history might reveal the presence of psychological conditions that might otherwise not be immediately apparent. In discussing legal issues, it is also useful to explore whether the client is involved in any current or pending litigation. Such knowledge might buffer against any future surprise when one's therapy work and notes are subjected to court review, or when one might be asked to testify during divorce or child custody proceedings. In the event that litigation is likely and that the therapist might be called to supply testimony, it is important to discuss with the client the advantages and disadvantages of providing evidence or opinion during ongoing therapy.

- "Have you ever had any legal difficulties?"
- "Have you ever been arrested?"
- "Are you currently involved in any legal proceedings that might have relevance to our work together?"
- "Do you anticipate any future litigation, such as divorce proceedings or child custody disputes?"

Health and Medical Status

Several studies have indicated that physical health is associated with overall well-being (e.g., Moak & Agrawal, 2010; Zvolensky & Smits, 2010). A variety of medical conditions can also produce signs and symptoms that strongly resemble psychological disorders. Hypoglycemia, hyperthyroidism, or acute caffeine intoxication, for example, are associated with signs or symptoms that can resemble anxiety or depression (Chueire, Romaldini, & Ward, 2007; Simon et al., 2002). Conversely, some psychiatric disorders increase the risk for health-related problems. In the case of bulimia nervosa, for example, the use of purging compensatory methods can result in electrolyte abnormalities, impaired renal functions, and esophageal weakening or rupture. Before initiating therapy, it is advisable for the client to seek a medical consultation in the event there are current untreated medical difficulties or an indication that current symptomatology may be due to or exacerbated by an underlying medical condition.

- "Do you have any current medical problems?"
- "Have you had any medical problems in the past?"
- "What medications are you currently taking?"
- "How would you describe your health at present?"

Current Life Situation and Quality of Life

Quality of life is another factor that can be considered during initial assessments as well as throughout therapy. Quality-of-life factors not only influence one's overall sense of well-being but can also pose threats to ongoing therapy (e.g., no money for housing, arrests for criminal behavior). Behaviors that interfere with quality of life, threaten the viability of ongoing treatment, or are associated with risk and safety issues should be actively targeted in therapy (Linehan, 1993a).

- "Where do you currently live?"
- "Whom do you live with?"
- "What is your financial situation like?"
- "Do you have recreational interests? How often do you participate in these?"
- "Have you had any recent changes in your life?"
- "How would you describe a typical day for you?"
- "Are you satisfied with your current situation? Would you like for anything to be different?"

Suicide Risk and Other Risk Areas

The assessment and evaluation of risk are important aspects a client's ongoing therapy. In the initial stages of assessment, suicidal and homicidal ideation and intention should be assessed, as should other indicators of risk such as thinking anomalies (e.g., hallucinations and delusions), substance abuse, mania, and self-harm tendencies. The client's history in relation to these areas should also be evaluated (e.g., past suicide attempts, past acts of aggression). In the event that there is a suggestion of child or elder abuse, or abuse of any vulnerable person, the therapist must thoroughly explore the issue and take appropriate action, such as notifying appropriate authorities, if such abuse is acknowledged.

If a client reports suicidal or homicidal thoughts or self-harm behaviors, the original plan for the initial session should be suspended, and these areas addressed in great detail. Included within this assessment might be an evaluation of the frequency, intensity, and duration of these thoughts as well as the strength of the urge to act on such ideation. Any plans for action should be evaluated, together with associated means and the availability and potential lethality of such means. In the event that the client is at imminent risk for harming self or others, appropriate action should be taken to ensure the safety of the client or others.

When a situation is not urgent or imminent (e.g., low urge to act on suicidal ideation, ability to tolerate emotional pain, suicidal behavior viewed by client as ineffective coping, unavailability of lethal means, willingness to act in accordance with an established suicidal prevention plan; see Chiles & Strosahl, 2004), further detailed exploration is warranted. For those who report suicidal ideation, for example, one might take time to determine what the client feels hopeless about or what problems the individual believes suicidal action or parasuicidal behavior may solve. Protective factors, such as reasons for living, are also important to explore (Linehan, 1993a).

- "Have you had thoughts of wanting to hurt or kill yourself? Have you ever acted on these thoughts? Do you have these thoughts now?"
- "Have you ever wished that you were dead?"
- "Have you had thoughts of wanting to hurt others? Have you ever acted aggressively toward another person?"
- "Sometimes people do things to cause pain to themselves, whether or not they have a desire to kill themselves. Have you ever done anything to intentionally inflict pain on yourself?"
- "Have you ever had feelings of rage to the extent that you lost control?"
- "How strong is your desire to live currently?"

THE BEHAVIORAL INTERVIEW

Behavioral interviews are often conducted within the first few sessions by behaviorally oriented therapists as a means of gathering information relevant to the development of a behavioral case formulation. The focus of such interviews is frequently on the designation of the client's problem areas (e.g., problematic emotional responding, ineffective interpersonal or coping behavior), an identification of specific behavioral patterns related to these problem areas, an exploration of possible precipitants and maintaining factors associated with these patterns, and an investigation into the possible commonalities across these problem areas. Although behavioral interviews take many different forms, a number of similarities can be identified (Kanfer & Saslow, 1969; Morganstern & Tevlin, 1981; Spiegler & Guevremont, 2010). An underlying philosophical assumption that guides the interview is that behavior is determined—current behavior is jointly influenced by immediate environmental factors and the culmination of a lifetime's worth of experiences. There is also an emphasis on current behavior and functioning. Relevant aspects of the client's history might also be explored to place problem behaviors in a historical perspective and to aid in the identification of possible current contexts and maintaining factors associated with these behaviors.

During the behavioral interview, the therapist frequently adopts an active approach. As the client provides new information about himself or herself, the therapist continuously develops, tests, and refines the case formulation in accordance with existing knowledge (e.g., by predicting a client's responses to questions posed, or predicting behavior in certain situations as recounted by the client). Consistent with this active approach, there is an ongoing evaluation of potential target behaviors. In the initial stages of assessment, a therapist might consider client behaviors in terms of broad, inclusive categories such as excesses or deficits, and strengths or assets (e.g., areas of competence or skill, effectiveness of coping behavior, social support network). In addition to thinking about potential target behaviors in relation to their frequency, intensity, severity, and generality, one might consider the antecedents that precede behaviors of interest and the consequences that follow them. Examples of interview questions for investigating areas typically addressed in the early phases of behavioral assessment are outlined in Exhibit 2.1.

FUNCTIONAL ANALYSIS: CLARIFYING THE CONTEXT AND PURPOSE OF BEHAVIOR

A functional understanding of clinically relevant behavior attempts to isolate the conditions under which behavior is most likely to occur and identify the consequences that function to maintain it over time. The products of such an analysis are, in turn, integrated into a hypothetical model about the client's behavior and subsequently used to inform decisions concerning which behavioral interventions might be most appropriate for this client at this time.

EXHIBIT 2.1
Examples of Questions Used in Behavioral Interviews for Evaluating
Possible Target Behaviors and Their Associated Features

For Identifying Possible Target Behaviors and Their Frequency and Severity:
"What brings you here today?"
"What is the problem as you see it?"
"Please tell me about types of problems you have been having that you wish to
    address here."
"Are there things going on in your life right now that make you unhappy?"
"How often does the problem occur?"
"How serious do you see the problem as being?"
"Have others suggested that this is a problem?"
"Are there things that you used to enjoy doing that you no longer do?"
"Are there often situations you are in when you are unsure of how to respond?"
"Because of this problem, has there been any impact on your family life? Your work?
    Your relationships with important persons in your life? In your overall sense of
    well-being?"
"Has anything important changed in your life since this problem has occurred?"

For Establishing Antecedents of Target Behaviors:
"When, or in what situations, does the problem occur?"
"What is happening right before the problem occurs?"
"If you think back to the last time that the problem took place, what was going
    on then?"
"Does this problem typically happen when you are around other people, or by
    yourself?"
"Before the problem occurs, do you typically experience certain thoughts of feelings?"
"Before doing this, do you have any thoughts about what might happen as a result?"

For Identifying Possible Consequences Target Behaviors:
"What happens right after the problem occurs?"
"What do you get from doing this?"
"When the problem occurs, are you aware of any changes in how you feel?"
"If the problem takes place around other people, how do they respond when it
    occurs?"
"Are there times when the problem gets better? If so, what is going on then that is
    different?"
"Are there longer term effects associated with the problem?"

**For Evaluating Associations That Learning History or Person Variables Have
    With Target Behaviors:**
"When did the problem first begin?"
"Do you recall other times in your life when you had this same problem?"
"What was going on in your life then?"
"Is the problem today different in any way from what it was in the past?"
"When you had this problem in the past, was there anything you tried that helped?"
"Has anyone in your family, including grandparents and cousins, ever had this
    problem?"

For Assessing the Effectiveness of Coping Behaviors:
"What have you tried to reduce or eliminate the problem?"
"How has that worked?"
"Tell me how you cope with difficult situations."
"When you do that, does it help? Does that way of coping cause other problems?"

(continues)

"Do you find yourself coping with the problem through avoiding or withdrawing in any way?"

"Are you more likely to do certain things when the problem is present? If so, what do you do?"

"Is it difficult to be with those painful feelings when they are there? If so, what do you when you're feeling them?"

For Evaluating the Consistency of Problem Behaviors With Values or Goals:

"How might life be like if this were not a problem for you?"

"If you think about it, are your actions consistent with what you want your life to be about?"

"What might you be doing in your life right now if this was not a problem for you?"

"Is there anything missing in your life right now that is important to you?"

"If therapy is successful, how would things be different for you?"

For Assessing the Client's Ideas for Addressing His or Her Problem Areas:

"What do you think might be done to improve your situation?"

"Can you imagine yourself doing anything that would make the situation better?"

"If you didn't have this problem, what would you be doing differently?"

"Do you know of anybody who had problems similar to yours? What did they do?"

"What might contribute to other people feeling satisfied with their lives?"

In the sections that follow, we describe four essential components of a functional analysis of behavior: (a) antecedent stimuli (i.e., discriminative stimuli and establishing operations), (b) person variables (i.e., physiological makeup, heritable biological characteristics, and learning history), (c) behavior (i.e., cognitive-verbal, physiological, emotional, and motor responses), and (d) consequences (reinforcement and punishment, both immediate and delayed). These four components represent the foundations of a hypothetical model of a client's problem area in which a person's behavior is regarded as a joint function of immediate environmental variables (antecedent stimuli and response consequences) and person variables that the individual brings to a situation (Goldfried & Sprafkin, 1976).

The Antecedents of Behavior

From a behavior therapy perspective, there are two general types of antecedents that set the occasion for behavior. These are discriminative stimuli and establishing operations.

Discriminative Stimuli

Discriminative stimuli (or S^D) are events that provide information about the likelihood that reinforcement or punishment will follow the engagement in some type of behavior. The informational value of S^D is based on a person's previous experiences for behaving in certain ways in the presence of those or related stimuli. When a given behavior has typically been reinforced or punished in the presence of S^D, those S^D will often acquire influence over behavior by signaling the likelihood of reinforcement or punishment. Displays of disruptive behavior in the classroom, for example, are frequently reinforced and maintained by attention from peers. The presence of peers in a classroom setting, then, often creates S^D that occasion disruptive behavior for children who have been previously reinforced for such behavior by peers in similar settings.

Establishing Operations

Establishing operations (EOs), sometimes referred to as *motivational operations*, constitute another type of antecedent that sets the occasion for certain behaviors. EOs reference the influence that environmental events or conditions have on behavior by altering the reinforcing or punishing properties of other environmental events (Laraway, Snycerski, Michael, & Poling, 2003; Michael, 2000). If, for example, a person is deprived of water for a long time, the reinforcing value of water or similar substances (e.g., juice, soda, beer) increases as a result of the deprivation. Conversely, a person who has just consumed a lot of water might find the act of drinking even more water to be unpleasant. The reinforcing value of water for such an individual has been diminished by satiation.

Internal events that arise from certain environmental events, such as thoughts and emotional states, are common EOs for some behaviors (Michael, 1982; Miltenberger, 2005). Among people who frequently binge eat, for example, common EOs that occasion binge episodes include negative mood states, negative thoughts related to self, sleep deprivation, and food cravings associated with prolonged food deprivation (Farmer & Latner, 2007). The experience of anger, perhaps as a result of painful or aversive stimulation (e.g., a slap across the face), might serve as an EO for aggressive behavior. Similarly, deprivation of attention from others might function as an EO that increases the likelihood that the deprived person will enact a variety of behaviors that have in common an attention-obtaining function (Michael, 1982, 2000).

EOs also include rules that influence behavior (Schlinger, 1993). Rules are verbal stimuli, transmitted through spoken word or writing, which specify consequences or outcomes associated with acting in particular ways. Rules include instructions, commands, demands, "if-then" statements, advice, oral traditions, moral teachings, and modeled behavior (Baum, 2005). Technically speaking, a rule is a verbal description that specifies an antecedent condition or context, a particular behavior or set of behaviors, consequences for behavior, or a combination of these (Anderson, Hawkins, Freeman, & Scotti, 2000). In this respect, rules are regarded as stimuli that, in the presence of which, a response specified by the rule will result in either reinforcement or punishment. *Rule-governed behavior*, then, refers to those behaviors influenced by verbal rules that specify the operating contingencies associated with behavior. A client with fears about public speaking, for instance, might have his or her behavior guided by the following rule: "If I speak [the behavior] in front of a large audience [the antecedent condition or context], I will be evaluated negatively and humiliated [the consequence]." Such a person might avoid public speaking as a result of this rule, even if it is not accurate. The rule-governed behavior concept is used to account for behavior influenced by delayed consequences and provides a framework for how thoughts or self-directed speech might promote goal-oriented actions (Malott, Malott, & Trojan, 2000).

The Consequences of Behavior

Behavior is usually performed to produce particular outcomes. Whether behavior is successful in producing that outcome, however, will influence its likelihood of being performed under similar circumstances in the future. In this section, we describe consequences of behavior and the influence that these consequences have on future behavior.

Factors That Increase or Maintain Behavior

Often in CBT, the focus is on behaviors that occur frequently and are problematic. Many of the behaviors dealt with in clinical contexts are reinforced behaviors, which is why they persist and become more frequent or intense over time.

There are two types of reinforcement that *increase or maintain behavior*: positive reinforcement and negative reinforcement. The terms *positive* and *negative* in relation to both reinforcement and punishment (described in the following list) do not connote a type of evaluation (e.g., good or bad); rather, they refer to whether behavior results in the application of something (i.e., positive) or the removal of something (i.e., negative). Given the technical definitions of these terms, we can define positive and negative reinforcement as follows:

- *Positive reinforcement* occurs when behavior results in the application or provision of a reinforcing event, which increases the probability of the behavior in future similar situations.

- *Negative reinforcement* occurs when behavior results in the removal or termination of an aversive event or condition, which increases the probability of the behavior in future similar situations.

Positive or negative reinforcement processes often maintain *behavioral excesses*, or behaviors that occur with such frequency or intensity that they become problematic. To understand what function the excessive behavior serves for the individual, it is important to understand *why* the person engages in the behavior. Theories on the functional properties of addictive behaviors, for example, have emphasized two processes, both of which Fowles (2001) has conceptualized as an "abuse of reinforcers." When substance abuse is instrumental in producing pleasant or desirable consequences (e.g., euphoria), it is regarded as positively reinforced behavior. Conversely, when substance use produces relief (escape) from aversive states or environments (e.g., negative emotion, social anxiety), it is regarded as negatively reinforced behavior. Although the positive and negative reinforcing effects of substance use are likely instrumental in the maintenance of addictive behaviors, individuals vary as to which type of reinforcing consequence most influences their behavior. Consequently, in the process of understanding the problematic behavior targeted in therapy, we must understand why the person engages in the behavior. Such knowledge will likely inform decisions concerning which interventions are most appropriate for a given individual.

Problematic binge eating is another example of a behavior that might be maintained by different consequences depending on the individual. Some models on the maintenance of binge eating emphasize the avoidance function that binge eating serves for the person. Generally speaking, when we talk about behavior maintained by avoidance, we are usually talking about negative reinforcement processes in which behavior results in the elimination or removal of something aversive. In relation to binge eating, various theoretical models have emphasized the role that binge eating has on the avoidance of or escape from aversive self-awareness (Heatherton & Baumeister, 1991) or negative emotions (Johnson, Schlundt, Barclay, Carr-Nangle, & Engler, 1995). Other models of binge eating emphasize the positive reinforcing functions that establish and maintain binge eating. Possible reinforcers for binge eating include the taste of desired foods and reinforcement provided by others in the social context of eating. Additional research suggests that the degree to which the taste and consumption of food might be reinforcing varies as a function of the type of eating disorder a person displays. Those with binge eating disorder, for example, have reported greater enjoyment associated with eating during binges compared with those with bulimia nervosa (Mitchell et al., 1999).

Factors That Decrease or Extinguish Behavior

There are two types of punishment, both of which *decrease* the future likelihood of punished behavior under similar stimulus conditions:

- *Positive punishment* occurs when behavior results in the application or provision of an aversive event or condition, which decreases the probability of the behavior in future similar situations.
- *Negative punishment* occurs when behavior results in the removal or termination of a reinforcing event or condition, which decreases the probability of the behavior in future similar situations.

Another type of process that results in a reduction or elimination of behavior is *extinction*. Extinction of behavior over time occurs when previously reinforced behavior reliably fails to produce reinforcing consequences. If a behavior repeatedly fails to produce reinforcing consequences, then it will simply "drop out" and no longer be displayed over time.

In an example of the role of extinction, some models of depression (e.g., Ferster, 1973; Lewinsohn, 1974) emphasize a low rate of response-contingent positive reinforcement (RCPR) for social behaviors that, in turn, effectively extinguishes these behaviors over time. As behavior frequency becomes reduced because of low RCPR, the opportunities to receive reinforcement for social behavior correspondingly become less and less. This resultant progression is a true downward spiral in which a low rate of RCPR for social behavior becomes associated with a low rate of emitted behavior that further reduces the likelihood of reinforcement for behavior.

The consequences that affect behavior are summarized in Table 2.1. In this table, forms of behavioral consequation are compared and contrasted in terms of the type of consequence, the effect the consequence has on behavior (i.e., increase or decrease), and the behavior–consequence relationship.

Additional Considerations Associated With Behavior Consequences

When examining the consequences of behavior, there are two other important considerations. The first is that the definition of what constitutes a reinforcer or punisher is solely determined by the effect the consequence has on future behavior. A *reinforcer* is, by definition, an operation that increases behavior frequency or intensity over time. A *punisher*, in contrast, is an operation that decreases a behavior over time. Although an event might appear to be either rewarding or punishing on the basis of its surface features, we can only infer the nature of the consequent event by observing the effect that it has on future behavior. Among some individuals, for example, attention from

TABLE 2.1
Behavioral Operations and Their Effects

Operation	Type of consequence	Effect on behavior	Behavior/consequence relationship
Positive reinforcement	Rewarding	Increase	Behavior → Receive rewarding event
Negative reinforcement	Relieving	Increase	Behavior → Removal of aversive event
Extinction	Frustrating	Decrease	Behavior → No reinforcing consequence
Positive punishment	Aversive	Decrease	Behavior → Receive aversive event _spanks_
Negative punishment	Penalizing	Decrease	Behavior → Removal of rewarding event _Time out_

Note. Adapted from *Personality–Guided Behavior Therapy* (p.60), by R. F. Farmer and R. O. Nelson-Gray, 2005, Washington, DC: American Psychological Association. Copyright 2005 by the American Psychological Association.

others can be either a reinforcing or punishing consequence for behavior. For those who experience attention from others as reinforcing, behaviors that produced attention will become more probable in the future. In contrast, persons who experience attention as punishing will be less likely to display behaviors that previously resulted in attention.

A second consideration is whether the consequences are *short-term or immediate* versus *long-term or delayed*. In the case of problematic behaviors, short-term consequences often maintain such behaviors, whereas long-term consequences make those behaviors problematic (Nelson-Gray & Farmer, 1999). When conducting a functional analysis, assessments might emphasize both the short- and long-term consequences of problematic behavior.

Person Variables and Learning History Within a Functional Analysis

Person variables, sometimes referred to as *organismic variables* (Goldfried & Sprafkin, 1976), include biological characteristics of the individual and the effects of past learning. Examples of biological characteristics include genetic predispositions, temperament, physical appearance, and the effects of aging. Learning history refers to the influence that a lifetime of environmental learning has on one's behavior, knowledge of which can aid predictions about how a person might behave in particular environmental contexts.

As an example of the potential importance of biological characteristics in developing a functional understanding of problematic behavior, abnormalities in appetitive and metabolic functioning have been suggested to influence overeating among some individuals with bulimia nervosa and binge eating disorder (Latner & Wilson, 2000). Similarly, many of the symptoms and features of anorexia nervosa and bulimia nervosa can be accounted for by the common long-term physical effects of starvation. An undernourished individual's behavioral and neurocognitive functioning will often be impaired (Fowler et al., 2006), which may or may not be reversible once weight and nutrition return to more normative levels.

Many psychological conditions, such as schizophrenia, bipolar disorder, attention-deficit/hyperactivity disorder, and major depressive disorders, have been suggested to have some genetic influences (Cross-Disorder Group of the Psychiatric Genomics Consortium, 2013). Although genes cannot themselves be directly manipulated, knowing one's family history with reference to a particular problem behavior might suggest possible biological influences on behavior, such as those that result in an individual being especially sensitive to the reinforcing effects of certain substances or environmental events (Tabakoff & Hoffman, 1988).

With regard to learning history, many forms of problematic behaviors persist for years or decades due to the high concentrations of positive and negative reinforcers that usually follow such behaviors. Examples of such behaviors include eating disorders and substance abuse. Given the abundant reinforcers associated with such behavior, successful treatment effects are often difficult to achieve or maintain, perhaps because such behaviors are not experienced as especially troublesome or because they provide considerable relief (Miller, Forcehimes, & Zweben, 2011; Vitousek, Watson, & Wilson, 1998).

Knowledge of learning history might reveal the functional development of a person's problem areas, suggest variables that might influence these problem behaviors in current contexts, or imply additional problem areas not readily apparent but consistent with prototypical histories associated with certain forms of psychopathology. In an example of the latter, a majority of individuals with borderline personality disorder (BPD) have histories of deliberate self-harm or suicidal behavior, which are sometimes not readily acknowledged in early interviews. In the event that someone exhibiting BPD features does not volunteer information concerning past self-harm or suicidal behaviors during an initial interview, the therapist might consider exploring these areas given the commonality of this type of behavioral history.

When historical etiological antecedents to problematic behavior can be identified, they might have little or no relevance for the maintenance of those behaviors over time. That is, we cannot assume that factors instrumental in the initial establishment of a set of problematic behaviors exert influence on current behavior. Consequently, to understand current behavior, one needs to identify contemporary influences on behavior.

Examples of a Clinical Functional Analysis

mention analysis chain analysis of specific behavior

Now that we have described the key components of a functional analysis of behavior, we provide an example of a functional analysis of a clinically relevant behavior. "Adam," a 24-year-old ranch hand, came to the clinic for assistance with alcohol dependence. Before undergoing a medically supervised detoxification as a precursor to a course of CBT, he met with a psychologist who assessed the descriptive and contextual aspects of his drinking behavior, among other areas.

In reviewing Adam's drinking history, the therapist learned that he began episodically drinking at age 12. He cited peer influences as his main reason for drinking at the time (e.g., "All of my friends were doing it"). After a period of heavy drinking, he and his friends would typically go downtown and vandalize property, verbally harass people, and steal low-value items. Adam commented that he enjoyed the psychoactive effects of alcohol, felt that alcohol facilitated camaraderie with his mates, and took pleasure in the effects of what he did while intoxicated (e.g., the reactions on the faces of people whom he harassed, possessing stolen objects). He added that he was always an impulsive individual and enjoyed a good time.

When the therapist sampled several episodes of excessive drinking over the past few weeks, a fairly consistent pattern emerged. Adam's drinking was more or less continuous in that he would drink on four or more occasions during a typical day. Common antecedents to drinking would include reduced tissue concentrations of alcohol and associated feelings of discomfort (nausea, feelings of edginess, lethargy) linked to withdrawal, strong alcohol cravings, and negative drink-related thoughts related to himself ("I'm just a drunk and I'll never amount to nothing"). He also reported that he would also drink immediately before he met with the ranch owner, stating that "It's just easier for me to get along with him if I'm a little crocked" and "When I'm juiced, it's easier for me to joke around with him." Further probing of these disclosures indicated that Adam typically felt some mild to moderate anxiety immediately before beginning a social exchange with the ranch owner. He also indicated that when he joked around with the rancher and others, he felt a stronger bond with them. Regarding the latter, he reported that others responded to him more positively when he was intoxicated.

When other consequences of intoxication were explored, Adam described a mixed picture. On the one hand, he reported that he would feel a little euphoric once he started drinking, and that his discomfort and cravings would quickly lessen and then go away. Similarly, as the intoxicating effects of alcohol took hold, he reported that he felt less anxious when interacting with others and, in fact, was able to "be himself," which he described as being more socially outgoing and funny. Adam also reported that he enjoyed the taste of alcohol. Whiskey was his favorite, and he would usually consume about four standard drinks on each drinking occasion.

On the other hand, within an hour of a drinking episode, Adam reported, "I would start to feel bad again." The euphoria would have lessened or be completely gone, cravings would return, and negative self-thoughts would again surface. As time progressed, physical withdrawal symptoms would intensify. The ability to work would typically be impaired as these aversive effects became more pronounced. On the basis of past experiences, Adam learned that he could terminate the aversive experiences by consuming more alcohol.

Figure 2.1 illustrates the functional analysis of Adam's alcohol use. In this model, dots that appear in between components in the response chain indicate a probability function denoting the degree of influence that the preceding component will have on the following component. Items listed within the Reinforcing Consequences components that are followed by (+) indicate positive reinforcing consequences, whereas items followed by (−) indicate negative reinforcing consequences, both of which maintain or strengthen preceding behavior.

Functional Response Class Analysis

One of the goals of performing functional analyses of problem behaviors is to facilitate the client's attention to the contextual flow within which such behavior is embedded. As a result, clients are more likely to understand the influences on their behavior and the notion that they do what they do because of the effects that their behavior produces.

When grouping behaviors, behaviorally oriented clinicians typically do so according to the purpose that behavior serves. Functional response classes are groups of behaviors that produce similar outcomes, even though they may assume several forms (Follette et al., 2000). Phobic behavior, dissociation, intentional self-harm, and substance abuse, for example, are vastly different forms of behavior. They often, however, have a similar underlying function for individuals who engage in them—namely, experiential avoidance (Hayes, Wilson, Gifford, Follette, & Strosahl, 1996). Individuals who display these and other forms of avoidant behavior might be regarded as having a strong or excessive behavioral avoidance repertoire.

EXAMPLES OF OTHER BEHAVIORAL ASSESSMENT METHODS

Several behavioral assessment methods exist, and depending on the client's presenting problems, some methods might be more appropriate than others. In this section, we discuss two commonly used behavioral assessment methods: self-monitoring and direct observation. Other approaches to behavioral assessment

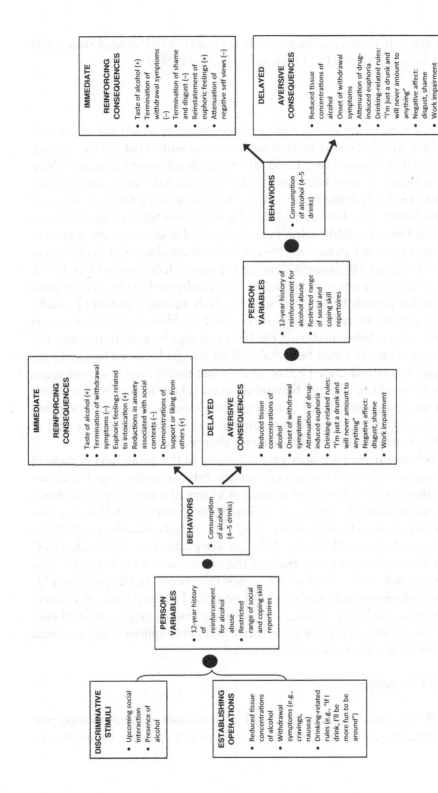

Figure 2.1. Functional analysis of Adam's drinking behavior.

are described in Hayes, Barlow, and Nelson-Gray (1999); Haynes, O'Brien, and Kaholokula (2011); and R. O. Nelson and Hayes (1986b).

Self-Monitoring

Self-monitoring is an assessment procedure in which the client collects data on behaviors of interest as they occur within naturalistic settings (Korotitsch & Nelson-Gray, 1999). To engage in self-monitoring, the client must be clear as to what behaviors should be monitored; that is, target behaviors must be clearly defined and the client familiar with the range of exemplars of the behavior. The client must also be able to notice when the target behavior occurs and record it. Although commonly regarded as an assessment therapy approach, the simple act of self-monitoring has also been observed to result in changes in behavior frequency in desirable directions (Korotitsch & Nelson-Gray, 1999).

As an assessment tool, self-monitoring can be used to identify the antecedents that precede behaviors of interest. Such information might be useful for determining the types of contexts in which problematic behavior is most likely to occur. Self-monitoring methods can also be used to monitor the frequency of certain target behaviors. When data on behavior frequency are collected before and during active therapy, self-monitoring assessments can be used to evaluate whether therapy is having a beneficial effect. Similarly, when the treatment consists of multiple components, self-monitoring data might reveal which among the treatment components was most useful or effective in producing desirable behavior change.

Self-monitoring methods vary according to the nature and purpose of the assessment. If the frequency of a specific behavior is the object of assessment, then a tool such as a golf counter or a piece of paper where hash marks are recorded might be sufficient. Perhaps more commonly, self-monitoring forms such as thought records (e.g., J. E. Young, Rygh, Weinberger, & Beck, 2014), mood charts (Miklowitz, 2014), or diary cards (e.g., McCrady, 2014) might be developed to keep track of the occurrence of clinically relevant behaviors and the contexts within which they occur. In the published literature, self-monitoring methods have been used to keep track of a variety of behaviors, including instances of self-harm, hallucinations, alcohol consumption, classroom participation, binge and purge episodes, and insomnia (Korotitsch & Nelson-Gray, 1999).

Direct Observation

When direct observation is used as an assessment methodology, persons other than the client monitor the frequency of target behaviors, the contextual features associated with target behaviors, or some combination of these. The observers can be family or friends of the client, or other persons who enter the client's natural environment for assessment purposes. In the published literature, examples include parents as participant-observers of aspects of their children's behavior, spouses in couple's therapy who monitor the frequency of certain partner behaviors, and assistants who enter the classroom environment to observe disruptive behaviors displayed by a child (Hayes et al., 1999).

Direct observation methodologies can be devised in such a way that they reveal important information about a client's target problem area. During in vivo exposure for agoraphobia, for example, a therapist will often accompany the client to a number of anxiety-evoking environments, such as a town center or shopping mall. During the exposure process, the therapist will often assist the client in monitoring his or her level of anxiety to determine the extent to which the client's anxiety habituated during the exposure session.

Functional analytic psychotherapy (FAP; Kohlenberg & Tsai, 1991), an interpersonally oriented behavior therapy, is premised on the notion that the therapeutic environment is a social context that has some similarities to interpersonal situations that clients participate in outside of therapy. As such, clinically relevant behaviors in FAP are evoked and observed, then responded to in a manner consistent with the client's treatment goals. For behaviors to strengthen, displays of clinically relevant behaviors are responded to with natural reinforcers (e.g., natural expressions of warmth or support from the therapist). Instances of problematic behaviors are not reinforced and instead are placed on an extinction schedule (e.g., the therapist may respond to a client's complaints by ignoring the client, in the event that complaining is a problem behavior of the client's that reliably leads to difficulties in important relationships). In this example, the therapist is acting as a participant-observer because he or she is part of the client's current environment, with one of the roles of the therapist being to notice clinically relevant behaviors.

Role-play situations are another example in which therapists act as participant-observers. Role-plays permit the therapist to observe the client's social behavior in a simulated environment that resembles aspects of his or her natural environment in which the problem occurs. A client, for example, might role-play some type of target behavior (e.g., assertive action) in the therapeutic setting, with the therapist adopting the role of a significant other in this situation. After the role-play, the therapist can provide feedback on the client's performance and offer suggestions for how to improve the effectiveness of the behavior on future occasions.

CLOSING THE INITIAL INTERVIEW

Before closing the initial interview, it is often useful to provide the client with an opportunity to raise anything else he or she regards as important (e.g., "Is there anything that we have not discussed so far that would be important for me to know?"). It is also helpful to check in with the client to evaluate whether he or she has any questions (e.g., "Do you have any questions for me?") or whether he or she has any discomfort associated with events that transpired during the session (e.g., "Is there anything that happened or came up during today's session that was unpleasant?"). In addition to providing an opportunity for the client to express himself or herself in these areas, such questions convey a spirit of collaboration and an interest in the client's welfare. It is also useful to summarize the main points raised during the session and anticipate the next steps in the process with the client (e.g., continue assessment, develop a formulation of the client's problem areas, generate a therapy plan based on the formulation).

SUMMARY

In conducting initial behaviorally based assessments of a client's presenting complaints, it is often helpful for a therapist to do the following:

- Provide the client with a description of what to expect during the first few sessions, and work with the client to establish a warm and collaborative therapeutic relationship.
- Convey that CBT is an action-oriented therapy and that the client will have an active role in making decisions about his or her treatment and in carrying out therapy-related activities.
- Broadly assess the client's functioning, including strengths and behavioral skills.
- Emphasize what the client does and describe relevant behaviors in behavioral terms.
- Identify the circumstances or situations in which the client is more likely to engage in clinically relevant patterns of behavior.
- Explore the consequences that clinically relevant behavior patterns often produce, with emphasis placed on the processes that account for the maintenance of these behaviors over time.
- Assess the history associated with the client's problem areas; consider any biological conditions that might be associated with such behavior patterns.

- Evaluate the level and pervasiveness of impairment associated with clinically relevant behaviors.
- Consider and implement methods for assessing behaviors of clinical interest.
- Continue to develop, explore, and refine hypotheses concerning how clinically relevant behavior patterns might be related; that is, work toward the development of a case formulation.
- Inquire about the existence of other important areas that were not discussed before closing the initial interview, explore the client's overall sense of the therapeutic process thus far, and anticipate with the client what the next meeting or two might cover.

3

BEHAVIORAL CASE FORMULATION AND TREATMENT PLANNING

In this chapter, we address the process of developing a behavioral case formulation and offer guidelines for translating the formulation into a plan for therapy. We begin by discussing approaches for reducing large amounts of information obtained during initial assessments into a manageable set of problem areas and a workable case formulation. We also describe approaches for sharing and exploring the validity of the formulation with the client. This is followed by a presentation of guidelines for translating the case formulation into a plan for therapy and procedures for selecting appropriate intervention components. We also provide an overview of strategies for strengthening the motivation to change long-standing behavior patterns, anticipating therapeutic obstacles, and evaluating the effectiveness of therapeutic interventions. We conclude this chapter with a detailed case example that illustrates our main points.

http://dx.doi.org/10.1037/14691-003
Behavioral Interventions in Cognitive Behavior Therapy: Practical Guidance for Putting Theory Into Action,
Second Edition, by R. F. Farmer and A. L. Chapman

TAILORING ASSESSMENTS AND INTERVENTIONS TO THE CLIENT'S NEEDS, GOALS, AND STRENGTHS

Standardized therapy protocols have been developed and evaluated for use in the treatment of specific psychiatric disorders, and those that have demonstrated efficacy are regarded as empirically supported (cf. Barlow, 2014). These *empirically supported therapies* (ESTs) have typically been developed and evaluated with reference to a specific psychiatric disorder (e.g., major depressive disorder, panic disorder). In practice, decisions as to which EST to use are typically based on the client's presenting symptomatology or diagnosis, with the guiding rule being something such as, "If the client has diagnosis x, then use treatment y," provided that an effective therapy exists for that diagnosis or collection of symptoms. The use of ESTs in this way often results in successful outcomes for persons whose needs are consistent with the therapeutic objectives of the treatment protocol (Tarrier & Calam, 2002).

ESTs often represent a good starting place for clients who meet criteria for a single disorder for which ESTs exist. Often, however, clients present with multiple problem areas or several diagnoses. In these instances, there is little guidance regarding the order in which separate protocols should be applied and insufficient evidence that such a sequential approach is useful. For some disorders such as depression, there is more than one EST (A. T. Beck, Rush, Shaw, & Emery, 1979; Klerman, Weissman, Rounsaville, & Chevron, 1984; Lewinsohn, Antonuccio, Steinmetz-Breckenridge, & Teri, 1984; Martell, Dimidjian, & Herman-Dunn, 2010). It is also common for clients to present with problem areas for which there are no ESTs. In these instances, ESTs provide little guidance as to which interventions to select.

In contrast to the EST approach, which is protocol driven and variable centered (i.e., on diagnosis or symptom presentation), behavioral assessment is tailored to the individual client (Hayes, Nelson, & Jarrett, 1986). Individualized assessments are performed in acknowledgment that each person is distinctly different from any other in terms of inherited biological factors and learning history and that each person exists within a unique context. Diversity among persons is recognized and valued, and client assessments and intervention strategies are tailored to the therapy goals that are best suited to the client's problem areas and strengths.

Another aspect of the behavioral assessment approach is that ongoing assessment of the client's behavior and progress guides the selection and modification of interventions throughout treatment. As such, the process of assessment is ongoing, iterative, and adjustable and often results in the modification of hypotheses concerning factors influencing client behavior. Assessment and the resulting case formulation typically suggests the use of certain types of interventions, and the client's response to those interventions helps to refine the formulation and might suggest the need to modify or adjust subsequent interventions. Therapy, therefore, is much like the scientific process, where hypotheses are confirmed or disconfirmed and new experiments arise to address shortcomings or to extend the findings of previous experiments. Additionally, the behaviorally oriented therapist typically uses repeated assessments to evaluate the impact of interventions and the maintenance of therapy gains over time.

An individualized or case formulation–based approach to therapy is especially well suited to clients with multiple problem areas. A therapist who works within this approach is not limited to the use of a particular treatment protocol designed for a specific disorder and has the flexibility to select appropriate interventions from many empirically supported protocols (Persons, Roberts, Zalecki, & Brechwald, 2006). This flexibility allows the therapist to address multiple problem areas in an efficient manner. A therapist who sees a client, for example, with major depression and significant symptoms of worry and generalized anxiety might draw from behavioral activation approaches as well as behavioral experiments and other interventions for worry. The case formulation approach also suggests alternatives in the event that initial interventions prove unhelpful.

When therapists make decisions about therapeutic interventions for multiproblem clients based on person-centered (vs. diagnostic) data, cognitive behavior therapy (CBT) principles, and empirically supported CBT interventions, the therapeutic outcomes are often similar to those reported for clients treated with ESTs developed for specific diagnostic categories (Persons et al., 2006). Limited research is also mixed as to whether the tailoring of therapeutic interventions to the client's specific problem areas produces improved therapeutic outcomes compared with instances in which therapy follows a standardized protocol (Hallam, 2013; McHugh, Murray, & Barlow, 2009).

NARROWING DOWN THE CLIENT'S PROBLEM AREAS

In this section, we briefly summarize phases of assessment over the course of therapy. As we note, initial client assessments are quite broad in scope. As the clinical picture emerges, however, the focus increasingly narrows. This refinement process and the nature of behavioral assessments over the course of therapy are summarized in Exhibit 3.1.

Broadly Surveying Possible Problem Areas

In some respects, the initial assessment procedure can be likened to a funneling process (R. P. Hawkins, 1986). Within the first phase of assessment,

EXHIBIT 3.1
Phases of Behavioral Assessment

- *Broad survey of problem areas.* This involves screening possible problem areas in addition to those acknowledged by the client. Broad-bandwidth assessments might be used, such as diagnostic interviews, personality inventories, or symptom surveys. Within this phase, problem areas are conceptualized in general terms, and decisions concerning therapy are generally rudimentary (e.g., "Is therapy indicated? If so, which therapeutic modality or modalities would be most appropriate?").
- *Description of the client's problem areas.* This consists of a conceptualization of the client's primary problem areas within descriptive categories (e.g., diagnostic labels, functional response classes, topographical descriptions of behavior). Ideas for therapeutic approaches are still fairly broad and focused on classes of intervention strategies that might be appropriate (e.g., exposure therapy, skills training).
- *Identification of behavior patterns to target in therapy.* This consists of the delineation of specific behavior patterns to address in therapy as well as the situations where they are most likely to be observed, the generation of hypotheses concerning behavioral principles that are relevant to the maintenance of particular behavior patterns (e.g., positive reinforcement, negative reinforcement), and the development or design of intervention approaches for addressing these problem areas.
- *Implementation of an intervention and continuous evaluation of intervention effectiveness.* This includes an evaluation of the effectiveness of therapy as it is taking place. Assessment data gathered before and during the active intervention phase indicate whether behavior is changing as therapy progresses, and whether adjustments in the therapeutic approach should be undertaken to increase the likelihood of beneficial therapeutic outcomes.
- *Posttreatment assessment of behavior patterns targeted in therapy.* This consists of assessments on behavior patterns targeted in therapy once the active treatment phase has concluded. These assessments might be performed immediately after the conclusion of therapy and at spaced intervals thereafter (e.g., 1-, 3-, 6- and 12-months posttreatment). The main purpose for these assessments is to evaluate the maintenance of therapy gains over time and to detect instances when targeted behavior patterns reemerge or regain strength, suggesting the need for additional therapy or booster sessions.

for example, several potential problem areas might be screened. In addition to the client's chief complaint, broadband questionnaires (e.g., Brief Symptom Inventory; Derogatis, 1992) or diagnostic interviews (e.g., Structured Clinical Interview for the *Diagnostic and Statistical Manual of Mental Disorders*; First, Spitzer, Gibbon, & Williams, 1997) might be administered. Such assessments could reveal problem areas that would otherwise go unnoticed. At this point in the assessment process, decisions concerning treatment are fairly general, such as whether therapy is indicated or whether a referral should be considered.

During the early phases of assessment, it may be useful for the therapist to clarify with the client what aspects of his or her behavior are problematic. Inquiries into this area are often fairly broad at first. The therapist, for example, might ask if the behavior is happening too much, is too intense, or goes on for too long, all of which might suggest behavioral excesses (Follette, Naugle, & Linnerooth, 2000). If the client wishes to behave in a certain way but does not, this might suggest behavioral deficits or perhaps reflect the influence of rules related to the consequences of behavior that, in turn, suppress future action (e.g., "If I do _____, nothing good will come from it" or "If I do _____, I'll be humiliated"). Inquiries about the degree of impairment or distress associated with problematic behaviors (or nonengagement in behaviors that are pleasurable or rewarding) are also useful for gauging the severity of the problem area.

Transitioning From Broad Survey to Focal Assessments

In the second phase of assessment, the focus narrows. The end of this phase might include a definition of the client's problem area, a diagnosis, or some other means of classification (R. P. Hawkins, 1986). Once the general problem areas have been identified, intervention approaches might be considered in broad terms (e.g., exposure therapy, skills training, medication referral).

In the third phase, the assessment focus narrows further. The basic goals of this phase are the identification of specific target behaviors and the design of intervention strategies linked to assessment information (R. P. Hawkins, 1986). The selection of target behaviors, particularly among multiproblem clients, can be a challenge. Multiproblem clients, for example, often display some combination of the following:

- *behavioral excesses* (e.g., anxiety frequently experienced in situations that are objectively nonthreatening, substance misuse, pleasure-seeking behavior);
- *behavioral deficits* (e.g., impoverished coping skills, limited social skills);
- *difficulties in stimulus control* as evidenced by displays of inappropriate behavior in specific contexts (e.g., sexual provocativeness in inappropriate settings, inappropriate self-disclosures to strangers);
- *failures to display appropriate behavior in relevant contexts* (e.g., frequent failures to carryout responsibilities at work, refusal to perform household responsibilities);
- *excessively high or low performance standards* (e.g., perfectionism that interferes with task completion, frequent critical remarks directed at oneself); and
- *problems in self-regulation or control* (e.g., poorly controlled or impulsive behavior such as compulsive gambling or binge eating, frequent emotional outbursts).

During the first few phases of this process, it is often useful to consider the potential relevance of general principles of behavior as well as general scientific and clinical knowledge about the behavior patterns displayed by the client. These general, or *nomothetic*, principles can guide the case formulation by suggesting hypotheses about possible influences on the client's behavior and the appropriateness of therapeutic strategies. The clinician may then follow up on hypotheses with a more individualized, person-centered (or idiographic) assessment, further refining his or her case conceptualization and treatment plan. Ongoing assessment also ideally addresses the severity, impairment, and risk to the client or others associated with the client's problem areas because these factors can influence therapy goals (Goldfried & Sprafkin, 1976).

The last two assessment phases are primarily concerned with the assessment process itself (R. P. Hawkins, 1986). In the fourth phase, the effects of interventions on targeted areas or behaviors are continuously assessed. The main data derived from these assessments might be the severity, frequency, or pervasiveness of the problem behavior. In the fifth phase, assessments are performed posttreatment to evaluate the maintenance of therapy gains over time.

DEVELOPING THE CASE FORMULATION

A case formulation consists of the identification of a set of problem areas and the generation of hypotheses about factors associated with their development and maintenance (Eells, 2007). To arrive at these hypotheses, the therapist must first sift through and organize information gathered during the initial assessment phase. Although multiple determinants of behavior are generally assumed, behavioral case formulation approaches tend to emphasize operant and classical conditioning processes and social learning principles in the conceptualization of such influences. A clear understanding of these areas facilitates the therapist's development of a case formulation that will, in turn, inform the therapist's selection of appropriate interventions.

In this section, we begin by highlighting basic assumptions that underlie a behavioral case formulation. We then provide a general framework for developing a case formulation grounded in behavioral theories and principles. After this, we include a section that describes how information collected during initial interviews can be integrated to yield a cohesive case formulation that, in turn, informs the subsequent selection of therapy interventions.

Assumptions Associated With Behavioral Formulations

From a behavioral perspective, there are several central assumptions about the client in relation to his or her problem areas. In behavior assessment and therapy, for example, the primary level of analysis is the whole person in interaction with his or her environment (Hayes, Strosahl, Bunting, Twohig, & Wilson, 2004; Martell et al., 2010). From this perspective, behavior and the environmental context are not seen as "parts" to be analyzed separately. Rather, behavior and context are analyzed as a unit (Martell et al., 2010). Many of an individual's most important behaviors occur internally and include one's thoughts, emotions, or bodily sensations. To understand these internal behaviors as well as overt behaviors, one needs to understand the contexts both within and outside of the skin. For these reasons, one cannot neatly separate "person" from "environment" when understanding and changing the behavior of another. As summarized by Martell and colleagues (Martell, Addis, & Jacobson, 2001): "A contextual view . . . leads us to focus on changing actions and contexts. We're interested in what people are doing . . . when they're doing it, how they're doing it, and what the consequences are" (p. 16).

A central focus of behavioral interventions has historically been on the current situational determinants of behavior. There are two primary reasons for this. First, volumes of experimental research indicate that behavior varies in accordance with the contexts within which it occurs, and consequences associated with behavior affect its future occurrence (e.g., Catania, 2013). Second, one cannot change the past. That is, therapy cannot eliminate a client's prior learning and the resultant effects that such learning has had on his or her current actions. Therapeutic interventions, however, can promote new learning. Similarly, there are aspects of the client's physiological makeup that cannot be altered (e.g., genetic endowment). Accumulating evidence, however, indicates that brain structures and functions, and possibly gene expressions, can be modified by environmental events (Roth & Sweatt, 2011; Schneider, 2012) and that psychosocial therapies, when effective, can alter brain functioning such as neurochemistry and regional blood flow (Etkin, Pittenger, Polan, & Kandel, 2005; Thomaes et al., 2014).

Another important assumption of behavioral interventions involves the distinction between etiology, or the development of a psychological condition, and the maintenance of the condition over time. Historical factors that are responsible for the development of certain behavioral patterns are not necessarily responsible for the maintenance of those patterns. Although it is important to understand a client's learning history, it is imperative to assess and understand the current influences on behaviors that will be subsequently addressed in therapy. Such a view is consistent with the here-and-now focus of behavioral interventions.

Finally, problematic behavior often indicates the absence of alternative and more effective behaviors in the person's behavioral repertoire or the influence of contemporary environmental factors (e.g., environmental reinforcement for behavioral excesses, environmental suppression of infrequently occurring behaviors). Depending on the situation, therapy might emphasize the teaching of new behaviors (e.g., coping skills, more effective actions), alteration of current environments (e.g., eliminating reinforcement for frequently occurring problematic behaviors, increasing reinforcement opportunities for appropriate or effective behaviors), or modification of faulty thoughts or rules (e.g., helping individuals become aware of the actual contingencies associated with their behavior, supplying more accurate rules related to behavior in certain contexts).

A General Framework for the Development of a Case Formulation

Within CBT, the case formulation approach involves the development of an in-depth and individualized formulation of the client and his or her problem areas. The formulation approach presented here involves the conceptualization of the client's particular problem areas along functional and structural domains (R. O. Nelson & Hayes, 1986b; Persons & Tompkins, 2007). That is, this approach takes into account both the contextual features within which clinically relevant behavior occurs and the topographical (or descriptive) features of these behaviors.

Once established from pretreatment assessments, the therapist and client continually evaluate and refine the initial case formulation. That is, the case formulation is dynamic rather than static and is modified in accordance with new information or observations. The validity of the case formulation is supported by the following:

- *The ability of the formulation to account for areas on the problem list.* Does the formulation yield a convincing and coherent story about the problem areas in terms of their emergence, maintenance, and manifestation in some situations more than others, as well as the client's vulnerabilities that contributed to these problems (Persons, 1989)? If the formulation does not provide a logical account supported by existing client data, additional assessments might need to be performed, or additional work on the formulation might be required.
- *The ability of the formulation to predict clinically relevant behavior.* A formulation also has validity to the extent that it helps the clinician accurately predict a client's behavior in specific situations. When new data appear that are inconsistent with the

formulation, the clinician and client modify the formulation as needed. The validity of the case formulation, then, is subsequently evaluated in terms of its explanatory power, comprehensiveness, ability to account for items on the client's problem list, and accuracy in predicting future behavior in specific contexts (Persons et al., 2006; Wolpe & Turkat, 1985).

- *The client's reaction to the proposed formulation.* In the event that the client agrees with the formulation and supports it with additional examples or evidence, the validity of the formulation is supported. If the client disagrees with formulation, it is often useful to take time to understand what aspects of the formulation the client disagrees with and how he or she would modify the formulation to make it more accurate (Persons, 1989; Wolpe & Turkat, 1985).
- *The effectiveness of the interventions on the basis of the formulation.* The case formulation provides guidance for the selection and adaptation of empirically supported interventions for the client's problem areas (Persons et al., 2006). From a behavioral perspective, the primary aim and best test of any case formulation is whether it results in effective interventions. In instances in which the intervention is not effective, it is likely that either the formulation was incorrect or the intervention was inappropriate given the factors that established and maintained the behaviors targeted in therapy (Hayes & Follette, 1992). When the therapist believes the formulation was correct, he or she might try and evaluate an alternative intervention consistent with the formulation. Alternatively, the therapist might reexamine the underlying hypotheses and assumptions on which the formulation is based.

In this section, we provide a model of case formulation influenced by Persons (1989; Persons et al., 2006; Persons & Tompkins, 2007). In keeping with the focus of this book, emphasis is placed on contextual factors associated with problem behavior. We therefore organize our presentation according to the following formulation elements: (a) the problem list, (b) precipitants and activating situations, (c) hypothesized origins, (d) the working hypothesis, and (e) sharing and exploring the formulation with the client. The last four elements of the case formulation, (f) the treatment plan, (g) establishing a motivation for change and securing a commitment for action, (h) potential obstacles to effective therapy, and (i) procedures for evaluating the effectiveness of therapy, are discussed later in this chapter. Components of this model of case formulation are presented in Exhibit 3.2.

EXHIBIT 3.2
Steps in the Development of a Behavioral Case Formulation

- *The problem list.* This list contains no more than 10 problematic behavior patterns to address in therapy.
- *Situational determinants of targeted problem areas.* This includes a description of antecedent conditions that reliably set the occasion for problem behavior, as well as the consequences that follow behavior that, in turn, influence its future frequency, intensity, or duration.
- *Hypothesized origins.* This includes a delineation of hypotheses concerning relevant biological characteristics and learning histories associated with the primary problem areas.
- *Working hypothesis.* This is an integrated and cohesive case formulation that addresses interrelations among the various problem areas.
- *Sharing and exploring the formulation.* This involves sharing the therapist's understanding of the client's problem areas, including ideas about factors associated with onset and maintenance of these problems. The client's agreement with formulation is also explored, with the formulation modified in accordance with client feedback.
- *Treatment plan.* This includes the provision of a rationale for the therapeutic interventions suggested, followed by an evaluation of the client's understanding of the rationale. Therapeutic goals in behavioral terms are also specified, as is the therapeutic framework, interventions, and between-session activities that comprise the suggested treatment approach.
- *Strengthening motivation for change and securing a commitment for action.* This involves nonconfrontational and empathic discussions with the client about the effects and consequences of the problem behavior. The therapist and client also explore the potential benefits of change.
- *Potential obstacles to effective therapy.* The therapist offers one or two hypotheses concerning potential therapy obstacles. This is done to increase the likelihood that problems posed by potential obstacles can be anticipated and problem solved in advance of their emergence.
- *Procedures for evaluating of the effectiveness of therapy.* Movement toward measurable therapy goals is repeatedly assessed to determine whether sufficient progress is being made as therapy unfolds.

The Problem List: Behaviors for Targeting in Therapy

The assessment process begins with the generation of a problem list, which is often defined by a set of topographically defined behaviors that might be subsequently targeted in therapy. This list is often substantially informed by the client's chief complaint but also may include other problem areas that emerge during the assessment process.

Persons and Tompkins (2007) suggested that problem lists typically consist of five to eight items and should not contain more than 10 items, or the list may become unwieldy. If there are more than 10 potential problem areas, the therapist might work with the client to prioritize potential areas so that therapy will be more focused. Although not all items on the problem list may be actively or explicitly targeted in therapy, it is often useful to monitor nontargeted areas throughout. The therapist and client might discover later on that nontargeted areas are therapeutically relevant or that they change as modifications occur in other primary problem areas targeted in therapy. Improvements in emotion regulation skills might, for example, result in improvements in interpersonal skills or problem solving, even when therapy has not focused on interpersonal functioning (Dixon-Gordon, Chapman, & Turner, in press).

Persons and Tompkins (2007) also suggested that items on the list, whenever possible, be summarized with no more than a few words (e.g., depressed mood, panic attacks, binge eating, marital conflicts) and supplemented with a short topographical description of associated behavioral, cognitive, or mood components of the problem (e.g., frequently sleeps more than 10 hours per day and avoids social interactions, with accompanying negative self-referential thoughts such as "I'll never amount to anything" and feelings of emptiness). Additionally, to monitor change in the problem area as therapy progresses, the therapist needs to quantify the problem area in some way (e.g., frequency counts of problem, problem intensity ratings, scores on a relevant self-report measure, activity log record).

Even though not necessarily identified as problem areas by the client, other areas in which quality of life is adversely affected in some way (e.g., daily alcohol use, unemployment, health-related problems) might represent potential problem areas. These areas should initially be included in the list. An inclusive list allows the therapist to consider the wide range of potential factors that might be associated with the client's primary problem areas and may consequently aid in the development of working hypotheses about these areas (Persons, 1989).

Once a problem list is generated and the therapist and client agree on its content, the therapist should take time to consider possible common themes that run through these various problem areas (Persons, 1989). That is, the therapist might question, "What do all of these problems have in common?" Although the list might contain a number of diverse or topographically distinct behaviors (e.g., bingeing, purging, agoraphobic avoidance, dissociation, intentional self-injury), they might all have in common similar functional properties or relations (e.g., experiential avoidance). In addition to listing problem behaviors on the basis of topography, they can also be organized according to their associated functional properties, as behaviors that have similar functions can often be effectively addressed through the same therapeutic interventions.

Situational Determinants of Behavior: Precipitating Events and Behavioral Consequences

Precipitating events refer to antecedent conditions (e.g., discriminative stimuli, establishing operations) that set the occasion for behavior. Consequences are the events that follow behavior, which influence the frequency, intensity, or duration of future behavior in these situations (e.g., reinforcers or punishers).

Functional analyses, reviewed in Chapter 2 of this volume, help identify antecedent and consequent events that influence behavior. Such analyses also facilitate the development of hypotheses concerning a particular form of problem behavior (Sturmey, 2008). Steps in generating a functional formulation of specific problem areas involve the following:

- use of questionnaire measures, behavioral observations, and clinical interviews to obtain information about the form and function of problematic behaviors;
- ongoing self-monitoring and recording of target behaviors and their associated contexts in initial assessments and during therapy; and
- generation of hypotheses about the functions of problem behaviors and the exploration of the validity of these hypotheses with the client.

In addition to immediate environmental contingencies, there is another class of determinants that influence behavior. These are verbal rules that specify associations between antecedent events and behaviors, behaviors and consequent events, or a combination of these (Skinner, 1969). In fact, it is quite possible that for most individuals, behavior is more strongly influenced by contingency-specifying rules than actual environmental contingencies. When verbal rules function as an antecedent of behavior, such behavior is *rule-governed*. Examples of rules that could influence behavior include the following: "If I make myself vomit, I won't get fat," "If I have a few drinks, I'll be less anxious and more funny around others," and "When someone acts like they want to get to know me, they're actually looking for ways to take advantage of me."

Verbal rules in some circumstances are analogous to self-efficacy expectations and outcome expectations in social cognitive theory (Bandura, 1986). *Self-efficacy expectations* are a set of beliefs about one's ability to perform certain behaviors. Such expectations often result from personal knowledge concerning actual behavioral deficits. Alternatively, such expectations might be erroneous and underestimate the client's actual behavioral capacities. In this latter case, an individual might incorrectly conclude that there are deficits in his or her behavioral repertoire because of faulty early learning (e.g., frequent statements by the client's father that conveyed the idea "You'll never amount to anything") or inaccurate feedback concerning performance by others (e.g., overly harsh and unrealistic evaluations by a job supervisor). Regardless of the accuracy of one's thoughts about his or her behavioral efficacy, when self-efficacy is low, the likelihood that a person will engage in a particular behavior in a certain context is likewise low (e.g., "Why should I try? I know I can't do it").

Outcome expectations refer to a person's estimate that a given behavior will result in certain outcomes. In social cognitive theory, positive outcome expectations function as incentives for behavior (e.g., "If I try hard and persist, I'll eventually get what I want"). Negative outcome expectations function as disincentives and reduce the likelihood that an individual will perform behavior in certain contexts (e.g., "Even if I work really hard on this, nothing positive will come from it").

Rule statements also have some similarity to A. T. Beck's notion of *primary assumptions* (also referred to as *personal rules* or *core beliefs*) in his cognitive model of therapy:

> During his [sic] developmental period, each individual learns rules or formulas by which he attempts to "make sense" of the world. These formulas determine how the individual organizes perceptions into cognitions, how he sets goals, how he evaluates and modifies his behavior, and how he understands or comes to terms with events in his life. In essence, these basic assumptions form a personal matrix of meaning and value. (A. T. Beck et al., 1979, p. 244)

A review of Chapter 12 ("Depressogenic Assumptions") of A. T. Beck et al.'s (1979) landmark work reveals that core assumptions often take the form of rule statements that specify a behavior, a consequence associated with that behavior, an antecedent condition in the presence of which a behavior will produce a specified outcome, or some combination of these (e.g., "If I am nice [suffer for others, appear bright and beautiful], bad things [divorce, poorly behaved children] won't happen to me"). Rules or assumptions that a client holds about his or her behavior have influence as to whether behavior will be performed and how it is evaluated.

As we discussed in the Chapter 2, establishing operations also can affect the likelihood of behavior by altering the reinforcing properties associated with engaging in certain forms of behavior. If, for example, one has not had anything to drink for a long time, the reinforcing properties associated with drinking water or other beverages are much greater. Conversely, if one has just consumed large amounts of water, the act of drinking more water would likely be experienced as aversive. Many forms of problematic behavior are more likely following certain establishing operations (e.g., binge eating after a period of food deprivation, purging after the consumption of large amounts of food, aggressive acts when feeling angry in response to a frustrating event, consumption of a large amount of alcohol when feeling acutely stressed).

Hypothesized Origins

Hypothesized origins refer to what we described as person variables in Chapter 2—that is, one's biological characteristics and learning history as related to the primary problem areas. Person variables often constitute predisposing or vulnerability factors associated with the development, recurrence, or maintenance of problem areas. Clarifying the client's predisposing factors might illuminate why she or he developed the problem in question, whereas someone else under similar circumstances would not have developed the problem.

Biological characteristics include genetic predispositions, temperament, and other physiological characteristics that might have some relevance for the problem area (e.g., normal effects of aging on cognitive abilities, the effects of disease). Several psychological conditions, for example, have been observed to run in families, a finding that has often been interpreted as indicating a genetic influence (Rhee, Feigon, Bar, Hadeishi, & Waldman, 2001). Similarly, variations in temperament are often regarded as the result of biological influences (Fowles, 2001) and are also observed to run in families (e.g., Olino, Klein, Dyson, Rose, & Durbin, 2010). There are further indications that variations in temperament partially account for individual differences in the sensitivity or responsiveness to rewarding and punishing outcomes (Corr, 2008; Gray & McNaughton, 2000). Temperament factors might be considered when developing hypotheses about the client's behavior and designing interventions.

Aspects of the client's early learning history also frequently account for the development of current problem areas. Among such potential influences are modeling experiences, social and cultural values or practices, or a history of reinforcement for engagement in the problematic behaviors. Individuals with more chronic patterns of psychological disorder often have extensive learning histories, behavioral deficits, and behavioral excesses that appear to be linked to the problem area. Persons with some forms of personality disorder, for example, often report histories of significant interpersonal loss, neglect, rejection, or abuse (Zanarini et al., 1997). Therapy might, therefore, target resultant behavioral deficits or excesses as well as long-standing vulnerabilities associated with such histories.

One way to initiate the collaborative process of developing a formulation and, more specifically, to generate hypotheses about the origins of the problem, is to ask the client what his or her thoughts are about how the problem came about. By the time a client comes to therapy, it is likely that he or she has spent a good deal of time thinking about the problem. Questions for exploring this area include the following:

- "When did you first notice this problem?"
- "What was going on in your life when this first occurred?"
- "Do you have ideas about how this problem came about?"
- "How have people responded when this problem is present?"

- "Can you recall a time when this problem helped or benefited you in some way?"
- "Since this problem first occurred, has it had any lasting effects on you?"

Working Hypothesis

The working hypothesis represents the heart of the case formulation and seeks to tie together each of the client's problem areas into an integrated and cohesive formulation (Persons, 1989). The formulation ideally addresses the interrelations among the various problem areas through the consideration of similarities in etiological, predisposing, precipitating, and maintaining factors. In relation to behavioral interventions in CBT specifically, a working hypothesis seeks to explain the function of problematic behavior for the individual and to specify the forms or topographies of problematic behavior that share similar functions. The degree of distress or impairment associated with these problem areas might also be assessed because these considerations have implications for what treatment setting or treatment modalities are most appropriate for the client as well as the appropriate duration of treatment. *Treatment settings* refer to whether the client would best benefit from weekly outpatient sessions or more frequent contacts, if a crisis plan should be developed and whether it can be successfully carried out on an outpatient basis, or whether inpatient or other forms of institutional care (e.g., day hospital) are required. *Treatment modalities* are exemplified by individual therapies (e.g., weekly outpatient CBT, supportive therapy), group or milieu therapies, biological interventions (e.g., medications, electroconvulsive therapy), or some combination of these.

Psychiatric diagnoses can inform the case formulation and treatment decisions. Given that diagnostic categories are often defined by collections of covarying behavior, cognition, and emotion, they are not necessarily incompatible with cognitive or behavioral approaches to assessment. Diagnostic concepts, however, are nomothetic. That is, they are group or variable centered, whereas behavioral assessments within CBT tend to be idiographic, or centered on the individual and his or her uniqueness (Nelson-Gray & Paulson, 2003). A diagnosis without an accompanying individualized formulation leaves the therapist with little guidance on how to best help the client (Persons, 1989). Consequently, from a CBT perspective, a diagnosis is largely regarded as a supplement to, not a substitute for, an individually focused case formulation that includes consideration of contextual factors associated with the problem area.

Similar to psychiatric diagnoses, psychological test findings are sometimes a useful supplement to an individualized case formulation. Test findings can, for example, be used to validate a client's diagnosis or aspects of the formulation. Tests, such as self-report measures, can also be used to index pretreatment functioning in clinically relevant areas, assess any progress during treatment, and evaluate maintenance of therapeutic gains posttreatment.

EXPLORING THE PROBLEM FORMULATION WITH THE CLIENT

Behavioral assessment and intervention are collaborative endeavors in which the client and therapist work together to understand and ameliorate problems that are important to the client. Because the case formulation serves as a road map for subsequent therapeutic interventions, it is important for the therapist to give the client a clear description of this road map as well as the opportunity to add to it or modify it. The following are several tasks for the therapist related to communicating the formulation to the client: (a) presenting the formulation in an open and collaborative manner, (b) distinguishing the client from the problem, (c) using effective communication strategies, and (d) dealing effectively with the issue of diagnosis.

Presenting the Formulation in an Open and Collaborative Manner

When exploring a formulation of the problem area with the client, the therapist may find it useful to describe his or her understanding of the etiology of the problem area; any hypothesized predisposing factors; a description of the development of the problem over time; and how manifestations of the problem may have changed in terms of expression, antecedent triggers, or consequences. Primary emphasis, however, should be placed on factors that currently function to maintain problems.

The therapist ideally offers his or her views in a manner that conveys openness to exploration. The case formulation should be presented at a level that is easily understandable to the client and that minimizes the use of technical terms and jargon (e.g., negative reinforcement, automatic thoughts). Often, however, a formulation that is grounded in core CBT principles and concepts will require the use of some associated terminology. When using technical terms, the therapist should define key concepts clearly and use actual examples from the client's life to illustrate their application. Educating the client about the rationale of behavioral approaches to treatment is, after all, part of the therapeutic process.

When reviewing the formulation, the therapist should distinguish the client from the problem. Doing so conveys to the client the idea that the problem area is the focus of therapy. Such an approach also conveys that the client's problems are understandable and that both the client and the therapist are united to solve the problem (Wolpe & Turkat, 1985). If the client disagrees with the formulation, the therapist must take great care to assess why before proceeding. Given that the formulation is based on a wide variety of information obtained during pretreatment assessments, it is likely that disagreements will be based on small details that can be easily clarified rather than on larger, differing views of core assumptions.

Using Effective Communication Strategies

To facilitate the client's understanding of the formulation, the therapist may find it helpful to supply a diagram that summarizes the overall model or to develop a diagram while discussing the formulation (Persons & Tompkins, 2007). Such a diagram can take several forms, such as a time line that represents the onset of critical events or a functional representation of the client's problem behavior (as exemplified in Chapter 2). Ideally, the emphasis of the diagram should be on factors that can be changed or modified during therapy, assets that can be strengthened, or a combination of these. In addition, once a formulation has been developed and discussed, it is often useful to check the client's understanding by asking him or her to explain it (Persons, 1989). One way to do this is to ask a client to imagine that he or she is discussing his or her problem and formulation with a friend or family member.

Dealing Effectively With the Issue of Diagnosis

A question often arises as to whether the therapist should share diagnostic labels with the client. Some clients feel relieved and optimistic when they hear that their problems have a name (Addis & Carpenter, 2000). Some diagnostic labels, however, are not always appropriate to share. In particular, personality disorder diagnostic labels might not be appropriate to share given the many conceptual and psychometric difficulties associated with these concepts (Farmer, 2000; Widiger, 2011) and their associated stigmatizing properties. The label that the therapist provides the client for his or her problem does not necessarily need to be a diagnostic label. Rather, the label can refer to the collection of behaviors the client exhibits that will be targeted in therapy (e.g., chronic pain, excessive stress, intentional self-harm, marital distress).

INITIAL STEPS IN DEVELOPING A COLLABORATIVE PLAN FOR THERAPY

In some respects, the process of treatment planning and formulation is like an exercise in problem solving and decision making (Kanfer &

Busemeyer, 1982). Whereas problem solving involves coming up with alternative approaches for responding to problems, decision-making processes involve using rules or guides to make selections among available alternatives. When viewed from this perspective, the client and therapist first work together to identify problems. Upon reaching consensus as to the nature of the problem areas, the therapist and client decide collaboratively how to best approach these areas on the basis of a detailed understanding of the client's problems and knowledge of the most effective treatment guidelines available.

A number of factors influence which interventions are optimal for a particular client with a given problem area. Among these are characteristics of target behaviors, characteristics of the client, social-environmental factors, diagnosis, treatment history, and characteristics of interventions (Haynes, 1986). Client characteristics include motivation for therapy, goals for treatment, personal resources and skills, and thoughts about whether the social environment will positively support therapeutic change. Behaviors that compete with therapeutic goals may also reduce the likelihood of successful treatment and thus should be targeted in therapy. Social-environmental factors are important to consider, particularly if the problem behavior coincides with particular social or environmental contexts. When situational influences are evident, they might be addressed as part of the intervention program. Characteristics of interventions include features that define the interventions as well as associated qualities such as cost-effectiveness, side effects, and the magnitude, generalizability, and maintenance of treatment effects.

In this section, we provide general guidelines associated with developing a collaborative plan for therapy that uses behavioral interventions within a CBT framework. In doing so, we are cognizant that there is currently no single method or empirically supported approach for integrating an array of assessment data and, from this, designing an effective intervention. We also note that before coming to therapy, clients often have already tried many ways of coping with the problem. If a client has been in therapy before, it is often useful to clarify why he or she previously entered therapy, what issues therapy primarily addressed, how these issues were approached in therapy, and to what effect. Interventions that were previously tried and appropriately administered but failed to produce desirable outcomes might be considered only after alternative interventions are tried.

Reaching Consensus on the Goals of Therapy

In planning treatment, it is important for the therapist and client to clarify and explicitly agree on the goals of therapy. Goals may include the content focus of therapy (e.g., which topics will be of central importance), which target behaviors to pursue, which interventions or strategies will best realize therapy goals, the within-session structure of therapy, engagement in therapy-related activities in between sessions, the duration and frequency of therapy, and the use of follow-up or maintenance sessions. Reaching agreement in these areas not only establishes an implicit therapy contract but also ascribes the client's and therapist's roles, tasks, and responsibilities (Otto, Reilly-Harrington, Kogan, & Winett, 2003).

Orientation also should address the focus and structural aspects of therapy. Therapists using a CBT approach may find it useful to orient the client to the fact that therapy will largely emphasize current behaviors and problems areas, and to provide a rationale for this emphasis. The relatively short-term nature of CBT and the expected number of sessions to reach therapy goals is also important to review. Finally, CBT should be described as an active approach to therapy within which the therapist and client participate together.

When the client's goals for therapy are not explicitly conveyed by his or her chief complaint, therapists can ask about how therapy might ideally be helpful. Questions such as the following, taken from Persons (1989, p. 327), can help the client identify goals:

- "How will you know when you have solved this problem?"
- "How might your life be different when you solve this problem?"
- "What will you do differently once this problem is solved?"

Suggesting Areas to Address That the Client Does Not Acknowledge as Problems

Although clients often come to therapy for assistance with relatively specific problems (e.g., mood disturbance, lingering effects of trauma), therapists sometime learn about other behaviors that are problematic. Examples include suicidal behavior, self-injury, binge–purge behavior, substance abuse, or other behaviors that interfere with the client's quality of life. When such behaviors are evident, the therapist might highlight them, assess their impact on the client's functioning, and ascertain whether the client wishes to change these behaviors. Clients may not wish to change some problem behaviors (e.g., non–life-threatening substance use), and it might be reasonable for these behaviors not to be targeted in therapy. In other cases, some behaviors (e.g., suicide attempts or self-injury) are likely to be life threatening or to significantly interfere with the quality of the client's life, and the therapist might make them high priority treatment targets out of necessity. Generally, the client is more likely to accept the inclusion of these behavioral targets if the therapist is able to provide a cogent rationale for doing so.

The Overarching Therapeutic Goals of Psychological Flexibility,
Freedom, and Effectiveness

Whenever possible, therapists should emphasize in therapy the development of effective behaviors or behavioral repertoires and place less emphasis on the elimination of behaviors (Goldiamond, 1974; R. P. Hawkins, 1986). This approach contrasts with other approaches that emphasize eliminating something, such as emotional distress, rather than acquiring something. Behaviorally oriented clinicians often find it helpful to build behavioral repertoires and skills that provide the client with more behavioral options and greater flexibility for responding to situations that arise (Hayes & Strosahl, 2004; Linehan, 1993a). Rather than eliminate emotional distress, for example, a therapeutic goal might be to assist the client in coping more effectively when distress is present. A benefit of building behavioral repertoires (e.g., coping skills) is that it often lessens the frequency, intensity, or duration of the problem area (e.g., emotional distress). By strategically developing or strengthening certain behavioral repertoires, therapists provide clients with more effective behavioral options and, correspondingly, greater flexibility.

Albert Bandura (1986), the primary developer of social learning and social cognitive theories, regards freedom as having choices among options, with available options determined by prior learning experiences. As the client gains more behavioral options and, correspondingly, greater flexibility, his or her freedom also becomes that much greater. Behavioral interventions in CBT seek to increase an individual's freedom by providing him or her with more skills, abilities, and options for responding to the events in his or her life than were previously available (Kazdin, 2012). Multiple abilities, capabilities, and behavioral alternatives increase an individual's opportunities for greater flexibility in responding and increase likelihood for effective action across varying contexts. Similarly, therapists often attempt to facilitate clients' sense of personal freedom by helping them understand contextual factors that influence their behavior, articulate their goals and values, and realize that problem behaviors or dysfunctional ways of coping are often inconsistent with these goals and values (Kazdin, 2012).

Prioritizing Problem Areas

Most clinicians agree that high-risk behaviors, such as suicidal or self-injurious behaviors, should receive immediate priority. In her description of dialectical behavior therapy (DBT), for example, Linehan (1993a) outlined a schema for prioritizing behaviors to attend to during individual therapy sessions. Her within-session hierarchical framework during the first stage of therapy prioritizes treatment targets in terms of their potential to threaten the life of the client or others, disrupt or reduce the effectiveness of therapy, or interfere with the client's ability to attain a reasonable quality of life.

In Linehan's (1993a) hierarchical arrangement of Stage 1 treatment targets, behaviors regarded as most urgent or of the highest priority are *life-threatening behaviors*, including suicidal behaviors and nonsuicidal self-injury. Examples of behaviors that fall within this class are suicide crisis behaviors, suicide attempts, suicidal ideation and communication, suicide-related beliefs, and nonsuicidal self-injury. On similar footing in terms of urgency and priority are homicidal plans or indications of aggressive, neglectful, or otherwise abusive actions toward individuals who are unable to protect themselves (e.g., children, elderly adults).

The next class in her schema consists of *therapy-interfering behaviors* on the part of the client or therapist (Linehan, 1993a). Examples of such behaviors for the client include frequent missed sessions, chronic lateness, strong emotional outbursts or aggressive behavior directed at the therapist, or failure to complete homework assignments; examples of behaviors for the therapist include routinely starting sessions late or frequently gazing at the clock during sessions. Behaviors that fall within this class would likely undermine therapy, result in therapy being less effective, lead to therapist burnout, or diminish the interest that the therapist or client has in continuing therapy (in Chapter 11, we discuss strategies for effectively responding to therapy-interfering behaviors).

The third class consists of *quality-of-life interfering behaviors* and includes substance abuse, unprotected sexual behavior, financial problems, criminal activities, and dysfunctional interpersonal behaviors. Finally, an additional class consists of *behavioral skills to increase*. In DBT, skill training usually takes place within a separate skills training group. Individual therapy sessions, however, might facilitate the integration of these skills into the client's daily life.

The hierarchical arrangement of therapy priorities in DBT are provided as examples for how a therapist might think about sequencing therapy in relation to treatment targets over time. Even though the specifics of this approach may not be applicable to all clients with multiple problems, some sort of hierarchical and sequential approach is usually indicated.

With clients who have fewer problem areas or problems of a more acute nature, other guidelines for target behavior selection might be considered (R. P. Hawkins, 1986; Linehan, 1993a; R. O. Nelson & Hayes, 1986b). These include selecting behaviors for attention in therapy that

- are given priority by the client,
- are endorsed by the client as behaviors he or she is willing to work on,
- are related to higher order treatment targets,

- belong to a similar functional response class as the primary problem behaviors,
- are widely regarded as desirable by others,
- have the greatest likelihood of being reinforced in natural environments,
- facilitate entry into natural environments in which other important behaviors might be taught or reinforced (e.g., hygiene; appropriate conduct for maintaining job),
- have a high degree of general utility across situations (e.g., problem-solving skills),
- maximize the flexibility of the client's behavioral repertoire and promote long-term benefit to the person, and
- occur lower in a skill hierarchy (i.e., foundation skills) and are necessary to establish before modifying skills higher in a hierarchy.

DECIDING WHICH INTERVENTIONS TO SELECT

Whereas disorder-specific EST protocols might be useful for individuals who have a single and specific problem area or diagnosis, they might be less applicable to individuals who have multiple problem areas. With such clients, a therapist might elect to administer several relevant ESTs simultaneously or sequentially; however, such an approach can be cumbersome and have many redundancies. There is also little in the way of guidance as to which problem area to target first (Persons et al., 2006).

Additionally, some clients who have a specific problem area with an associated EST do not require all therapy components in the EST protocol. A client with panic disorder, for example, may not engage in shallow and rapid breathing when anxious. For such an individual, treatment components on breathing retraining may not be particularly relevant or helpful. As this example illustrates, therapy selection based on diagnosis alone might result in the application of therapeutic approaches that are not optimally effective or might result in the application of more therapy interventions than are necessary (Eifert, Schulte, Zvolensky, Lejuez, & Lau, 1997). Ultimately, this may result in lengthy and costly treatment interventions, when a briefer and more targeted course of therapy could have been equally effective. In addition, when the relevance of particular interventions is not apparent to the client, he or she may lose interest in or become pessimistic with regard to therapy and consequently drop out prematurely.

Finally, many problem areas do not have an associated EST. In these circumstances, a strict empirically informed protocol-driven approach is not available. When confronted with such a situation, a therapist is left with several options: (a) do not treat the client, (b) refer the client to another provider, (c) use a collection of techniques or components of ESTs for problems that are similar to those of the client, or (d) use evidence-based cognitive and behavioral principles in the development of a client formulation that subsequently informs the selection of interventions. We suggest that strategies (c) and (d), when combined, are more likely than other options to address important idiographic features of the client and his or her life context that influence treatment outcome. In essence, behavioral case formulation and treatment planning are principle driven and empirically informed rather than strictly protocol-driven endeavors.

In this section, we highlight two principle-driven case formulation approaches to the selection of interventions: clinical functional analysis and the case formulation–driven modular approach. These approaches contrast with the client-matching-to-EST method because they are both idiographic and guided by behavioral and cognitive principles, or formulation driven, and not exclusively protocol driven. Although we present these approaches separately, they are not necessarily exclusive and can be combined to produce a formulation that takes into account both functional and topographical aspects of the client's problem areas.

The Role of Functional Analyses in the Selection of Interventions

Clinical functional analysis is an ideal method for identifying the sequence of events that precede and follow problem behavior. Knowledge of such influences can, in turn, inform the design of an intervention that is conceptually linked to the assessment findings. The components of a clinical functional analysis are reviewed in Chapter 2. Procedurally, the therapist and client might first work together to clearly identify links or sequences between antecedent events and problem behaviors as well as immediate and delayed reactions to the problem behavior displayed by the client and others. Once these have been defined in reasonable detail, specific junctures in the sequence are identified in which opportunities exist for alternative responses that, if enacted, might produce more desirable outcomes and avert conditions that occasion the problem behavior.

Findings from such analyses can also be used to facilitate a cost–benefit profile of specific problem behaviors in which current problem behaviors are analyzed in terms of their negative and positive consequences as well as the extent to which such outcomes are consistent with long-term goals or values. Once established, alternative behavioral routes are explored that have a reasonable chance of producing similar reinforcers as problematic behaviors but without the associated negative costs. Building competencies and behavioral repertoires increase the likelihood that therapy will produce lasting gains because effective behaviors should produce their own reinforcing consequences that function to maintain them over time.

As suggested by Haynes (1986), the selection of interventions based on a clinical functional analysis should be strongly influenced by a client's therapeutic objectives because interventions that result in outcomes incongruent with the client's goals are often doomed to fail. A well-designed intervention takes into account the client's skill and ability level and other strengths and resources that he or she brings to the therapeutic situation (Haynes, 1986).

Evaluating the Functional Similarity of Different Forms of Problem Behavior

Upon performing a set of functional analyses for different problem areas, a therapist might notice that several behaviors in which a client engages (e.g., excessive and ritualistic house cleaning, binge eating, excessive alcohol consumption, dissociation) often occur under similar circumstances (e.g., when feeling stressed, after a disagreement with a partner) and produce similar outcomes (e.g., a reduction in the intensity or frequency of unpleasant thoughts or emotions). Such diverse behaviors might constitute a functional response class. *Functional responses classes* consist of groups of behaviors that, although different in form or expression, share functional relatedness because they are often influenced by similar classes of environmental variables, including the outcomes or consequences they produce.

Experiential avoidance, for example, has been described as a functional response class characterized by an unwillingness to remain in contact with painful emotions, thoughts, or memories, as evidenced by a tendency to actively alter these experiences through some other behavior (Hayes, Wilson, Gifford, Follette, & Strosahl, 1996). Behaviors used to alter these experiences (e.g., substance use, dissociation, self-injury) often attenuate or terminate unwanted internal experiences and are consequently maintained by the relief they produce (negative reinforcement) or by other reinforcing outcomes (e.g., the experience of euphoria in the case of substance use, which might positively reinforce drug consumption). Farmer and Nelson-Gray (2005) and Follette et al. (2000) described several examples of functional response classes.

An awareness of the functional similarity that multiple problem behavior patterns serve can help pinpoint the core processes that maintain their occurrence. These core processes, in turn, can be addressed therapeutically by similar intervention strategies (cf. McHugh et al., 2009). If shared functions exist among diverse patterns of behavior (e.g., substance use and intentional self-injury), it is also important to establish what, if any, alternative behaviors are present in the client's repertoire that have similar functions and are more adaptive, health promoting, and consistent with the client's personal goals. As therapy works to reduce or eliminate the problematic behavior patterns, adaptive alternative behaviors are ideally targeted for strengthening. When the client's repertoire is deficient of behavioral alternatives, therapy might be focused on teaching new skills that can eventually substitute for problematic behaviors.

A Case Formulation–Driven Modular Approach to Intervention Selection

A modular approach to intervention selection has been described as a strategy for developing an individualized approach to treatment planning and implementation based on assessment information (Chorpita et al., 2013; Henin, Otto, & Reilly-Harrington, 2001; McHugh et al., 2009). With this approach, empirically supported CBT interventions are dismantled into their associated components. The selection of CBT modules for clients is individualized, with selection based on pretreatment assessments, a consideration of the client's needs, progress in therapy, and the client's therapy goals.

Before selecting appropriate modules, the therapist ideally performs detailed assessments within a given area (e.g., does a client who is depressed demonstrate highly negative views of self, excessive worry, social skills deficits, problem-solving deficits, nonengagement in previously enjoyable activities, or some combination of these?). From these assessments, a problem list is developed that outlines areas tied to the overall problem area that is of greatest concern. After the collection of pretreatment assessment information, a treatment approach is constructed by assembling modules that are relevant to the client's needs and goals, with between-session therapeutic activities (e.g., self-monitoring of target areas, therapy-related homework) as the "glue" that holds the modules together and provides continuity across treatment elements (Van Brunt, 2000).

A depressed client who displays negativistic views of self and future, for example, might be assigned to a cognitive restructuring model. Another client who is depressed and displays primary deficits in the area of social skills might undergo a skills training module. Similarly, a third depressed client, who has become withdrawn, stays at home, and worries a good part of the day might undergo a therapy program that emphasizes worry reduction and behavioral activation. Rather than receiving a complete CBT treatment package that involves cognitive restructuring, social skills training, and behavioral activation, a client would receive only those components that are most appropriate for him or her from an all-inclusive treatment package.

Compared with an EST protocol–driven approach, the case formulation approach is more individualized and flexible (see, for example, Chorpita et al., 2013). Rather than using all treatment components within a single EST protocol, for example, a therapist might instead use intervention strategies from several EST protocols that have particular relevance for the client's problem areas (Persons et al., 2006).

Some General Intervention Guidelines

In Chapters 4 through 10, we describe several behavioral interventions and the circumstances under which they are most appropriate and likely to be effective. In this section, we briefly discuss some general considerations in the design of therapies that use behavioral interventions. The relevance of these nomothetic guides for a given client should first be established before selecting interventions to use in therapy.

Interventions for Behaviors Maintained by Positive Reinforcement

Problematic behavior maintained by positive reinforcement processes is often effectively addressed by interventions that involve environmental change. To support new or infrequent positive behaviors (e.g., socially affiliative behaviors, health-promoting behaviors as a substitute for illicit drug use), one might also seek alternative environments that naturally reinforce behaviors one wishes to increase and do not reinforce or otherwise support behaviors one wishes to decrease (Cunningham, 1998). Chapter 4 describes approaches to changing behavior by changing the environment.

Interventions for Clients Who Are Depressed or Who Experience Behavioral Inertia

Some clients engage in a low rate of behavior, particularly behaviors that were once enjoyable or pleasurable. This is especially true of individuals who are depressed or who experience low self-esteem (Kuppens, Allen, & Sheeber, 2010; Martell et al., 2001). Many clients also display a low sense of self-efficacy or do not believe that they are capable of engaging in certain forms of behavior. Similarly, many clients do not believe that behavior they are capable of performing will lead to positive outcomes; that is, they have negative outcome expectations. In Chapter 5, we discuss behavioral experiments as a method for increasing behavior and testing thoughts about behavioral capacities and behavioral outcomes. In Chapter 8, we discuss behavioral activation strategies for individuals who engage in avoidance behaviors that reduce access to positive reinforcers and, in turn, have a negative effect on mood.

Interventions to Increase Effective Behavior and Ameliorate Behavioral Deficits

Therapy goals often include learning to be more effective through one's behavior, to increase both objective and subjective mastery, or to enhance behavioral skills. Invention strategies that are intended to develop, increase, or strengthen behavioral repertoires often involve direct instruction, advice, modeling, behavioral rehearsal, and skills training. Examples of behavioral interventions that develop or strengthen behavioral repertoires in these ways can be found in Chapters 6 and 7.

Interventions to Target Unhelpful Thinking Patterns

Clients with a variety of psychological conditions often display *overly rigid rule governance*; that is, they are strongly influenced by thoughts or statements from others that inaccurately specify associations between behaviors and consequences. This reduces flexibility in responding to certain environmental events and results in ineffective or aversive outcomes. For such clients, the accuracy of these rules or assumptions can be challenged, or clients might be encouraged to attend to and bring behavior more in line with the actual contingencies associated with behavior. Other clients may have uncertain or ambivalent long-term goals or, for whatever reason, may not act in accordance with their own goals or values and instead respond more strongly to immediate environmental contingencies. In Chapter 5, we describe intervention approaches for altering faulty assumptions or appraisals, modifying inaccurate rules that influence behavior, and developing awareness of and bringing behavior more in line with long-term goals and values.

Interventions That Target Ineffective Interpersonal Behavior

Poor social support and ineffective interpersonal behavior are risk and maintaining factors for a wide variety of psychological difficulties (e.g., Campbell, Hansen, & Nangle, 2010; Lewinsohn & Gotlib, 1995). The ability to skillfully interact with others is critically important for the development of social networks and, consequently, for the availability of social supports. Social skills deficits, environmental suppression of social behavior, behavioral inhibition related to inaccurate rules about behavior–consequence relations, or the routine display of behaviors others find aversive can each contribute to impair or deficit social relationships. In Chapter 7, we describe behavioral interventions for enhancing relationship quality and strengthening prosocial behaviors.

Interventions to Target Emotional Difficulties

Many clients evidence problems with excess negative emotions, particularly anxiety. Among these persons, some respond to a range of situations with high levels of anxiety, panic, behavioral avoidance, avoidance of private experiences (e.g., emotions, memories, physiological sensations), or some combination of these. Exposure-based therapies are often effective interventions for addressing excessively high anxiety maintained by avoidance or conditioning processes. These therapies are reviewed in Chapter 9.

In Chapter 10, emotion regulation interventions for responding to acute and intense emotional experiences or situations associated with negative affect are described.

Additional Intervention Considerations

Before closing this section, we also note that it is frequently useful to consider whether a medication evaluation referral or a medical examination would be appropriate for some clients. These considerations are especially pertinent for persons who exhibit severe psychological disorders (e.g., psychotic disorders), behavior problems that can adversely affect biological functions (e.g., substance abuse, anorexia nervosa, bulimia nervosa), or behavioral or emotional problems that might have their origins in physiological functions (e.g., hypothyroidism in the case of depression, hypoglycemia in the case of anxiety or panic).

DISCUSSING THE THERAPY PLAN WITH THE CLIENT

As noted by Addis and Carpenter (2000), clients often have a variety of reactions to therapist's suggestions for a treatment plan and description of the therapy rationale. Among these are hope and optimism, self-doubts, expectations of failure, uncertainty about whether one is able to carry out the therapy, and apprehension as a result of not fully understanding the process of therapy in the initial stage. A credible therapeutic rationale provided by the therapist can promote a client's hope and optimism about subsequent therapy (Addis & Carpenter, 2000). Doing so might convey to the client that the problem is understandable, that he or she is not the only one who has struggled with this problem, and that there are effective therapies for his or her problem areas. If a client is hopeful that change is possible, he or she might be more willing to try something new or persevere in the face of obstacles. In this section, we discuss three primary areas therapists frequently review with the client before initiating therapy: the rationale for the therapy, appropriate therapy modalities, and the justification for between-session assessment or therapeutic activities (e.g., homework).

Discussing the Therapy Rationale

Discussing the rationale for therapy and the selection of specific therapeutic interventions with the client can be a delicate task. Such discussions usually involve issues such as etiology of the client's problem area (or why the problem came about), and why this problem is perhaps best addressed by the modes of therapy suggested by the therapist. As reviewed by Addis and Carpenter (2000), a client's acceptance of the treatment rationale is usually associated with greater therapeutic benefits.

When the interventions selected for therapy have been empirically evaluated and found to be useful for persons with problem areas similar to those of the client, it is important to convey this information. For many clients, knowledge that the therapeutic approaches planned for use have been widely tested and found to be effective for many can promote a sense of optimism about therapy and its prospects for success (Kazdin & Krouse, 1983).

Because the treatment rationale is an important aspect of therapy, it is useful for the therapist to spend time verifying that the client understands the rationale and assess whether he or she agrees with it. Addis and Carpenter (2000, p. 151) provided examples of questions that a therapist might ask the client once the rationale has been discussed:

- "What is your understanding of why you are having this problem?"
- "What are your reactions to what you know about this therapy so far?"
- "What parts concern you?"
- "What parts seem positive or potentially helpful?"
- "If you were to explain to a friend or family member how this therapy works, what would you say?"

When the client does not accept the therapy rationale, or if he or she voices doubts, the therapist might take time to carefully explore the client's doubts in a nonthreatening and validating manner. The therapist should objectively consider the client's view and, if relevant, incorporate his or her perspectives into a modified plan. Among the more common client reactions is that CBT interventions are superficial and do not deal with the "real problem" (Addis & Carpenter, 2000). One way for the therapist to respond to this reaction is by distinguishing between problem etiology and maintenance. The therapist might note, for example, that causal factors associated with the development of problems are multifaceted and complex. Why problems persist over time, however, might be completely different issues from those associated with their development. The therapist might further stress that therapy will likely be more effective if it addresses current determinants of the problem area because there is currently no evidence to suggest that an underlying problem, if present, must be solved to get one's life back on track (Addis & Carpenter, 2000). Providing the client with a summary of research findings on the effectiveness of the approach suggested might also be helpful, as would the adoption of a "let's give it a try and see" approach. Regardless of the approach taken, it is important first to hear the client and consider the potential kernel of truth that can, in turn, be incorporated within the CBT framework and treatment plan.

Deciding Which Therapy Modes to Use

Clients vary in terms of the number of problem areas they have and the degree of severity and impairment associated with problem areas. For clients with multiple and severe problems in particular, it is often useful to establish structural framework for therapy given the many areas that would likely be targeted for therapy and the many therapeutic challenges and complexities that are likely to arise with such individuals.

In DBT, there are four primary treatment modalities (Linehan, 1993a). *Individual outpatient therapy* usually consists of one or two weekly sessions, each 1 to 1.5 hours in length. The primary focus of these sessions is on problem areas targeted for therapy (e.g., self-injury, therapy-interfering behaviors, substance misuse, repeated entry into harmful environments). The *skills training group* is a separate treatment modality and primarily involves instruction in coping skills. Groups are typically composed of six to eight clients, and sessions take place weekly for about 2 hours. A third treatment modality, *telephone consultation,* involves contact between the therapist and client by phone in between sessions. Either the client or the therapist can initiate contact, with conversations intended to be opportunities for therapist consultation concerning methods and approaches for coping with difficult situations (other than through self-injury or suicidal behaviors), promoting the use of behavioral skills to everyday situations, and repairing any disruptions in the therapeutic relationship before the next session. *Case consultation meetings* constitute the fourth treatment modality, and are analogous to supervision meetings and usually take place on a weekly basis.

Even though the inclusion of each therapy modality may not be necessary for many clients, DBT treatment modalities exemplify the various levels and methods of therapy available for a given purpose. Recent innovations in technologies have expanded the range of service modality options, including those that are Internet based or delivered through mobile platforms such as ecological momentary assessments, text messaging, and apps (Aguilera & Muñoz, 2011; Rusby, Westling, Crowley, & Light, 2013).

Discussing Between-Session Activities as an Integral Part of Therapy

CBT interventions typically involve between-session activities carried out by the client. Examples of typical activities include self-monitoring, completing questionnaires, filling out thought records, or engaging in self-initiated exposures. Studies that have examined the association between carrying out such between-session activities (or homework) and therapeutic outcome often show robust positive associations (Kazantzis, Whittington, & Dattilio, 2010). Therefore, if homework is part of a therapy plan, it should be regarded as an integral part of the therapeutic process.

The likelihood that a client will carry out homework in between sessions increases when the therapist provides a detailed rationale, including an explanation of how the activity is tied to therapy goals. Time should be dedicated to an exploration of the client's reaction to therapeutic work between sessions as well as potential obstacles to homework completion. When clients complete homework assignments, the therapist must also take time to review these activities with the client during therapy sessions. The therapist might inquire about how the activity went, explore what the client learned from the activity, or query whether he or she had any difficulties in relation to the activity. A failure on the therapist's part to acknowledge and reinforce the client's efforts in this regard will likely lead to less adherence to prescribed activities in the future and, in turn, result in a less efficacious therapy (Bryant, Simons, & Thase, 1999).

STRENGTHENING MOTIVATION TO CHANGE AND SECURING A COMMITMENT FOR ACTION

If the motivation to be actively involved in therapy is low or if the client is conflicted or ambivalent, the likelihood for meaningful therapeutic change is similarly low. One strategy for facilitating motivation for therapy is motivational interviewing (MI; Miller & Rollnick, 2013). MI is a non-confrontational, empathic, and minimally intrusive approach for discussing the effects and consequences of the problem behavior and exploring the benefits of change. MI also includes strategies to minimize the likelihood of eliciting resistances or defensiveness. Components of MI frequently include (a) challenging the client to identify reasons for changing, (b) providing the client with feedback about personal risk or impairment associated with problem behavior, (c) teaching the client problem-solving strategies for promoting change, (d) helping clients identify their own strengths and resources, (e) providing advice, and (f) strengthening the client's sense of self-efficacy and optimism (Miller & Rollnick, 2013; Sobell & Sobell, 2003).

The following are examples of MI-consistent questions or statements associated with problem drinking provided by Sobell and Sobell (2003, pp. 218–219):

- "Tell me about your alcohol use."
- "What would you like your drinking to be like a year from now?"

- "Tell me about the good things and less good things about your drinking."
- "It sounds like you might have some ambivalence about changing your drinking."
- "If you continue drinking like you have in the past year, where do you see yourself in two or three years?"
- "You have managed to cut down your drinking considerably. How did you manage to do that?"

In using motivational strategies, it is important not to come across as judgmental or confrontational (e.g., "You don't seem to be taking your drinking very seriously" or "You have a serious drinking problem that you are denying"; Sobell & Sobell, 2003, p. 219). Although MI is not typically regarded as a behavioral intervention, it is often a useful strategy for helping clients evaluate the consequences of their behaviors, formulate more accurate rules related to their behavior, and identify goals or values that might function as guides for altering behaviors targeted for change (see Chapter 5 for detailed discussions of strategies for developing new rules and for bringing behavior under the influence of values or distal goals). In these respects, the therapeutic goals of MI are both complementary to and compatible with the goals frequently associated with behavioral interventions.

Another strategy for enhancing motivation for treatment is the use of treatment contracts (Otto et al., 2003). Once the client and therapist collaboratively establish the goals and parameters for therapy, a formal treatment contract might be developed. Such a contract is usually written and typically specifies the responsibilities and expectations of all parties within the contract. Otto and colleagues (2003) suggested three benefits associated with therapy contracting. First, therapy contracts promote adherence with therapy procedures by solidifying goals for the client. The client can subsequently refer to these written goals during times of stress or setbacks. A written contract also constitutes a public stand on what the client is working toward. Second, particularly during times of stress, it provides the client with a reminder of therapy options, therapeutic principles, coping skills, and treatment contingencies. When used in this way, the therapy contract might consist of a checklist of coping strategies the client may use in stressful situations or a sequence of steps the client can take to resolve crisis periods. A contract might also delineate specific and centrally important therapeutic procedures (e.g., methods for monitoring mood and steps to take when mood begins to elevate or sleep becomes impaired, as in the case of bipolar disorder) or specify consequences for the client's engagement in some sort of target behavior (e.g., a client receiving treatment for substance abuse cannot come to a session intoxicated). Third, in times of crisis, the contract can provide a framework for crisis resolution and a consent form for treatment team members, family members, and support services (e.g., crisis agencies, social work agencies) to act for the benefit of the client. This is of particular relevance for clients who have difficulty taking appropriate action themselves during times of heightened stress. When contracts serve these purposes, they often include a suicide crisis plan and a checklist that family members can follow to help protect the client during particularly vulnerable periods. An example of this is a client's agreement to refrain from actively engaging in suicidal behavior and instead contact the therapist, crisis counselor, family member, or caregiver if other coping efforts have not succeeded. Ideally, the client actively collaborates with the therapist in the development of any treatment contract. An example of a treatment contract can be found in Otto et al. (2003).

Securing a commitment for change in the early stages of therapy might simply involve the therapist asking about the client's willingness to participate in a set of therapeutic procedures for a short period of time and to reevaluate progress during and after the initial stages. A brief, short-term commitment does not ask a lot of the client and allows the client and therapist the opportunity to review the therapy plan and the commitment to it if necessary.

RAISING POTENTIAL OBSTACLES TO EFFECTIVE THERAPY

Persons (1989) suggested, and we agree, that the case formulation can assist in generating hypotheses about potential obstacles that might challenge therapy. Anticipation of such obstacles allows for the opportunity of preplanning and increases the likelihood that the therapist can prevent or solve the problems that obstacles pose.

After the sharing of the case formulation, the therapist might suggest one or two potential obstacles that might adversely affect therapy (Persons, 1989). These can be suggested as potential problems, and the therapist might (a) explore with the client the degree to which he or she also perceives these as obstacles, (b) examine whether other potential obstacles are anticipated by the client, and (c) invite the client to brainstorm with the therapist about how these obstacles should be addressed if and when they occur or how related issues might be addressed in therapy so that the anticipated obstacles do not arise.

The client, for example, who holds the view "I'm not able to cope with stress" might experience difficulty completing between-session activities and offer stress as a reason. Similarly, such a client may be more likely to present to therapy sessions with a series of crises and demand that the therapist assist in resolving those. With such clients, difficulty in effectively responding to stress may represent a potential obstacle to therapy. When such obstacles are anticipated, however, they can be translated into therapeutic goals and represent opportunities for genuine change. Chapter 11 describes approaches for navigating challenges to effective therapy.

EVALUATING THERAPY EFFECTIVENESS

Therapy goals agreed on by the client and the therapist before the initiation of therapy suggest the nature and type of outcome indicators that might be repeatedly assessed before the initiation of therapy, during therapy, and after the active phase of therapy has concluded. Ideally, therapy goals should be measurable so that the therapist and client can determine together whether sufficient movement is being made toward the realization of treatment objectives as therapy progresses (Persons et al., 2006).

The process of evaluating therapy effectiveness includes the selection of an appropriate assessment framework and appropriate dependent measures (Hayes, Barlow, & Nelson-Gray, 1999). For most clients, the A–B or A–B–C assessment framework is generally the most appropriate. The "A" phase is the baseline phase, in which the frequency, intensity, or duration of a particular behavior is assessed and recorded before the application of an active intervention. The "B" phase represents the intervention phase. The "C" phase covers a period of time after the active phase of therapy has been discontinued. Intermittent assessments during the "C" phase are often useful for evaluating the degree to which therapy gains have been maintained or whether there is any evidence suggestive of a lapse or relapse.

When desirable change is observed between the "A" and "B" phases, it is possible that the therapy contributed to this change. We cannot necessarily conclude, however, that therapy was the cause of this change. That is, change may have been influenced by factors that, although independent of the intervention, occurred during the intervention phase. Stated another way, we cannot infer causation from correlation. Despite this limitation in inference, we strongly suggest that therapists repeatedly collect data related to the client's main problem areas throughout therapy. Repeated assessments not only help inform or guide treatment, they also promote responsible clinical practice. If the client is having a negative reaction to a given therapeutic intervention, the therapist may not be aware of this unless data were collected during therapy. Similarly, it would not be ethical to continue a therapy over an extended period of time when it is not producing any therapeutic gains or benefits.

R. O. Nelson and Hayes (1986b) provided some guidelines to evaluate therapy efficacy. Among these are recommendations that measures should accurately assess the primary behavior(s) targeted in therapy, measurement should occur frequently, and, if possible, before initiating treatment. Repeatedly administered measures should be convenient to take or complete, and data obtained should be graphed by either the client or the therapist and regularly reviewed as part of the therapeutic process, with significant events that might account for marked variability noted on the graph. Dependent measures can include data collected through self-monitoring, direct observation, or repeated questionnaire assessments or checklists.

For some problem areas, it is useful to assess target behaviors at least a few times a day. Some depressed clients, for example, report that they are depressed all the time. They may not discriminate variations in their mood over the course of a day and, correspondingly, variations in environmental contexts that influence such mood fluctuations. For such clients, it may be useful to self-monitor mood at prescribed points during the day (e.g., morning, early afternoon, late afternoon, and evening). For example, the client might make a rating along a 7-point scale indicating the degree or intensity of depressed mood experienced at the time of self-assessment (from 1 = *not at all depressed* to 7 = *the most depressed I ever get*). Many persons, even those with relatively severe psychological disorders, evidence considerable variability in mood when assessed repeatedly during waking hours (cf. Trull et al., 2008). Variations in mood ratings might help the client identify factors that influence mood as well as provide a challenge to the view that some clients have that they are depressed or distressed all the time.

EXTENDED CLIENT ILLUSTRATION

In the case example that follows, we illustrate elements of the behavioral case formulation and treatment planning process outlined previously. The formulation approach presented here is primarily informed by the work of Persons (1989; Persons et al., 2006; Persons & Tompkins, 2007) and Haynes (1986; Haynes, O'Brien, & Kaholokula, 2011).

Background Information

"Robert" is a married 24-year-old accountant who lives in the Pacific Northwest region of the United States. His primary physician referred him for a psychological evaluation and possible therapy related to a fear of heights.

Chief Complaint

During the initial interview, Robert reported his primary problem as a long-standing fear of heights, which has become more pronounced in recent years. Robert is seeking therapy now because he was recently awarded a job promotion that necessitates travel to another office in a neighboring city. Commuting to the new job requires that he travel across a long bridge that spans a wide river and gorge. Robert estimated that the bridge was some 500 feet above the water and about a mile long. He further reported that the only alternative routes to his new office would add about 100 miles round trip to his commute each day. Because of his fear of being on the bridge and the associated avoidance of it, Robert has taken vacation leave and delayed the start of his new job, as he believes that it is currently impossible for him to drive over the bridge.

Psychological and Psychiatric History

Robert reported a largely unremarkable psychiatric history. The only problem area he acknowledged was a fear of heights. He reported falling from a second-story patio deck at age 5. Apart from a mild concussion, Robert reported no significant injuries from the fall.

After the incident, Robert recalled that his mother seemed overly protective and typically did not allow him to go out and play without her close supervision. She also had a tendency to exhort caution frequently (e.g., "If you get too close, you'll fall and break your neck!" and "Be careful or you're going to get hurt!"). Although Robert denied any lasting psychological impact from the fall (e.g., no troubling memory flashbacks), he reported that as a child he found himself mentally imagining and rehearsing the hypothetical consequences described in his mother's admonishments (e.g., imagining himself falling and seeing himself with a broken neck or head injuries). In relation to his present-day fear of heights, Robert reports that as he approaches heights, many of the same type of images come to him and exacerbate his level of distress. When in or approaching high places, Robert also reported that he experiences recollections of seeing one of his friends fall from a bicycle. This incident occurred when Robert was about 12 years of age. His friend experienced a moderate gash in the head that produced a lot of blood. Robert added that he tends to recall this incident only when in or around high places.

A timeline analysis of the development of his fear of heights revealed that since the fall at age 5, he has been more apprehensive when in high places. Within a few years of the incident, however, Robert reported that he would occasionally climb on trees and playground equipment, although he also described incidents during this time when he refused to approach high locations. Avoidance of heights and escape from high places gradually increased over the years and became well entrenched by his middle adolescent years. By then, Robert reported that he avoided almost all high places, including airplane travel as well as open-view elevators.

Robert reported that he has always been somewhat "jumpy." As an example, he reported that sharp, loud, and unexpected sounds, such as a car backfiring, cause him a strong physiological reaction. Robert added that many of the sensations he experienced immediately after being startled are the same type of experiences that he has when he is on or near a high location (i.e., panic, palpitations, depersonalization, dizziness, feeling frozen and unable to move, and shortness of breath). When Robert experiences these sensations around heights, they reportedly only gradually go away once Robert has left the situation. He had difficulty recalling when he last remained in a high location when feeling panicky, adding that he fears he could go crazy or do something embarrassing in those situations (e.g., shout out loud, faint).

Other reports from Robert suggested some dependent characteristics. These included difficulty making everyday decisions without first seeking advice, difficulty expressing disapproval out of fear of losing support or approval, and feeling helpless when alone. When asked, Robert said that he felt he overly relied on others, particularly his wife, which he believed caused some strain on his relationships. He added that he wished he were more independent.

Robert received therapy on one previous occasion, principally for his fear of heights. This occurred 4 years ago for about 3 months and took place at his university student counseling service. Robert reported that counseling largely consisted of talking, mostly about his past and particularly about his relationship with his mother. He reported that his fear of heights did not improve as a result of this therapy.

Family and Social Relations

Robert grew up in an intact home. His father worked as a long-haul truck driver and was home about one third of the time when Robert was growing up. His mother worked at home and primarily took care of Robert and his two younger siblings. She maintained a small home business that centered on the crafts she made. Robert described his siblings as "more anxious than most." He indicated, however, that he was the only one with a phobia. Robert described a history of good relations with family members, which continues to this day.

Robert recalled some periods of anxiety during his elementary school years. He felt non–height-related anxieties most acutely when his mother dropped him off at school each day. He reported that although there was a twinge of anxiety upon being dropped off, which usually passed within a few minutes. Although he reported not having many friends during his school years, he indicated that he has always had two or three close friends.

During late high school, Robert began dating and met his future wife during his second year at university. The most significant current strains in their relationship are related to Robert's fear of high places because they have not pursued activities and interests together that involve heights (e.g., traveling in a plane, dining at upper level restaurants in the downtown area).

School and Occupational Functioning

Robert reported that his academic performance was above average, typically near the top of the class. Since graduating from university with a bachelor's degree, he has been steadily employed as an accountant by the same firm. His performance reviews have always been good. His recent reassignment to the main office was regarded as a promotion for his good work.

Health and Medical Status

Robert's health status is unremarkable. A medical evaluation carried out by his physician ruled out any significant vestibular influence on phobic symptomatology or any other medical problem (e.g., impairments in visual acuity) that might account for Robert's experience.

Impairment, Distress, and Coping

Robert's current primary impairments are anxiety related and associated with his fears concerning traveling to places he would like to go. This situation has become more acute in recent weeks as a result of a change in work setting that requires daily travel over a bridge. He also acknowledged that he relies too much on others, particularly his wife, and that his fear of heights has caused some strain on their relations as he avoids participation in some leisure activities as a result. Although Robert has always had some degree of distress related to his fear of heights, this distress has increased markedly in recent weeks because he sees no viable way to cope with his fear other than through avoidance.

Case Formulation

Following two sessions of clinical interviews as well as between-session self-monitoring assessments and a number of questionnaire assessments, Robert's therapist came up with the following formulation.

The Problem List (Descriptive and Functional Features of Problematic Behavior)

1. *Exaggerated fear of heights*. Experiences panic-like symptoms when in high places.

2. *Catastrophic thoughts and images related to being in high places.* Thoughts and images often involve personal injury as a result of falling from high places.
3. *Avoidance of high places.* Passive avoidance of high places is associated with an absence of fear and panic; escape from high places is associated with a reduction of fear and panic as well as images and thoughts related to personal injury.
4. *Avoidance of travel when heights are involved.* Inability to participate in some leisure activities (e.g., plane travel) or commute to new job; the experience of relief when travel or leisure activities that involve exposure to heights is no longer considered.
5. *Frequent reliance on others for advice and support.* Difficulty making decisions or taking action without advice or reassurance; difficulty tolerating being alone and tendency to "go along" with others rather than experience disapproval.
6. *Strained marital relations related to height phobia.* Difficulty in traveling and engaging in some leisure activities have contributed to some marital discord and resentments.

Situational Determinants of Problem List Behaviors:
Precipitating Events and Consequences

Problem Areas 1 through 4 identified constitute behavioral excesses and are all related to situations that involve heights. Avoidance and escape behavior is reinforced behavior as it produces immediate relief (i.e., reductions in anxiety or panic, lessening of unpleasant physiological sensations, attenuation of catastrophic thoughts and images). These functional properties of escape and avoidance behavior likely maintain their occurrence as well as Robert's fears and catastrophic thoughts and images. Problem 5 also includes some behavioral excesses (e.g., frequently asking others for advice, acting in an overly compliant manner). The reassurance provided by others appears to result in a lessening of apprehension and anxiety, thus likely making advice seeking a negatively reinforced behavior. The social support and reassurance provided by others is also pleasing to Robert and suggests that this reaction from others also positively reinforces his reassurance seeking. "Going along with others" similarly results in a reduction of anxiety associated with conflict and is likewise negatively reinforced. Robert's tendency to seek out others or distracting activities (e.g., TV watching) when alone is similarly associated with a reduction in and relief from feelings of helplessness.

Hypothesized Origins (Person Variables and Learning History)

Robert's fall from the patio decking at age 5 was associated with a change in his mother's behavior. In particular, his mother became more vigilant for potential dangers that might cause injury to Robert, notably heights. She would frequently be physically present and watchful when he played. She also relayed a number of verbal rules that implied serious injury if care was not taken around high places (e.g., "If you get too close, you'll fall and break your neck"). In response to these statements, Robert stayed away from high places and also mentally rehearsed the behavior–consequence relations implied in these statements (e.g., he imagined himself falling and badly injuring himself). This mental imaging, plus recollections of his friend's bleeding face after he fell from a bike, might have further covertly conditioned associations between certain environmental situations (high places) with certain behaviors (falling) and associated consequences (serious physical injury or death).

Also during his childhood, Robert learned that one way to make uncomfortable emotions and physical sensations go away is to passively avoid or actively escape from the situations that evoked them. Although this method of coping was effective in reducing anxiety and fear, it did little to facilitate the development of alternative responses that would allow him to cope and perform effectively in anxiety-evoking situations.

There is also a suggestion that Robert might be temperamentally prone to anxiety. That is, there are some indications that he shows a higher degree of autonomic reactivity to unexpected events than persons typically experience. He also appears to have been more anxious than other children regarding separation from his parents. These, in combination with the observation that his other siblings are also somewhat overly anxious and that Robert scored high on a trait measure of anxiety, suggest that he might be temperamentally predisposed to the experience of anxiety and prone to magnify and overemphasize the likelihood of possible negative outcomes associated with everyday events.

Working Hypotheses

Dominant themes present among Problem Areas 1 through 5 include coping with anxiety-evoking situations (e.g., heights, conflict, uncomfortable inner states) through escape and avoidance behaviors. Although escape and avoidance are associated with immediate reductions in anxiety and fear, such behaviors prevent the extinction or habituation of unjustified anxiety and fear in the environments in which they are experienced. Problem Area 6 appears to be long-term aversive consequence associated with Problems Areas 1 through 5. Robert indicated that he very much loves his wife and would like to share a close and satisfying life with her.

High levels of fear and panic, exaggerated estimations of danger associated with high places, and escape and avoidance from these places appear to be accounted for by three primary processes: (a) experiencing a fall from a high area at age 5 that resulted in some injury and observing a friend sustain an injury at age 12 after falling from a bike; (b) learning rules from his mother that convey heights are dangerous (e.g., "If you get too close, you'll fall and break your neck"); (c) covert conditioning processes that repeatedly linked certain environmental contexts (high places) with particular actions (falling) and associated aversive consequences (serious bodily injury), and a history of reinforcement for avoidance or escape from high places. Figure 3.1 graphically represents several aspects of the working hypothesis of Robert's fear of heights.

Robert also revealed that he finds emotions such as anxiety and associated physiological reactions such as elevated heart rate, depersonalization, shortness of breath, and dizziness to be unpleasant. Robert added that he actively seeks to get away from situations that produce these experiences, in part, because the experiences themselves are aversive and associated with unpleasant outcomes (e.g., fear of going crazy).

The anxiety-reduction function of avoidance and escape behaviors was hypothesized as the primary maintaining factor for Robert's phobic anxiety. Avoidance and escape in the presence of heights provide immediate relief and are consequently effective means of short-term coping. The cost, however, is that overreliance on escape and avoidance as a method of coping has resulted in the avoidance of an increasingly wider range of situations over time that is now beginning to adversely affect Robert's marriage and work.

Robert met *Diagnostic and Statistical Manual of Mental Disorders, Fifth Edition* (American Psychiatric Association, 2013) criteria for Specific Phobia, Natural Environment Type (Heights). This type of phobia has historically been referred to as acrophobia. As with most phobias, exposure and response prevention is widely regarded as the treatment of choice given its high effectiveness rate in eliminating phobic fears. This intervention also conceptually maps onto the individualized working hypothesis of Robert's fear of heights (see Figure 3.1).

It was hypothesized that a therapy program that exposes Robert to high places but blocks associated escape and avoidance behavior would provide new learning and, consequently, reduce or eliminate the fear and unpleasant physiological sensations and images he currently experiences in these settings. Skills training elements will also be included, such as diaphragmatic breathing, to provide Robert with coping alternatives to escape and avoidance. Although acknowledging a desire to reduce his interpersonal dependency on others, Robert indicated that he would rather focus therapy on his fear of heights, particularly given the urgency to resolve this problem. The therapist agreed and noted that some approaches used to overcome his fear of heights might also be applicable to situations in which overly dependent

Figure 3.1. Functional analysis of Robert's fear and avoidance of heights. Dots between components of the response chain indicate a probability function in which a dot represents a probability that the preceding component will influence the following component. Items listed within the *Immediate Reinforcing Consequences* components followed by (+) indicate positive reinforcing consequences, whereas items followed by (−) indicate negative reinforcing consequences, both of which function to maintain or strengthen preceding behavior.

ANTECEDENTS
- A high area
- Height-related rules (e.g., "If you get too close, you'll fall and break your neck")

PERSON VARIABLES
- 11-year history of reinforcement for avoidance/escape
- Fall from patio deck at age 5
- Observing effects of friend's fall from bike at age 12
- History of mentally rehearsing catastrophic outcomes associated with falls from high places
- High physiological reactivity

BEHAVIORS
- Anxiety
- Panic
- Palpitations
- Depersonalization
- Dizziness
- Frozen in movements
- Shortness of breath
- Images of self falling and resultant bodily injury
- Images of injured friend
- Images of self being injured due to falling
- Passively avoid high places
- Actively escape from high places

IMMEDIATE REINFORCING CONSEQUENCES
- Reduction of anxiety and panic following escape or avoidance (−)
- Reduction of unpleasant physiological sensations following avoidance or escape (−)
- Cessation of catastrophic images of injury due to falling following avoidance or escape (−)
- Cessation of fear of going crazy following avoidance or escape (−)
- Receive reassurances from others that high areas are safe (+ and −)

DELAYED AVERSIVE CONSEQUENCES
- Marital tension and discord associated with having to limit activities to accommodate avoidance
- Does not participate in some leisure activities that are enjoyable (e.g., travel)
- Work impairment (cannot travel to new job)

behavior is more probable because such behavior also appears to include an anxiety-reduction function.

Treatment Plan

Goals include the following:

- Substantially reduce or eliminate fear of heights
- Reduce the intensity and incidence of physiological sensations (e.g., palpitations) and unpleasant images (e.g., falling and injuring oneself)
- Substantially reduce or eliminate avoidance of and escape from high places
- Facilitate and support approach behavior to high areas
- Teach and support alternative coping methods when anxious in high situations
- Participate in pleasant or necessary activities not currently engaged in because of avoidance of heights (e.g., drive car over bridges, travel in airplane)

Therapeutic framework includes the following:

- Two 1.5-hour assessment sessions
- Two 1-hour sessions of preexposure preparation (includes development of fear hierarchy involving high situations or places ordered in terms of level of associated distress)
- Training in diaphragmatic breathing

Five 1.5-hour sessions of in vivo exposure sessions that will consist of the following:

- Meeting at a mutually agreed on public location that corresponds with items on the client's hierarchy or feared situations or places
- Review of between-session therapy-related activities
- In vivo exposure
- Debrief of exposure session
- Planning next session and between-session activities
- Between-session activities that involve skills practice, self-monitoring, and self-initiated graded exposures
- Three monthly follow-up sessions after discontinuation of active therapy
- One 6-month follow-up after the last monthly follow-up session

Interventions include the following:

- Self-monitoring
- Breathing retraining and mindfulness training
- Therapist modeling of skill and mastery associated with being in and coping with high places
- Exposure plus response prevention
- "Think aloud" procedure during exposure sessions (i.e., say out loud what one is thinking and covertly experiencing during exposures)
- Hierarchically ordered in vivo self-initiated exposures in between sessions
- Going on "dates" with wife, which include exposure to high places (e.g., dining in a top story restaurant and intentionally sitting by a window)

Motivation for Therapy and Commitment to Therapy Goals

Robert recognizes the negative effect avoidance coping has on his life. He further recognizes that if he does not do something about it now, it may have irreversible effects on his job, his relationship with his wife, and his goals of traveling. His motivation for therapy is high.

Potential Obstacles to Effective Therapy

On the basis of his self-reports, it is possible that Robert might excessively seek reassurance from the therapist or from others during exposure sessions. To reduce the likelihood of this, Robert and the therapist reached an agreement that he may ask the therapist only once during an exposure session if the situation is safe and the therapist will honestly reply. If Robert should ask again, his query will go unanswered and he will be encouraged instead to focus closely on his experiences during the exposure. Robert also agreed to relay these instructions to any persons present (e.g., his wife) during self-initiated exposures in between sessions.

Given Robert's history of avoidance and escape and that a small but significant proportion of persons who undergo exposure therapy prematurely quit, Robert and his therapist agreed to spend some time during pre-exposure sessions discussing this possibility. These discussions will include problem solving, during which Robert and the therapist will develop a plan for action if Robert should consider leaving therapy in response to the exposure sessions.

Procedures for Evaluating the Effectiveness of Therapy

Two sets of assessments were used. One set consisted of measures that were administered before the initiation of therapy and immediately after the discontinuation of active therapy as well as at follow-up assessments conducted 3 and 9 months after therapy. Robert completed another set of measures on several occasions during active treatment. Measures from both of these assessment sets are listed in the following section.

Assessment Measures Administered Pre- and Posttherapy, and at 3- and 9-Month Follow-Ups

- *Behavioral Avoidance Test* (BAT; Borkovec, Weerts, & Bernstein, 1977) is administered before and immediately after active treatment and at 3- and 9-month posttreatment assessments, Robert will be asked to approach and enter into the same anxiety-evoking situation. The setting he and the therapist agreed on for this assessment is the footpath on the bridge that he will eventually need to drive over to get to work. The following will be evaluated during the BAT at both pre- and posttherapy: (a) whether Robert will be able to walk onto the footpath at all, (b) how far along the footpath he will walk, (c) how long he will be able to remain on the footpath, and (d) his peak levels of subjective distress as intermittently assessed during the test.
- *Individualized fear and avoidance hierarchy* will be developed before the initiation of the in vivo exposure sessions. This includes a list of situations that Robert often encounters that are associated with anxiety or panic, with items on the list arranged in order of the amount of distress that the situation typically evokes using a scaling system in which 0 = *no anxiety or avoidance at all* and 100 = *very severe anxiety or avoidance*. Pretreatment ratings of associated distress will be used to hierarchically organize the content of the exposure sessions, with the less distressing situations being those that Robert is exposed to first. After discontinuation of active treatment, Robert will be asked to provide distress ratings for situations listed on the hierarchy, with pretreatment ratings used as referents to evaluate therapy effectiveness at posttreatment and follow-up.
- *Dyadic Adjustment Scale* (Spanier, 1976) is widely used to assess marital distress. Both Robert and his wife will be administered this test pre- and posttreatment and again at 3- and 9-month follow-ups.

- *Pleasant Events Schedule* (MacPhillamy & Lewinsohn, 1974) consists of a listing of 320 activities that are potentially enjoyable to a wide range of individuals. On this measure, individuals are asked to indicate the frequency of engagement in each activity over the past month and the degree to which such activities were experienced as pleasant. A subset of these activities involves participating in enjoyable activities with other people.

Measures Administered Repeatedly (Before, During, and After Active Therapy)

- *Subjective Units of Distress Scale* (SUDS; Wolpe & Lazarus, 1966) ratings are self-report ratings of overall distress that Robert feels during exposure sessions, with 0 = *no anxiety or panic* and 100 = *extremely intense anxiety and panic*. SUDS ratings will be collected every 3 minutes during exposure sessions. Change in SUDS ratings during exposure sessions will be used to index the degree of habituation or extinction of anxiety during exposure sessions and will also provide a guide to the therapist as to when it is appropriate to discontinue the exposure (e.g., not before several consecutive ratings of self-rated distress are 50% below pre-exposure levels).
- *The Trait Scale of the State–Trait Anxiety Inventory, Form Y-2* (Spielberger, Gorsuch, Lushene, Vagg, & Jacobs, 1983) will be completed by Robert once a week and will reflect the degree of anxiety he has generally felt over the past 7 days.
- *Self-monitoring assessments* will be completed each day. Printed on a set of 5- by 7-inch index cards is a table within which Robert will record behaviors of clinical interest and associated features for each day of the week. On each diary card, Robert will be asked to indicate if he approached or entered a high place that day, identify the high place, record his SUDS rating immediately following approach or entry, write down how long he remained in the situation, indicate his SUDS rating at the time he left the situation, and record a mastery rating related to his ability to skillfully remain in the situation. He was also asked to list coping skills that he used that were helpful in that situation. Data corresponding to between-session planned self-initiated exposures are recorded on this card, as are any unplanned exposures that Robert initiated.

SUMMARY

When developing a behavioral case formulation, it is often useful for therapists to

- broadly assess the client's functioning and then continuously narrow the focus of assessments as problem areas become clearer;
- develop a problem list that identifies behavior patterns to be addressed within therapy;
- consider basic behavioral principles that might apply to the client's problem areas, particularly with reference to behavior maintenance;
- share with the client the working hypothesis of his or her problem area and explore his or her perceptions concerning the accuracy and completeness of this hypothesis;
- continuously evaluate and refine the case formulation, particularly with reference to whether the formulation accounts for areas on the client's problem list, predicts clinically relevant behavior, and explains the effectiveness of therapeutic interventions; and
- consider how problem areas will be assessed before, during, and after treatment because assessment data will provide useful information concerning the effectiveness of therapy and the maintenance of therapy gains once the active phase of therapy has concluded.

When designing a treatment plan, it is often helpful for therapists to

- reach consensus with the client as to the problem areas that therapy will address, the goals of therapy, and how therapy will be structured to realize these goals;
- consider prioritizing problem areas when a client presents with multiple problems, with the highest priority areas being those associated with the greatest risk of harm to self or others;
- consider treatment goals primarily in terms of building behavioral repertoires or skills whenever possible (rather than goals that primarily involve the elimination of already established behaviors);
- consider whether there is an effective EST available for behavior patterns targeted for therapy and, if so, whether such a treatment approach would be appropriate for this particular client;

- contemplate designing an individually tailored therapeutic program based on the case formulation if there is no EST for a client's problem areas or a relevant EST is not appropriate for the client;
- collaboratively evaluate the proposed treatment plan with the client, including a provision of a rationale for suggested treatment elements and a discussion about the role and possible therapeutic benefit of activities carried out by the client in between sessions;
- work to strengthen a motivation for change and secure a commitment for action in case either of these are minimal or lacking; and
- suggest a couple of potential obstacles to effective therapy and explore with the client how these might be effectively addressed should they arise.

4

CHANGING BEHAVIOR BY CHANGING
THE ENVIRONMENT

A fundamental set of behavioral intervention strategies involves helping people change their behavior by changing aspects of their environment.
This group of behavioral interventions, collectively referred to as *contingency
management strategies*, involves altering environmental conditions that occur
before (antecedents) or after (consequences) behaviors of clinical interest.
Contingency management procedures have been used effectively as core
components of contemporary cognitive behavior therapies (CBTs; e.g.,
Higgins et al., 1993; Kohlenberg & Tsai, 1991; Linehan, 1993a; Petry, Alessi,
& Rash, 2013); they can be used effectively to modify environments outside
of therapy and to ensure that contingencies operating within the therapeutic
relationship promote positive therapeutic change.

In this chapter, we discuss contingency management strategies and how
therapists can use these powerful approaches to help their clients make meaningful changes and reach their goals. We begin by describing key concepts

http://dx.doi.org/10.1037/14691-004
Behavioral Interventions in Cognitive Behavior Therapy: Practical Guidance for Putting Theory Into Action,
Second Edition, by R. F. Farmer and A. L. Chapman

and assumptions associated with the use of contingency management strategies. This is followed by the presentation of guidelines for implementing these interventions. We also describe several examples of contingency management interventions commonly found in many CBTs.

OVERVIEW OF CONTINGENCY MANAGEMENT PROCEDURES

In this section, we first discuss the concept of contingency management as well as some of the important assumptions, concepts, and considerations associated with the use of these procedures to change behavior. Next, we describe general guidelines for implementing contingency management procedures.

Key Terms and Concepts

One central concept associated with contingency management is the behavioral contingency. A *behavioral contingency* is a relationship between events that occasion a behavior, the behavior itself, and the consequences that the behavior produces. "Gabrielle" is a single mother struggling to maintain employment and raise her son, "Xavier." Xavier has attention-deficit/hyperactivity disorder, frequently does not attend to Gabrielle's instructions or requests, and often engages in defiant behavior (refusing to get dressed for school, yelling and stomping out of the room) when Gabrielle asks him to take his dishes to the kitchen following meals. When Xavier exhibits disruptive behavior on these occasions, Gabrielle often becomes silent and carries out the task she asked Xavier to perform.

In this case, there are at least two behavioral patterns worth investigating further if we are to help Gabrielle solve this parenting problem. The first is her tendency to stop asking Xavier to do things when he yells, and the second is Xavier's yelling and noncompliance. When it comes to Xavier's yelling and noncompliance, the behavioral contingency consists of (a) situations that occasion Xavier's yelling and refusal, such as Gabrielle asking Xavier to put away his dishes or get dressed for school, as well as other features of the contexts in which this behavior occurs (e.g., at the dinner table following a meal, with the sibling present or absent, nighttime), (b) the behavior of Xavier yelling and refusing to perform the task, and (c) the consequences of Xavier's behavior, primarily Gabrielle's ceasing further requests or doing the work task for Xavier (e.g., bringing his dishes to the kitchen).

The *consequences* of clinically relevant behaviors are important elements of the contingency. As discussed in Chapter 2, there are two categories of consequences that influence behavior: (a) those that increase the likelihood that similar behaviors will occur in future comparable contexts (i.e., reinforcers) and (b) those that decrease the likelihood that similar behaviors will occur in future comparable contexts (i.e., punishers). When describing the type of reinforcement or punishment, a further distinction is made. A consequence, either a reinforcer or a punisher, is characterized as *positive* when the behavior results in the application or provision of consequences. Conversely, a consequence is considered *negative* when the behavior results in the removal, cessation, or termination of some event. In the example of Gabrielle, she is inadvertently strengthening (reinforcing) Xavier's opposition and yelling by ceasing her requests for him to clean up once he engages in disruptive behavior. Extinction is another procedure for decreasing behavior and involves the removal of reinforcers that previously maintained the behavior. Behavior that no longer results in reinforcement becomes less frequent over time and may extinguish entirely.

Another important concept is *stimulus control*. A behavior is under stimulus control when it reliably occurs in the presence of a particular stimulus but not in its absence. Consider Xavier's disruptive behavior when Gabrielle makes requests for him to carry out certain acts, such as cleaning up after dinner. Interestingly, when Xavier's father, "Griffin," makes similar requests of Xavier after dinner in Gabrielle's absence, Xavier usually complies immediately without engaging in defiant behavior. Xavier's behavior varies considerably depending on which parent is making the request, which suggests that his disruptive behavior is under stimulus control. Xavier has learned that he can successfully avoid chores when his mother makes a request if he acts out because she will usually withdraw the request and carry out the actions herself. Griffin, however, has a history of consistently responding differently to Xavier's behavior: He does not provide any reinforcement for oppositional behavior.

Recall that in Chapter 2, we briefly described two general classes of antecedents: discriminative stimuli and establishing operations. *Discriminative stimuli* (S^D) are events that signal the likelihood of reinforcement or punishment for behavior based on previous learning experiences. Whereas requests by Gabrielle are S^D for oppositional behavior, requests by Griffin are not. To reduce Xavier's disruptive behavior when Gabrielle makes requests of him, she will need to learn different ways of consistently responding to his non-compliance that do not involve reinforcement for such actions.

In Chapter 2, we defined another class of antecedent stimuli, *establishing operations* (EOs), as events that alter the reinforcing or punishing properties of consequences. "Amanda" has a history of engaging in unprotected sexual activities with men whom she has just met. She grew up as an emotional child in an unemotional family. Her mother often told her she did not understand why Amanda was getting so upset, emotional, or even excited about so many things, and her siblings seemed cool, calm, and collected much of the time. Amanda often did not receive adequate emotional support or care when she needed it, and she did not learn to effectively seek such support as a young adult. As a result, she often felt emotionally disconnected even from her close friends. Amanda was also attractive; she found that she could easily solicit the attention of men and that the physical intimacy of sex was a good substitute for the emotional intimacy that she felt was lacking in her relationships. Through therapy, she began to have safer sex and more recently had gone for 3 weeks without engaging in casual or risky sex with acquaintances. Recently, however, her best friend moved back to another state, resulting in a loss of social support and intense feelings of deprivation related to the loss of attention and intimacy provided by her friend. This loss of her friend and the caring and support the relationship provided constituted a potent EO that increased the reinforcement value attention and intimacy from others. When a coworker invited her back to his place a few days later, she said yes and had sexual relations with him even though she thought at the time that doing so was a bad idea. Her consent, however, was more likely in this situation given the absence of in-person contacts with her close friend and the resultant heightened reinforcing properties of attention and physical intimacy from others. If her best friend had remained in town, and she was not experiencing social deprivation, she would have been less likely to say yes in this instance. To reduce Amanda's state of deprivation, and her vulnerability to risky promiscuous sex, therapy examined ways that she could strengthen existing positive relationships with others who lived and worked nearby.

Key Assumptions of Contingency Management

The primary assumption underlying contingency management interventions is that the target behavior in question is under the influence of direct-acting environmental antecedents or consequences. This is in contrast to behavior influenced by rules, which may operate differently from actual environmental contingencies. A person with panic disorder and agoraphobia, for example, might avoid public or crowded places from which escape may be difficult in the event of a panic attack. The behavior of staying inside her home and avoiding these places might be under the influence of rules such as "If I go to the park, I will have a panic attack"; "If I have a panic attack in the park, it will be humiliating, everyone will think I'm crazy, and my neighbors will avoid me and give me bad looks later on"; or "If I stay at home, I will be safe." Implied in these rules is the idea that aversive consequences will occur if the individual goes to the park and that staying home will prevent these consequences from happening. When the behavior–consequence relations specified in this rule are contrasted with the environmental contingencies, there usually is a discrepancy. Indeed, the individual may not actually have a panic attack in the park, and even if she does, the consequences are unlikely to be as dire as specified in the rule. Contingency management procedures are most effective when behaviors targeted in therapy are under the influence of direct environmental contingencies, not verbal rules that specify environment–behavior relations.

When contingency management procedures are used to increase certain behaviors, another important assumption is that the client has the targeted behaviors within his or her behavioral repertoire. If the client has not previously learned the target behaviors, the client's behavioral deficit should be addressed (see Chapter 6), and contingency management procedures should emphasize shaping principles (discussed later in this chapter). Once the novel behavior becomes part of the individual's repertoire, contingency management procedures can be used to increase, refine, or maintain the behavior.

Steps in Applying Contingency Management Interventions

Contingency management procedures have several important steps. We outline these steps as a general guide for clinicians, but therapists may elect to use various combinations of them given the circumstances of particular clients. These steps include (a) specifying and defining target behaviors and relevant contextual factors, (b) orienting the client to contingency management, and (c) monitoring and attending to target behaviors.

Specifying and Defining Target Behaviors and Relevant Contextual Factors

Before using contingency management procedures, a therapist needs to clearly specify and operationalize the target behaviors. *Target behaviors* are those behaviors that are to be altered, either increased or decreased in frequency, intensity, or duration. As discussed in Chapter 2, a thorough behavioral assessment involves collecting detailed data on the various target behaviors. Contingency management strategies generally work best when the target behavior is clearly defined, is directly observable, and can be recorded or monitored.

In using contingency management, a therapist must remember that a behavior cannot be divorced from its context. Indeed, the context is the primary focus of contingency management. "Sally," for example, struggled with alcohol use and drank a bottle or two of wine every evening. The behavioral excess in this case was alcohol use. In describing this behavior, it was important to specify (and monitor) precisely how frequently she drinks, what she tends to drink, how much she drinks on each occasion, as well as when, where, and with whom she drinks. Importantly, the therapist strives to understand how excess drinking "works" for Sally. What are the consequences that maintain this behavior (e.g., the high, a reduction in tension or stress, social approval)? As contingency management interventions modify the context of behavior (antecedents and consequences), it is important to specify the range of contextual variables associated with her problematic alcohol use.

For Sally, relevant S^D consisted of an empty house when she returned home from work, the presence of a bottle of her preferred wine on the wine rack in the living room, the time of day (she tended to only drink between 5:00 p.m. and 7:00 p.m.), and other such factors. EOs consisted of urges or cravings to drink, hunger or thirst, social deprivation, or other factors that seemed to enhance the reinforcing properties of alcohol. The context for a particular form of behavior (e.g., excess alcohol consumption) as well as appropriateness of interventions for modifying such behavior are idiographic and must be clearly specified for each individual client before embarking on a contingency management program.

Orienting the Client to Contingency Management

It is important to first orient the client to the use of contingency management strategies. Clients often enter therapy with some understanding that positive consequences or rewards might increase certain behavior, whereas negative consequences or punishment might decrease certain behavior. Often, however, clients need more information to fully consent to and engage in the modification of their behavior through contingency management procedures. In our experience, it is helpful to make two key points about learning principles.

The first point is that reinforcement, punishment, and extinction procedures are defined by their effect on behavior. A reinforcer is not a reinforcer if it does not increase the likelihood that a behavior will occur again under similar circumstances. Similarly, a punisher is not a punisher if it does not reduce behavior. Some clients believe that they are "reinforcing themselves" just because they are engaging in pleasurable activities or "punishing themselves" by intentionally harming themselves in some way because of what they did (e.g., cutting their arm with a razor in response to a situation associated with the emotions of guilt or shame). It is often useful for the client to understand, for example, that a behavior that might appear to result in punishment (e.g., self-cutting) may actually result in reinforcement, particularly if the behavior occurs frequently, takes place over an extended period, or is done with great intensity or vigor.

The second point is that persons do not always participate in behavior with the intention of receiving reinforcement from the environment. In fact, persons are often unaware of many of the factors that influence their behavior (Nisbett & Wilson, 1977). This is a particularly important point to make with clients who have a history of being called "manipulative" for engaging in unpleasant interpersonal behaviors. Consider the following example of "Alan," who frequently talked about suicide to people in his social network. When he mentioned topics related to suicide, such as disclosing that he has a new suicide plan, wants to kill himself, wishes that he were dead, and so forth, certain friends and family members reacted with shock, asked him what was wrong, and went out of their way to help and spend time with him. When he was not talking about suicide, these people generally did not provide this degree of focused attention, support, or concern. Even though Alan had no intention of talking about suicide in a manipulative manner to get attention or support from others, he and his therapist over time observed that suicide-related talk was increasing in frequency commensurate with the amount of time he spent with people who expressed shock and concern. As an experiment, the therapist asked Alan to make suicide an off-limits topic with these particular friends and family members (a crisis plan, however, also involved seeking help when he was imminently suicidal), and a plan was generated for gaining support and attention without talking about suicide. Rather than focusing on the "manipulativeness" of the suicide talk, it was more effective to clearly identify associated reinforcers, define and determine the function of Alan's behavior (e.g., to elicit support from others), and tailor the contingency management intervention to these factors. See Exhibit 4.1 for an example of how a therapist might communicate these points to a client.

EXHIBIT 4.1
Educating the Client Regarding Reinforcement

One way to get closer to reaching your goals in therapy is to use reinforcement. Have you ever heard of the word *reinforcement*? Reinforcement is any consequence that increases the likelihood that you will do a particular behavior again in the future. For example, let's say you took yourself out to your favorite place for coffee every time you exercised each day for a whole week. You noticed that, over time, you had more and more weeks of exercising every day. In this case, going out for coffee would be a positive reinforcer for exercising. If, however, you found that going out for coffee had absolutely no effect on how often you exercised, then going for coffee would not be a reinforcer. A reinforcer has to be something that actually increases a behavior—it's not just something that's enjoyable or pleasant.

Another important point is that reinforcement can work without your even knowing it. Also, just because your behavior produces positive results doesn't mean that you did it with the *intention* of getting those results. For example, I know that when you ask your children to do something and they say no, yelling at them works to get them to say yes and do what you ask. Of course, you may have no interest in or intention or desire to yell at them at all. In fact, from what I know about you, you feel badly about yelling, and you would rather not do so. But, unfortunately, yelling actually works. Your yelling is reinforced by your children saying yes and doing what you asked them to do.

Monitoring and Attending to Target Behaviors

Positive therapeutic outcomes are more likely if the therapist remains alert to occurrences of the target behavior(s) both within and outside of sessions. The therapist can facilitate this task by using self-monitoring or observational methods, consistently inquiring about key behavioral targets each week, and observing in-session behavior to determine whether target behaviors are occurring during sessions. Being alert to the occurrence of target behaviors is useful in both the assessment (e.g., for determining the contexts that reliably occasion these behaviors and establishing their frequency) and treatment stages of therapy. In treatment, when the therapist notices target behaviors, he or she has the opportunity to respond in an effective manner that will influence the frequency of these behaviors over time.

CHANGING BEHAVIOR BY ALTERING ANTECEDENTS

Intervention strategies described in this section involve altering antecedent events to change behavior. These strategies involve arranging, modifying, or otherwise changing the amount of contact clients have with particular stimuli to increase the likelihood of desired behaviors, reduce the likelihood of undesired behaviors, or both. There are several approaches for modifying antecedents, and we provide some examples of these procedures in the following sections.

Removing or Avoiding Antecedents

One approach to altering antecedents involves the removal, elimination, or avoidance of cues that occasion certain target behaviors. This approach, sometimes referred to as *cue elimination*, is especially useful for reducing problematic behaviors occasioned by certain environmental cues, such as addictive behaviors. When applied for this purpose, cue elimination involves having the client remove all drug-associated stimuli from his or her environment and completely avoid environments in which drugs are used (Cunningham, 1998). Avoiding "high-risk" situations is also a central feature of relapse prevention strategies (Marlatt & Gordon, 1985) and CBT for substance use problems (McCrady & Epstein, 2013).

The client also might sever ties with friends who use drugs or alcohol. An adaption of dialectical behavior therapy (DBT; Linehan, 1993a) for persons who are dependent on opiates and other substances (e.g., Linehan et al., 1999, 2002) involves a strategy called *burning bridges*, which involves the client cutting off his or her contact with drug-using people and drug dealers, thereby reducing the likelihood of encountering stimuli signalling that drug use will lead to reinforcement (Dimeff, Rizvi, Brown, & Linehan, 2000). In more severe instances in which drug use has become associated with a large number of environmental stimuli in an individual's community, relocating to another location might be the only effective way for eliminating a substantial number of cues that occasion drug use.

"Joanie," for example, was previously a sex worker and was trying to stop using heroin. Initial therapeutic work involved reducing Joanie's contact with signals or cues for drug use, such as paraphernalia, people with whom she previously used drugs, and places associated with drug use. One major challenge was that Joanie lived, volunteered, and engaged in community outreach and advocacy work in a part of town known for a high population of persons with addictions or serious mental illness. A walk down the street at almost any time of day brought her in contact with several people actively using or selling drugs, often including friends and drug dealers from whom she used to purchase heroin. Although her volunteer activities were consistent with her values and an important part of her recovery, she found it increasingly difficult to stay off heroin while living and working in this community. Therefore, one potential solution raised was for Joanie to find ways to continue her meaningful volunteer work while relocating to another area. Fortunately, Joanie had financial support from her family to do this. Many people in a similar situation do not have this option because they can only afford to live in communities in which drug use cues are plentiful. In these cases, the therapist and client may need to be creative to devise appropriate cue elimination strategies.

Modifying Antecedents

Another strategy involves *modifying the antecedents* for problematic behaviors, which entails making changes in attributes of stimulus situations that are related to the occurrence of the undesired behaviors. Some people who struggle with alcohol or drug abuse, for example, have repeatedly used substances in particular situations or with particular people. As a result, these situations or people have become contexts that set the occasion for substance use, and the individual has a tremendously difficult time avoiding substance use in these contexts. Modifying drug use cues might involve encouraging the client to ask drug-using peers to stop using or offering drugs in his or her presence.

Similarly, persons who struggle with binge eating similarly have a difficult time avoiding bingeing if they are in an environment rife with foods on which they often binge (these are often processed, fatty, or sugary foods). "Mark" was a young adult trying to reduce binge eating, but he lived with his parents, who often stocked the kitchen shelves with cookies, crackers, and other foods on which Mark often binged. Although he was reluctant at first to disclose to his parents that he had been bingeing, he soon found out that they were already onto him because of the rapidly diminishing food supply in the kitchen. Mark and his parents discussed ways to make it easier for him to stop bingeing, and his parents agreed to remove (or hide) the cookies and crackers and to replace these items with fruits and vegetables. Although Mark initially spent some time searching for the missing cookies, he eventually had an easier time avoiding bingeing, as the regular cues or antecedents for bingeing (the presence of sugary or processed foods) had changed. Therapy also had to address the possibility that Mark would purchase binge foods on his own. Additional interventions to alter antecedents involved Mark using smaller plates, bowls, and glasses during mealtimes. Over time, Mark reported a steady decrease in binge-eating episodes.

Introducing Stimulus Cues to Alter the Frequency of Behavior

In some instances, the therapist might help the client rearrange cues in his or her environment in a manner that increases the likelihood of desired behaviors or decreases the likelihood of problematic behaviors. These strategies can be especially helpful when the client is motivated to change particular behaviors or engage in new behaviors but forgets to do so, has not established a routine of practicing new skills, or is busy and overwhelmed with life.

Cues, for example, might be introduced into a client's typical environment to increase target behaviors. Cues might include items such as sticky notes placed in key places around the home to serve as reminders for the client to engage in or practice particular behaviors. Similarly, a client might carry around a "coping card" that lists new behaviors to use in certain situations (e.g., in a crisis, use the following skills to cope with emotions), or use mnemonic or other strategies (e.g., the "method of loci") from cognitive psychology to enhance recall of details regarding specific behaviors and when to use them. Smartphone technology presents possibilities for the use of cues (reminders, alarms, calendar entries, and so on) to guide behavior in the client's natural environment, and many apps exist for this purpose. Some examples of clients using this strategy of introducing stimulus cues are below:

- To reduce her likelihood of self-injury, "Amanda" placed a paper listing the pros and cons of self-injury on her bathroom mirror because the bathroom was a high-risk environment due to the presence of razors, scissors, and other such implements.
- To remind himself to use breathing-related relaxation strategies to better cope with anger and anxiety, "Alfred" set an alarm on his smartphone to go off every 2 hours, with the word *breathe*.

- "Rebecca" had the phrase "This, too, shall pass" tattooed on her ankle as a reminder for effective coping.
- "Mark" put his anxiety management binder on his bedside table to help remind and encourage him to practice his skills before going to bed and after arising in the morning.
- "Rachel," who struggled with depression and had great difficulty getting out of bed in the morning, put two separate alarms in her bedroom, one next to her, and the other across the room, so that she would need to get up physically to turn the second alarm off. The second alarm was on her smartphone and was set to go off every 10 minutes even if she turned off the initial alarm.

Discrimination Training

Discrimination training involves the delivery of reinforcers or punishers for behavior in a given stimulus situation (S^D) but not in other stimulus situations (S^Δ). As used here, S^Δ denotes a discriminative stimulus that signals the *unavailability* of reinforcement or punishment for a particular behavior. When discrimination training is successful, an individual learns to discriminate between situations in which certain behavior is appropriate (e.g., results in reinforcement) or not appropriate (e.g., does not result in reinforcement). As a result, the client will more likely attend to relevant cues (S^D) in a given situation and ignore irrelevant cues (S^Δ).

Persons with some forms of anxiety disorder, for example, may associate many stimuli with aversive events or outcomes and hence experience aspects of the world as threatening. Therapy might, therefore, involve helping the individual learn cues that reliably signal aversive outcomes. That way, the client only engages in avoidance behavior in the presence of cues that signal actual or probable threats or dangers (S^D). When cues are evident that are not associated with actual threats or danger (S^Δ), the client either ignores them or responds in a manner that does not involve avoidance.

As a therapeutic tool, discrimination training is probably most appropriate when the client's problem behaviors result from *inappropriate stimulus generalization*. Technically speaking, stimulus generalization occurs when a behavior that has been reinforced in one context increases in frequency or intensity in other contexts in which the behavior has not been previously reinforced. As a general rule, previously neutral stimuli that have similarities with the physical or sensory qualities of the established S^D are especially susceptible to stimulus generalization.

Stimulus generalization can become problematic when individuals experience different environmental features as functionally similar when they are not and respond in a rigid, inflexible, and ineffective manner. When discrimination training is used to reduce stimulus generalization, behavior that has generalized to inappropriate cues becomes more narrowly confined to situations in which it is appropriate and less likely in situations in which it is not.

One central feature of posttraumatic stress disorder (PTSD) is the generalization of trauma-related associations to cues that were previously neutral. As a result, individuals with PTSD often respond to sets of cues that do not actually signal forthcoming dangerous events. Individuals who have developed PTSD as a result of events experienced during combat, for example, might sometimes respond to aspects of current environments as if they were in a combat situation (e.g., ducking for cover when a helicopter flies overhead; experiencing intense fear or panic, accompanied with a strong desire to flee or escape, upon hearing a car backfire). As a result of stimulus generalization, the individual acts as if large numbers of stimulus cues in his or her typical environments signal a danger or threat.

Behavioral therapies for persons with PTSD often involve discrimination training to reduce stimulus generalization that has occurred since the traumatic events. This might include, for example, noticing and discriminating other contextual features in the environment that indicate danger is likely. When such training is successful, the client responds to common cues that are not associated with an increased risk or danger as S^Δ rather than S^D.

Sometimes individuals demonstrate deficits in discriminating among different emotional states. For instance, a person might apply the word *anger* to an experience that is more appropriately labeled *anxiety*. As a result of mislabeling the experience of anxiety as anger, a person might behave in a manner that is incongruent with the actual emotional experience but consistent with the misapplied label, such as verbally or physically attacking another person. Follette, Naugle, and Linnerooth (2000) and Linehan (1993a) described other problems associated with discrimination deficits, such as emotionally responding to events or people, inappropriately expressing to others the emotional impact of their actions, difficulty regulating one's emotions, or trouble "motivating" appropriate action (whereby the mislabeled emotion state serves as an EO for a different emotion that the client does not experience). In short, the functional potential associated with emotions cannot be fully realized among persons who have deficits in their ability to discriminate and accurately label their emotional experiences.

Arranging Establishing Operations to Decrease Behavior

Some behaviors can be reduced by altering EOs. Many of us have, for example, learned to avoid grocery shopping on an empty stomach after discovering that we end up purchasing highly caloric "junk" foods or go beyond our intended grocery budget. When we are feeling satiated on food, perhaps as a result of having a meal beforehand, the reinforcing qualities of the fat-tening foods on the grocery shelves is lessened.

One example of arranging EOs to decrease behavior is the use of metha-done to decrease heroin use. Among other properties, methadone suppresses narcotic withdrawal symptoms, reduces drug cravings, and blocks the high from heroin while not itself producing euphoria. Methadone, then, reduces EOs that occasion heroin use and reduces the positive reinforcing properties of heroin. Given these effects, methadone use results in a decrease in behav-iors that have historically been used to obtain heroin as well as a reduction in heroin use (Mattick, Breen, Kimber, & Davoli, 2009; Poling & Gaynor, 2003), in part because of the influence it has on altering EOs that historically occasioned heroin use.

Satiation therapy, perhaps more appropriately termed *oversatiation ther-apy*, involves the delivery of more reinforcers than is optimal or preferred (Bowers, 2003). The provision of an excessive amount of reinforcers might eventually make them less desirable or less likely to influence behavior. With this approach, reinforcers are delivered in a manner that is not con-tingent on the occurrence of a target behavior. Ayllon (1963) published the first description of satiation therapy. In this case study, a psychiatric inpatient frequently hoarded towels. The hospital staff's initial attempts to suppress this behavior were ineffective. When satiation therapy was imple-mented, hospital staff provided towels noncontingently over several weeks, with more towels delivered to the client's room each successive week. As the program progressed, the client's towel hoarding decreased in frequency. In fact, she frequently attempted to give back or remove towels given to her by hospital staff.

One strategy for reducing behaviors that are maintained by positive reinforcement, especially social reinforcement, is the *noncontingent* delivery of events, actions, or objects that normally reinforce problematic behavior. Noncontingent means that reinforcers are delivered on the basis of the pas-sage of time and are independent of displays of the target behavior (Vollmer & Wright, 2003). Because this intervention does not involve the establish-ment of alternative behaviors, it is not a particularly useful technique by itself. Rather, it might be part of a larger treatment package geared toward the reduction of a specific set of behaviors. Chiles and Strosahl (1995), for example, outlined an approach to treating chronically suicidal individuals that includes the noncontingent delivery of attention and support from their therapist in the form of the *random support call*. This intervention is based on the idea that some clients have a history of receiving attention and sup-port from others (positive reinforcers) when they engage in self-injurious acts (target behavior to decrease). These phone calls involve the therapist telephoning the client from time to time simply to check in and inquire how things are. Phone calls are brief, just a couple of minutes, and convey the message that the therapist is engaged in and genuinely supportive of the client's therapy. The rationale for this intervention is that noncontingent support and attention from the therapist lessens the association between suicidal behavior and the provision of support and attention by the therapist. In this way, noncontingent attention might also be an effective strategy because it provides the client with valued social support that has been primarily accessible only by talking about suicide or engaging in suicide attempts.

Arranging Establishing Operations to Increase Behavior

Later in this chapter, we discuss behavioral contracting as a contingency management procedure. For our purposes here, we note that behavioral contracts are sometimes used to make explicit a client's goals, the behavioral steps that facilitate the realization of those goals, and the consequences of acting toward a goal (e.g., delivery of specified reinforcer) or moving away from a goal (e.g., loss of specified reinforcers, or response cost). Contracts also represent a publicly expressed commitment to act in the manner outlined in the contract. When thought of in this way, the contract can possibly function as an EO that increases the frequency of behaviors specified in the contract (Miltenberger, 2004). The contract, for example, might occasion an aversive state (e.g., anxiety, tension) when the client observes that he or she is not behaving in a manner consistent with the provisions of the agreement, contemplating the therapist's reaction to his or her failure to follow through with agreed-on provisions, or thinking about what it would be like not to realize personal goals. Acting in accordance with the contract under these conditions, then, would be negatively reinforced behavior because doing so would reduce any anxiety or tension elicited by the contract (Malott, Malott, & Trojan, 2000; Miltenberger, 2004).

In another example of arranging EOs to increase behavior, consider a client who is depressed, reports having little energy, and takes lengthy naps (2–3 hours) during the day. At bedtime, however, the client typically has great difficulty falling asleep and usually lies in bed restlessly for several hours. As part of the client's treatment for sleep disturbance, the therapist instructs him to avoid naps during the day, even if he feels very tired. The therapist reasoned that the extended naps during the day might have removed an important EO (feeling tired or desiring sleep) that makes falling asleep a reinforcing activity. Falling asleep is not reinforcing when the client is not tired. Blocking sleep during the day might increase feelings of sleepiness at nighttime, thus increasing the likelihood that at bedtime, the client will fall asleep (Miltenberger, 2004).

Altering Consequences to Influence Behavior

Applying or altering consequences to effect behavior change primarily involves reinforcement, punishment, or extinction-based strategies. As noted previously, when the goal is to increase behavior, the best therapeutic strategy is to use reinforcement. In contrast, when the goal is to decrease behavior, therapy may involve extinction or punishment. There are several ways to incorporate the modification of consequences into treatment, but across many different behavioral and cognitive behavior treatments, the most common strategies often boil down to three essential steps: (a) determine which contingencies are under the control of the therapist and the client; (b) establish ways to block or prevent the reinforcement of maladaptive or undesirable behaviors, or extinguish or punish these behaviors; and (c) establish ways to reinforce adaptive or desirable behaviors.

Issues in the Application of Reinforcement Contingencies

When using contingency management strategies, a therapist needs to be aware of several issues that are particularly applicable to reinforcement, punishment, and extinction procedures. One important point about reinforcement strategies is that reinforcement is idiographic. What is reinforcing to one client may not be reinforcing, and indeed may be punishing to another client.

The timing of reinforcement influences the degree to which it will effectively increase behavior. Generally, reinforcement that occurs soon after the behavior of interest (i.e., immediate reinforcement) is more likely to lead to behavior change, compared with delayed reinforcement. For instance, if a parent is helping his daughter learn to say "please" when asking for treats at a party, the child may be more likely to say "please" if the parent gives her a treat immediately after she does so. If, however, the parent gives his daughter a treat the next day, the treat is less likely to influence the child's likelihood of saying "please." Similarly, if a client comes in after completing an arduous therapy homework assignment and the therapist waits until the following week to acknowledge the client's completion of it, attention from the therapist might not influence or maintain "homework behavior."

In addition to timing, the scheduling of reinforcement influences the extent to which it increases future behavior. There are several types of reinforcement schedules and two that are particularly relevant for the following discussion:

- A *continuous schedule* involves providing reinforcement after each instance of a particular behavior. The therapist might provide praise, attention, or other forms of reinforcement every time the client, for example, successfully completes his or her therapy homework, avoids using drugs, or spends time outside the home (e.g., for agoraphobic clients).

■ A *variable ratio schedule* involves providing reinforcement after a varying number of responses. In this case, the therapist on occasion provides reinforcement after a couple of effective responses; on other occasions, the therapist waits until the client has emitted the behavior several times. For a client working on binge eating, for example, a therapist might provide reinforcement after she has demonstrated a few days of regular, scheduled eating and has practiced mindful eating a few times. At other times, however, the therapist might provide reinforcement only after the client has engaged in scheduled, mindful eating five or six times.

When considering the use of reinforcement schedules to influence client behavior, a therapist should remember four important principles:

■ A continuous reinforcement schedule is most effective at helping a client learn a new behavior and will initially lead to the highest frequency of responses.
■ Behavior on a continuous reinforcement schedule is vulnerable to extinction when the reinforcement schedule is thinned (made less frequent).
■ The variable ratio schedule is associated with the most resistance to extinction.
■ The best way to help a client learn new behaviors and maintain them in the face of low or absent reinforcement (i.e., to produce "extinction-resistant" behavior) is to first reinforce a new behavior continuously and then thin reinforcement to a variable ratio schedule.

The characteristics of the reinforcer also influence the extent to which reinforcement influences behavior. Generally, reinforcers that are larger in magnitude are more effective than reinforcers that are smaller in magnitude. If, for example, a gambler wins $1,000 at the slot machines, he or she is more likely to play the slots again than if the winnings are more meager (e.g., 10 cents). However, sometimes reinforcers can be too large. Overly enthusiastic and emotionally intense praise by the therapist or an unrealistically large reward for performance on schoolwork (e.g., providing an A+ for C+ level work) may actually be less effective than reinforcers that are more realistic and moderate.

There also has been some suggestion that using natural reinforcers (when available) is preferable to using arbitrary reinforcers (Kohlenberg &

Tsai, 1991). *Natural* reinforcers have an inherent connection with the behavior of interest. In contrast, *arbitrary* reinforcers are not naturally connected with the behavior and generally would not occur in the client's natural environment. Rewarding a client with praise (e.g., "Thank you so much for sharing with me your past trauma") for open self-disclosure often represents arbitrary reinforcement because it may be unlikely that people would respond this way to the client in his or her natural environment. In contrast, natural reinforcement might involve leaning toward the client, conveying interest, listening and responding empathetically, nodding, reciprocal self-disclosure, and other such behaviors that are more naturally connected with disclosure of emotionally intimate details.

As we noted earlier, *satiation* (an EO) is another factor that can influence the effectiveness of reinforcement. The client may simply not respond to S^D that signal a type of reinforcement that has already been delivered at a high volume. In fact, after satiation, stimuli that would have previously functioned as reinforcers might, in fact, function as punishers.

Determine Which Consequences Are Under the Influence of the Therapist

Often it is helpful for therapists to be aware of the types of consequences they can use in reinforcing desirable behaviors or extinguishing or punishing undesirable behaviors. The therapeutic relationship offers many opportunities to use principles and practices of reinforcement, punishment, and extinction. Among contemporary behavioral therapies, functional analytic psychotherapy (Kohlenberg & Tsai, 1991) and DBT (Linehan, 1993a) perhaps most explicitly use reinforcement, punishment, and extinction in the context of strong therapeutic relationships. Exhibit 4.2 is a list of different therapist behaviors that may reinforce, extinguish, or punish client behaviors. This is not an exhaustive list, but it does include many of the most frequent strategies therapists use in standard outpatient CBT.

Prevent the Reinforcement of Dysfunctional or Undesirable Behaviors

Once the therapist and client have decided to work on reducing particular target behaviors, it is important for the therapist to avoid reinforcing these behaviors when they occur. Let us say that a client is working on anger management and reports an angry outburst toward another driver. The therapist finds the nature of the client's outburst itself to be amusing, and from what the client describes, the recipient seemed deserving (e.g., the recipient had cut the client off and yelled expletives at the client). A therapist in this situation would want to be careful to avoid laughing at the comical nature of the client's outburst or otherwise tacitly indicating agreement that the other driver was deserving of this behavior, as these behaviors might function

EXHIBIT 4.2
Consequences Under the Control of the Therapist

Positive	Negative
Reinforcement strategies	
Increasing session length or frequency	Decreasing session length or fre-
Praise, encouragement	quency (for those who experience
Increasing eye contact, smiling	therapy as aversive)
Validation	Reducing or withdrawing demands
Contact between sessions	or expectations (e.g., homework)
Warm tone of voice or demeanor	Eliminate or modify aspects of the
Expressing caring and positive regard	therapy that the client does not
Doing things for the client	like
Making changes in the therapy when asked	Not talking about a behavior that
Attentiveness	a client feels ashamed of (e.g.,
Therapist self-disclosure	self-harm) when it is not
	happening
Punishment strategies	
Expressing disapproval or disappointment	Withdrawing warmth
Expressing frustration	Withdrawing validation
Nonverbally expressing disapproval	Reducing session length or frequency
Confronting the client	(for those who experience therapy as
Increasing demands on the client	reinforcing)
Talking at length about the maladaptive	Reducing contact between sessions
behavior	Avoiding extending session time when
Increasing session length, frequency, or	client is tardy
contact between sessions (for clients	
who find contact aversive)	
Extinction strategies	
Ignoring dysfunctional behavior	
Using a neutral or matter-of-fact tone of voice	
Being less available to the client after dysfunctional behavior	
Limiting or withdrawing warmth	
Sticking to the treatment plan despite the occurrence of distress or maladaptive behavior	

Note. Whether events listed in this table actually function as reinforcers, as punishers, or extinguish behavior would need to be idiographically determined for each client. Data from Linehan (1993a).

to reinforce the client's actions. Similarly, a therapist treating a client who repeatedly arrives late for therapy might want to avoid extending the session beyond the normal stop time to avoid reinforcing tardiness.

Not all target behaviors are amenable to reinforcement from the therapist, however, and not all clients will increase behavior in response to presumably reinforcing actions on the part of the therapist. For some clients, if the therapist provides attention, praise, support, and warmth after the occurrence of maladaptive behaviors, these behaviors may increase. For other clients, attention, praise, support, and warmth may have no effect on certain behaviors or might even function as punishers.

In other cases, the therapist may not reinforce the right behaviors. One client remarked that the therapist's praising of her going a week without self-injury actually made her want to self-injure the next week. She explained that the focus on self-injury without sufficient validation of her emotional pain and efforts to cope with alternative behaviors felt invalidating. When the therapist began to validate these difficulties while praising the client's use of coping strategies other than self-injury, the client showed evidence of more sustained abstinence from self-injury.

Reinforce Adaptive Behaviors and Progress

The therapist can use contingency management strategies in a variety of ways. As illustrated by Linehan (1993a) and Kohlenberg and Tsai (1991), two key ways for doing this are to (a) use consequences within the therapeutic relationship and (b) set up formal or informal reinforcement, extinction, or punishment systems, or assist the client in doing so.

If the therapist notices that undesirable target behaviors are occurring during the session or have occurred since the last session, the therapist might use extinction procedures. There are several ways to use extinction. One method is simply to ignore or restrict the degree to which the therapist responds to the target behavior. As another example, a therapist treating an angry client who displays outbursts in sessions might ignore the angry behavior and respond to the client as if he or she is behaving in a "normal" manner (if it is possible that angry behavior has inadvertently been positively reinforced in the past by the therapist or other people).

An important consideration is that providing reinforcement within sessions is more likely to influence behavior occurring during sessions than it is to influence behavior occurring outside of sessions (Kohlenberg & Tsai, 1991). As previously mentioned, the closer in time that the reinforcement occurs to the behavior, the more effective it is in increasing the probability of a particular behavior being repeated in the setting within which it was reinforced. Verbal praise, encouragement, or other such therapist behaviors may increase the client's verbal reports of progress or positive behaviors but may not increase the actual behaviors being described.

There are several examples in the clinical literature of reinforcing adaptive behavior and progress. In their behavioral intervention for cocaine dependence, Higgins et al. (1991) evaluated the effectiveness of a treatment approach that offered reinforcement for cocaine abstinence. When clients produced clean urine specimens at scheduled meetings, they earned points that were worth the equivalent of 15¢ per point. Points were redeemable for retail items. The first negative specimen was worth 10 points, or $1.50.

Each successive negative specimen was worth an additional 5 points, with an additional $10 bonus offered after each set of four consecutive negative specimens. Urine samples were collected four times per week, and the maximum an individual could earn if consecutively abstinent over the 12-week course of therapy was $1,038. A dirty urine sample indicative of cocaine use would reset the point scale back to the initial $1.50 level. In this study, 11 of 13 (85%) clients completed the 12-week intervention. Of these, 10 (91%) achieved abstinence for 4 continuous weeks, 6 (55%) were abstinent for 8 continuous weeks, and 3 (27%) were abstinent for the entire 12 weeks. Overall, persons who received this contingency-based behavioral intervention produced a significantly larger number of clean urine samples compared with control participants who received 12-step counseling. Although treatment programs that offer monetary incentives for progress can be expensive, they are often much less expensive than several weeks of inpatient treatment.

Other examples of this approach are presented in Petry et al. (2001). In their case examples, Petry and colleagues described the use of a "prize bowl" to reinforce drug abstinence. In one example, a client with opioid and cocaine dependence was allowed one draw from the prize bowl for each urine specimen that was clean of one of the substances, and four draws if the specimen was clean of both substances. The prize bowl contained slips of paper, on half of which was written "good job" with no additional prize. Forty-four percent of the slips indicated a "small prize" (e.g., $1 food vouchers, lipstick, nail polish), 6% a "large prize" (e.g., sweatshirt, watch, a voucher for books or CDs), and 0.4% a "jumbo prize" (e.g., television, DVR). Urine samples were collected two to three times per week, and for each week of consecutive abstinences of both substances, bonus draws were awarded (e.g., five bonus draws for the first week, six bonus draws for the second week, seven bonus draws for the third week, etc.). A total of 200 draws were possible when the client was completely clean of substances for the 12-week study period.

INTERVENTIONS TO DEVELOP, INCREASE, OR STRENGTHEN BEHAVIOR

In this section, we describe several behavioral interventions that use reinforcers to develop, increase, or strengthen behavior. These strategies largely involve shaping and modifying reinforcement contingencies.

Shaping

Shaping involves the reinforcement of successive approximations to a final, desired response and generally is used to develop a skill or establish a behavior not currently in the person's repertoire (Ferguson & Christiansen, 2008). An initial step is to identify a complex behavior or sequence of behaviors that the client needs to learn and then to break down the sequence or components of the behavior in to smaller elements. When working with a couple ("Margarita" and "Anita") learning active listening skills, for example, the therapist in collaboration with the clients might first specify the desired behaviors of effective, active listening. Smaller elements of this sequence of behavior could include (a) providing Anita with time to speak; (b) appearing to listen to what Anita is saying without interruption; (c) effectively using nonverbal behavior, including nodding and eye contact, to convey that she (Margarita) is listening; (d) paraphrasing the meaning of what Anita has just said; and (e) calmly and nonjudgmentally describing an opinion, fact, or feeling.

During shaping, the client must progressively engage in more elements of the desired behavioral sequence to receive reinforcement. When the client is establishing the initial behavioral elements, a reinforcer is delivered on each occasion on which the client engages in the initial behavior in a sequence of behaviors. If Margarita were just learning new communication skills, the therapist might highlight and provide potentially reinforcing remarks or praise when Margarita has simply listened to Anita for a short period without interrupting her.

Once the client has established the initial behavioral element, the therapist prompts the next behavior and withholds reinforcement until the client engages in that next behavior or makes an effort to perform it. The next behavior might involve Margarita not only allowing Anita time to speak but also nodding or effectively using other nonverbal signals that she is listening actively to Anita. Each time, it takes a closer approximation to the desired behavioral sequence for the client to receive the reinforcement. During the next practice trial, for example, Margarita may need to demonstrate effective paraphrasing of what Anita has just said before she receives positive feedback from the therapist. This process would continue until Margarita reliably performs the entire sequence of behavior. At that point, the emphasis shifts from the acquisition of behavior to the maintenance of behavior (Ferguson & Christiansen, 2008). During this maintenance phase, the therapist might deliver reinforcement not for each instance of the target behavior but instead for some fixed number of instances of the target behavior (e.g., reinforcement is delivered every fourth time the behavior is displayed).

As a primary method of teaching new behaviors, shaping has been successfully illustrated in several clinical investigations (e.g., Kazdin, 2001; Miltenberger, 2004), including studies in which persons with schizophrenia were taught appropriate social behaviors (Pratt & Mueser, 2002). In most applications of CBT, however, shaping processes tend to be more informally carried out. When teaching new or alternative social behaviors, for example, behavior therapists might use behavioral rehearsal, otherwise known as role-playing. This approach is most useful for teaching new behaviors or skills, or demonstrating how to perform a particular behavior, and consists of the following components (Goldfried & Davison, 1976):

- willingness of the client to learn new and relevant behaviors in areas of skill or ability acknowledged as currently deficit or noneffective;
- identification of situations in which deficit or noneffective responding is a source of distress or impairments in functioning;
- participation in role-plays in a clinical context, which involves the enactment of behaviors aided by instruction (e.g., telling the client what to do), therapist modeling, or shaping processes and feedback provided by the therapist; and
- performance of rehearsed behaviors in natural environments, coupled with self-evaluations as to whether the behavior was performed skillfully and resulted in desirable consequences.

Other considerations and guidelines associated with shaping procedures can be found in Ferguson and Christiansen (2008), Kazdin (2012), and Miltenberger (2004).

Increasing Reinforcement for Desired Behaviors That Occur at a Low Rate

In some instances, desired or adaptive behavior occurs at a low rate because reinforcers are unavailable from the client's natural environment. In theories of depression, low rates of reinforcement have been used to account for the low rate of activity often observed among depressed persons (Lewinsohn & Gotlib, 1995). Theoretically, the absence of reinforcers over time might result in extinction of previously adaptive behavior, such as spending time with other people, engaging in previously enjoyed activities, and working toward life or occupational goals.

When desired behaviors occur at a low rate, it is first important to assess why this might be the case. Such assessment might reveal that the environment is impoverished (i.e., reinforcement is simply not frequently available), the individual lacks the skills to engage in behaviors that result in reinforcement (e.g., is socially unskilled), the individual avoids situations in which reinforcement may occur, or some combination of these or other factors. In other cases, the problem is that the individual is responsive to only a narrow range of reinforcers, such as those associated with drug use and the acquiring of drugs and related items. Understanding these factors will highlight potentially effective interventions.

Gaining access to potential reinforcers might involve entering into new environments that potentially offer more reinforcers than current environments, avoiding punishing or aversive environments that decrease or suppress behavior, becoming more behaviorally active, or some combination of these strategies. One approach for realizing these therapeutic goals might involve having the client reenter situations that he or she avoids but that were previously associated with reinforcement. Another approach might involve pleasant events scheduling, with emphasis placed on increasing the frequency of behaviors that were previously associated with pleasure and enjoyment (Lewinsohn, Antonuccio, Steinmetz-Breckenridge, & Teri, 1984). In Chapter 8, we describe strategies for increasing behavioral activation.

One important behavioral principle to keep in mind is the *matching law*, originally demonstrated by Herrnstein (1961). According to the matching law, the frequency, intensity, and time that an individual spends engaging in a particular behavior is directly proportional to the reinforcement value of the behavior. Essentially, people "match" their behavior to the available schedule of reinforcement. Lejuez and colleagues (Hopko, Lejuez, Ruggiero, & Eifert, 2003; Lejuez, Hopko, & Hopko, 2001, 2002) applied this principle to the treatment of depression. If reinforcement is more frequent, accessible, or immediate for engaging in depressive behaviors (e.g., staying in bed all day, avoiding people, watching hours of television) than it is for engaging in nondepressive behaviors (e.g., going out, socializing, working, engaging in enjoyable recreational activities), the individual will devote more time and effort to engaging in depressive behaviors. "Sam," a depressed client who spent most of her days in her room on her tablet or smartphone, for example, had to find ways to make behaviors involving leaving the home and interacting with others more reinforcing. Over time, these behaviors would ideally become well-rehearsed, easy, and more reinforcing than staying at home on electronic devices.

Another approach for increasing low-rate behaviors is to make engagement in high-frequency behaviors contingent on engagement in the low-frequency behaviors targeted to be increased. This procedure is sometimes referred to as *Premacking*, named after the individual who first described the procedure (Premack, 1959). An assumption underlying this approach is that a behavior that occurs with low frequency (or less preferred) becomes more probable when high-frequency behaviors (or more preferred) are contingent on performance of the low frequency behavior.

Therapists might assist clients in using Premack principles to modify behavior occurring both within and outside of sessions. Sam's spending time on her smartphone is a higher frequency behavior than is getting out of the home and engaging in other activities. When using Premacking, Sam might allow herself an hour on her smartphone only if she has gone out for an hour's walk, spent time talking with a friend, or visited her favorite coffee shop or the library. Many of our graduate students have committed to similar plans that involve allowing themselves time on Netflix or the Internet only after they have completed a certain amount of writing or studying. Within therapy sessions, the therapist might consider deferring topics of discussion that the client prefers until higher priority topics have been addressed. An example of this occurs in DBT (Linehan, 1993a), where the therapist might defer discussions of a client's fight with her boyfriend (if this is the preferred topic) until a thorough discussion and assessment of a recent self-harm episode has occurred (see Naugle & O'Donohue, 1998, who observed the similarity of this procedure in DBT to Premacking).

PROCEDURES FOR DECREASING OR WEAKENING BEHAVIOR

In this section, we describe several behavioral interventions that use extinction and punishment procedures to decrease or weaken behavior. These interventions include extinction and differential reinforcement, covert sensitization, and response cost procedures.

Extinction and Differential Reinforcement

One way to decrease the frequency of problematic target behaviors is to eliminate the reinforcers that maintain them. When a behavior previously maintained by reinforcement no longer produces reinforcing outcomes, the behavior will likely decrease in frequency and perhaps be eliminated (or extinguished) altogether.

An important first step in using extinction procedures is to identify the reinforcers that maintain the behavior. Functional analyses of the problem behavior will often identify the reinforcers that support the behavior. Once the therapist and client have decided to eliminate reinforcers that maintain the problem behavior, the next step is to consider how to respond when the target behavior does not occur. When extinction procedures are used to reduce the frequency or intensity of a target behavior, reinforcement is usually used to strengthen an alternative, more desirable behavior. Examples of reinforcement contingencies that might accompany extinction procedures include the following:

- *Differential reinforcement of other behavior* (DRO) is delivered when the target behavior does not occur within a specified interval. Reinforcement, then, is contingent on the target behavior not occurring over a specified period, or the absence of the target behavior.

- *Differential reinforcement of alternative behavior* (DRA) is delivered after the display of an alternative behavior that is functionally similar to the target behavior but different in topography (form). This method is used when the therapeutic goal is to replace problematic target behaviors with more adaptive behaviors that produce similar outcomes.

In the case of DRO, the therapist and client determine how long the client must go without engaging in the target behavior to obtain the reinforcement. When DRA is used, the client and therapist need to agree on the alternative behavior or acceptable range of behavioral alternatives. Under ideal circumstances, the alternative behavior is already within the client's behavioral repertoire and is naturally supported (reinforced) by the client's social environment (Wallace & Robles, 2003). If the alternative behavior is not currently in the client's repertoire, the therapist might first use shaping or other contingency management procedures to establish the behavior before embarking on the DRA approach. The therapist and client also collaboratively decide on the nature of the reinforcer. In the case of DRA, the same natural reinforcers that supported the target behavior ideally are accessible through the alternative behavior. In the case of DRO, an ideal reinforcer is one that is just as potent or even more so than the reinforcers that maintained the target behavior. Reinforcers are most effective when they occur immediately and continuously after displays of the desired alternative behavior (e.g., with DRA) or after the client does not display the undesired behavior within a specified interval (e.g., with DRO; Wallace & Robles, 2003).

Remember Alan, whose frequent talking about suicide resulted in attention and social support? Therapy with Alan around this target began with a functional analysis and self-monitoring of suicide talk. After it was clear as to how the suicide talk functioned in Alan's social environment, the therapist discussed the importance of Alan developing and using alternative means to obtain social and emotional support and attention. Once Alan agreed to work toward this goal, therapy included a combination of practice with interpersonal skills, DRO (reinforcement following intervals without suicide talk occurring), and DRA. Using DRA, the therapist worked with Alan to express his needs effectively. When Alan used interpersonally skillful communication instead of suicide talk (either within or outside of therapy sessions), the therapist provided praise as well as naturally reinforcing consequences. For example, if Alan asked the therapist whether she would be available for a quick call to help him get through a difficult time (in the past, he would have discussed his suicide plan), she commented on his effective use of skills and provided him with the extra telephone time (within reason). During this process, extinction procedures were used, in that the therapist would not respond to suicide talk and ask Alan to describe what he wants or needs. Of course, during this work, the therapist remained mindful of Alan's suicide risk (he had attempted suicide in the past) and conducted ongoing risk assessment.

Initially, when Alan began to communicate his needs without suicide talk, those in his social network unfortunately sometimes ignored or did not respond to him (as long as he was not making extreme or worrisome statements, they seemed to take a breather from communication with him). To solve this problem, he chose a family member and a close friend with whom to discuss his therapy goal of expressing his needs without talking about suicide, and these individuals began to be more attentive and supportive when Alan asked directly for what he wanted (e.g., "I'm feeling really lonely and down today. I was wondering if there's any way that we could talk or go for coffee this evening").

As we have illustrated, DRA is often combined with extinction procedures. In Alan's case, this involved the withdrawal of typical reinforcers for suicide-related talk. One important consideration in using extinction procedures, however, is that the undesired target behavior sometimes temporarily increases in frequency or intensity after positive reinforcement is withdrawn. This common, temporary side effect of extinction procedures is referred to as an *extinction burst*. In the example of Alan, an extinction burst might involve a temporary increase in the frequency or intensity of suicide-related talk, but it might also involve actual suicidal behavior. The same type of phenomenon happens all the time at vending machines. If a person puts money into a vending machine and it does not produce the soda or treat, he or she might press the buttons harder, hit, or kick the machine. This is not particularly good for the vending machine, but is much less of a concern than the threat of an escalation in Alan's suicidal behaviors. Therefore, it is important to remember that the initial response to the implementation of the extinction procedure is often a sudden increase in the frequency or intensity of the target behavior, which gradually declines as reinforcers continue to be withheld. When the target of extinction involves self-damaging behaviors, the therapist must have an effective crisis plan, assess ongoing risk, and be willing to abandon the contingency management procedures to ensure the client's safety, if needed.

When a behavior is placed on an extinction schedule, reinforcement for the behavior under extinction must be continuously withheld, even within the period of an extinction burst (if it is safe to do so). A behavior that is incompatible with or alternative to the behavior undergoing extinction could also be reinforced, which might further facilitate the extinction process while establishing a different, and perhaps more adaptive, behavior. Additional procedural guidelines concerning extinction and differential reinforcement can be found in Malott et al. (2000), Miltenberger (2004), and Wallace and Robles (2003).

Positive Punishment Procedures

Positive punishment procedures (i.e., those that involve the application of an aversive event or stimulus following the performance of a behavior targeted for weakening) are infrequently used in CBT. Aversion therapies based on the principle of positive punishment historically included mild electric shocks and the use of chemicals or drugs to produce nausea. These techniques have largely been abandoned because of their equivocal effectiveness and a host of negative effects such as the dehumanization of the client, fear or mistrust of the therapist, and impracticality when applied in natural client settings (Kearney, 2006).

Positive punishment in contemporary CBT, although rare, may occur in response to the client's behavior. Examples of this include confronting the client regarding rude or disrespectful behavior, lateness or therapeutic absences, or other behaviors targeted for change. Confrontation itself, even when delivered in a compassionate manner (which is what we recommend), could be experienced as aversive and function to suppress or reduce a behavior. Another potential positive punisher could be more therapy session time (if therapy is experienced as aversive by the client), or therapy session time spent discussing undesirable topics (from the client's perspective), such as self-injury. It is important, however, when using aversive procedures, to remember that distal reinforcers may not affect out-of-session behavior as much as the therapist hopes. Confrontation or other positive punishment procedures occurring several days after the targeted behavior (e.g., drug use) might simply suppress the client's talking about problem behavior rather than altering the target behavior. A client reporting drug use who is confronted by her therapist, for example, might not stop using drugs but might stop reporting accurately on her drug use.

Another positive punishment procedure is *covert sensitization*. This approach has been used primarily to reduce some behavioral excesses (e.g., abuse of substances, gambling, sexual deviations such as pedophilia or exhibitionism, nail biting, overeating). With this procedure, the therapist instructs the client to imagine participating in the target behavior. As the client does so, the therapist asks him or her to imagine the co-occurrence of some type of aversive event (e.g., becoming nauseous to the point of vomiting, the experience of ridicule or horrified stares from others). The aversive event the client imagines acts as an aversive consequence or punisher for engagement in the maladaptive behavior. Although the consequence itself is covert, occurring in imagination, there is some indication that behavior change as a result of this process occurs at the overt or publicly observable level (Kearney, 2006; Upper & Cautela, 1979). See Kearney (2006) and Upper and Cautela (1979) for detailed descriptions of covert sensitization procedures.

Negative Punishment and Response Cost Procedures

When punishment procedures are used in CBT, they are most frequently based on the principle of negative punishment, or the removal of a reinforcing event following the enactment of behavior targeted for weakening. Behavioral interventions based on this principle and carried out for this reason are described as *response cost* interventions. An assumption associated with response cost procedures is that the client already has access to reinforcers and that the therapist or some other person (e.g., a participant-observer) is in a position to remove reinforcers contingent on displays of targeted behavior. Whenever a punishment procedure is used, including those involving response cost, it is often useful to simultaneously reinforce a desired behavior while the target behavior is being weakened.

Examples of response cost in nonclinical settings are quite common. These include fines for engaging in a behavior that violates a relatively minor social code or law (e.g., speeding ticket, fine for the late return of a library book). Similarly, some parental discipline strategies are based on this principle, such as time out. A shorthand label for "time-out from positive reinforcement" (Friman & Finney, 2003), *time out* is a procedure that involves the removal of an individual from a reinforcing context contingent on the display of an undesired target behavior. In the application of this procedure, a child might be immediately removed from a situation in which the targeted problematic behavior occurred and placed for a period of time (e.g., 1 minute per age in years) in a situation in which the reinforcers that maintain problematic behavior are absent (e.g., attention) and there is nothing to do (children often experience doing nothing as aversive; see Friman & Finney, 2003). Once the child associates engagement in the target behavior with a change in situation, from preferred to nonpreferred, the frequency of the problematic behavior usually decreases.

Another example of the use of response cost includes the use of a "donation jar," in which an individual who is seeking to decrease a behavior (e.g., cigarette smoking) contributes to the jar (e.g., $1) for each instance of the targeted behavior beyond that day's goal (e.g., number of cigarettes smoked in excess of the goal amount for that day). To make the response cost procedure aversive, the therapist or other person donates all contributions in the jar at the end of the intervention period to a charitable organization whose actions or values are offensive to the client (e.g., the campaign committee of a political candidate whom the client opposes).

Other examples of response cost procedures include those used to manage treatment-interfering or self-destructive behaviors. When a client repeatedly arrives late for sessions, one response cost procedure is to allow the client only the remaining session time (e.g., the remaining 30 minutes of a 50-minute session). This procedure has elements of response cost, in that a portion of the session time to which the client would otherwise be entitled is withdrawn.

Another example involves DBT (Linehan, 1993a), in which the therapist is available by telephone (or e-mail, text-messaging, or other forms of communication) between sessions to assist clients struggling to apply their new behavioral skills. One rule regarding between-session contact is the 24-hour rule, in which the client is not permitted contact with the therapist for a 24-hour period following an act of self-injury or a suicide attempt. If the client does call the therapist during this period, the therapist keeps the telephone call short, with the main purpose being to determine whether injuries are life threatening and whether medical emergency services should be summoned. The primary aim of this rule and procedure is to avoid providing immediate social reinforcement for self-injury or suicidal behavior. The 24-hour rule can also be considered a response cost procedure, however, in that between-session time with the therapist is withdrawn for a period (for recent discussions of telephone procedures in DBT, see Linehan, 2011, and Manning, 2011).

ADDITIONAL APPROACHES FOR CHANGING BEHAVIOR THROUGH CONTINGENCY MANAGEMENT AND SELF-MANAGEMENT STRATEGIES

In this section, we describe four strategies for modifying behavior through contingency or self-management procedures. As we note in the following subsections, each procedure involves some sort of alteration of the context within which targeted behavior occurs or does not occur to influence the frequency of behavior in desirable directions.

Self-Management Strategies

Clients often engage in impulsive acts to obtain short-term rewards, often with apparent disregard for the immediate or delayed aversive long-term outcomes that accompany such behavior. Within laboratory-based studies, self-control has been defined as "choice of a larger but more delayed outcome over a smaller but less delayed outcome" (Logue, 1998, p. 252). Impulsivity is regarded as the opposite of self-control, in which smaller immediate outcomes are preferred over larger delayed outcomes.

One approach for reducing the influence of immediate reinforcers on behavior in favor of long-term goals involves the use of *self-management strategies*. Self-management is evident when a person engages in a behavior or set of behaviors to influence the occurrence of another behavior (i.e., the target behavior) on a later occasion (Miltenberger, 2004). To illustrate, a client wishes to reduce the amount of cigarettes he or she smokes and eventually stop smoking altogether. Cigarette smoking in this example is the target behavior. To reduce the target behavior, the client engages in several other behaviors (e.g., self-monitoring of cigarette use, goal setting, regular exercise, healthier food choices) to increase the likelihood that he or she will successfully decrease his or her use of cigarettes.

Other strategies to improve self-management and reduce impulsivity involve helping the client to bring more distal consequences of behavior into awareness. Teaching the client how to effectively consider short and long-term pros and cons for different courses of action (before acting) might increase the salience of possible aversive outcomes associated with impulsive actions. It can also be helpful to have the client entertain the pros and cons of potentially more effective behavior and then to compare the pro versus con profile of the effective versus impulsive behavior (Linehan, 2015).

Behavioral (or Contingency) Contracting

Behavioral contracting is a method for formalizing agreements reached between a client and therapist concerning the client's behavior. When using behavioral contracts, the client and therapist first collaboratively establish goals for particular behaviors. "Monique," for example, struggles with anger management and engages in angry outbursts. She and her therapist might identify "reducing angry outbursts" as a therapy goal. They might also specify "practicing anger management skills four times per week" as a goal that is consistent with reducing angry outbursts. In coming up with a behavioral contract, Monique and her therapist might specify that if she goes for 1 week without engaging in an angry outburst, she will reward herself by renting a video that she has been hoping to watch. Alternatively, they might specify that if she practices her anger management skills three times per week for 2 weeks in a row, she can have an extra-long therapy session (if therapy is reinforcing), buy herself a small gift, or obtain some other type of reinforcer. The therapist might also agree, as part of the contract, to be available by phone to assist Monique in inhibiting angry outbursts or to perform some other action to facilitate Monique's movement toward her goals.

Behavioral contracts can be written or established through a verbal agreement. As summarized in Houmanfar, Maglieri, and Roman (2003), behavioral contracts have at least four central functions:

- formalization of behavioral goals,
- provision of an accessible reference that serves as a reminder of behavioral goals,

- specification of the responsibilities of each individual involved in the contract, and
- a public statement signifying a commitment to the goals specified in the contract.

Effective behavioral contracts have several crucial ingredients. First, it is important to clearly specify some threshold level of performance (e.g., in terms of frequency or duration) required for certain positive consequences. Second, the consequences associated with reaching specified levels of performance should involve some form of positive reinforcement or negative punishment (i.e., response cost). Third, the behavioral contract would ideally specify how consequences will be administered and by whom, as well as the duration of the contract period. Fourth, the therapist and the client should establish methods for monitoring progress, such as behavior charting or some other form of self-monitoring or participant observation. A final consideration has to do with focusing on the positive aspects of the client's behavior (Houmanfar et al., 2003). The contract would ideally identify what the client should do rather than what he or she should not do. This might involve, for example, reconceptualizing a client's problem area in terms of goals (Heinssen, Levendusky, & Hunter, 1995). Once a behavioral threshold specified in the contract is reached, the reinforcer specified in the contract should be delivered as soon as possible. Houmanfar et al. (2003) provided an example of a behavioral contract used in family therapy, and Heinssen et al. (1995) provided guidelines for the use of contracts in institutional or milieu setting for clients with severe psychological disorders.

Habit Reversal Procedures

Habit behaviors generally fall into one of three categories: nervous habits (e.g., nail biting, skin picking, hair pulling, teeth grinding, mouth biting), motor or vocal tics, and stuttering (Adams, Adams, & Miltenberger, 2003; Miltenberger, 2004). Habits such as these are often maintained by negative reinforcement processes linked to anxiety or tension reduction or to automatic reinforcing processes associated with self-stimulation. Stuttering, however, is linked to interrupted airflow through the vocal cords and is often reduced through regulated breathing methods (Miltenberger, 2004).

Several methods have been used to effectively reduce behaviors associated with habit disorders (Miltenberger, 2004). According to Adams et al. (2003), two features associated with habit control procedures are most strongly linked to positive treatment effects. The first of these is *awareness training*. This involves training in the ability to detect and discriminate instances of the habit behavior when it occurs. Various manifestations of the habit behavior are clarified, as are the conditions that typically occasion such behavior. The second component is *competing response training*. This involves instruction in ways to immediately stop the target behavior as soon as the client is aware that it is happening and is immediately followed by performing an alternative behavior that competes with the target behavior. When nervous habits and tics are the target behaviors, competing behaviors appear to primarily operate as punishers for the target behaviors (Miltenberger, 2004).

To decrease nail biting, for example, a client might first self-monitor instances of nail biting. This includes discriminating among the various forms and manifestations that nail biting might have and also noticing the situations in which nail biting is most likely to occur. Once the client has demonstrated adequate awareness of his or her nail biting and the antecedents associated with its occurrence, competing behaviors that can be used in these situations might be identified. Depending on the situation, this might include putting on gloves, placing lotion on one's hands, or grasping a pencil. The competing behavior, regardless of its form, should functionally result in the hands being unavailable for nail biting (Adams et al., 2003).

SUMMARY

The following principles and guidelines are useful to consider when therapeutic interventions target environmental factors to help clients reduce unwanted behaviors or increase behaviors consistent with their goals:

- Contingency management procedures involve changing antecedents to increase or decrease particular behaviors and include stimulus control strategies (e.g., cue elimination, discrimination training) and procedures for arranging or modifying establishing operations.
- Interventions that involve altering consequences to influence behavior include reinforcement, punishment, or extinction-based strategies.
- Natural responses on the part of the therapist can function as reinforcers for client behavior targeted to increase.
- A variety of therapist behaviors can also weaken or reduce problematic client behavior targeted to decrease.
- When using the forms of contingency management outlined in this chapter, the therapist must clearly specify the target behavior(s), orient the client to the contingency management procedures, and be alert to the occurrence of target behaviors.
- Knowledge of and facility with the application of learning principles can complement the use of therapeutic interventions designed to bring the client's behavior in line with his or her personal goals and values.

5

TARGETING THE FUNCTIONAL ASPECTS OF MALADAPTIVE THINKING

Cognitive therapy has traditionally emphasized the importance of altering inaccurate or biased thought content to bring about therapeutic change. Questions have been raised, however, as to whether cognitive interventions in cognitive behavior therapy (CBT) that explicitly target thought content result in symptomatic improvements beyond those realized by behavioral interventions (e.g., Ilardi & Craighead, 1994; Longmore & Worrell, 2007). If belief change has uncertain or negligible influence on symptom change, questions arise as to whether there are other aspects of thoughts or thinking patterns that might influence psychological symptoms. One behavioral perspective on this question, which we develop in this chapter, emphasizes the functional properties associated with certain thoughts or patterns of thinking.

The behavioral intervention strategies reviewed in this chapter explicitly attempt to alter functional aspects of maladaptive thinking patterns by reducing avoidant or detrimental modes of thought and increasing goal- and

http://dx.doi.org/10.1037/14691-005
*Behavioral Interventions in Cognitive Behavior Therapy: Practical Guidance for Putting Theory Into Action,
Second Edition,* by R. F. Farmer and A. L. Chapman

value-directed behavior. To illustrate the functional approach, we describe intervention strategies for testing the validity of thoughts that associate behavior with anticipated (usually aversive) outcomes. We also discuss strategies for reducing rumination and for altering or inhibiting problematic behavior by promoting the development of sustained patterns of behavior consistent with one's goals and values. We conclude the chapter with a client illustration that demonstrates several of the intervention strategies reviewed. We begin this presentation with an overview of thinking and thoughts from a cognitive perspective.

THINKING AND THOUGHTS FROM A COGNITIVE PERSPECTIVE WITHIN CBT

Traditional cognitive therapy is primarily concerned with the content of thinking. Centrally important to the cognitive theory of psychiatric disorders is the concept of *schema*. Cognitive schema have been characterized as "organized structures of stored information that contain individuals' perceptions of self and others, goals, expectations, and memories" (A. T. Beck & Dozois, 2011, p. 398). When a disorder-specific schema is activated, information processing becomes biased at all levels (e.g., what information is attended to; what stored information is retrieved; how incoming information is categorized, interpreted, or processed) in a manner consistent with schema content (i.e., core attitudes and beliefs; D. A. Clark & Beck, 2010).

Schemas that are specific to particular emotional or behavioral disorders are considered inactive or dormant until triggered by stress. The cognitive theory of disorders, then, is an example of a *diathesis-stress model* of psychopathology in which the diathesis (e.g., depressogenic schema) predisposes an individual to certain emotional or behavioral disorders (e.g., major depressive disorder) or related experiences (e.g., pessimism or hopelessness). Once the diathesis is triggered by an external stressful event, a series of presumed physiological events are initiated that result in schema activation (A. T. Beck & Dozois, 2011).

The influence of schema is perhaps most readily evident in the content of *automatic thoughts*, which are characterized as consciously available ongoing thoughts related to proximal events in day-to-day life (A. T. Beck & Dozois, 2011). Automatic thoughts that are by-products of depressogenic schema, for example, are often thematically related to personal loss, deprivation, and failure (A. T. Beck & Dozois, 2011). Among those with a schema-vulnerability to anxiety disorders, automatic thoughts are usually thematically related to environmental risk or danger, personal vulnerabilities, or potential future catastrophic outcomes.

In cognitive therapy, symptomatic relief is thought ultimately to result from the weakening dysfunctional schema or schema change (D. A. Clark & Beck, 2010). This is primarily accomplished by assisting the client in shifting his or her biased and maladaptive cognitive appraisals to ones that are accurate and adaptive and by treating thoughts as hypotheses to be tested rather than literal truths (A. T. Beck & Dozois, 2011; D. A. Clark & Beck, 2010). Traditional cognitive therapy, as outlined by Sacco and Beck (1995) and J. E. Young, Rygh, Weinberger, and Beck (2014), accomplishes these objectives by

- identifying examples of maladaptive thoughts;
- helping the client identify relationships between maladaptive thoughts, emotion, and behavior;
- objectively evaluating the content of the client's maladaptive thoughts by
  - examining the evidence for or against that thought,
  - appraising the value of thinking in a particular way,
  - searching for alternative explanations for an event to which the thought is related,
  - evaluating what the real implications are if the thought is accurate, and
  - regarding maladaptive beliefs as hypotheses to be tested rather than as "facts";
- challenging the client to substitute more reasonable beliefs in place of maladaptive automatic thoughts; and
- identifying and evaluating core underlying assumptions or schemas that globally influence the client's perceptions and interpretations of persons and events.

The primary focus of cognitive therapy, then, is on the content of thinking, and this content is targeted for change to bring about additional changes in emotion and behavior.

In contrast to the central assumptions of the theory underlying the cognitive therapy model, research findings have been mixed as to whether changes in dysfunctional thinking patterns precede or mediate treatment outcome in cognitive therapy (e.g., Kleim et al., 2013; Longmore & Worrell, 2007; Maxwell & Tappolet, 2012; Smits, Rosenfield, McDonald, & Telch, 2006). Overall, there is little solid evidence that changes in cognition have strictly unidirectional effects on emotion and behavior (Longmore & Worrell, 2007). Additionally, change in dysfunctional thinking concurrent with symptom reduction has been observed in other therapies that do not explicitly target maladaptive thoughts or thinking patterns. Rather, change in cognition, emotion, and behavior appear to be concurrent or correlated processes, and targeting maladaptive thinking patterns may not afford additional benefit beyond that derived from behavioral interventions (Ilardi & Craighead, 1994; Longmore & Worrell, 2007).

THINKING AND THOUGHTS FROM A BEHAVIORAL PERSPECTIVE WITHIN CBT

Behavior therapy and cognitive therapy each emphasize the importance of learning processes in the development and maintenance of psychiatric disorders. Both approaches also utilize similar interventions, such as psycho-education, behavioral experiments, behavioral activation, problem solving, cognitive disputation, and role-playing. As we have just reviewed, however, cognitive theory attributes psychopathology to cognitive schema that bias thinking and information processing. Cognitive therapy accordingly emphasizes the use of intervention strategies that weaken the influence of dysfunctional schema or produce schema change.

In addressing how thinking processes and thoughts are handled from a behavioral perspective within CBT, we first need to distinguish between the content of thoughts and the function of thinking behavior (Addis & Martell, 2004). The *content* of thinking refers to *what* a person is thinking about. Consider the example of an executive who has been worrying about the presentation she is going to give at work. The content of thinking would refer to the actual images, scenarios, and covert verbal statements she experiences as she worries. The *function* of thinking, however, refers to *why* a person is thinking in terms of the purpose it serves or the consequences it produces. In this instance, worrying might be a form of avoidance behavior, similar to procrastination, that is negatively reinforced on the basis of the consequences that worrying produces. This executive, for example, might worry because doing so minimizes or blocks contact with self-doubts she has concerning her competencies in the areas that she will present. The act of worrying can also be a way to avoid expending the effort required to put the presentation together. Similarly, worrying may provide relief from feelings of frustration associated with having to do something she would rather not do (i.e., develop and deliver a presentation). Although worrying might be associated with some discomfort (e.g., anxiety), it may also provide relief from a number of other experiences that, in the aggregate, are even more uncomfortable or uncontrollable.

Behavioral approaches, in comparison to cognitive approaches, typically emphasize the purpose or functions associated with the client's thinking. For example, is a person who is engaged in worry productively thinking about strategies for solving problems in his or her life, or is the act of worrying functioning as a distraction method used to avoid something? Is this individual trying to figure out how to respond most effectively in this situation by weighing the likely consequences associated with responding one way versus another way? Or is he or she applying a rigidly held rule that may or may not apply in this situation? Compared with traditional cognitive therapy, behavioral interventions place less emphasis on altering the content of one's thinking and more emphasis on understanding what thinking is doing for the individual in a given moment (Addis & Martell, 2004). From a behavioral perspective, the act of thinking is a form of behavior and, similar to other behaviors, thoughts can have any of the following functions (Miltenberger, 2004):

- a *discriminative stimulus* for behavior (e.g., the thought "I'm beginning to feel overwhelmed. I had better slow down my breathing" might be followed by the behavior of breathing more slowly and deeply);
- an *establishing operation* that alters the consequences for behavior (e.g., "If I eat that delicious looking cake, my blood sugar levels will go up, and I'll probably feel sick");
- a *conditioned stimulus* for an emotional response (e.g., when the act of imagining a dog produces anxiety-related autonomic arousal for someone with a fear of dogs); and/or
- a *reinforcing or punishing consequence* for another preceding behavior (e.g., after dropping a favorite coffee mug onto the tile floor and watching it break, a person covertly exclaims to herself, "You're such a stupid klutz. You need to be more careful!").

In this chapter, we discuss several behavioral interventions that are primarily directed at altering the functional aspects of clinically relevant patterns of thinking.

ALTERING THE FUNCTIONAL ASPECTS OF THINKING THROUGH BEHAVIORAL EXPERIMENTS

Behavioral experiments can be regarded as a form of exposure therapy framed as a cognitive test in which dysfunctional thoughts are explicitly challenged through a real-life experiential learning process (McMillan & Lee, 2010). Within the cognitive therapy framework, behavioral experiments are often used to evaluate the therapist's cognitive formulation of the client's problem areas or to help the client test his or her maladaptive thinking content and develop more accurate thoughts (A. T. Beck, Rush, Shaw, & Emery, 1979; Bennett-Levy et al., 2004). Emerging but limited research suggest that behavioral experiments, when coupled with exposure-based treatment elements (see Chapter 9, this volume), are effective means for changing thoughts and behavior (McMillan & Lee, 2010).

Take, for example, the following thought that a depressed client might express: "Nothing makes a difference. I feel equally terrible all day." There are at least three assumptions associated with this thought: (a) mood or some other physiological sensation is invariant over the course of an entire day, (b) these sensations are consistently and persistently negative to the extreme (i.e., "terrible"), and (c) nothing can be done to alter this negative mood or physiological sensation. Such thinking also conveys both hopelessness and helplessness for the possibility of eventual relief from painful emotions or sensations. Functionally, such a thought might be associated with passivity, submission, avoidance, and withdrawal, all of which result in reduced access to positive reinforcers for behavior. If the client expresses this thought, other people might get the impression that they cannot help, or they might avoid this individual because some persons experience expressions of intense suffering or hopelessness as aversive. Unfortunately, such loss of social support might result in a further intensification of depressive experiences.

When rigidly held and untested, a single thought such as the one just discussed can have a wide-ranging detrimental impact. Such thoughts, however, are often premised on a number of assumptions that may not be valid. When thoughts are viewed as hypotheses to be tested rather than as facts, new opportunities arise as a result of being freed from the constraints associated with such thinking.

Central concept [handwritten marginalia]

Types of Behavioral Experiments Within CBT

Bennett-Levy et al. (2004) distinguished between two types of behavioral experiments: (a) those that resemble true experiments and involve the manipulation of the environment through action (i.e., the *hypothesis-testing approach*) and (b) those that are akin to an observational study, in which information is gathered that is either consistent or inconsistent with a specific belief (i.e., the *discovery-oriented approach*). In an example of the hypothesis-testing approach, a client might have the thought that she cannot eat ice cream, a desired but forbidden food, because of the immediate impact that doing so might have on her shape and weight. A CBT-oriented therapist would approach this thought as a hypothesis, and a test might be constructed to evaluate the validity of the assumptions associated with this thought. When at home, for example, the client might be encouraged to weigh herself and measure her stomach or hips with a tape measure before eating a standard portion of ice cream. Soon after eating the ice cream, she might weigh and measure herself, and perhaps again several hours later in the day, as a means to evaluate whether the initial thought was accurate.

In an example of the discovery-oriented approach, the question "Will I gain weight if I incorporate sensible portions of ice cream into my regular diet one to two times a week?" can be investigated by seeking out relevant information, such as from a nutritionist or a physician. For clients who do not wish to conduct a hypothesis-testing–oriented behavioral experiment, a discovery-oriented experiment might be a good starting point, and the resultant information might be sufficient to allay unwarranted fears and concerns.

Behavioral experiments can experientially demonstrate to clients that activities or events can influence mood, thinking, and behavior. Behavioral experiments can also be helpful with clients who demonstrate low *self-efficacy expectations* (Bandura, 1997). Self-efficacy is influenced by a set of beliefs that connote the ability to execute actions to produce desired outcomes. Bandura (1997) suggested that the building or strengthening of self-efficacy beliefs is a central transdiagnostic mechanism of therapeutic change that underlies most successful psychological therapies. Evidence of low self-efficacy expectations is evident in verbal statements that connote doubts about one's ability to carry out a behavior or sequence of behaviors (e.g., "If it weren't for my anxiety, I would be able to go to the shopping mall"). When clients doubt that they can carry out a behavior, they often will not try or will avoid the activity altogether. A behavioral experiment (e.g., having the client go to the shopping mall despite anxiety) can demonstrate that these doubts are unfounded and that the client can engage in effective action despite the presence of doubts. *Mastery experiences* often follow from successful behavioral experiments, in which tests of dysfunctional cognitions produce outcomes that are different from their content, thus demonstrating to the individual through participation in real-life events that he or she does have the ability to accomplish important life-enhancing tasks.

Behavioral experiments can also be especially useful for clients who exaggerate the potential for negative outcomes associated with certain actions. Bandura (1997) defined ideas concerning the outcomes or consequences of behavior as *outcome expectations*. When anticipated consequences are negative, aversive, punishing, ineffectual, or unpleasant, there is less incentive to engage in behaviors that could result in those consequences. Behavioral experiments can be arranged to evaluate whether certain behaviors, in fact, result in negative outcomes or, alternatively, result in desirable or effective outcomes in certain situations.

Procedures for Conducting Behavioral Experiments

When behavioral experiments are used to test hypotheses linked to specific thoughts, generally one of two types of interventions are used: *in vivo experiments* and *simulated experiments* such as role-plays (Rouf, Fennell, Westbrook, Cooper, & Bennett-Levy, 2004). With either approach, the overall therapeutic goal is to test and evaluate the validity of certain thoughts. Features can also be built into the behavioral experiment in which the validity of an alternative thought—one that might serve as a more accurate substitute—is simultaneously tested. A moderately depressed client, for example, might think that he is too depressed to clean his house. The specific thought regarded as a hypothesis to be tested might be, "I cannot clean my house so long as I'm depressed." In working with the client around this thought, his therapist might suggest an alternative belief, such as, "I am capable of cleaning a portion of my house even when I am feeling depressed." An experiment might subsequently be devised for testing this competing thought. Such an experiment should be well planned before implementation and include a detailed description of the activity (e.g., pick up and put away clothes on bedroom floor, make bed, and pick up and put away papers and books scattered throughout bedroom between 7:00 p.m. and 7:30 p.m. on Wednesday evening) as well as guidelines for evaluating performance (e.g., rating mood quality both before and after engagement in a specified task, rating the degree to which the activity was effectively carried out and accomplished).

When behavioral experiments are conducted to gather evidence or information in relation to a specific thought, emphasis is placed on assisting the client to discover the processes that maintain a problem or to find out what happens when one acts in a novel or different way (Rouf et al., 2004). Observational strategies used to promote discovery include direct observation of models, surveys or data gathering, and information acquisition from other public sources (Rouf et al., 2004). An example of an observational experiment involves the therapist modeling a behavior that would be highly anxiety evoking to a client. In such an exercise, the client's role is to simply observe or to gather information (Rouf et al., 2004). At this point in the process, the client would not be an active participant in the experiment. For a client with obsessive-compulsive disorder who has excessive and debilitating fears of contamination, for example, the therapist might model the competent handling of a can of insecticide while the client watches (Steketee, 1993). Similarly, for those with intense anxiety reactions when in the presence of certain stimuli, such as dogs, simply observing the therapist interact with the dog without fear often produces change in phobic behavior among clients (Bandura, 1986).

Observational strategies associated with surveys and data gathering involve collecting factual information or opinions concerning some matter of interest (Rouf et al., 2004). A client with body dysmorphic disorder, for example, might believe that physical attractiveness is the primary determinant of relationship satisfaction and long-term relationship stability. For such a client, a survey task might be devised in which the client informally asks friends what they see as the most important determinants of satisfying and close interpersonal relationships.

Rouf et al. (2004) stressed the importance of planning as a precursor to conducting behavioral experiments to maximize the likelihood of success. Included among their considerations for adequate preparation are the following:

- Are the rationale and purpose of the experiment clear to the client?
- Have relevant and specific thoughts been identified for examination during the behavioral experiment?
- When appropriate, have more realistic alternatives to the problematic thought been explicitly identified?
- Have the specific elements of the experiment been identified (e.g., setting, time, place, resources required, activities to be performed)?
- Have the possible outcomes of the experiment, and how these might be interpreted in relation to the target thought, been discussed?
- Have possible problems that might arise during the experiment been anticipated and addressed through problem solving or perspective taking?
- Have the client's reservations about carrying out the experiment been solicited and responded to?
- Is the level of exposure required by the experiment consistent with what the client can effectively tolerate at this time?

In addition to the previous considerations, Rouf et al. (2004) suggested that when active experiments are undertaken, clients should record the outcomes of the experiment. The client might, for instance, record ratings of how strongly he or she believed the target thoughts both before and after completion of the experiment (e.g., where 0% = *do not believe the content of the thought at all* and 100% = *complete and total agreement with the content of the thought*). Similar self-ratings might be collected on the level of emotional intensity associated with the thought, given that one of the primary objectives of behavioral experiments is to facilitate emotional change. Records of such information can provide direct evidence as to whether the experiment weakened the influence of the targeted thought.

For clients to achieve maximal benefit from behavioral experiments, they should also be aware of and focused on their environment and experience during the exercise (Rouf et al., 2004). This includes full attention to the stimulus features of relevant environmental cues present when carrying out the experiment, awareness of internal reactions (e.g., cognitive, emotional, physiological, behavioral) during the experiment, and any shifts that might take place in these areas as the experiment progresses. Also important is the blocking of any avoidant or escape behaviors during the exposure (e.g., distracting, dissociating, scanning for safety signals from the environment) because full immersion in the experiment will likely produce greater therapeutic effects.

After the experiment is complete, clients should be encouraged to verbalize and discriminate what happened (Rouf et al., 2004), with special attention given to antecedent–behavior and behavior–consequence links. Such an emphasis helps reinforce the contextual focus on behavior and promotes new learning when the experiment produces outcomes inconsistent with targeted thoughts.

A final component of the behavioral experiment is the promotion of rule generalizability to other relevant situations (Rouf et al., 2004). This might be enhanced through discussions with the client about what he or she has learned from the experiment that could be applied to future situations. Contrasting the outcomes of the experiment with preexisting expectations may help the client develop alternative and more accurate rules to influence future behavior. The therapist might also take time to discuss plans for following up on the experiment (Rouf et al., 2004). That is, how might the client expand on his or her progress gained from the experiment? What other assumptions need to be evaluated or tested for further progress to be possible? What might constitute the next experiment? Quite often several experiments are required before a primary belief is sufficiently weakened or contradicted to the point that the client is ready to abandon it.

Hypothesized Mechanisms of Change Associated With Behavioral Experiments

From both cognitive and behavioral perspectives, the primary therapeutic benefit of behavioral experiments is derived from the client actually doing something different from what he or she did before (Addis & Martell, 2004; Bennett-Levy, et al., 2004). In cognitive therapy, the act of doing something differently is believed to result in cognitive change that, in turn, is regarded as the underlying basis for therapeutic change (A. T. Beck et al., 1979). From a cognitive perspective, then, behavioral experiments produce cognitive change by establishing the validity (or lack thereof) of specific beliefs or in helping clients develop more accurate beliefs. Cognitive change is thought to directly influence emotional states and facilitate more effective means for confronting life's problems (Rouf et al., 2004).

Another mechanism of change associated with behavioral experiments may involve *decentering*. Decentering refers to shifting one's perspective on aversive thoughts and emotions, through which they come to be viewed as transient or passing events that are neither necessarily valid reflections of reality nor the central core feature of the self (Segal, Williams, & Teasdale, 2002). Segal et al. (2002) and others have speculated that this process of altering one's relationships within one's inner experiences, as opposed to changing the content of one's thoughts, is more strongly associated with therapeutic change in cognitive therapy. Decentering is evident in behavioral experiments, in which thoughts are viewed as hypotheses to be tested and not necessarily as valid facts. These interventions help facilitate an awareness that thoughts and emotions are transient and ever changing as well as the perspective of a self separate or distinct from the experiences of the self (e.g., "the person who observes your experiences, your thoughts and feelings, is different from those experiences").

From a behavioral perspective, the simple act of changing aspects of one's behavior allows for change in other co-occurring behaviors (e.g., thinking and emotion). Such changes in behavior may, in turn, alter how the environment responds to the individual, such as by making sources of reinforcement more accessible or available (Martell, Addis, & Jacobson, 2001). Behavioral experiments often encourage the client to confront avoided activities and events through action. Acting rather than avoiding involves doing something different and allows for the possibility of outcomes that are different from what the client expects.

ALTERING THE FUNCTIONAL ASPECTS OF THINKING BY PROMOTING BEHAVIORAL FLEXIBILITY

As we discussed in Chapter 2, environmental antecedents that have been associated with reinforcement for certain behaviors in the past often set the occasion for similar behaviors when present in current situations. *Verbally represented rules* are another important class of antecedent conditions that influence behavior. In this section, we discuss the influence of verbal rules, their relevance as establishing operations, and various behavioral interventions used to alter their influence. We also discuss strategies for developing desirable behavior patterns that are more strongly influenced by distal consequences (e.g., goals, values) implied in rule statements.

An Overview of Rule-Governed Behavior

A *rule* is "something that tells us what to do, when to do it, and what will happen when we do it" (Forsyth & Eifert, 1998, p. 53). Rules can consist of statements that an individual applies to himself or herself (e.g., "If I get this job, then I'll be a worthwhile person") or aspects of his or her world (e.g., "It's impossible to get ahead in life if one is honest and plays by the rules").

Rules can assume several various forms, including instructions, advice, commands, demands, propositions, laws, moral injunctions, myths, and modeled behavior (Baum, 2005).

How Rules Might Influence Behavior

Rules can have several different functional features (Barnes-Holmes et al., 2001; Baum, 2005). Rules might specify, for example, the consequences of acting in a certain way (e.g., "Mom said if I eat all of my dinner tonight I'll get a special dessert"). Rules also may strengthen, weaken, or otherwise alter the influence of the environment on a person's behavior (e.g., "Although I usually end up losing on the slot machines, today I have my lucky gemstone pendant, so things should go better"). Rules may also influence sequences of behavior over time by specifying distal consequences (e.g., "If I do nice things for Melissa and spend a lot of time around her, maybe she'll eventually go out with me"). When rules are accurate, they can result in efficient and effective forms of behavior as they eliminate the need for trial-and-error learning. If one is told, for example, "Do not touch the stove when it is hot because you will be burned" and adheres to this rule, it is not necessary to discover for oneself through actual experience that touching a hot stove is painful.

When behavior is under the influence of verbal stimuli such as rules (rather than immediate environmental contingencies), the behavior is said to be *rule governed*. From a functional perspective, the rule is technically regarded as an antecedent, typically an establishing operation (Malott, Malott, & Trojan, 2000; Schlinger, 1993). Rules are verbal descriptions of a behavioral contingency within which a behavior is specified as well as a consequence associated with that behavior. Alternatively, a rule can describe an antecedent condition, in the presence of which a particular behavior will produce a specified outcome (Anderson, Hawkins, Freeman, & Scotti, 2000). A rule, then, might take the form of something like, "When it is x, y is the right thing to do" or "If I do y, then z will occur" where x is some type of antecedent condition, y refers to some behavior, and z is some outcome that could be reinforcing or punishing.

Among persons with sufficiently developed verbal repertoires, most behavior is under rule control rather than immediate contingency control. If it were not, our behavior would be haphazard, erratic, and highly changeable from one situation to the next. The fact that much of our behavior is under rule control accounts, in part, for the stability evident in behavior across time and situations. The principle of rule-governed behavior also accounts for why behavior might be influenced by distal outcomes. In these instances, however, it is not the actual distal outcome that directly influences behavior. Rather, it is the rule statement that describes the behavior—consequence contingency that exerts direct influence on behavior (hence the term *rule governed*). A rule statement, then, directly influences behavior, whereas the consequence implied in the rule indirectly influences behavior (Malott et al., 2000).

A person, for example, might feel confident on the basis of previous experiences that if he mails a subscription card with a check for a magazine, about a month later, the magazine will begin to arrive at his house (Malott et al., 2000). The act of mailing in the subscription card and check caused the magazine to be received a month later, and receiving the magazine may have functioned as a reinforcer. The delivery of the magazine is not, however, a reinforcer for the act of mailing in the subscription card and check because the outcome of this behavior is too delayed. Rather, in this example, the person who subscribed to the magazine might have said to himself when filling out the subscription card, "If I complete this card and enclose a check, I'll start receiving this magazine in 1 month." This rule statement is what is directly influencing the act of filling out the card and check, whereas the reinforcer implied in the rule (i.e., receive a magazine) has only an indirect effect. Whether an outcome of an action carried out under the influence of a rule subsequently confirms or contradicts the rule will, however, influence whether one acts in accordance with that rule in the future (Malott et al., 2000).

Although rule statements often have a direct influence, and the outcomes implied or specified in the rule have an indirect influence, there are some conditions under which rules might affect behavior in other ways. When an individual, for example, verbalizes a rule statement to himself or herself and when that statement implies negative outcomes if the rule is not followed, an aversive physiological state such as tension or anxiety can result (e.g., "If I don't work on this project tonight, I'll be so far behind I'll never get it done before tomorrow afternoon's deadline"). In such instances, rule following might represent a form of escape behavior in which rule adherence results in a lessening of the aversive physiological states of anxiety or tension (Malott, 1989).

Individual Differences in Rule Following

Individuals vary in the degree to which their behavior is influenced by rules, and this is, in part, influenced by the extent to which rule following has been previously reinforced and rule statements have been historically proven to be accurate. As a result of experience, people will often generate and verbalize rules about possible behavioral contingencies. Behavior guided by such rules might accurately describe behavior–consequence relationships. Sometimes, however, individuals are overly influenced by rules, to the extent that they become relatively insensitive to immediate environmental contingencies that operate differently from the environment–behavior relations characterized in the rule statement (Follette & Hayes, 2000). That is, some individuals may be overly concerned about rule following and correspondingly less observant of what behavior actually works in their current situations. *Excessive or overly rigid rule adherence* in such instances can result in excessively inflexible and noneffective behavior.

Deficits in rule following, conversely, can also be problematic. Such deficits, in turn, might be associated with problems in other areas, including the following:

- deficiencies in verbal ability, attention skills, or concentration skills, all of which are requisite abilities for discriminating features of a rule statement (e.g., the specified behavior, consequence, or both);
- hypersensitivity and responsiveness to immediate environmental cues, as is evident among members of some groups, such as those with attention-deficit/hyperactivity disorder (Johansen, Aase, Meyer, & Sagvolden, 2002);
- deficits in the skill of discriminating behavior–consequence relations (individuals who do not discriminate the effects of their actions are less likely to have future behavior influenced by their outcomes, with subsequent behavior less effective as a result [Farmer & Rucklidge, 2006; C. M. Patterson & Newman, 1993]; discrimination of behavior–consequence relations might also facilitate the rule-generation process or contribute to the refinement and accuracy of rules and thus occasion more effective behavior [Barkley, 1997]);
- failure to generate self-rules, which often takes the form of prepositional statements that link particular forms of behavior to outcomes (e.g., "If I study hard, I'll likely get good grades and a higher paying job once I graduate") and are important for self-management and self-regulation; and/or
- substance intoxication, which interferes with all forms of behavior, including thinking and language use.

Generally speaking, overly rigid rule governance is more characteristic of internalizing disorders, whereas deficits in rule generation and adherence are more strongly associated with externalizing disorders. Individuals who are elevated in both internalizing and externalizing features, such as those with borderline personality disorder (Røysamb et al., 2011), often demonstrate rigid rule adherence, difficulties in self-management, and strong reactivity to immediate environmental experiences, among other challenges.

Assessment of Rules That Influence Behavior

One initial approach for working with problematic thinking patterns is to monitor and record them. Self-monitoring not only provides information relevant to ongoing therapy but also has associated therapeutic functions. Research suggests that the act of simply noticing and recording behavior often results in beneficial changes in the frequency of the behavior being monitored (R. O. Nelson, 1977). The self-monitoring thoughts and thinking patterns, in particular, might assist clients in identifying the types of rules that influence their behavior, help them evaluate the degree of correspondence between their rules and actual behavior—consequence relations, and facilitate the development of more accurate rules that influence future behavior. To accomplish these objectives, a therapist might begin with traditional cognition assessment techniques, such as the daily thought record, to identify automatic thoughts. From a behavioral perspective, however, the functional aspects of one's thinking are more important than the content or the type of logic error evident in one's thinking. In the case illustration provided at the end of this chapter, we suggest some modifications in the thought-recording process that provide additional information on the function of the client's thinking.

Interventions for Altering Rigid Adherence to Faulty, Inaccurate, or Harmful Rules

Sometimes rules may not accurately state the true relation between behavior and consequences. Even when actions are guided by inaccurate rules that repeatedly result in ineffective outcomes, they are nonetheless resistant to change (Hayes, Brownstein, Zettle, Rosenfarb, & Korn, 1986) and consequently can become quite problematic. Rules, when rigidly or excessively applied, can also contribute to personal distress or ineffective behavior. Some clients, for example, might be overly conscientious as evident by persistent efforts to not disappoint or offend, please others or be good, or be overly compliant. Self-rules for such overly conscientious people might include statements such as, "If I am good to others, then I will be liked and valued" and "If I make waves, I'll disappoint others." Similarly, some clinical groups are primarily defined by their tendency to rigidly adhere to rules, such as those with obsessional, perfectionistic, workaholic, and paranoid tendencies.

Two general therapeutic approaches can be used to reduce overly rigid rule following: (a) strengthening the influence of immediate reinforcement contingencies on behavior or (b) weakening the influence of rigidly held rules. Chapter 4 discusses methods for strengthening the influence of immediate reinforcement contingencies. For weakening rules that result in rigid and maladaptive behavior patterns, traditional cognitive therapy techniques might be helpful, such as the behavioral experiments described earlier in this chapter. In this section, we describe additional therapeutic approaches that can be used to weaken the influence of maladaptive or inaccurate rules.

Working With Cognitive Distortions From a Behavioral Perspective

In cognitive therapy, *cognitive distortions* refer to persistent errors in reasoning or systematic misinterpretation of situations (Sacco & Beck, 1995). Another way to view these distortions from a behavioral perspective is to regard them as faulty rules defined by inaccurate associations between antecedents and behaviors, or behaviors and consequences. Examples include the following:

- *All-or-none thinking, dichotomous thinking, black-or-white thinking* is evident when thinking patterns are polarized, and outcomes are only possible at the extreme ends of a continuum (e.g., "You're either with me or against me"; "I'm a complete loser").
- *Personalization* is the tendency to inaccurately relate events or circumstances to oneself (e.g., "My boss didn't smile at me when I walked by him; I bet he's thinking of firing me").
- *Overgeneralization* involves making broad and sweeping conclusions based on outcomes of single events. The use of certain words in some contexts might suggest the presence of over-generalization; these include *all, none, every, always,* and *never* (e.g., "All men are untrustworthy" or "Whenever I try to get ahead, nothing good ever comes from it").
- *Disqualifying the positive* involves minimizing or negating positive experiences or outcomes that conflict with rules that are negative (e.g., after the delivery of a presentation, when a junior colleague offers praise, the presenter concludes, "She's only saying this because she wants to get in good with me").
- *"Should" statements* consist of a set of inflexible rules about oneself or others concerning how one should act. The presence of "should" rules results in a greater tendency to judge, often against unrealistic or inflexible standards (e.g., "I should never make mistakes"). Other words that suggest the presence of inflexible rules for action include *ought, must,* and *have to.*
- *Catastrophizing* involves predictions of highly negative outcomes related to small events rather than viewing these events in perspective. Catastrophizing is often revealed by the use of words such as *awful, dreadful, terrible, horrible,* and *horrendous* to denote an anticipated outcome (e.g., "It would be horrible if people noticed I was anxious").

Perhaps the most direct way to approach such inaccurate or faulty ways of thinking is for the therapist to appeal to the client's actual experience by examining instances from the client's life to determine whether these rigid rules are uniformly accurate. When approached in this way, the therapeutic issue becomes whether the client's rule fits the events or the context to which it refers. To this end, there is no need for the client to learn the complex skill of applying name labels to the type of cognitive distortion evident. More important, we believe, is the skill of accurately matching up thinking related to a given context to the actual events of the context itself—that is, the generation of accurate antecedent–behavior–consequence relations as they actually occurred or unfolded (or seeing oneself or the world the way it actually is). An individual, for example, who rigidly embraces the view that "I should never make mistakes" might be comforted by noticing what happens when he makes mistakes, both big and small, and the proximal and distal outcomes of those actions. Do mistakes *always* result in negative outcomes? Are there occasional benefits to making a mistake (e.g., the resultant new learning; being viewed by others as more human or approachable)?

Another related way for therapists to respond to these thoughts is to examine with the client the effect that such thinking has when present. That is, when the client distorts actual experience, what does he or she do in relation to the distortion? Does avoidance or escape behavior follow? Does the client characteristically withdraw or give up? Does the client ruminate or become passive? If maladaptive behaviors accompany distorted modes of thinking, then a therapeutic goal might be to (a) heighten awareness of such modes of thinking and the effects that such thoughts characteristically have on behavior, (b) block any maladaptive behavior patterns that are associated with such thinking, and (c) engage in an alternative behavior that is more directly geared toward solving the problem that occasioned the distorted thought. Another approach is for the therapist to test the thought through behavioral experimentation.

Perfectionistic thinking is another example of a thinking pattern that often contributes to overly rigid rule-governed behavior. Evidence of perfectionistic thinking might be revealed by thoughts such as "I have to do a perfect job on this" or "I have to accomplish at the very highest of my abilities" or "If I'm not at the top of the class, then I'm a failure." With this pattern of thinking, there is a tendency for the client to see oneself or world in dichotomous, black-and-white, or all-or-nothing terms. In addition to reducing the client's evaluation of one's behavior to the narrow categories of "success" or "failure," excessively high self-standards for performance often result in frequent disappointment, a consequence of an inability to realize unattainable goals (Bandura, 1986). Such a frame of reference also makes alternative evaluations of one's behavior more difficult, such as from the perspectives of "partial success" or "effectiveness." Excessively high performance self-standards are common among persons with certain psychological characteristics or disorders, such as obsessive-compulsive personality disorder, Type A personality, anorexia nervosa, or depression.

Burns (1980) described several strategies for challenging the effectiveness or benefit of perfectionistic thinking. These include the following:

- *An objective evaluation of the utility of perfectionistic thinking.* Does such thinking result in more effective outcomes, or does it result in negative emotions and self-appraisals?
- *Participation in behavioral experiments geared toward the exploration of outcomes related to lower standards.* The purpose of these types of experiments is to see what effect, if any, acting in accordance with lower performance standards has on personal or performance satisfaction. Such experiments might also evaluate the effects of intentionally making a mistake or acknowledging personal flaws to others. When a mistake is made, for example, are the outcomes as negative as expected? When flaws, vulnerabilities, or potentially embarrassing information about oneself is disclosed to others, does that result in ridicule or negative evaluation, or does it promote a deepening of relationships?
- *Explore other ways of representing naturally occurring events other than through dichotomous categories.* This type of experiential exercise might involve the client intentionally taking notice of situations, events, or objects to see if they can all be categorized in a certain way. That is, can one point of view be completely correct and another competing view be completely wrong? Are there some arguments within both perspectives that ring true to some degree? Do other arguments come across as weaker? Do other persons appear all one way in some area, such as calmness, intelligence, attractiveness, or competence? Do such individuals shine in some areas, but have weaknesses in other related areas?

Shifting the Focus From Behavior Performance to Behavior Effectiveness

Another therapeutic approach to perfectionistic thinking or excessively stringent rules for self-reinforcement is to shift the focus of behavioral evaluation away from the topography (or form) of behavior (e.g., "Was the threshold for acceptable performance reached?") to a consideration of behavioral effectiveness (i.e., "What are some of the positive outcomes that resulted from my actions?"). When such a shift in orientation occurs, the emphasis moves away from getting the form of behavior correct, doing the "right" thing, or realizing of some end-state goal. From this alternative frame of reference, the focus is instead on the evaluation of behavior in terms of the outcomes it produces (Follette & Hayes, 2000).

Shifting the Focus From Thought Content to Other Experiences

In another example of behavior under the influence of faulty rules, the hallmark of paranoid modes of thinking is "an intense, irrational, but persistent mistrust or suspicion of people, and a corresponding tendency to interpret the actions of others as deliberately threatening or demeaning" (Fenigstein, 1996, p. 242). Because paranoid thinking often persists even when there is frequent evidence to the contrary, it is likely that such thinking is under the influence of faulty rules. As with other forms of rigid thinking, a client might be asked to consider alternative explanations (e.g., "Are there any other possibilities that might explain why she acted this way toward you?" or "Is there any evidence that is inconsistent with this way of viewing the situation?"). Along these lines, a feature of therapy might emphasize the development of hypothesis-generation skills in which the client is challenged to come up with more than one possible explanation for events that occasion suspicious thinking. Alternatively, the content of the thinking may not be as important as the emotion that accompanies the thought. Rather than directly challenging the thought, it might be useful for the therapist to directly focus on the accompanying emotion in a reflective and validating manner (e.g., "It sounds like you were very angry when the attendant did not respond to your question. Tell me more about what you did when you were having the feeling of anger in this situation").

Developing Rules That Are More Consistent With Actual Experience

Inaccurate rules held by people who are especially vulnerable to depressed or anxious moods tend to be evident by their overly negative thinking patterns. Often, this process involves formulating more accurate rules that incorporate some positive aspects of a situation. A cognitive technique geared toward the development of alternative or balanced thinking can be used to identify more accurate ways of thinking about the situation (Greenberger & Padesky, 1995):

- If a rule statement appears to be inaccurate because it is not supported by objective evidence, then generate an alternative rule that is more consistent with what has been observed.
- If a rule statement is partially accurate, identify the aspect of it that is supported and note the specific evidence that is consistent with it. Then identify the aspect of the rule statement that does not appear to be accurate and generate an alternative statement in its place that is more consistent with the evidence.

- Rate the degree to which you think the new rule is accurate (on a 0%–100% scale).
- Practice or apply this new rule in situations within which it might apply. New rules can be written down on index cards, carried in a pocket or purse, and referred to when indicated.

"William," for example, had the self-rule "If I am among a group of people, I will have a panic attack and do something uncontrolled that will be embarrassing [85%]." After considering occasions when he was among groups of people, William acknowledged that this statement was too absolute because he was able on several occasions to be with a group of people and not have an attack. He also could not recall any occasion when he had a panic attack and did something uncontrolled that drew attention to him. Consequently, he revised the self-rule to be, "Sometimes when I am among a group of people, I get panicky. When I'm panicky, I often think that I'll lose control, but so far I have not acted in an out-of-control way during a panic attack [90%]." As he reflected on his therapy experience, he decided to revise the self-rule even further: "Sometimes I get panicky when I'm in a group of people. If this should happen in the future, I know what I can do to cope with my panicky feelings and to reduce their intensity. Given my past history, it is unlikely that, even if I do have a panic attack, I will lose control and draw attention to myself [95%]." The goal of such an exercise is to develop more accuracy in one's thinking, which does not necessarily mean the same thing as being more positive in one's thinking. Rather, this process involves the development of a skill for seeing oneself or the world the way it actually is.

Other clients might have rules that suggest that certain types of events or private experiences are threatening. Examples of such rules might be, "Anxiety is bad because it might cause me to lose control or freak out" or "I can't go to the party because I won't know what to say to people and I'll come across as a dolt." Avoidant thinking is often associated with avoidant behavior, whether it be external (e.g., passive avoidance, active escape) or internal (e.g., dissociation, rumination, distraction). Individuals who regard certain private experiences as threatening might take dramatic steps to avoid coming into contact with them such as by engaging in ritualistic compulsive behavior, intentional self-injury, and substance misuse. Paradoxically, however, although such avoidance often provides short-term relief, the avoided experience usually becomes more common or frequent in the future. In recent years a number of behavioral interventions have been developed that target the avoidance of private events. One such intervention is acceptance and commitment therapy (ACT; Hayes, Strosahl, & Wilson, 2012). In ACT, the therapist emphasizes the verbal functions that contribute to experience avoidance. These include evaluation (e.g., "Thoughts about sex are bad and should be avoided at all costs"), reason giving (e.g., "If it wasn't for my anxiety I would go to the concert tonight"), and literality ("I feel like I'm an evil person so I must be").

Establishing Rules That Bring Behavior in Line With Desirable Distal Outcomes

In this and the following sections, we discuss therapeutic interventions for transcending the influence of immediate environmental events in favor of bringing behavior in line with desirable distal outcomes. As we previously noted, distal outcomes only influence current behavior indirectly; the direct-acting influence is a rule that associates current behaviors with distal outcomes. In the next two sections, we are primarily concerned with two general classes of verbal rules: those related to goals and those related to values. Before describing intervention strategies for increasing goal- and value-directed behavior, we first distinguish the concepts of goals and values from a behavioral perspective.

Distinguishing Goals and Values From a Behavioral Perspective

When people speak of goals and values, they generally do so in terms of what an individual has. From a behavioral perspective, however, both goals and values are evident in one's action. That is, goals and values are regarded as verbal rules that are associated with verbally constructed consequences that make some behaviors more appetitive and others more aversive (Twohig, Masuda, Varra, & Hayes, 2005). Evidence of the influence of goals and values is seen in one's behavior that is, in turn, influenced by contingency-specifying rules.

As used here, *goals* refer to concrete events, situations, or objects. They can be realized, achieved, or completed (Hayes & Smith, 2005). Goals are attainable and can specify a directional course that has value for the individual. Ideally, goals that an individual pursues should be consistent with or complementary to his or her values. *Values* refer to areas of life that one cares about or regards as important (Twohig et al., 2005). Unlike goals, values are not something to be achieved or completed; rather, a person's values are made manifest in his or her day-to-day actions (Hayes & Smith, 2005). In this respect, values are choices or selections among alternatives, and they, too, suggest a directional course. Values often represent the outgrowth of cultural teachings or practices. One's values, however, might diverge from cultural practices as a result of personal experience.

In an example from Twohig et al. (2005), a client with obsessive–compulsive disorder might value being a good mother and wish to be free of the anxiety that occasions compulsive behavior. Being free of anxiety might be a goal that is temporarily realized through engagement in ritualistic behavior. Participation in compulsive actions, however, takes time away from living in accordance with the value of being a good mother because time spent on rituals is time that is not available for being with her daughter. Although the client may regard being anxiety-free as a personal goal, she may value the time spent with her daughter even more.

In another example, Hayes and Smith (2005) illustrated the distinction between goals and values with reference to a person with a drug addiction. Such an individual might take drugs to "feel good" or for their immediate positive reinforcing effects. Although this might represent the goals of drug use, being high and feeling good may not necessarily be valued outcomes for such an individual. Rather, this person might value being physically with and psychologically close to other people. Taking steps in the direction of establishing, maintaining, and deepening relationships, however, might occasion significant anxiety. Because anxiety is experienced as aversive, the person stops moving forward and instead takes drugs to deal with the anxieties associated with moving in a valued, yet frightening, direction. Initial movements in a valued direction, then, might not "feel good" in the short term, whereas drug consumption might produce immediate "good feelings" and relief.

In the next section, we describe techniques for realizing goals, or potentially achievable outcomes that result from a series of actions. After discussing techniques associated with goal setting, we offer examples of values-based intervention strategies in a following section.

Goal Setting and Time Management

Goal setting in behavior therapy is always individualized in accordance with the needs and therapeutic objectives of the client. Selected goals are ideally related to one's values or ideals and should represent something the client is willing to spend time and effort working toward (Hayes et al., 2012). Goals should also be achievable within a practical time frame and progress toward the realization of goals should be evident in each step taken. Goals also might be conceptualized in terms of things to work toward rather than away from (M. Davis, Eshelman, & McKay, 2000). In the case of goals related to alcohol abuse, a practical goal might be complete abstinence or controlled drinking, with the parameters of what constitutes "complete abstinence" or "controlled drinking" clearly defined. This would be more desirable than the goal of "avoiding alcohol."

Goal setting is often carried out in conjunction with self-monitoring and some type of contingency-management program. Consequently, a list of goals might be drawn up and subdivided into short-term goals (e.g., goals that one might work toward in the days and weeks ahead) and long-term goals (e.g., goals that will require sustained effort over longer periods of time).

Once goals are clearly identified, the therapist and client might consider together how to go about realizing these goals. What rewards, for example, will be available for efforts directed toward the realization of goals, or what will the costs be when efforts are not made? Consideration might also be given to the inclusion of other people. Social reinforcement from others can be a potent influence on behavior and often increases the likelihood that the program will be carried out. Addis and Martell (2004) summarized the steps associated with goal setting.

- *What are the steps for working toward a goal?* The path to realizing a goal is more likely to be followed if the points along the way are clearly spelled out. Smaller and clearly defined steps are better than bigger and vague ones.
- *In what sequence should these steps be organized?* Once steps have been clearly identified and delineated, they should be arranged in a logical sequence that maximizes the likelihood for reaching the goal. Consideration should be given to what needs to be completed first before another step can be taken. In this regard, steps can be thought of as separate actions that, in the aggregate, link up to a chain of behaviors that collectively move one toward the realization of a goal.
- *Commit to carrying out each of the identified steps*. This involves specifying the day and time that the first step will be taken. In doing so, thought should be given to what the step would involve in terms of resources or time and arranging for these in advance. Consideration should also be given to potential obstacles that might arise and how these will be overcome, as well as how progress at each step will be monitored.
- *Work through any barriers*. Regardless of mood, inhibiting thoughts, or other psychological barriers, the goal is to take a step.
- *Reward oneself*. This involves acknowledging one's efforts and what one has accomplished after the completion of each step by providing a reward or pat on the back.

Part of goal setting and working toward goal realization is *time management*. Effective management of one's time is a necessary skill if one is to get one's work done and have time left over to do elective enjoyable activities. A related goal might be to manage one's time so that time and energy is spent on valued activities and not on procrastination or avoidant activities.

The effective use of time requires prioritizing activities, clarifying one's values, and comparing the worth of activities on the basis of their relationship to those values. This also involves daily planning, in which one makes a specific plan each day to accomplish goals and activities that are highest in priority. *Time logs* can be used to organize one's daily plan. A time log is a listing of activities that one plans to carry out over the course of the day, an estimate of how much time is required to carry out each of the activities, and a priority rating for each activity. Priority ratings might be based, for example, on the degree to which the activity is tied to important goals or values or the significance of consequences associated with carrying out or not carrying out the activity (M. Davis et al., 2000).

As Hayes et al. (2012) observed, persons who attempt to shift their behavior from immediate contingencies to long-term goals are often confronted with a challenge: the immediate outcomes that follow goal-directed behaviors. On some occasions, the immediate consequences for acting in a valued direction might be experienced as aversive, even though the behavior performed is related to desirable goals. Take, for example, an individual who wishes to no longer passively avoid or actively escape from situations that occasion anxiety. To accomplish this, she will likely experience immediate significant anxiety as she enters into and remains within anxiety-evoking situations. For her to remain in such situations, she must value the non-immediate or distal outcomes associated with exposing herself to situations that evoke such uncomfortable experiences.

Behavioral intervention strategies designed to facilitate action toward valued or long-term goals include *acting toward a goal* (Martell et al., 2001). Related therapeutic goals are the facilitation of the client's engagement in previously established behaviors that have been extinguished or the acquisition and enactment of new behaviors. For individuals whose behavior is often guided by immediate contingencies or experiences, such as current emotions, a therapeutic goal would be to help them shift their behavior away from responding to immediate events. That is, clients might be encouraged to act in accordance with values or long-term goals rather than with immediate emotional experiences. Expressed a different way, "the goal is the action itself, rather than the outcome of the action" (Jacobson, Martell, & Dimidjian, 2001, p. 261). Helping the client find a good job, for example, may not be the focal goal of therapy; rather, a goal consistent with a behavioral activation approach would be to help the client develop and maintain a pattern of behavior or routine that increases the likelihood of finding a good job, regardless of how he or she might feel while doing so (Jacobson et al., 2001).

Long-term goals often involve valued outcomes related to health, career, family, relationships, finances, leisure and personal interests, and general satisfaction. Acting in accordance with long-term goals, then, often involves acting in accordance with what one values. In the next section, we discuss intervention strategies that facilitate the development of behavioral habits or routines that are consistent with one's values.

Values-Based Intervention Strategies

Although values-based interventions have been central features of therapies developed from the human potential movement during the 1950s through the 1970s, they have only recently surfaced within CBT therapies. Values connote what holds meaning for the individual, what is good versus bad, or what is moral versus immoral (Baum, 2005). One's values are often evident in responses to questions such as the following (Hayes et al., 2012):

- What do you want your life to stand for or be about?
- What are your hopes, aspirations, or wishes for yourself during your lifetime?
- How do you want people to think about you after you're gone?

Values can be regarded as a special form of verbal behavior that specify, either directly or indirectly, the contingencies of behavior linked to the value. As related to their directional or purposive qualities, values are verbal rules that connote desired life consequences and are based on a set of behavioral practices. This quality of value-based rules both coordinates and maintains values-related behavior over long periods of time.

In behavior therapies such as ACT, the act of valuing is regarded not as a feeling or even thought. Rather, the act of valuing is manifest through action (Hayes et al., 2012). Consequently, ACT-based interventions facilitate the development of behavioral trajectories that move and sustain behavior in a direction consistent with a client's values. To this end, a good deal of therapeutic activity in ACT is directed toward helping clients identify their values and act in accordance with these even in the face of psychological obstacles. Because values, in contrast to goals, are not fully realizable or permanently achievable, they have greater potential applicability across time and situations and are less likely to give way to satiation or change (Hayes et al., 2012).

Motivational interviewing or *motivational enhancement therapy* is an approach to therapy that has primarily been associated with the treatment of alcohol abuse and dependence (Miller, Zweben, DiClemente, & Rychtarik, 1995), although it has recently been applied to several other domains (e.g., Arkowitz, Westra, Miller, & Rollnick, 2008). When interpreted from a behavioral perspective, motivational interviewing helps clients establish connections between current harmful behavior patterns and more distal outcomes as a way to lessen the influence of immediate environmental contingencies. In the first phase of therapy, the primary objective is to establish a motivation for change. Among the techniques used to accomplish this is the provision of information to the client about the level of his or her alcohol use and the likely effects it will have in the future if current use patterns continue (Miller & Rollnick, 2013). Within this phase, the therapist provides the client with information about his or her personal risk and degree of impairment while emphasizing the client's personal responsibility for bringing about a change in drinking behavior.

In the second phase, emphasis is placed on the facilitation of a commitment to change. During this phase, the therapist explores with the client his or her readiness for change and whether a decision to change has been made. The therapist, in an empathic and supportive manner, provides clear advice that encourages a change in drinking behavior. When the client expresses an interest in change, various change options are discussed and considered. A significant other might be included within change plans to increase the likelihood that action plans will be carried out. Consequences associated with taking action toward change versus inaction are also contemplated.

In the last phase, the client and therapist discuss and test change-oriented strategies. Also within this phase, any progress or gains are reviewed, and the client's motivation and commitment for change are frequently reassessed and reaffirmed.

Inhibiting Problematic Behaviors Through Rule Generation and Adherence

Rules can also be useful for promoting restraint (Alessi, 1992). Societies, for example, often enact laws that demarcate the division of what constitutes acceptable and unacceptable behavior. Other examples of cultural rules that frequently restrain behavior include values, warnings, taboos, and admonishments, all of which imply negative social consequences for instances of noncompliance.

Some persons' behaviors are inordinately influenced by immediate environmental cues, resulting in behavior that is primarily stimulus driven and influenced by short-term contingencies. Such individuals may appear to be impulsive, erratic, and pleasure seeking. For individuals who are overly reactive to immediate environmental cues, one therapeutic task might be to shift the influence of behavior away from immediate environmental contingencies to the influence of rules that specify alternative distal outcomes. One consequence of this might be that individuals will be in a better position to develop and sustain behavior patterns that assist in achieving long-term objectives.

To facilitate this, the therapist might direct early work toward goal or value identification. Once identified, the therapist and client work together to identify patterns of behavior that would be required to realize such values and goals. Once so identified, the client might be encouraged to act in a manner that is consistent with his or her values (Hayes et al., 2012; Martell et al., 2001). Included among these techniques is acting *"as if."* In short, acting "as if" involves acting in line with how one would ideally like to be. Approaches such as this increase the salience of distal consequences and weaken the influence of immediate environmental events.

Another approach is *behavioral contracting*. A behavioral contract is a rule or statement, often written, that specifies a behavior to increase or decrease, when the behavior should or should not take place, the method used to monitor behavior, and the consequences associated with either performing or not performing the behavior (Malott et al., 2000; Miltenberger, 2004). In this respect, the contract serves as an establishing operation that brings behavior in line with the parameters set forth in the contract. Rules that are easier to follow describe immediate outcomes that are both sizable and probable. In contrast, rules that describe immediate outcomes that are relatively small in magnitude or improbable are more difficult to follow (Malott et al., 2000). In dialectical behavior therapy (Linehan, 1993a), variations of the basic behavioral contracting strategy are used during the process of orienting the client to therapy, clarifying therapy-related expectations for the client and therapist, and establishing guidelines for responding to crisis situations.

REDUCING WORRY AND RUMINATION

Borkovec (1994) and others (e.g., Newman & Llera, 2011; Nolen-Hoeksema, Wisco, & Lyubomirsky, 2008) have conceptualized habitual worry and rumination as a style of thinking that is often negatively reinforced as a result of the escape or avoidance function it serves in relation to the amelioration of anxiety. Worry and rumination also preclude opportunities for dealing with problems directly and actively (Addis & Martell, 2004). To determine, however, whether someone who is worrying or ruminating is actually avoiding (rather than some other adaptive alternative such as problem solving), it is important to first understand *why* the person is thinking about certain events over and over at this particular point in time.

Clarifying the Function of Rumination and Worrying

Rumination and worry are often different in form than problem solving (Addis & Martell, 2004). When persons ruminate or worry, they mentally repeat some event, circumstance, issue, or scenario and the actual or hypothetical associated negative consequences. In problem solving, however, the focus is on identifying the problem, generating solutions to the problem, choosing one or two potential options that are most likely to be effective in the given situation, acting on the selected solution option, and evaluating the consequences of the approach. Rumination often involves few, if any, of these elements. Instead, rumination is often a way to avoid taking actions that might potentially solve the life problems that occasion rumination (Addis & Martell, 2004).

Worrying and ruminating are strongly associated with anxious, depressed, and angry moods. One important commonality across ruminating and worrying is that both involve repetitive and unproductive thinking that is either focused on the past or a hypothetical future, respectively. As a result, the individual who is ruminating or worrying is not focused on the present moment and may have difficulty responding to what is happening in his or her immediate environment (Martell et al., 2001). From a behavioral perspective, central questions in relation to this process are, "Why is this person psychologically disconnecting from the environment now?" and "How is disconnecting through rumination helping this person?"

Targeting the Functional Aspects of Rumination and Worry

If rumination is a form of avoidance, and if the outcomes of rumination are more harmful than beneficial, therapy might target rumination. This is perhaps best accomplished by coming up with alternative coping options for tolerating or accepting anxiety associated with the problem, identifying what the client is avoiding through rumination, preventing avoidance behaviors, and taking action to solve the problem (even if anxiety is present; Addis & Martell, 2004; Forman et al., 2012).

In behavioral activation interventions (Addis & Martell, 2004; see also Chapter 8, this volume), once clients can identify instances of unproductive rumination, they are encouraged to label it as such (i.e., "this is ruminating"), and use the act of ruminating as a cue for alternative and more effective actions that are more closely related to current problems in their lives. As a part of this approach, the client and therapist might generate a list of alternative activities, with activities selected on the basis of their associated mood-enhancing features or potential effectiveness for dealing directly with the problem at hand.

In ACT (Hayes et al., 2012), the tendency to worry or ruminate exemplifies a type of psychological inflexibility that results from emotional and behavioral avoidance, the attempted control of internal events (emotions, thoughts, physiological responses), and difficulties distinguishing self from experience (e.g., "I am anxious" vs. "As I think about my financial situation, I'm noticing that my experience of anxiety increases"). ACT-based interventions for rumination and worry include cognitive defusion (experiencing thoughts as transient and changing events rather than literal truths); observing, describing, or accepting thoughts (rather than actively working to change them); acting with increased awareness (or mindful actions); and strengthening behavior patterns that are aligned with one's values.

Other behavioral interventions have been developed and evaluated for their effectiveness in reducing rumination. These include the exposure-based interventions (e.g., Steketee, 1993), reviewed in Chapter 9.

CASE ILLUSTRATION

"Jenny" is a 24-year-old married woman who is employed as a retail clerk at a local department store. All of her adult life, she has exhibited a pattern of behavior consistent with generalized anxiety disorder. This is most evident in her persistent worry about something bad happening. The content of her anticipatory thoughts ranges from doing things incorrectly or making mistakes to being negatively evaluated by others, to a preoccupation with her own faults and shortcomings, to exaggerated pessimism about the future. Worrying is related to sleep disturbance (particularly in getting to sleep at night), fatigue, difficulty concentrating and sustaining attention, and feelings of tension most of the time. Jenny also reported some features consistent with major depressive disorder, social anxiety disorder, agoraphobia, and avoidant and dependent personality disorders, but not to the level of diagnostic threshold for these conditions.

In her initial explorations of the function of Jenny's worrying patterns, her therapist inquired about how worrying might be helpful. The therapist made the assumption that worrying was helpful to Jenny in some way because it occurred with high frequency, suggesting that some sort of reinforcement process functioned to maintain worrying. Jenny offered several reasons for worrying (listed in the "Establishing Operations" section of the functional formulation provided subsequently), including the view that "worrying helps me figure out what to do" and "worrying calms my mind a bit." As she and her therapist examined this further, Jenny's additional disclosures were consistent with the view that worrying is sometimes associated with a short-term reduction in anxiety or other negative emotions; however, worrying did not solve her problems. Rather, Jenny reported that she characteristically tends to replay various scenarios of how negative events might unfold and how they will affect her, with little time spent considering how to solve these problems if they actually arose.

Jenny disclosed that she sought therapy at this time because she sees herself becoming increasingly avoidant of situations or places, particularly those in which other people are present. Her worrying is also associated with impairment because it interferes with her sleep and takes time away from other activities. Although reassurances from others often provided her with limited short-term relief, they had little long-term effect on her worrying patterns. Jenny described that she was tired of going to people, particularly her husband, over "small matters."

During the assessment phase of therapy, Jenny's therapist asked her to self-monitor situations that accompany worrying. A self-monitoring form was developed based on the daily thought record used in cognitive therapy. Slight modifications in this form were made to assess Jenny's behavior in the context of worrying and the consequences associated with such behavior.

Jenny's recordings over 3 days are displayed in Exhibit 5.1. Upon giving the completed form to her therapist, Jenny indicated that this record was fairly representative of her worrying patterns. As they reviewed the form together, several observations were noted.

- Jenny is more vulnerable to worrying when time is unstructured, that is, when she is alone, uncertain what to do, or bored.
- Sometimes emotions that accompanied worrying decreased in intensity when she worried.
- Her "emotion intensity" ratings were consistently higher than her "evidence" ratings, suggesting that her degree of emotional reactions were considerably stronger than the evidence in support of her thinking in these situations.
- Even though Jenny thought she was addressing her problems through worrying, much of her rumination involved amplifying unlikely negative outcomes associated with the scenarios she worried about, with little time actually spent on constructive problem solving.
- In situations in which she worried, Jenny often did "nothing" in response to her worries or the contexts that occasioned them.
- In one instance in which she actively responded to a situation that occasioned worry, an argument with her husband (see Situation 2 in Exhibit 5.1), she observed that actually doing something about the problem helped resolve it, whereas worrying alone usually does little to address her concerns.

As a result of the clinical interview, self-monitoring, and other pretreatment assessments, Jenny's therapist developed the following functional formulation of her pattern of worrying.

Antecedent Conditions

Antecedent conditions included the following:

- *discriminative stimuli,* which are situations in which there are few pressures for alternative behavior to worrying (e.g., when alone or when there are no customers to attend to); situations in which there is no clear indication of how to respond or what

EXHIBIT 5.1
Jenny's Functional Daily Thought and Feeling Record

Situation	Emotions	Thought	What is troubling about this thought?	Action	Consequences of action
What happened? Where were you? Who were you with?	Label your emotions in this situation and rate their intensity (from 0 = *no feeling* to 10 = *most intense feeling possible*)	What were you thinking in this situation around the time you had the unpleasant emotion?	What does this thought mean to you? If the thought is true, what are the implications? Also rate the degree of evidence for this thought (from 0 = *no evidence* to 10 = *clear objective evidence*)	What did you do in this situation after you had the emotion or thought? (If you did nothing, just write "nothing")	What happened after you acted? (If you did not act, did the situation change, or did your thoughts or emotions change?) Were your actions helpful or unhelpful? If so, how?
1. At home, sitting, and largely doing nothing but thinking.	Anxious (8)	I'm going to get a negative quarterly job evaluation.	I might get fired. (3)	Nothing (just continue to worry).	Anxiety went down a little. Did nothing about problem.
2. Argument with husband at home (finances).	Angry (5) Anxious (7) Sad (4)	Sometimes we just don't seem compatible.	We might drift apart, divorce. (3)	Went to husband and suggested we need to work this out rather than leave situation as is.	We worked out disagreement. Anxiety and anger gone. Feel more positive toward him.
3. At work, boss frowned at me when I walked by.	Anxious (7)	He's got it in for me.	I'll be fired for sure. (4)	Nothing (continued to worry).	No changes until customer came along.

(continues)

EXHIBIT 5.1
Jenny's Functional Daily Thought and Feeling Record   (Continued)

Situation	Emotions	Thought	What is troubling about this thought?	Action	Consequences of action
4. At work, manager is teaching me a new inventory method.	Anxious (7) Pressured (8)	Why can't I get this? I must be stupid or slow.	I'm not competent or intelligent and won't amount to much. (6)	Told manager I need to go to the bathroom (but I really didn't need to).	Went to bathroom. Felt less anxious. Came back. Eventually learned method.
5. At home, watching TV and feeling bored	Bored (7)	My mother's going to fall and break her hip.	She might have to be hospitalized, or she might die. (6)	Called mother to talk (really to see if she's okay).	Relieved. Mother says she's getting around fine.
6. In bed, trying to sleep.	Anxious (9)	My mother's going to fall and break her hip.	She might have to be hospitalized, or she might die. (6)	Tried to stop worrying. Imagined myself at her funeral.	Couldn't stop worrying. Feel more anxious as well as sad. Didn't get to sleep for 3 hours.
7. Getting ready for work, by myself, thinking about finances.	Anxious (8) Sad (6)	If I lose my job, we won't be able to make mortgage payments.	We'll be homeless, and I won't have a job. (4)	Continued to get dressed and think more about these possibilities.	Felt a little less anxious, worrying decreased. Finished getting dressed.
8. At home by myself (husband away for "poker night"), don't know what to do.	Bored (7) Anxious (5) Uncertain (7)	The world is really falling apart. Wars, terrorism, crime, corruption.	The world isn't a safe place anymore. (6)	Nothing. Just thought about these issues.	Still alone. Boredom went down, but anxiety and feelings of uncertainty went up. Also feel sad and hopeless now.

to do; situations that require a response that is not clearly established within Jenny's behavioral repertoire; the presence of
other people, particularly persons in positions of authority; and
- *establishing operations*, which include the experience of anxiety,
boredom, or uncertainty (regarded by Jenny as aversive) as well
as rules related to worrying, such as:
  - "My worrying prevents bad things from happening."
  - "Worrying is a useful way to solve my problems."
  - "Worrying calms my mind somewhat."
  - "If something bad happens that I didn't anticipate, I won't
be able to handle it [with "it" referring to the intensity of her
anxiety and the situation she is in]."
  - "I can't manage this situation by myself."
  - "Forcing myself to stop worrying is the only way to make
worries go away."

Person Variables

Jenny had a family history of various problems related to anxiety; a
long personal history of anxiety and worry, with some indication of a history
of negative reinforcement for worry (e.g., occasionally results in an immediate decrease in anxiety level and some reductions in catastrophic thoughts
and images); a lifelong hypersensitivity and responsiveness to cues associated with punishment, threat, and danger; and a lifelong history of excessive
behavioral inhibition and hypersensitivity to other's evaluations.

Responses

Jenny's responses included worry, with content of worries tending to
shift from one domain to the next and occurring often in a continuous flow
that can go on for relatively long periods of time; disengagement from the
immediate environment to attend to worries. Agitation and restlessness, difficulties going to sleep, muscle and psychic tension, and problems with concentration and attention accompany periods of worry; she also often seeks out
reassurance and support from others following prolonged episodes of worry.

Consequences

Reinforcing outcomes associated with worrying include the following:

- *Negative reinforcement:* Jenny experiences an immediate reduction in anxiety, boredom, or uncertainty as well as reductions
in catastrophic thoughts and images as worrying progresses
over time.

- *Positive reinforcement:* She receives support and reassurance from others and is accompanied by others when she expresses uncertainty as to whether she can perform a particular activity or engage in a certain event.

Immediate aversive outcomes include the following:

- Because worries are attended to when present, her behavior is less effective in relation to immediate environmental events; she is unable to sleep even though she feels fatigued.

Delayed aversive outcomes associated with worrying include the following:

- Jenny experiences fatigue after periods of worry, increasingly avoids places where others are present, loses time for valued activities because of time spent worrying, and experiences ongoing distress related to the current situation.
- Therapy with Jenny included several behavioral interventions not further described here, such as diaphragmatic breathing to promote present moment awareness and reduce tension; exposure to specific recurring worries (presented in her own voice via a cassette tape); response prevention (cessation of reassurance and support seeking as well as seeking the physical accompaniment of others as a means of coping with anxieties and worries); and the promotion of decentering, or the perspective of thoughts and feelings as separate from self, through experiential and mindfulness exercises. The following summary describes her therapy as it relates to techniques explicitly used to alter the functional aspects of her worrying behavior.
- In therapy, Jenny and her therapist first discussed features that distinguish unproductive rumination from problem solving. With some assistance, Jenny was able to identify several features, and she listed these on an index card as they were discussed. Her therapist suggested that when she notices herself worrying on the basis of the presence of these features, she was to correctly label her behavior (e.g., "This is unhelpful worry"). On the basis of the hypothesis that worrying was a form of avoidance behavior that helped Jenny cope with certain contexts or situations, Jenny and her therapist developed a list of activities other than rumination that Jenny could do if she caught herself ruminating. These were written down on a separate index card, and Jenny was encouraged to refer to this card for ideas for alternative behavior when she found herself worrying and

unsure about what else she could do. The act of worrying, then, was transformed to the status of a cue that signaled alternative action. Alternative behaviors listed on the card were chosen on the basis of their likelihood of producing positively reinforcing outcomes. Because these alternatives were listed on a small index card, she could carry this list with her wherever she went and consult it when needed.

- In initial sessions, Jenny and her therapist devised some behavioral experiments to test some of the rules that served as establishing operations for worrying. Some of these rules, such as "Worrying is a useful way to solve my problems," were already revealed to be inaccurate through the self-monitoring exercise depicted in Exhibit 5.1. As a result of self-monitoring, Jenny revised this rule to suggest, "Worrying does not solve my problems."

- One behavioral experiment targeted the rule "Telling myself to stop worrying is the only way to make worries go away." The experiment was based on the assumption present in Jenny's statement that suggested verbal control is an effective means of suppressing private events such as thinking (i.e., "Telling myself to stop worrying . . ."). An experiment was set up in which Jenny's rule was tested against an alternative rule, "Trying to stop myself from thinking or feeling something only makes it more 'there'." The experiment involved noticing what happened when she took part in the Chocolate Cake Exercise from ACT, and then deciding whether what she noticed was more consistent with her rule or the alternative rule. For this exercise, Jenny was asked to do the following:

Suppose I tell you right now that, I don't want you to think about something. I'm going to tell you real soon. And when I do, don't think about it even for a second. Here it comes. Remember, don't think about it. Don't think of . . . warm chocolate cake! You know how it smells when it first comes out of the oven . . . don't think of it! As the warm, moist piece crumbles and crumbs fall to the plate . . . don't think of it! . . . It's very important—don't think about any of this! (Hayes et al., 2012, pp. 185–186)

Jenny acknowledged that the more she tried not to think about the chocolate cake, the more it was "there" for her, and that the image became increasingly more threatening as she was unable to get rid of it despite all efforts. Her therapist appealed to Jenny's other experiences with suppression of private events, and whether it was true that such efforts generally worked that way. Jenny eventually concluded that trying to get rid of thoughts and feelings really does not work. After the exercise and when reflecting on her past experiences, Jenny accepted the alternative rule and discarded the old one.

Another behavioral experiment targeted the rule "The world is threatening and dangerous," which, when further dissected, was refined to suggest, "People are threatening and will harm me." For this experiment, Jenny and her therapist agreed that to test the validity of this thought, she would sample various downtown locations where people congregated. They agreed that this would be a therapist-guided activity, whereby the therapist would join Jenny on a walk to several predetermined and nearby locations where people gather: a shopping mall, grocery store, city park, central city square, and bus station. They set aside 2 hours for this exercise, with the goal being to look for evidence either in support of or inconsistent with the view that people are threatening and will inflict harm. The therapist's role in this exercise was to provide support and encouragement, to monitor and discourage the use of any safety behaviors (e.g., rushing through the experiment, reassurance seeking, distraction), and to guide the exercise to ensure that Jenny took in available information relevant to her rule.

As they visited these predetermined spots, Jenny was encouraged by her therapist to notice the people, their movements and actions, their posture, the expressions on their faces, the tones of their voices, and the content of their speech. Her task was to detect whether there were any indications of danger or threat originating from the people she observed, and whether others she watched appeared fearful or threatened. During these experiments, her therapist also monitored her level of anxiety and sampled her thinking in alternating 2-minute intervals. As the experiment went on, Jenny reported that she became less and less anxious. She noticed that others did not come across as threatening or appear to be threatened. Rather, she observed that most people appeared to be having a good time as they went about their business. Before the experiment, Jenny's belief in the rule "People are threatening and will harm me" was 70%. Upon the conclusion of the experiment, she rated it at 20%.

As therapy progressed, increasing emphasis was placed on identifying Jenny's values, or what is centrally important to her, and what she wanted to be known for or her life to be about. Values identification was subsequently emphasized on the basis of her expressed wish to "Do things that I'm not doing because of all of the time I spend worrying." When asked, Jenny indicated that she would be willing to experience tension and anxiety if it meant no longer having her life sidelined by worries. For Jenny, this represented a shift away from the predominant short-term goals of reducing tension and anxiety and toward a life direction that had importance to her, even if this meant experiencing some degree of discomfort.

As a starting point, Jenny and her therapist focused on relationships, something that she valued greatly but an area that she regarded as largely neglected. In her relationship with her husband, for example, she wanted to increase the level of intimacy, as she felt that many of their day-to-day interactions revolved around her anxieties and worries (e.g., reassurance seeking). Although the idea of strengthening intimacy in her relationship with her husband was somewhat threatening, she speculated that doing so would not only enhance her relationship with her husband but also eventually shift her away from being preoccupied with worries.

Initial steps in the process of deepening her relationships with others, starting with her husband, involved setting goals that moved her in a valued direction (Hayes & Smith, 2005). Short-term objectives involved doing more leisure activities with her husband (e.g., going out to a restaurant once a week, going for walks in the park). Time logs were used to organize these events. Long-term goals included having children and establishing a family environment that was consistent with their wishes and aspirations. Jenny also expressed a commitment to spend a little time each day—time that she would typically take up with worrying—to consider ways to enhance the quality of her life with her husband. She also committed to experimenting with being more open and vulnerable with her husband and sharing her values with him. Although the thought of doing so occasioned worries related to rejection, Jenny maintained that she would not be alienated from her values by her unfounded concerns in this area of her life. By the time therapy ended, Jenny had taken steps to shift her life away from entanglements with her worries and anxieties to building the type of life she wanted to have.

SUMMARY

When the functional aspects of thoughts and thinking patterns are considered for targeting in therapy, it is often useful for the therapist to do the following:

- Evaluate possible functional relations between certain patterns of thinking and the client's problem areas.
- Investigate whether certain patterns of thinking preclude opportunities for dealing with life problems more directly and actively.
- Assist the client in noticing and labeling occurrences of unproductive thought, and use such occasions as cues for engaging in alternative actions.

- Devise behavioral experiments that have potential for modifying both the form and function that unproductive thinking has on behavior.
- Consider the possible utility of other intervention approaches for altering adherence to inaccurate, faulty, or harmful rules.
- Identify goals and values that might suggest alternative behavior patterns that are incompatible or inconsistent with the client's problem behaviors.
- Design and implement intervention strategies that facilitate engagement in behavior patterns that are consistent with one's goals or values.

6

CHANGING BEHAVIOR
BY BUILDING SKILLS

As with other behavioral interventions discussed in this book, the primary aim of skills training is to increase clients' effective engagement in behaviors that help them move toward important goals. Unlike contingency management procedures, in which consequences are manipulated or modified to influence behavior in desirable directions, the primary targets in skills training are deficits in the client's behavioral repertoire. An assumption of skills training is that, for the client to reach important goals, she or he needs to learn new behaviors or to refine and sharpen her or his engagement in behaviors that are already within the repertoire. To play tennis effectively, an individual may need to learn not only how to serve or hit a backhand, but how hard to swing, how to optimally position the racquet and properly position her or his body, and so on. Clients who have interpersonal difficulties might need to learn how to strike up conversations with people, make assertive and appropriate requests rather than yelling or passively avoiding,

http://dx.doi.org/10.1037/14691-006
Behavioral Interventions in Cognitive Behavior Therapy: Practical Guidance for Putting Theory Into Action,
Second Edition, by R. F. Farmer and A. L. Chapman

and to engage in appropriate small talk. People who have difficulty managing emotions might need to learn how to identify their emotional states and what to do to up- or down-regulate emotional arousal.

We begin this chapter by covering some background and research findings on the application of skills training approaches. We define and discuss key principles and terms as well as when to use skills training. In the latter part of the chapter, we provide some practical guidance on how to apply skills training interventions to help clients acquire and strengthen skills and achieve their goals.

SKILLS TRAINING: BACKGROUND AND EVIDENCE

In the sections that follow, we provide a brief history of skills training interventions in behavior therapy and cognitive behavior therapy (CBT). We also highlight some contemporary treatments in which skills training plays a prominent role. In addition, we outline some of the research evidence on the efficacy of skills training.

A Brief History

Skills training has been a feature of behavior therapy practically since its inception. Mary Cover Jones (1924), a student of John B. Watson, described an early application of skills training used in conjunction with exposure therapy, called *social imitation*. Originally reported in a case study, social imitation involved having peers demonstrate the handling of feared objects for a phobic child ("Peter"). Subsequently, in the 1930s, mental health workers began to use social skills training to increase the social competence of individuals who were transitioning from psychiatric institutions back into the community. Phillips and Zigler are credited for their seminal work on social skills training in the 1950s (summarized in Phillips & Zigler, 1961), which has evolved and been adapted quite effectively for a variety of clinical problems, with notable examples including depression (Becker, Heimberg, & Bellack, 1987; Rehm, 1979) and schizophrenia (Benton & Schroeder, 1990; Mueser, Levine, Bellack, Douglas, & Brady, 1990).

Skills training is potentially applicable to several clinical problems and areas of life, including everything from parenting difficulties to anger management problems, sexual problems, and job functioning, among other domains. In fact, there are probably as many potential applications of skills training as there are clinical problems. Regardless of the problem area, skills training interventions usually involve teaching or changing a set of behaviors (e.g., deliberate self-harm) as well as promoting the implementation of effective alternative behaviors (e.g., emotion regulation and problem-solving skills). Any of these effective behaviors could be conceptualized as behavioral skills (e.g., the skill of coping effectively).

Empirical Basis of Skills Training Interventions

Skills training interventions have demonstrated effectiveness for a variety of clinical problem areas. Generally, evidence-based treatments involve skills training in two primary ways: (a) as a stand-alone treatment and (b) as a component of a larger treatment package. As a stand-alone treatment for persons with schizophrenia and other psychotic disorders, social skills training has demonstrated efficacy for reducing relapse rates of psychotic episodes and rehospitalization (Bellack, 2004), level of functioning and negative symptoms (Granholm, Holden, Link, & McQuaid, 2014), and anxiety, depression, and psychotic symptoms (Cui, Yang, & Weng, 2004). A meta-analytic review indicated that social skills training has generally been associated with medium effect sizes for improvements in social and daily living skills, community functioning, and negative symptoms (Kurtz & Mueser, 2008). Social skills training also has demonstrated efficacy for reducing depression among adults (Becker et al., 1987; Rehm, 1979) and adolescents, even when compared with active but nonspecific control treatments (e.g., J. F. Young, Mufson, & Gallop, 2010). A couple of treatments for substance abuse with strong empirical support use skills training focused on enhancing interpersonal communication and emotion regulation (Higgins, Sigmon, & Heil, 2014; Monti et al., 1990). In addition, skills-based anger management programs have demonstrated efficacy for reducing the emotion of anger as well as overt anger-related behaviors (Novaco, 1975; see also Saini, 2009, for a review).

Skills training interventions also constitute components of larger CBT treatment packages that have considerable evidence of efficacy. Progressive muscle relaxation and diaphragmatic breathing skills, for example, are key components of CBT for panic disorder and agoraphobia (Craske & Barlow, 2014). Up to 78% of persons who complete the full course of CBT in clinical outcome studies are free of panic by the follow-up assessment phase (Craske & Barlow, 2014). The research is unclear, however, as to whether training in relaxation or diaphragmatic breathing skills is an essential component of CBT for panic disorder and agoraphobia. Similarly, stress inoculation training (Meichenbaum, 1996), cognitive processing therapy (Resick & Schnicke, 1993), and prolonged exposure (Foa & Rothbaum, 1998) all have demonstrated efficacy in treating posttraumatic stress disorder, and each includes training in muscle relaxation and diaphragmatic breathing skills (for a review, see Olatunji, Cisler, & Deacon, 2010).

Other evidence-based treatment packages include skills training as a key component. The treatment for couple discord and dissatisfaction that has the strongest empirical support is an approach called behavioral marital therapy (BMT; Jacobson & Margolin, 1979), which heavily emphasizes training couples in effective communication and problem-solving skills. Dialectical behavior therapy (DBT; Linehan, 1993a) is currently the psychosocial treatment with the most empirical support for treating women with borderline personality disorder. DBT includes a weekly outpatient skills training group that teaches skills in mindfulness, regulating emotions (emotion regulation skills), tolerating distress and surviving crises (distress tolerance skills), and navigating interpersonal situations with an effective degree of assertiveness (interpersonal effectiveness skills). Again, as with panic disorder and posttraumatic stress disorder, it is unclear whether skills training is an essential component of BMT or DBT; nevertheless, it is firmly embedded in these evidence-based treatments.

Another issue with regard to skills training has to do with whether simply providing a person with information rather than training in skills constitutes a sufficient intervention. A couple of studies have addressed this question. In one study, clients with schizophrenia were randomly assigned to a group CBT skills-oriented program or to a group psychoeducation program that involved education on mental health and schizophrenia but no formal training in skills (Bechdolf et al., 2004). Both the CBT skills program and the psychoeducation program were related to improvement in problems related to schizophrenia, but the CBT skills group demonstrated lower relapse and higher treatment adherence at posttreatment and follow-up as well as a lower rehospitalization rate at follow-up. In another study, investigators randomly assigned substance-abusing, dually diagnosed adolescents to a CBT coping-skills group or a psychoeducation group. Both conditions were associated with reductions in substance use, but only those clients in the CBT condition demonstrated fewer positive urinalyses at follow-up (Kaminer, Burleson, & Goldberger, 2002). Although the research in this area is somewhat sparse, at present, it appears that simply providing information in a psychoeducational format is not as effective as actually teaching skills.

KEY PRINCIPLES AND TERMS

Within this section, we discuss some key principles that therapists can use to guide their use of skills training interventions in CBT. We also discuss definitions of key terms, such as *skills*, *performance*, and *effectiveness*. Because an important goal of skills training is for the client to display skills in an effective and adaptable manner across varying contexts, we also discuss the concept of flexibility as applied to skills training.

Key Principles

Skills training interventions are based on the assumption there are deficits in the client's behavioral repertoire. The clinician often first notices such behavioral deficits when the client is not performing actions that, if performed, would help her or him to reach important goals. A client who wishes to meet people and expand his social network, for example, might attend parties but not talk with anyone. In this case, before selecting skills training as the most appropriate intervention, the therapist must determine what factors are contributing to the client's lack of talking. Is the client intensely anxious and avoiding social interactions? Does the client have a history of experiencing aversive consequences for making small talk at a party? Is the client's behavior influenced by inaccurate rules (e.g., "If I talk to people, they will think I'm weird and reject me")? Or does the client not know how to strike up a conversion with someone, how to engage in small talk, make appropriate eye contact, and so on. If the client is unsure of how to perform such behaviors, then skills training would be the most appropriate intervention. The assumption is not that the client is unmotivated, that fear or avoidance reduces his willingness and ability to socialize, or that contingencies in the environment are suppressing her or his behavior, but rather that the client needs to learn how (and often when) to talk with people at parties. In clinical practice, many of these factors are operating in concert and serve as barriers to the client's effective social functioning; thus, skills training is often one component of a broader treatment approach.

Important Terms and Concepts

The word *skill* encompasses a wide variety of definitions, with most including terms such as *proficiency*, *capacity*, *capability*, and *ability*, among others. O'Donohue and Krasner (1995) suggested that whether a person has skills is related to whether he or she has the capacity to perform specific behaviors that fit within a general class of skills. The general class of social skills, for instance, includes a large variety of subskills such as displaying polite, courteous, and assertive behavior. According to many definitions, to say that a client has social skills would mean that he or she possesses the capability to perform these behaviors.

Although clients do not "have" or "possess" skills in the same way that they might have or possess a tool such as a hammer, this focus on what a client is capable of doing has pragmatic value in practice. When assessing and conceptualizing a client's problem areas, it is important to determine what the client is capable of doing. A client undergoing exposure therapy for social phobia may require skills training if she or he lacks essential social skills to successfully converse with other people (otherwise, exposure to party scenarios might result in feared consequences, such as ostracism or rejection). Clients who do not have the skills to label their emotions might have difficulty applying new coping or emotion regulation skills. When a client is incapable of engaging in a certain behavior (e.g., the client does not know how to be assertive with her boss), then skills training is an appropriate intervention choice. If the client is capable of engaging in the behavior but does not do so, however, then treatment might involve finding ways to remove the barriers to effective action (e.g., increasing motivation, modifying contingencies).

There are, however, a couple of common pitfalls to the use of terms such as *capabilities* and *abilities*. One pitfall is that these terms are often not behaviorally specific and can be misleading. The only way to know whether a client is able to do something is to observe the client's behavior or review credible evidence that she or he actually performs certain behaviors. A second pitfall of such terms is that they contain the implicit assumption that the abilities or skills are inherent features or characteristics of the individual. This assumption can obscure important contextual variations in behavior. A person might, for example, have the skills to make assertive requests when her partner leaves his dirty socks on the floor but may not know how to negotiate a raise at work. Even though a client may "have" the skills to perform a certain task (e.g., the client knows how to ask the boss for a raise and to negotiate if the boss waivers), other factors such as anxiety can interfere with the client's performance. Skills training ideally takes into account the contextual variations in the client's display of particular skills as well as factors that might inhibit or enhance the performance of skillful behavior.

Situations that impinge on clients in their daily lives are often in a state of flux, and one of the key challenges involves adapting to changes and applying skills effectively. Along these lines, a final concept regarding skills training is the notion of *flexibility*. Whereas *effectiveness* refers to the degree to which behavior resulted in preferred outcomes within a particular context, flexibility is the extent to which the client adapts to differing contexts or changes in contexts and performs behavioral skills effectively. The concept of flexibility is useful for practitioners because it highlights the need to avoid carrying out skills-oriented guidelines in a lockstep fashion that fails to take into account changes or differences in contextual factors. When therapy involves social skills training, for example, emphasis tends to be placed on teaching topographies or forms of social behavior. A client might be taught, for instance, one assertive response that might be effective in a particular situation. Often, however, several alternative responses produce similar and effective outcomes (Follette & Hayes, 2000). There may be many roads to Rome, so to speak. For this reason, the effectiveness of particular behaviors within particular contexts should be emphasized in skills-training programs, perhaps more so than the performance qualities of the behavior. It is important, therefore, not only to provide clients with a potentially useful toolbox of skills and the rules needed to use them but also to help them track and adapt their behavior in response to changes in the environment.

HOW DOES SKILLS TRAINING WORK?
MECHANISMS OF CHANGE

When it comes to mechanisms of change, the emphasis is on how or why the intervention of skills training leads to desirable outcomes. Understanding the mechanisms through which skills training affects outcomes can help the therapist target treatment toward those mechanisms. Because skills training, as a general class of interventions, is intertwined with the specific skill domains taught to clients (e.g., coping skills, interpersonal skills), it is difficult to separate the effects of skills training generally from the effects of changes related to specific types of skills.

As a general class of interventions, skills training theoretically works by addressing behavioral deficits and broadening the client's repertoire of adaptive behavior. The client learns new behaviors through the processes of instruction, modeling, shaping, reinforcement, and coaching by the therapist. In this way, skills training may be considered a means to an end. Alternatively, skillful interpersonal behavior might lead to a greater frequency of positive reinforcement from the social environment, enhance an individual's sense of self-efficacy or confidence, produce changes in fear or threatening associations with social situations, and so on. These changes would be expected to improve the client's quality of life as well as to support the maintenance of new, skillful behavior. In the case of improved coping or emotion regulation skills, mechanisms might include negative reinforcement in the form of a reduction in aversive emotional states, greater self-efficacy regarding the regulation of emotions, reduced fear of emotions, and improvements in the client's ability to respond to the information provided by emotions in an effective manner (e.g., a client deciding not to avoid situations when the fear is maladaptive or unrealistic, or a client acting on adaptive frustration by assertively asking her partner to stop insulting her). Over time, ideally, new skills come under the control of natural contingencies operating in the client's everyday life, generalize to many relevant situations, and have a ripple effect, enhancing quality of life in several areas.

USING BEHAVIORAL ASSESSMENT TO GUIDE SKILLS TRAINING

As with any behavioral intervention, therapists most optimally use skills training after a thorough assessment has revealed deficits in the behaviors required to achieve preferred outcomes or goals within particular contexts. Precise behavioral assessment will help to determine the specific areas of difficulty and the behaviors that a client may need to learn. Assessment also should determine whether the client has already learned these behaviors because skills training is not the intervention of choice if factors other than skill deficits are interfering with the client's performance of desired behaviors. We discuss these and other considerations later in the chapter.

Precisely Specifying Apparent Behavioral Deficits

Among the first steps in evaluating behavioral deficits is determining which content areas are most relevant for possible skills training. Behavioral assessment often begins by broadly delineating the client's problem domains, such as difficulties with anger and anger management, interpersonal dysfunction or couple discord, problems with occupational functioning, and so on. With awareness of these broader categories, the therapist can narrow the assessment to better understand what goes awry in particular areas. A client who has difficulty with anger, for example, might have challenges in one or more of the tasks needed to effectively regulate anger or curb aggressive behavior. Some of these tasks could include identifying physiological signs of increasing anger, correctly labeling anger, using strategies to soothe or reduce physiological arousal, maintaining composure and effectively communicating to others without aggression, or any of a number of other such tasks. Clear specification of the behaviors that would be helpful to the client but are absent will help the therapist and client define exactly which skills need to be taught or emphasized.

Although many skills training approaches include a standard set of skills, behavior therapy is essentially an idiographic approach. Some skills may be less relevant to the client than others. As an example, interpersonal skills training usually consists of a combination of directions on how to ask others assertively to change their behavior with effective listening and communication strategies. We have seen clients who are already skillful at asking for what they want but have tremendous difficulty with listening skills, whereas others are stellar listeners but have difficulty asserting their needs. Even though many skills training programs are standardized, the therapist may selectively emphasize those skills with which the client needs the most help.

Determining the Presence of Behavioral Deficits

Once the client's specific difficulties with a particular skill domain (e.g., anger, interpersonal skills) have been clarified, another important step is to determine whether the client has already learned the skills that appear to be deficient. As outlined by Dow (1994), there are at least three hierarchically organized considerations for establishing that a behavioral deficit, in fact, accounts for nonoccurring behaviors. The first consideration is whether the client can demonstrate the relevant skill or behavior in the protected therapeutic environment. The therapist can determine this in a variety of ways. One strategy is to elicit the client's demonstration of particular skills. The therapist might, for example, ask a client having difficulty managing interpersonal conflict to engage in a role-play of a conflict scenario with the therapist. Clients who have difficulty identifying and labeling emotions might attempt to label their emotions in session or describe how they felt in a difficult situation in daily life. These strategies allow the therapist to observe and assess the client's behavior and (later on, during skills training) to provide coaching and feedback regarding effective, skillful behavior. Less direct methods might involve asking the client to monitor her or his behavior in target situations. Collateral reports from loved ones or other treatment providers, where feasible, also can be helpful.

If the client can effectively demonstrate the skill or behavior in the therapeutic environment but not in the targeted situation, then two additional considerations might be explored. The first has to do with the issue of *response generalization*. Although the client may have learned the relevant skills and how to apply them in certain contexts, he or she may not have learned how to generalize these skills to targeted situations. In this circumstance, therapy might emphasize the generalization of these skills to relevant situations. This might involve helping the client identify contextual features that, when present, suggest that such behavior would be appropriate and likely reinforced. Similarly, therapy might include instruction in how to perform the particular behavior in the targeted setting.

The other consideration has to do with the possible suppression of the skill by contextual factors. Antecedents that might inhibit behavior include establishing operations such as the presence of certain emotional states (e.g., anxiety) that may further intensify upon enacting the skill. Faulty rules could also inhibit the behavior in question (e.g., "Why should I try to get what I want? No good will come of it"). Similarly, the client may have previously been punished for displaying skillful behavior in a targeted situation. Assertive action in the presence of an abusive spouse, for example, is rarely reinforced and frequently punished. Other relevant factors include the possible influence of disability or disease on an individual's capability to carry out certain forms of behavior.

Each possibility for infrequent or absent behavior suggests different therapeutic approaches. Most generally, skills training may be an appropriate intervention when (a) the client rarely or never engages in particular behaviors; (b) the infrequency or absence of behavior is not due to environmental constraints (e.g., punishment for displays of particular behaviors, low rate of reinforcement for effective behaviors); and (c) the behaviors would lead to the attainment of personal, therapeutic, or situation-specific goals, or an increase in quality of life.

INITIAL STEPS: PLANNING AND ORIENTING THE CLIENT TO SKILLS TRAINING

As with many other interventions described in this book, some preliminary steps can help to maximize the effectiveness of skills training. Among the first steps are to define the skills to be taught and to structure the presentation of skills in a manner that best fits the client. Another important preliminary step involves orientation of the client to the rationale as well as the logistical and procedural aspects of skills training. We describe and discuss these steps in this section.

Defining and Structuring Skills Training

Among the first steps is to determine the format and structure of the skills training. For some clinical problems, evidence-based skills treatment protocols already exist and follow a defined format and structure. In this case, it is often best to stick with the format and structure used in the research to keep the clinical procedures as close as possible to the treatment package that has demonstrated efficacy. In other cases, various factors make it difficult to apply an evidence-based skills training package. For some clinical problems, established skills-oriented protocols may not exist, may not be tailored to the characteristics of the client, or may not have demonstrated efficacy for problems similar to those experienced by the client. In addition, providing skills training in the manner specified in a treatment manual is at times not feasible because of resource or time limitations or challenges within particular clinical settings. In these cases, the therapist may need to decide on the most effective format for teaching skills given the context of therapy, the client's skill deficits, and the client's characteristics and learning history. Some key related considerations might include the following:

- Will the therapist conduct skills training himself or herself or refer the client to another provider for this intervention?

- Will skills training occur within a formal format or informally as needed within therapy sessions? How often will skills training occur?
- How will the therapist integrate skills training and skills learned into typical therapy sessions?
- Will skills training occur in an individual or a group format?

Perhaps the most common decision has to do with whether skills should be presented in an individual or a group format. Skills training is most often conducted in groups, and there are several potential advantages to a group format. Groups can, for example, be more efficient than individual sessions, in that they reach a larger number of clients in a briefer period. Groups can be more cost-effective compared with individual therapy sessions, for both treatment providers and individual clients. Groups can also offer opportunities for modeling, social connectedness, normalization of client problems and experiences, role-playing, and the active practicing of skills—opportunities that might be limited in individual therapy. Socially anxious clients may benefit from both the formal and informal opportunities for exposure to feared social situations (e.g., speaking in a group) as well as from active practicing of interpersonal strategies with other group members. In addition, if the client has a large array of problems that are the focus of clinical attention and tends to experience frequent crises or intense life stressors, the therapist may spend so much time addressing crises and acute stressors that there is little time to teach new skills (Linehan, 1993a). In these cases, group-administered skills training can be a helpful ancillary intervention.

There are some advantages of conducting skills training on an individual basis, however. Individual skills instruction allows the therapist to tailor skills training to the issues, difficulties, and characteristics of the individual client. In a group format, clients in the group receive less individualized skills instruction and attention than they would if they were learning skills in an individual format. The individual therapist is likely to know more about the client (compared with a skills trainer who does not individually work with the client) and may be able to individually tailor suggestions regarding skills in a manner that best fits the client's idiosyncratic life difficulties, wishes, goals, strengths, and weaknesses. If the client has a strong need for individualized attention and validation, individually administered skills training may be more capable of addressing this need while teaching new skills. When a client's problems involve severe depression and behavioral inertia, he or she may have considerable difficulty maintaining active participation in a group. Although socially anxious clients can benefit from a group format, some clients are too anxious initially to digest the information provided in a group setting or to participate effectively within a group. In addition, clients who experience recurrent hallucinations, delusions, disordered thinking, or features of psychopathy or antisocial personality disorder, a group setting may not be the most effective mode for teaching skills.

Orienting the Client to Skills Training

An essential early step in skills training is to orient the client to several aspects of the intervention, including the rationale for skills training and related structural issues, format, and expectations. When orienting clients to skills training in a group context, we find it helpful to first meet with each new client individually for a brief period (e.g., 10–20 minutes) to provide the client with information on these topics and to address any of his or her questions or concerns. As noted later in this section, skills training sometimes occurs in an informal manner, in which case orienting may also occur in an ad hoc manner. Nevertheless, in all cases, a clear orientation to the skills and their rationale provides the client with a road map of where this intervention is going and how it relates to his or her specific goals, problems, and desires.

Provide a Rationale

One of the first steps in orienting a client to skills training involves providing a rationale. It is generally most effective if this orientation provides a compelling rationale for learning new skills that fits with the client's goals. For a client with anger management problems who wishes to improve his relationship with his wife and others, the therapist might draw a link between improvements in anger management and improvements in interpersonal functioning. Consider the following example.

> *Therapist:* Dan, you've said that one of the most important goals you have is to improve your relationship with your wife. You care for her dearly and would like to work better together as family and be good role models for your kids. Is that correct?
>
> *Client:* Yes, I would love to work toward that. Things have been so rough between us, and I'm afraid our arguments and blow-ups are really affecting the kids. They have this special signal word they say when we seem to be blowing up too much.
>
> *Therapist:* Right, I remember that. You might remember that we were going to discuss some new coping skills to work on together today. From what I've learned about you so far, it seems like anger plays an important role in problems with your wife. Would you agree with that?

Client: Yeah, I would. I mean, I just get so frustrated so fast. It's hard to do anything about it. She gets angry, too, but I get so revved up that it's sort of all over before it's started.

Therapist: That seems to be the case. She says something about how you didn't consult with her before getting the car fixed, or about where you put the laundry, and your immediate reaction seems to be pretty intense frustration. And when you're that frustrated, it's hard to think or communicate well, the other person gets defensive or sometimes scared, and the conversation just goes downhill quickly. I'm thinking that for things to get better between the two of you, and for you to feel like you're working as a team and doing well by your kids, we've got to get a handle on the anger.

Client: I've been dealing with this for so long. How are we going to do that?

Therapist: Well, there's good evidence that treatments for anger work. And, often, these treatments involve learning new coping skills or strategies. From what we've discussed, one new skill that could really help you is the ability to identify anger when it starts to rise—sort of improving your anger radar system. Other skills might involve ways to cool down when you're really revved up or how to gracefully leave a situation when you can't say anything nice. There are many strategies for dealing with anger. If you were to put these into practice, I think you would start to notice some real improvements between you and your wife.

In this example, the therapist used what she had learned during assessment to link anger management skills to important interpersonal goals. Notice that the therapist described how these skills might help, but in an interactive manner, involving questions and back-and-forth discussion, rather than in a purely lecture format. We have found clinically that this way of providing a rationale for skills training (or for other types of interventions) can facilitate a collaborative set and increase the client's commitment to treatment.

Orient to Structure, Format, Timing, and Expectations

Often it is helpful to inform the client about aspects of the structure, format, timing, and expectations of skills training. Some of this information involves when and where skills training occurs, how many and what type of clients are in the group, how long skills training sessions are, and the length of the entire skills training program. Frequently, there are also some specific expectations and agreements a therapist needs to clarify. Some groups for persons who struggle with substance use, for example, have a rule specifying that clients are not permitted to attend group while inebriated or to talk about using drugs with other group members. Many skills training programs give regular homework assignments and expect that clients will have completed them before the next session. In addition, skills training groups may have specific rules and expectations about conduct between group members (e.g., no sexual relations, issues regarding forming friendships outside of group) as well as the confidentiality of material discussed during the group. Providing specific orientation to these aspects of skills training gives the client a clear road map of his or her skills training experience and prevents misunderstandings. The following is a brief example of how a therapist might orient a client to the structure, format, and rules for an anxiety-oriented group.

Therapist: I'd like to spend a little time talking with you about how the anxiety group will go. Feel free to jump in if anything is unclear or if you have questions. The group occurs on Wednesdays from 6 to 8 p.m., and there are about seven or eight people in the group struggling with similar problems with social anxiety.

Client: So, like, nobody talks in this group?

Therapist: Ha, good question! Not exactly, but it's true that you won't be alone in your anxiety about other people. A lot of people find that it takes a couple of sessions to warm up, but after that, they contribute regularly to group discussions. I know that talking in a group of people might be the last thing you'd want to do, but as we have discussed, it's also a great opportunity to become less confined by your social anxiety.

Client: Right, I know. I'm sure I'll probably learn a lot, but it will definitely be hard.

Therapist: It probably will. So, as I was saying, the group is on Wednesday evenings, and usually it starts with practice of a relaxation strategy, either some of the breathing strategies we've already talked about or muscle relaxation. Then, we spend some time discussing the homework assignments you had from the previous week's group. Often, we will have a break at this point, and then we will spend more time teaching you about anxiety and skills to manage it during the last half of the group. We also might have you practice some skills with a partner from time to time. How does that sound so far?

Client: It sounds scary but pretty good. I'm glad I'll have a chance to practice things rather than just talk about stuff.

Therapist: Indeed, it's hard to learn new skills without actually practicing them. Imagine if you had to learn how to perform surgery simply from a book. As for the group, there are a few important rules to keep in mind. First, it's very important that you let us know ahead of time if you will be late or absent. That way, we'll know whether to expect to see you that week. Second, although you might find that you meet people you like in group, we ask that you keep any friendships you might develop platonic—no sexual relationships with other group members. Third, some of the folks in the group have previously had alcohol problems, and I know that's something you're working on, too. Another rule is to avoid talking in any detail about alcohol or drug use because sometimes that kind of detail can lead others to feel urges to use. Does that all make sense? Do you have any questions?

It is also important to remember that the therapist may need to revisit important group rules regularly and to coach clients on how to maintain compliance. We have seen many clinicians surprised that a client is breaking a group rule that was just discussed couple of weeks prior. This is not actually surprising. As discussed in Chapter 11, therapy-interfering behavior is a normal and expected part of the therapeutic process. Many factors can influence a client's lack of rule following, including not remembering the rules, lack of motivation or commitment to follow the rules, skill deficits, strong emotional reactions, and so on. Therapists can help clients get the most out of skills training by assessing these problems and devising solutions to help solve them.

Brief Orientation to Informal Skills Training

In some cases, skills training occurs in a less formalized manner. For instance, sometimes within particular therapy sessions, it is apparent that a client needs to learn a new skill, and the therapist might highlight this issue, provide brief instruction and orientation on the skill, have the client practice the skill, and then fine-tune it by providing feedback and coaching (discussed in greater detail later in this chapter). In this case, the orientation is quite brief and primarily captures the essence of the skill and a rationale as to why the skill might be helpful to the client.

CORE SKILLS TRAINING STRATEGIES

Helping clients acquire skills requires a variety of behaviors on the part of the therapist. Because skills training involves instruction in new behaviors, clear and effective teaching is essential. Skill acquisition also involves using behavioral principles of shaping, chaining, and reinforcement to help clients increase their repertoire of effective skills. In addition, skill acquisition often involves a variety of exercises designed to provide clients with opportunities to model and demonstrate effective behaviors. We describe these exercises (using didactic strategies, behavioral principles, and modeling) as well as other skill-acquisition strategies in this section.

Using a Variety of Didactic Strategies

Skills training essentially involves teaching, and an effective skills trainer performs a range of effective teaching strategies. Although effective teaching involves many component skills and behaviors, we highlight some of the most important skill-teaching behaviors in the following sections. We have organized these skills into three categories: (a) conveying information, (b) effective skill-teaching strategies, and (c) effective skill-teaching styles.

Conveying Information

Conveying information involves the therapist communicating when, how, and why the skill works and the specific circumstances under which a client should use the skill (i.e., the contexts in which the skill may be effective). To help the client determine the effectiveness of his or her behavior, the therapist can provide him or her with information on how to determine whether or how well a skill has worked. With a client working on social skills, the therapist might, for example, point out the likely results of the client's effective engagement in small talk. Among the possible positive results for the client to attend to include the conversation partner continuing to speak, listen, or otherwise convey interest or the conversation broadening to other topics or deepening to more emotionally intimate content.

Other types of information to convey include knowledge of psychology and behavioral science. One of us went in to see his physician last year with some minor medical symptoms to discuss. The physician carefully assessed the symptoms, made a tentative diagnosis, and then discussed what is known about this type of problem, how long it usually lasts, what the recent research articles have said about effective management, and so on. The patient left feeling well-informed, was confident that the physician was up to speed on the latest information and able to help, and also knew what to do (and what not to do) about the problem. Similarly, a therapist providing information about the client's problem areas, how certain skills might work, as well as relevant scientific information about behavior can instill confidence and help the client to gradually evolve into becoming her or his own therapist.

Many clients, for example, struggle with sleep problems. A well-informed therapist who knows about sleep cycles and efficacious interventions for insomnia might educate the client on the importance of setting a regular daily time to get out of bed, how fatigue and a negative mood upon awakening are more likely due to the client awakening during particular stages sleep than due to poor or insufficient sleep, and how stimulating activities in the bedroom might create a conditioned association of wakefulness with the sleep environment (Morin, 2004). Once the client knows this information, she or he is in a much better position to learn and apply skills to improve sleep and to generalize these principles to new situations.

Effective Skill Teaching Strategies

In addition to conveying relevant information, an effective skills trainer also uses a variety of *effective skills teaching strategies*. Particularly within group settings, it is important to recognize that different clients learn skills at different rates and have differing preferences in terms of learning styles and learning activities. Some clients prefer to sit and listen to information and instructions about skills and may learn best by doing so. Other clients learn best when they are engaged in experiential exercises or active practice. Therefore, within group settings, it can be useful to use a variety of teaching strategies to ensure that some of these strategies will resonate with each client in the group. Such strategies might involve posing interesting questions, providing interesting stories or examples to illustrate key points, commenting on the applicability of the material to an individual client's situation, or using humor to facilitate engagement and learning. Other strategies include preparing or devising on-the-spot experiential exercises that illustrate important points about particular skills or providing interesting examples or metaphors to illustrate key points. In addition, an effective skills trainer paces the presentation of material such that neither too much nor too little material is presented within a particular period, breaks complex concepts and ideas down into concrete and easily understandable components, and presents the material in a manner that is neither over the heads of the clients nor overly simplistic.

An effective skills trainer must also use effective communication styles. Some effective communication behaviors include conveying interest and enthusiasm in the skill-related material; using humor; making interesting, unexpected, or off-beat or irreverent comments; or offering vivid or gripping examples of important points. An effective communicator both grabs the attention of his or her audience (even if it is just an audience of one) and conveys information in a manner that sticks with the audience well after the skills training session. Another effective strategy is to display a range of intensity in terms of voice volume and tone and to include variability in the rate and rhythm of speech.

Modeling and Demonstrating Skills

Another way to facilitate skill acquisition is to use modeling strategies. *Modeling* falls under the category of observational learning, through which people can "acquire cognitive skills and new patterns of behavior by observing the performance of others" (Bandura, 1986, p. 49). Simply instructing someone on how to perform a new skill and providing information on that skill often is woefully inadequate in the absence of any demonstration (O'Donohue & Krasner, 1995). Think for a moment about how you might write instructions for how to effectively drive a stick shift and how many accidents would occur if your students had only your instructions to guide them. Without any demonstration at all, it would be hard to learn how to navigate challenging interpersonal situations (e.g., conflict or heated discussions), with all of their nuances, nonverbal signals and communication, and so forth. Indeed, therapists in training often benefit tremendously by observing or listening to other therapists' work either live or through video or audio recordings. Modeling provides invaluable information to the client on what the new behavior "looks like" and how it is supposed to work. By demonstrating a skill, the therapist (or others) can show an entire chain or sequence of behavior (Bandura, 1986), which is particularly important when the skill is complex or the client has significant deficits in his or her repertoire (Rakos, 1991).

A martial arts instructor, for example, often starts by breaking down and presenting the sequence of movements involved in the effective deployment of particular techniques, such as kicks, blocks, punches, throws, grappling, and so on. The instructor often then demonstrates the whole activity so that the students know what their goal is—namely, to perform the movements as a whole, smoothly, effectively, and powerfully. Such demonstrations often occur with a partner and are designed to show how the particular movements work to disarm or defend against an opponent. In addition, it is common for the instructor to provide rules that specify when and how to perform movements effectively. For example, a common rule is that kicking is most effective when there is at least a few feet between opponents, whereas punching, elbow and knee strikes, and grappling are more effective close-in fighting strategies. As training progresses, demonstrations might involve increasingly complex and less predictable self-defense scenarios.

There are a couple of primary ways to provide modeling experiences during skills training. One method involves demonstrating component behaviors that comprise the skill or skills. With this method, the therapist might demonstrate a component of a skill by providing an example while describing the skill. For instance, a therapist might say,

One of the most important aspects of assertively asking for what you want from someone involves first describing the situation that you are in. If I wanted to ask a friend for money, I might say, "I'm stuck without any money for the bus, my car has broken down, and I live 40 miles from the clinic. Is there any way that you could lend me some money to get a bus home?"

Another way to demonstrate a skill is to display the physical movements involved with the skill. When therapists, for instance, teach clients with anxiety problems how to use diaphragmatic breathing to modulate the physiological experience of anxiety, they often place their hands on their diaphragms and demonstrate how the diaphragm, rather than the chest, moves when they breathe in and out.

A second method of modeling entails a demonstration of a chain of behaviors that is involved in the skill or skills. There are several ways to demonstrate chains of behavior, but one common method is to role-play the situation. For instance, a therapist teaching assertiveness skills might role-play a situation in which these skills are called for with a cotherapist, the target client, or another client. Role-playing allows for flexibility in terms of presenting stimuli and modulating the difficulty of the situation. Role-playing also gets the client involved in actively observing and practicing the skills. Often, however, it is more difficult to role-play non–interpersonally oriented skills (e.g., anger management skills, anxiety management skills). In such cases, it can be effective for the therapist and client to talk through an imaginary scenario, indicating which skills would be used and when. The following dialogue is an example of this.

> Therapist: OK, let's say I'm you, and my wife has just asked me why I didn't do the dishes. I'm noticing muscle tension and irritation increasing, and I'm thinking it isn't fair that she is on me about the dishes when I do so much around here. I have the urge to snap back and criticize her about something. Now, I'm going to take a deep breath, focusing on my diaphragm or abdomen, temporarily look away (but not in a really obvious way), and count to five before saying anything. OK, now I'm looking at her, and I feel just a bit less edgy, and I'm saying, "I'm sorry I didn't get to the dishes. I know how busy you are and how hard it is to come home to a messy kitchen. I got so caught up in my work that I just forgot." What do you think? Do you think you could give that a try? Is there anything that we're missing?

A third, and more formalized, approach to modeling is called *self-instructional training* (SIT), developed by Meichenbaum and Goodman (1971). SIT involves five steps. The first step, called *cognitive modeling,* involves having the client observe while a model performs a task and having the client make statements out loud about the task. A client learning progressive muscle relaxation, for example, might observe a model demonstrating this skill by saying, "Now, I'm tensing my muscles in my foot, and now I'm relaxing my muscles in my foot." The second step in SIT involves *cognitive-participant modeling*, in which the client performs the skill while the model verbalizes instructions. A third step, called *overt self-instruction*, involves having the client perform the new skill while instructing himself or herself aloud. The fourth step, called *fading overt self-instruction*, involves having the client perform the skill while he or she whispers instructions to himself or herself. Finally, the fifth step involves having the client perform the skill while instructing himself or herself but not aloud (*covert self-instruction*).

A fourth method of modeling involves disclosure regarding skill use. When this method is used in a group context, the therapist might elicit examples of when and how clients have used particular skills. The therapist might select clients who are "veterans" in the use of particular skills (if the group involves both beginners and more advanced clients) and have them discuss times during which they applied these skills as well as the consequences of doing so. The therapist or other clients might provide examples of when and how other people have used specific skills. In addition, the therapist also might disclose his or her own use of a particular skill in a difficult or challenging situation.

There are several ways to enhance the effects of modeling. For instance, findings from several studies have indicated that modeling is most effective when the model is similar to the target individual (i.e., the client) in terms of sex and age. Findings also suggest that individuals who are high in status, prestige, or expertise are also effective models (Grusec & Mischel, 1966; Paradise, Conway, & Zweig, 1986; Zimmerman & Koussa, 1979). Modeling is also effective when positive consequences follow the model's behavior and when the client's attention is directed toward the most relevant elements of the skillful behavior (Bandura, 1986). Research further suggests that the modeling of coping skills for overcoming challenges or difficulties is more effective than the modeling of mastery or expertise (Schunk & Hanson, 1985).

This research also has important implications for how a therapist might use self-disclosure as a modeling procedure. For instance, a therapist normally qualifies as a high-status person with expertise, so he or she is already in a good position to be an effective model. In addition, it may be more effective for a therapist to disclose a scenario in which he or she coped with and overcame some difficulty (i.e., coping modeling) rather than a scenario in which the therapist effortlessly engaged in effective, skilled behavior (i.e., mastery modeling). In addition, we urge therapists to avoid modeling failure experiences. We have found it helpful to model the skill of coping effectively with adversity, but at times, therapists make the mistake of simply modeling the fact that they have experienced adversity, struggled with it, and then failed to cope effectively. When using self-disclosure or other forms of modeling, it is important to think, "What am I trying to demonstrate?" The answer is effective behavior. Along these lines, it is important to show how the skillful behavior resulted in specific, positive consequences.

Using Reinforcement and Shaping

In addition to effective teaching and modeling, skills training often involves the application of basic behavioral techniques, such as reinforcement and, more specifically, shaping. Most of these techniques are discussed in Chapter 4, but here we nevertheless briefly highlight the importance of shaping. Shaping involves reinforcing successive approximations of a desired behavior. In skills training, the desired behavior could be anything from effective assertiveness, to coping behaviors to manage emotions, to behaviors that involve refusing drugs or tolerating urges to use drugs, among others.

At the beginning stages of teaching a new skill, the client may be unfamiliar with steps for learning new behaviors. Shaping involves breaking complex skills into smaller subskills, teaching those subskills, and then providing reinforcement for small steps or approximations toward the desired behaviors. The therapist requires the client to keep upping the ante or displaying more and more of the desired behavior before he or she provides reinforcement. In working with a depressed client who stays in bed most of the day, for example, the therapist might first provide positive reinforcement for the client's setting an alarm, getting up, and brushing her or his teeth. Once the client has established this routine, the therapist might require more activity before providing reinforcement, such as the client showering, writing a schedule for the day, having a cup of coffee and breakfast, and getting dressed. It also can be effective for the therapist to teach the client about the principles of shaping and to have the client provide herself or himself with rewards (which may or may not be reinforcers, depending on their effects on behavior) contingent on increasingly large steps toward the goal of, for example, getting out of the house to go for a walk and to see friends.

When using shaping or any other contingency management procedure, it is important to remember that reinforcement is most effective after the occurrence, rather than the nonoccurrence, of a target behavior. Many therapists, we have found, forget this principle and "reinforce" the absence of a behavior, such as the absence of self-harm, drug or alcohol use, and so on. It can be much more effective to assess what the client did instead of the problem behavior (such as effective use of coping skills) and to highlight and reinforce those alternative actions.

Helping Clients Strengthen Skills Through Practice, Feedback, and Coaching

When a client is first learning a new skill, the therapist's job is often to help him or her understand the skill through teaching and modeling, to provide opportunities for the client to get a feel for the skill through some preliminary practice, and to use shaping procedures to establish the skill within the client's repertoire. Once the client is capable of performing the skill, emphasis then shifts to honing and sharpening the skill. Strategies for accomplishing this generally involve (a) facilitating effective skill practice and (b) coaching and providing feedback regarding skill performance. A therapist might also use contingency management strategies to strengthen effective behavior, increase the rate at which effective behavior occurs, or extinguish behavior that interferes with implementing newly developed skills. Although we focus here on skill practice strategies, coaching, and feedback, it may be helpful to review Chapter 4 for information on the use of contingency management procedures for strengthening behavior.

Facilitating Effective Skill Practice in Session

One of the primary strategies for strengthening skills is practice. Practicing skills can help the client become more fluid and proficient with effective new behaviors and can increase the likelihood that he or she will engage in these behaviors in an automatic manner in relevant contexts. Therapists encourage skill practice in two primary ways: (a) through in-session practicing of skills and (b) through homework assignments.

Therapists can promote in-session skill practice in several ways: (a) the therapist can have the client engage in the skill or approximations of the skill in individual or group sessions, (b) the therapist and client might role-play various skills, or (c) the therapist might have the client repeat the behavior over and over again, essentially helping the client "overlearn" the effective behavior. Other in-session practice strategies involve having the client imagine in vivid detail himself or herself engaging in effective behavior in a variety of situations, as well as the desirable consequences that follow displays of effective behavior.

Using Homework to Facilitate Out-of-Session Practice

Homework assignments can be particularly helpful in encouraging skill practice in clients' natural environments. As described by Lindenboim,

Chapman, and Linehan (2006), there are several types of homework assignments in behavior therapy. Many of these fall within four categories: (a) discrete homework assignments, (b) self-monitoring homework assignments, (c) skills practice assignments, and (d) conditional homework assignments. The homework assignments that are perhaps most relevant to the practice of new skills include skills practice assignments, conditional homework assignments, and homework to self-monitor skills practice.

Skills practice assignments encourage ongoing practice of new skills. This type of assignment is designed to strengthen skills to the point that they become overlearned and are emitted with little effort on occasions in which they are most needed, such as during crises. Indeed, learning and strengthening skills requires time and repeated practice under conditions that support new learning. Some clients experience repeated crises and chaos in their natural environments, such as interpersonal conflict, employment difficulties, suicidal crises, and other such difficulties. Learning a new skill in a time of crisis is akin to running a marathon while having pneumonia. Therefore, one key benefit of homework assignments that promote ongoing practice is that they assist the client in becoming an expert in new skillful behavior to the point that he or she can skillfully and effectively handle even the most challenging situations. As an example, one of us leads a group that involves the teaching of mindfulness skills. The group leader provides a standing homework assignment for all participants to practice mindfulness skills at least four minutes each day. In another example, a therapist might give a client struggling with substance use issues the *discrete homework assignment* to practice the skills of urge-surfing at least three times over the next week or to practice drug refusal strategies (e.g., refusing offers for drugs; Higgins et al., 2014) with a supportive friend or partner. An astronaut would want to learn, rehearse, and master emergency procedures to deploy in the case of a shuttle malfunction. Similarly, one goal of repetitive, continual skills practice assignments is for the skills to become so entrenched in the repertoire that the client can use them automatically when needed, with minimal effort or thought.

Another type of homework assignment involves *self-monitoring* skill practice. Self-monitoring assignments involve clients' monitoring and recording various behaviors on an ongoing basis, usually daily. Self-monitoring forms, for example, might involve the client keeping track of occasions when skills are practiced by noting the specific skill performed, how often or how long practice took place, and the level of mastery achieved when enacting skills. One advantage of this type of assignment is that it encourages the client to move toward increasing the regular practicing of skills, especially when the therapist also urges and reinforces such practice. It is also helpful for clients to keep track of the effectiveness of the skill in achieving some goal (e.g., reducing stress, improving relationships); doing so can encourage ongoing practice and help the client discriminate which skills work and when they work best.

Lastly, another relevant type of homework assignment is the conditional type. *Conditional assignments* are those that the client performs only when certain events happen. As such, conditional homework assignments involve "if, then" rules for homework practice, such as, "If you are feeling anxious and panicky, then practice diaphragmatic breathing skills." "Molly," for example, was depressed and had the goals of taking better care of herself, showering in the morning, getting dressed, and coming to therapy sessions. Her long-term goal was to return to work as a health care professional. One skill she was learning in her therapy group was mindfulness, or paying attention to experiences in the present moment. She was specifically working on the DBT skill of "one-mindfully" in which the client simply does one thing at a time in the moment. The therapist coached her on how to use this skill to successfully get out of bed when she was particularly tired, dreading the day, and feeling sad and lethargic. Her lethargy, thoughts that there was nothing to look forward to, and heavy sensations in her body were cues to practice this skill. She would remind herself to do one thing at a time, as if each task was the only thing she had to do in her entire life, and to temporarily avoid thinking about the larger, more overwhelming goal of getting herself to the therapy office (e.g., when putting on her socks, focusing completely on this task and nothing else). Over time, and with continued practice of this skill, Molly attended therapy regularly, began to gradually feel less depressed, reengaged in recreational activities (dancing, specifically), and planned a trip to Asia with a friend.

Providing Coaching and Feedback

Another way to strengthen skills is to provide coaching and feedback. The therapist might begin by asking the client to emit a particular skill-related behavior. Afterward, the therapist might provide feedback on several aspects of the behavior, including (a) how closely the behavior approximated the desired skill; (b) the likely effect of the behavior, as enacted by the client, on his or her environment (i.e., the effectiveness of the behavior); and (c) various aspects of the topography of the behavior, including frequency, duration, intensity, tone of voice, body posture, language, or other similar features. In conjunction with such feedback, coaching would involve the therapist offering suggestions, instructions, or recommendations to the client on how to improve skillful behavior.

It can be effective for the therapist to modulate her or his approach to coaching based on the client's placement on the learning curve for a new skill. When a client is just acquiring the skill and trying it out, the therapist works to help the client understand the basics of the skill while simultaneously encouraging her or him to essentially "play" with it and get a feel for it. Coaching and constructive feedback at this stage might focus more on what the client is doing right than what she or he could do to improve. Following the principle of shaping, the idea is to create opportunities to practice and reinforce successive approximations of the desired skillful behavior. Emphasizing positive feedback in the beginning might also encourage the client to keep practicing, whereas a lot of specific or corrective feedback in the absence of reinforcement can be demoralizing. Over time, as the client has acquired the skill and is now strengthening it, coaching might be more balanced, providing positive feedback on what the client is doing well and a greater frequency of constructive feedback on how to improve.

Skills coaching can also vary in terms of timing, density, and specificity. In terms of timing, it is most helpful for the therapist to provide coaching as close in time to the occurrence of the behavior as possible. Recall from Chapter 4 that reinforcement is most effective when it occurs close in time to the behavior. In terms of density of coaching, it is often most effective for the therapist to make one or two suggestions on how the client can improve his or her behavior rather than make numerous suggestions that are likely to overwhelm the client or that the client is likely to forget. Finally, regarding specificity, there has been some debate in the literature regarding whether it is more effective to provide very detailed feedback and coaching versus feedback that simply suggests whether the behavior was effective or ineffective (for issues related to specific vs. general feedback in training therapists, see Follette & Callaghan, 1995). One potential pitfall of very specific coaching is that it might encourage rigid, rule-governed behavior that the client does not flexibly modulate according to shifting contextual demands. Encouraging effective rule-governed behavior, however, may be helpful to the client in that it provides a road map that specifies what to do in particular situations.

Helping Clients Generalize Skills

Once a client has established and strengthened a set of behavioral skills, it is important to consider the array of life situations in which these skills may be needed. A client may be able to effectively assert her or his wishes in the therapy room or with a partner, but when called on to refuse drugs or to ask a friend to stop commenting on her appearance, assertiveness may become more challenging. A client who has learned emotion regulation strategies might use these effectively to manage anxiety, but anger may be a different story altogether. It is important, therefore, to facilitate the generalization of skills to a variety of relevant contexts.

There are several ways to facilitate the generalization of skills. It is most effective to use strategies based on a clear, idiographic conceptualization of the client. This work can begin during the assessment phase, even before skills training, when the therapist assesses whether problems that occur in one area also show up in other areas. One of us saw a client who was working on reducing her aggressive communication. When she wanted someone to do something for her, she tended to either avoid asking altogether or to make demands in a loud, aggressive manner. She periodically did this with the therapist, and before helping her learn new assertiveness skills, he assessed the various life domains in which this problem showed up. It turned out that this client had previous difficulties keeping jobs due to her aggressiveness with superiors at work. After the client practiced more effective assertiveness skills until she was able to reliably ask for what she wanted (e.g., a different appointment time, less or more homework, to talk about a particular topic) in an effective manner with the therapist, attention turned to how she might practice (both in vivo and in imagination) the new skills in work situations.

Another way to address generalization is to review where and how the client has practiced the new skills. If the client only has practiced the new skills in very specific situations, then generalization might involve listing other relevant situations and having the client practice the skills in those settings. The list also might include increasingly difficult or challenging situations. It is one thing to use anger management effectively when someone accidentally knocks over your coffee cup, but it may be another matter entirely when someone is yelling at or threatening you. Generalization and the practicing of skills in new situations sometimes progresses much like graduated exposure, from less to more evocative or challenging situations.

Additional ways to facilitate generalization involve principles of stimulus control, discussed in Chapter 4. The client may have learned and practiced new skills in a variety of situations but still have difficulty discriminating (or remembering) when to use such skills. In this case, reminders, cues, and prompts in the natural environment can help orient the client to effective behavior. Some of our clients, for example, have learned the skill of reminding themselves of the cons of self-harming behavior when they experience urges to hurt themselves, and yet, in certain situations, this skill does not even come to mind. As a result, some clients have found it helpful to post notes reminding them to use the skill in a variety of high-risk situations or places, such as the bathroom (where razors are stored), the car, or other such places. Many clients also use their smartphones in this way, programming reminders, prompts, and sayings that orient them to effective skill use in a variety of situations. In addition, the therapist might provide audio recordings or notes to the client after sessions. Such recordings can function as reminders of therapy and the various skills the client has learned and can facilitate generalization when the client listens to or views them in relevant situations.

SUMMARY

In summary, when using skills training, we recommend the following strategies:

- Clearly define the skills or sets of skills that the client would likely benefit from by learning.
- Determine an effective structure and format for skills training. Consider whether it would be most effective to teach skills in a group or individually and how often, where, and with whom skills training will occur.
- Orient the client to the rationale, structure, expectations, and goals of skills training as well as the nature of the skills that he or she will learn.
- Help clients acquire skills by using a variety of didactic strategies, by creating opportunities to demonstrate or model skills (or have other clients do so), and by using principles of reinforcement when shaping new behaviors.
- When strengthening skills, use homework assignments to encourage regular practice and provide appropriate feedback and coaching to help clients refine their new skills.
- When promoting skills generalization, instruct clients to practice skills in a variety of contexts (including increasingly difficult or challenging situations), and consider the use of stimulus control strategies to prompt skill use in the natural environment.

7
ENHANCING INTERPERSONAL EFFECTIVENESS

Social support is widely recognized as having beneficial influences on physical health, psychological health, and overall well-being. Higher levels of social support, for example, are associated with lower rates of disease morbidity and mortality (Berkman, Glass, Brissette, & Seeman, 2000) and better functioning of important physiological systems (e.g., cardiovascular, neuroendocrine, and immune system functioning; Uchino, 2006). Lower levels of social support, in contrast, are associated with poorer physiological health and adjustment (Moak & Agrawal, 2010) and an increased risk for psychiatric symptoms and disorders (Moak & Agrawal, 2010; Sheeber, Hops, Alpert, Davis, & Andrews, 1997; Stice, Ragan, & Randall, 2004).

The ability to develop and maintain social supports depends, in part, on one's effectiveness in the interpersonal domain. Ineffective social behavior has been implicated as a risk or maintaining factor for a broad range of psychological difficulties (Campbell, Hansen, & Nangle, 2010), including depression

http://dx.doi.org/10.1037/14691-007
Behavioral Interventions in Cognitive Behavior Therapy: Practical Guidance for Putting Theory Into Action, Second Edition, by R. F. Farmer and A. L. Chapman

(Coyne, 1976; Hammen, 2003), nonsuicidal self-injury (Nock & Mendes, 2008), and adult antisocial behavior (Kellam et al., 2008). The addition of social skills training to standard treatments has been shown to increase the overall effectiveness of interventions for several conditions, including anxiety disorders (Herbert et al., 2005), depression (Hersen, Himmelhoch, Thase, & Bellack, 1984), schizophrenia (Kurtz & Mueser, 2008), gambling problems (Sylvain, Ledouceur, & Boisvert, 1997), and substance abuse (J. D. Hawkins, Catalano, & Wells, 1986; Monti et al., 1990). Social skills training approaches are also effective stand-alone treatments for social anxiety (Wlazlo, Schroeder-Hartwig, Hand, Kaiser, & Münchau, 1990) and depression (Cuijpers, van Straten, Andersson, & van Oppen, 2008). In addition to contributing to symptomatic improvement, social skills acquired during therapy are often maintained in the weeks and months after treatment completion, generalize to other settings, and appear to make beneficial ongoing contributions to overall adjustment (Corrigan, 1991).

Given the centrality of social support and social skills to psychological health and well-being and their contribution to symptomatic improvement for a wide variety of conditions, this chapter emphasizes intervention approaches for enhancing interpersonal effectiveness. *Interpersonal effectiveness* refers to the coordination of several complex social skills and abilities necessary for social interaction, relationship maintenance, and the achievement of social goals across multiple situations and contexts (Linehan, 1993a). Interpersonal effectiveness necessarily implies an ability to attend to others and communicate effectively, to plan behaviors before taking action, to demonstrate flexibility by making continuous adjustments to others' actions as appropriate, and to display behaviors that are pleasing to others. Interpersonal effectiveness also involves the minimization of behaviors that others might experience as aversive, uncomfortable, punishing, or invalidating.

ASSESSMENT AND CONCEPTUALIZATION OF INTERPERSONAL EFFECTIVENESS

Like any other form of behavior, interpersonal behaviors are learned behaviors and a joint function of person variables (e.g., temperament, learning history, social behaviors currently in one's repertoire) and current environmental influences (i.e., behavior antecedents and consequences). Reinforcement of social behavior is almost exclusively provided by the social environment, typically through reinforcers that are themselves social in nature. Among the most potent social reinforcers are responses from observers that demonstrate attention or notice, convey approval or acceptance, or suggest that the actor's behavior is desirable, attractive, influential, or dominant.

What constitutes interpersonal effectiveness or success is largely culturally defined (Baum, 2005). Within cultures, the socialization process is partly guided by the influence of longer term, socially mediated contingencies (e.g., rules, laws, moral teachings) that support prosocial forms of behavior and discourage behaviors that depart from society's interests or welfare. Cultural practices or customs are transferred to members through a variety of processes, including rule provision and reinforcement for rule following. Whether behavior is consistent with social norms and customs is a key consideration in distinguishing between ineffective and dysfunctional interpersonal behaviors. Furthermore, whereas *ineffective interpersonal behaviors* usually fail to produce reinforcing outcomes related to socially mediated situational goals or objectives, *dysfunctional interpersonal behaviors* frequently produce immediate reinforcing consequences (e.g., compliance, attention) despite the behavior's unpleasantness to others. Because definitions of what constitutes interpersonally effective behavior vary across cultures and subcultures, training in social skills necessarily involves knowledge of appropriate cultural norms and practices. Similarly, the effectiveness of social behavior is evaluated not only in terms of the behavior's outcome but also its acceptability within the sociocultural context in which it occurs.

Assessment Approaches

When assessing social behavior, it is important to identify (a) the specific problem behaviors in clear and understandable terms, (b) situations in which problem behaviors are most likely to emerge, and (c) the consequences that follow problem behaviors that contribute to its maintenance. If behavior is recognized as problematic, it is also often useful to pinpoint (d) the specific aspects of the behavior that are problematic (e.g., in terms of immediate and distal outcomes, conflicts with cultural norms or personal values) and (e) possible behavioral alternatives that could be used in the situation that have a better chance of producing reinforcing short- and long-term outcomes without accompanying aversive consequences. With respect to these latter areas, it is often useful to clarify a client's goals or values in important social situations and relationships and to explore behavioral alternatives that are consistent with these.

Self-Report Questionnaires

Client responses to self-report questionnaires can suggest possible behavioral and situational targets for attention during therapy. There are several self-report questionnaires or measures for assessing social behavior (for reviews, see Herbert, Rheingold, & Brandsma, 2010; Nangle, Hansen,

Erdley, & Norton, 2010). Although responses to self-report questionnaires might suggest useful hypotheses to further explore with the client during interview or in behavioral simulations, they often provide little information about contextual factors within which problematic behavior occurs. For these reasons, relevant additional information might be sought from other sources, such as the following.

Interview Assessments

Interview-based assessments are also useful for generating ideas about important targets for therapy. Clients, however, may not always be accurate reporters of skill levels or deficits. As with self-report measures, other informational sources are ideally sought in order to develop a comprehensive and consensus view of the client's interpersonal strengths and weaknesses. Exhibit 7.1 provides examples of interview questions that can inform a contextual understanding of the client's interpersonal behavior.

Self-Monitoring

If the client's problematic interpersonal behaviors are few and easily identifiable, self-monitoring methods might provide useful assessment information. In self-monitoring, the client keeps track of target behaviors in between sessions by noticing the behavior when it occurs and recording its occurrence on a record form. Other contextual information related to the behavior might be included on the record form, such as antecedents to the behavior (e.g., "What happened before the behavior occurred?"), consequences that followed the behavior's occurrence ("What happened after you did this?" "How did others respond?"), and other clinically relevant experiences that might have co-occurred with the behavior (e.g., "How anxious were you in this situation?" "Rate your level of anger in this situation from 0 to 100"). In addition to its assessment function, self-monitoring also has therapeutic value, as observing and recording target behaviors often produce behavioral change in desirable directions (R. O. Nelson, 1977).

In-Session Role-Plays and Simulations

Clinical assessments of social behavior and skills often involve in-session role-plays or simulations. Roles-plays permit the therapist to directly observe the client's interpersonal skills in a protected setting. Because the therapeutic setting is a "safe" environment and because situations are simulated, however, there may be only a modest relationship between role-played and naturally occurring behavior (Bellack, Hersen, & Turner, 1979). They are, however,

EXHIBIT 7.1
Examples of Interview Questions Useful for Developing a Functional Understanding of Interpersonal Problems

For identifying historical information on social functioning:
- During your childhood, adolescence, and early adulthood, did you have many friends?
- Did you feel emotionally close any of these people? What made these relationships special?
- What were your relationships with your father, mother, brothers, and sisters like?
- Was there someone in your family you felt particularly close to? Who? What was it about that relationship that was special?
- Did you date much when you were younger? What was your experience with dating?
- Were you involved in social clubs or social activities? What kinds?
- Were there times when you were younger when you felt socially awkward? Can you describe these?
- When you were younger, were there particular problems in relationships that kept coming up? What were these?

For identifying specific problematic social behaviors:
- Are there people that you're close to now? Who? How often do you have contact with them? Is it easy for you to be open with these people, including disclosing more intimate aspects about yourself?
- Do you experience any difficulties in relationships today? What kinds of difficulties?
- When you have difficulties interacting with others, what problems do you have? What do you say? What do you do?
- Are there times when you find yourself not knowing what to do in a social situation? When does this occur?
- Is it easy for you to initiate and carry on a conversation with someone you don't know or know well?
- Are you socially anxious? Does anxiety cause problems in social situations? What kinds of problems does anxiety cause?
- When you're in social situations, are there things you say to yourself that make your situation more difficult?
- When you think back on the times when it's been challenging to interact with others, what were the greatest challenges in those situations (e.g., Keeping your emotions in check? Expressing your opinions or what you wanted from others?)
- How hard is it for you to ask people to do something, or to change their behavior in some way?
- Is it hard for you to say "no" when you feel like it?
- Have other people commented on your social behavior? What do they say?
- Have others said to you that you do things that are annoying or unpleasant? What things?
- Do you do activities with other people that you enjoy? How often?
- If you were to rate your overall level of social skill or interpersonal effectiveness from 0 to 100, with 100 being extremely skillful or effective, how would you rate yourself? What's happening to make your rating less than 100?

For identifying current situational contexts that are difficult or challenging:
- Are there types of social situations that you find particularly difficult or stressful? Which ones? How often do these occur?
- Are there social situations that you avoid?

(continues)

EXHIBIT 7.1
Examples of Interview Questions Useful for Developing a Functional
Understanding of Interpersonal Problems *(Continued)*

- Do you experience any difficulties at work? In public places? During social events like parties? At home? What about in intimate or dating relationships?
- Are there people with whom you find it difficult to talk with? Friends? Your spouse or partner? Coworkers?
- Can you think of a time recently when you were dissatisfied with how you handled a situation?
- What's your evaluation of how you handle conflicts with other people?
- Are there times when you stop yourself from acting because you have doubts as to whether your actions will be effective? When does this occur?
- If we were to focus on social situations that are most challenging or difficult for you, what would those be?

For identifying consequences:
- On occasions when you've been dissatisfied with how you interacted with others, what happened? How did others respond? How did you feel or react on those occasions?
- What do you say to yourself following social interactions that didn't go well?
- Are you usually able to accomplish what you set out to do in your interactions with others?
- When you ask people for something, what usually happens right afterward?
- When you do have conflicts or problems involving other people, how do they usually turn out?

For identifying interpersonal strengths:
- Have people commented on what they find appealing about you?
- How would people who know you well describe you?
- Even in situations that are particularly challenging for you, are there some things you do particularly well? What?
- In relationships you described as "close," what did you do that contributed to their being close relationships?
- What do you see as your strengths or areas of competence in relationships with others?

For illuminating the client's understanding of the sources of problematic social behavior:
- Is there something that blocks you for responding in a way that might be more effective?
- What do you see as the biggest obstacles to being more effective in social situations?
- Are thoughts or emotions present in these situations that interfere with carrying out what you know might work?
- Is there anyone to blame for the difficulties you have in social situations?

For identifying effective behavioral alternatives:
- Once time has passed after a challenging situation, are you usually able to think of other ways you could have responded more effectively?
- How might a person who is skillful or effective have acted in this situation?
- If you were not socially anxious or awkward in this situation, how might you have acted instead?
- Are relationships important to you? If so, what makes them important?
- How would relationships be different if current problems or challenges no longer existed?
- Are the values that are most important to you evident in your current relationships? How?

frequently useful for the assessment of possible skills deficits. If a client is unable to demonstrate some level of skill in a safe and protected environment, it is unlikely that he or she would be able to act skillfully in natural social environments.

Examples of role-plays include those that are focused on specific problem situations that, in turn, present opportunities for evaluating conflict management, emotion regulation, and problem-solving skills (Linehan, 1993a). Dyadic role-plays could involve other specific scenarios that are especially problematic for the client (e.g., "You are at a dinner party and want to strike up a conversation with the person sitting next to you. Let's role-play how you would go about doing this"). Brief (e.g., 10 minutes) impromptu discourses on a particular topic of clinical relevance can also be used to evaluate the client's self-expression skills and his or her ability to maintain a dialogue (e.g., "Beginning with your earliest recollections from childhood up through today, describe important relationships you've had with others over the years, and what it was about those relationships that made them important to you"). Such tasks not only provide relevant assessment information, they are also performance-based activities that can provide insight in how the client communicates (e.g., word facility, eye contact, gestures, posture, speech tone, self-expression skills, level of social anxiety) and what aspects of relationships he or she finds particularly rewarding.

Role-play and simulation assessments might also clarify whether some forms of social behavior have been learned but are suppressed in some current social contexts. What appear to be skills deficits, for example, may actually be the product of a punitive or coercive environment that functions to suppress or inhibit behavior (Dow, 1994). If a client, however, were unable to emit assertive responses in a protected environment (e.g., during an in-session role play), this would suggest a skills deficit. In such instances, therapy might emphasize skills development. Occasionally, individuals have learned relevant skills (i.e., they know what to do and how to do it); however, they fail to execute these skills in appropriate situations. In such instances, it is important to assess the client's views about factors that may inhibit their behavior. Does the client believe, for example, that he or she does not have the right to be assertive? Do emotions such as anxiety interfere with assertive action? Do others respond punitively to displays of assertion? Ultimately, the success of an intervention program that promotes interpersonal effectiveness will depend, in part, on the correspondence between that intervention's emphasis and the reasons underlying the client's difficulties in the interpersonal domain. A skills training program, for example, will have little benefit for a client who has already learned these behaviors but fails to exhibit them because of suppressive environments.

Functional Analysis and Functional Response Domain Assessment

As with any target behaviors in behavior therapy, the initial assessment process usually begins with a thorough functional analysis to gain an understanding of the problematic nature of the client's behavior and to gage the appropriateness of intervention alternatives (see Chapter 2). Ideally, findings from functional analyses should not only illuminate relevant target behaviors and the contexts within which they occur but also suggest appropriate replacement behaviors (Sturmey, 1996).

Although the range of interpersonal behaviors a person can display is potentially limitless, the functions associated with such behavior can be grouped into a small number of functional categories, or *functional response domains*. Functional response domains constitute a behavioral approach to classification in which behavioral groupings are arranged to emphasize the conditions under which problematic behavior is most likely to occur or the purpose that such behavior serves (Follette, Naugle, & Linnerooth, 2000; Naugle & Follette, 1998). Although various forms of behavior (or topographies) might appear different based on surface level features (e.g., social avoidance, rumination, substance abuse in social situations), they may have similar functional properties in which they produce similar outcomes (e.g., avoidance, escape, or the altering of social situations). Awareness of the conditions that facilitate problematic behavior and the functions that such behavior serve can, in turn, inform the design of intervention strategies that specifically target the contextual factors in which the problematic behavior is embedded and aid efforts to identify healthier forms of alternative behavior.

In the sections that follow, we review several functional response domains relevant to the assessment and conceptualization of interpersonal effectiveness. These include interpersonal patterns of behavior developed over one's learning history (e.g., social skills and deficits, behavioral excesses), the influence of interpersonally relevant establishing operations (e.g., rules and values), and characteristics of current social environments (e.g., supportive vs. suppressive environments, availability of reinforcement for social behavior). Although this list is not exhaustive, these functional domains highlight some of the primary learning and contextual factors that contribute to problems in the interpersonal domain.

SOCIAL SKILLS AND DEFICITS

Social skills develop and become refined during childhood and adolescence and are generally the product of interactions that take place between youth and caregivers, siblings, and peers. Several influences combine to develop, shape, and refine interpersonal behaviors during development. These include direct reinforcement (or operant learning), observational learning (or modeling), and rule following (including the transmission of cultural practices).

Social skills deficits are usually apparent when individuals do not display an adequate range or repertoire of social behavior necessary for effective functioning in a variety of contexts. Skills deficits among otherwise normally developing individuals imply at least one of the following historical processes: (a) failure of early social environments to model or shape appropriate social behaviors or (b) the punishment of appropriate social behavior, resulting in behavior elimination from the person's response repertoire.

Deficits in social skills have been regarded as an important risk factor for depression and other psychological disorders. A popular behavioral theory suggests that depression may, in part, be a consequence of an inability to produce reinforcement from the social environment through one's own actions (Lewinsohn & Gotlib, 1995). Effective therapeutic approaches based on this and similar models (e.g., the Coping with Depression Course; Cuijpers, Muñoz, Clarke, & Lewinsohn, 2009; Lewinsohn, Antonuccio, Steinmetz-Breckenridge, & Teri, 1984) typically include a social skills training component. Similarly, many of the stand-alone social skills-based therapies for depression emphasize instruction in assertiveness (Cuijpers et al., 2008) or social problem solving (Bell & D'Zurilla; 2009; Nezu, Nezu, & Perri, 1989).

Interventions for developing social skills are usually structured in much the same way as any other form of skills training (see Chapter 6) and typically involve the following: (a) skills acquisition (e.g., shaping, direct instruction, modeling), (b) skills strengthening (e.g., behavioral rehearsal, feedback), and (c) skills generalization (e.g., homework assignments to practice skills in relevant situations). Common features frequently found in social skills training programs are summarized in Exhibit 7.2.

When undertaking social skills training, we along with others (e.g., Follette & Hayes, 2000), place greater emphasis on behavior effectiveness (i.e., the flexible selection and implementation of behavior strategies to produce reinforcing outcomes) than on behavior topography (e.g., getting the form of behavior "just right"). This is because many variations in behavior can produce similar and effective outcomes. Sole emphasis on the form of behavior encourages mimicry and the inflexible application of behavior across situations. Emphasis on effectiveness also conveys to the client that "the performance" is less important to a situation than is accomplishing one's objectives. We have found that such a stance, once adopted by the client, goes a long way in reducing performance anxiety.

EXHIBIT 7.2
Common Components of Social Skills Training Interventions

Psychoeducation. Psychoeducation often involves skill description and some form of rule provision (e.g., the therapist describes the skill, its rationale for use, and the situations in which the skill is most relevant or appropriate). Information conveyed through psychoeducation can also establish the rationale and potential utility of various treatment components used during therapy.

Direct instruction, modeling, and coaching. Direct instruction involves illustrating for a client what to do, usually by the therapist telling or physically demonstrating how to perform a certain behavior or sequence of behaviors. When the therapist is modeling behavior, the client is asked to notice and discriminate the various elements of the behavior being modeled. Modeling approaches are particularly useful for teaching new behaviors that combine sets of existing behavioral repertoires.

Behavior shaping. Behavior shaping is one approach that can be used to facilitate the development of new behavioral repertoires. Shaping procedures involve the gradual development of complex behavior or behavior sequences through the reinforcement of closer and closer approximations to the final form of the behavior. Complex behavioral sequences are broken down into smaller component elements. As the client tries out these new elements, the therapist provides feedback and support. Once behavioral elements early in the sequence are established, reinforcement for those behaviors is faded while the next behavior in the sequence is prompted and, once appropriately displayed, reinforced. This process of fading, prompting, and reinforcement is continued until the final form of behavior is established.

Role-playing and rehearsal. Behavioral rehearsals and role-playing are often used to help clients learn and refine ways of responding in specific situations. Behavioral rehearsal and role-play can be done in the imagination or in vivo with supportive others. Goldfried and Davison (1976) described common elements usually found in behavioral rehearsal exercises:

- Client preparation, which involves recognition by the client of the relevant behavioral deficits and willingness to learn a new behaviors through rehearsal processes.
- Selection of a target situation (e.g., a situation in which effective behavioral responses are absent, which results in distress or impairment).
- Behavioral rehearsal in session, which involves developing and trying out the behavior while the therapist provides direct instruction, modeling, and feedback.

Practicing skills in natural environments and skills generalization. Once the client has demonstrated the ability to carry out the skill in a protected setting (i.e., within therapy sessions), he or she is encouraged to try it out in everyday situations in which its application is relevant. In helping clients carry out this phase of skills acquisition, emphasis is ideally placed on the effectiveness of the behavior in these situations (e.g., "Did it produce the desired consequences?") rather than getting the form of the behavior "just right."

Developing mastery. Mastery develops when one rehearses or practices actions that are consistent with one's objectives and goals and by noticing successes when they occur. Self-respect is enhanced when one observes oneself acting skillfully, expressing one's opinions assertively, or by realizing goals consistent with one's objectives or values through one's actions.

Communication Skills

When we communicate with other people, we contribute to the establishment of an environment in which the persons who are communicating and the messages conveyed are the central focus. The act of communication involves several component processes, such as attention skills, word knowledge, verbal fluency, expressive ability, receptive language skills, and the integration of multiple responses such as emotion, posture, and nonverbal gesturing. *Communication skills training* focuses on the development or refinement of skills related to the constructive sharing of thoughts and emotions.

Communication skills training might be considered when clients are deficit in basic interpersonal skills or when dysfunctional modes of communication (e.g., characterized by anger, frustration, and coercion) have become prominent to the point that communication efforts have become generally ineffective. Behaviors targeted for strengthening in communication skills training include those that draw people in rather than push people away. These include emotional self-disclosure ("I really am excited about this new job prospect"), demonstrations of understanding and support ("I see that you're really upset. Would you like to talk about what's bothering you?"), making positive requests (e.g., "I need someone to talk to now. Could we talk?"), and communicating positive regard (e.g., "I very much enjoyed the time we spent together today"). Strengthening constructive communication patterns is a common feature of empirically supported behavioral approaches to couple therapy (Benson, McGinn, & Christensen, 2012; Epstein, Baucom, Hunt, & La Taillade, 2002) and is a feature of several other therapeutic methods that emphasize the facilitation of interpersonal effectiveness.

Central to skillful communication is adherence to certain roles when communicating, namely that of the speaker and the listener. Listener skills include the ability to attend to the speaker while he or she is talking, to acknowledge the speaker's comments with appropriate non-verbal behavior (e.g., eye-contact, head nodding), and to refrain from interrupting the speaker or challenging his or her views while they are being expressed. Other basic listening skills include the following (Epstein et al., 2002; Oliver & Margolin, 2003):

- *Parroting:* The listener repeats back verbatim what the speaker has said.
- *Paraphrase:* The listener rephrases what the speaker said using his or her own words and communicates this rephrasing back to the speaker.

- *Reflection:* The listener identifies the emotion underlying the content of the speaker's words and queries the speaker as to whether his or her perception of the speaker's underlying emotional tone is accurate.
- *Validation:* The listener communicates to the speaker that his or her position is understood, which can be accomplished by conveying to the speaker the accuracy or validity of the message conveyed provided that the listener agrees with the content of what the speaker said. Even if the listener disagrees with the content of the speaker's communication, some form of acknowledgment that the speaker has been heard (e.g., via head nods or verbal statements such as, "I understand your position") is itself a form of validation.

During communication training, these listener skills are taught sequentially, as each builds on the previous skill.

Speaker (or expressive) skills involve the ability to accurately communicate verbally what one is thinking or feeling to another (Jacobson, 1982; Oliver & Margolin, 2003). To increase the likelihood that messages will be accurately received, the speaker's statements should be brief, clear, accurate, and to the point. More complex or nuanced statements might be chunked into smaller and more manageable units, thus providing the listener with a greater opportunity to check with the speaker about the accuracy of his or her understanding of each element of the underlying message. As skills acquisition progresses, clients can be encouraged to divulge more personal information about himself or herself, such as preferences, interests, hopes, or values. Examples of specific speaker skills include the following (Jacobson, 1982):

- *Disclosing personal experiences:* This involves the disclosure of personal experiences to another or opening oneself up to others. To do this effectively, the speaker notices emotions or thoughts as they occur, associates these experiences with particular situations or circumstances, and communicates the emotion–situation or thought–situation linkage to the listener (e.g., "When I'm at the lake, I feel so relaxed and at ease").
- *Negative emotion expression:* This involves the ability to express negative emotions in a nondestructive way (i.e., devoid of threats, demands, or put-downs). Negative emotion expression links specific emotions with certain events in a matter-of-fact style with the intent of producing positive behavior change in the other (e.g., "I feel hurt when you make statements that ridicule me").

- *Positive self-expressions:* These include statements that convey caring, affection, support, encouragement, acceptance, recognition, approval, affirmation, validation, gratitude, appreciation, and respect. Such statements by a speaker are usually experienced as highly reinforcing by the listener and often function over time to deepen the intimacy of a relationship and improve overall relationship quality.

When altering communication patterns, artificial or unnatural changes should be discouraged. Future relationship distress, for example, has been predicted by extreme increases in positive communication and similar decreases in negative communication (Baucom, Hahlweg, Atkins, Engl, & Thurmaier, 2006). Such extreme behavior can be self-invalidating when it involves negating or suppressing negative feelings in the service of remaining positive at all costs. Acting in an overly positive and inflexible way is also not natural or genuine and is likely to be perceived as such by others.

Communication skills such as these can be taught and practiced within sessions. When the client is accompanied by a significant other, each can take turns practicing the listener and speaker roles. When communication skills training only involves the client, the therapist and client can take turns in the listening and speaking roles in the context of role-play scenarios, with the therapist from time to time switching out of the speaker or listener role to model, prompt, provide feedback, and reinforce the client's efforts.

Conflict Management Skills

Conflicts involving others are an everyday part of life. How we negotiate such conflicts, however, can have profound implications for important relationships. Conflict management skills such as interpersonal problem solving can be useful means through which disagreements are acknowledged and worked through in a collaborative and consensual manner.

Acknowledging Conflict

During communication skills training, particularly when describing areas of conflict to others, the speaker is usually encouraged to use "I" statements. Additionally, the speaker is usually urged to state thoughts and emotions as aspects of his or her experience rather than as unbiased truths, to be brief and to the point in his or her descriptions of the conflict, and to limit the expression of negative emotions tied to the past (e.g., complaints, resentments) while emphasizing current problems, their potential solutions, and goals associated with problem resolution. When raising problems, it is generally helpful for the speaker to separate the problem from the persons involved.

The following represents a general framework for addressing and resolving conflicts:

- *A statement of the issue or need associated with the conflict.* The time frame emphasized in such statements is future-oriented. A rehashing of events that have already taken place is avoided (e.g., "I would appreciate it if we could sit down and talk about how we might address our disagreements more effectively together"; "Would you be willing to talk with me about how we might make it easier to work together in the future?").
- *A statement acknowledging the associated emotion.* When expressing associated emotions, it is important that the person avoids inflammatory and accusatory statements directed at the other party. A primary goal in this exchange is to produce an effective outcome, not to exact retribution or revenge on another (e.g., "It troubles me that this has become a problem"; "I feel uneasy that we still haven't resolved this issue").
- *A goal statement that indicates an ideal resolution to this issue.* This would include statements that describe a goal beneficial to both parties ("I don't want this incident to ruin our friendship"; "I hope we can work on this issue until we're both satisfied").
- *A statement or query that involves checking in with the other person.* Such statements or queries involve gathering an understanding of how the other person experiences resolution of the conflict ("Are you OK with that?" "Are we good?"). If conflict continues to be evident, then the process should be started again from the beginning.

A key to navigating this process is the willingness of both parties to listen to the other person and not to interrupt. Listening and speaking skills, as described earlier, are important prerequisites to conflict resolution approaches. Described in the following section is a more fine-grained approach for addressing problems that are a source of conflict or concern.

Interpersonal Problem Solving

Interpersonal problem solving is a common element of multicomponent treatment programs for decreasing relationship distress (e.g., Falloon et al., 1985; Oliver & Margolin, 2003) and is a centerpiece of an empirically supported stand-alone cognitive-behavioral intervention for decreasing depressive symptomatology (problem-solving therapy; Bell & D'Zurilla, 2009; Nezu et al., 1989). In this section, we highlight the central skills associated with the interpersonal problem-solving process.

Problem solving is a useful coping skill for addressing a variety of challenging situations, including interpersonal conflicts. Quite often, problems-solving skills are deficient among persons who are less interpersonally effective, leaving them with few skills for addressing and constructively dealing with conflicts as they arise. In Exhibit 7.3, we outline a six-step sequential approach for problem solving, conveniently summarized by the acronym SOLVES:

S = Specify the problem
O = Outline your goals
L = List the alternatives
V = View the likely consequences and select a promising alternative
E = Establish and implement a plan
S = Survey the outcomes

EXHIBIT 7.3
Elements of Effective Interpersonal Problem Solving

S (Specify the problem): The main feature of this step is to clearly define the problem or to delineate the core features contributing to conflict in a situation. When the problem involves some aspect of a relationship, the problem definition would ideally include recognition of role of both persons in the conflict and the consequences of ongoing conflict in this area on the relationship. Statements of problems are ideally based on objective and observable facts. Blaming other persons for the problem or expressing judgments about others' behavior should be avoided.

O (Outline your goals): Once the problem has been identified, the next step is to identify one's personal goals in this situation. The focus, then, is on what could be done to resolve the problem, and not on what is "right" or "they way things should be." Within this step, it is important to be as specific as possible.

L (List the alternatives): In this step, the primary task is to come up with a list of possible solutions for resolving the conflict. Because this stage is more concerned with identifying a list of possible solutions, brainstorming is encouraged and self-censoring discouraged. Once a provisional list is generated, it is often helpful to consider ways that separate useful ideas might be combined.

V (View the likely consequences and select a promising alternative): The primary task associated with this step is the consideration of possible solutions in terms of their associated likelihood for being effective in realizing goals. Each of the alternatives listed might be ranked according to the likelihood that the potential solution, if carried out, will be successful. The approach viewed as most likely to produce desired outcomes is then selected.

E (Establish and implement a plan): Once a decision is reached on a possible alternative to try, a plan is then generated for putting the potential solution into action. Once a plan has been formulated, it is carried out and, if necessary, refined and tried again.

S (Survey the outcomes): After trying out the selected course of action, consider whether the approach has produced the desired effect. If the desired effect has been achieved, the problem has been resolved. If the conflict has not been resolved, the process may be reentered at the third step ("L") and something different tried to produce the desired goal.

Epstein and colleagues (2002) outlined a similar approach for use with couples that involves the following: (a) reaching consensus on the problem, ideally expressed in terms of observable events or behavior; (b) generating, without accompanying evaluation, possible solutions to the problem; (c) discussing the pros and cons of possible solutions once the brainstorming process has concluded; (d) jointly deciding on the most feasible solution based on the ease with which the solution can be implemented and the likelihood that it would produce the intended results; and (e) developing a plan for implementing the solution that is satisfactory to both parties, which includes specifying the time period during which the alternative would be tried and a description of how progress will be evaluated. Within this framework, problems are identified and discussed one at a time, with large problems broken down into smaller and more manageable problems. Both parties must agree to avoid blaming or becoming fixated on past events and to focus on the problem as a source of distress rather than the persons involved.

Assertiveness Skills

A central objective of assertiveness training is the removal of barriers to open self-expression, primarily by learning how to express preferences, rights, needs, emotions, and desires in a manner that that maintains self-respect while demonstrating respect for the rights or dignity of other persons (Alberti & Emmons, 1990; Dow, 1994; Linehan, 1993a). Assertiveness is distinguished from passivity (e.g., when a person allows his or her rights or dignity to be ignored or violated by another person) and aggressiveness (e.g., when a person's interactions with others involve standing up for his or her rights or dignity while simultaneously disrespecting the rights or dignity of others). Practicing assertion not only facilitates skill building, it also appears to reduce anticipatory anxiety or counter negative self-statements that would otherwise inhibit attempts at effective social behavior (Dow, 1994; Sanchez & Lewinsohn, 1980).

Components of Assertive Behavior

Exhibit 7.4 lists behaviors that are typically targeted for strengthening or weakening in the development of assertiveness skills (Alberti & Emmons, 1990; Dow, 1994). When working on these behaviors with a client, emphasis is placed on the effectiveness of such behavior in social exchanges rather than on the correct form of the behavior.

EXHIBIT 7.4
Examples of Common Behavioral Targets in Assertiveness Training

Nonverbal Behaviors

Targeted for strengthening: smiles, relaxed forehead, eye contact (if tendency to is look down or away); appropriate hand gestures, posture (e.g., that conveys confidence and equality), nonverbal behaviors that convey attentiveness and focus on the other.

Targeted for weakening: overt indicators of anxiety (e.g., fidgeting, trembling), uncomfortable eye contact (e.g., persistent and accompanied by tense facial expressions), nonverbal behavior that is incongruent with speech content, intimidating posture (e.g., that conveys dominance or superiority).

Verbal Behaviors

Targeted for strengthening:
- *Features of verbal communication:* confident voice tone and volume, calm and deliberate expressive styles, use of appropriate speech inflections, talking time (if tendency is to say very little), verbal fluency (e.g., smooth and relaxed speech flow with few hesitations or pauses).
- *Content of verbal communication:* summaries or paraphrases of what others have communicated, clear and to-the-point descriptions or accounts, saying "no" or refusing inappropriate requests, appeals for change that convey respect for others, statements that seek clarification or more information, expressions of personal experiences (e.g., emotions, interests, preferences) and "I" statements, expressions of opinions or views, protests of unfair treatment or criticisms, negotiation and compromise skills, questions directed to others about their personal experiences, prosocial statements (e.g., those that convey caring, concern, support, affirmation, or a willingness to provide aid or support), giving and receiving complements, positively toned statements (e.g., about other persons or events), honesty.

Targeted for weakening:
- *Features of verbal communication:* speech pauses and latencies, dropping voice volume at the end of a sentence or not finishing a sentence, mumbling, complaining or whining, yelling or raising one's voice in a threatening manner.
- *Content of verbal communication:* self-enhancing statements made at the expense of others; coercive or threatening statements; put-downs, accusations, or invalidating statements; judgments or critical evaluations of others; mind-reading statements; inappropriate self-disclosures that substantially exceed the level of depth or intimacy present in the relationship; statements that connote self-denial or self-deprecation; comments that suggest an unwavering willingness to accommodating others' needs at one's own expense.

Components of Assertiveness Training

Dow (1985) and Duckworth (2003) outline steps in assertiveness training:

- *Provide a rationale for assertiveness training,* with emphasis placed on achieving relationship goals while respecting the rights and dignity of others.

- *Discuss the distinguishing features associated with passivity, aggressiveness, and assertiveness.*
- *Review guidelines for assertive self-expression* (e.g., requests are reasonable and specific; behavioral alternatives are proposed when requesting change in behavior by others; matter-of-fact statements of how behaviors requested for change affect the speaker, and how changes in these behavior might beneficially impact the relationship).
- *Identify behavioral targets for strengthening and weakening* (Exhibit 7.4).
- *Identify common situations in the client's life when acting assertively is a particular challenge.* This includes interaction with specific people (e.g., parents, spouse, boss, strangers) or features of particular circumstances (e.g., asking for help, expressing an opinion that is different from others, expressing personal preferences or needs) associated with difficulty in acting assertively.
- *Conduct within-session role-plays* that involve teaching and shaping assertive behavior through direct instruction, coaching, modeling, and the provision of performance feedback.
- *Continue to practice assertive behavior* between sessions through homework assignments. Such assignments ideally are graded in terms of the level of associated challenge and are consistent with the client's current skill level. Assertiveness exercises in between sessions can be performed in vivo or in imagination. Imaginary exercises allow one to "test out" several possible behavioral alternatives in a situation, thus increasing the likelihood of skillful performance when the situation actually occurs (Lewinsohn, Muñoz, Youngren, & Zeiss, 1978). Exercises in imagination, for example, can begin with visualizing a specific situation and other persons who are a part of it. The scene might first be imaged as a photograph that eventually turns into a movie in which the client acts assertively, followed by a response from another person in the scene. After the imaging exercise, clients could be asked to evaluate their level of comfort and skill in executing the assertive behavior, and likelihood that such behavior will be effective if carried out in similar real-life situations.
- *Evaluate the effectiveness of assertive behavior* when performed and *identify remaining challenges to acting assertively.* This step includes reinforcement for the client's efforts and for successive approximations to skillful performance (e.g., via natural expressions of praise and encouragement).

When helping clients practice assertion in relation to a specific situation, such as making requests of others, a framework similar to the following is usually suggested (Alberti & Emmons, 1990; Dow, 1994; Linehan, 1993a):

- *Describe the situation.* When requesting change, describe in objective terms what has happened or is happening. Descriptions are fact-based and free from judgment, blame, or criticism.
- *Talk about how you feel in relation to the problem.* Rather than complain about the other person's behavior, it is usually more effective to communicate how the other's actions affect one personally.
- *Do not make assumptions or mind read.* Don't make assumptions that others already know what you want or need (e.g., "I shouldn't have to ask you—you should know"). Similarly, don't assume the motives behind other's actions. Ask instead.
- *Ask for specific behavior change that is reasonable and respectful of the rights and dignity of others.* Clearly describe how one would prefer the other to act in a particular situation. The likelihood of getting what one wants is greater if one is clear and concise, with descriptions based on observable behaviors rather than presumed personality traits (e.g., it is more effective to say, "I would like you to pick up your clothes off the floor" rather than "I would like you to be less of a slob"). The request should not place an undo burden on the other person and should be consistent with the level of depth or intimacy currently present in the relationship.
- *Skillfully listen.* This involves the use of listening skills described earlier to communicate attentiveness and understanding. When listening, remain focused on the interaction, and refrain from getting distracted or pulled into an argument. Convey confidence by using appropriate eye contact and a firm voice tone. Do not look away, fiddle with your fingers, mumble, or trail off at the end of sentences. Ask for clarification or additional information if what the other person is saying is unclear.
- *Negotiate and compromise.* Convey a willingness to give a little to get part of what you want. Explore possible alternatives that would be agreeable to both parties. Look for a workable solution if a compromise cannot be reached (e.g., "Let's do it my way this time, your way next time"). If an agreement cannot be reached, agree to disagree without challenging the wisdom or validity of either perspective.

- *Reward people who respond positively when asked to do something.* Compliment others on what they do that you like. Doing so reduces defensiveness and conveys important information about alternative behaviors that are positively regarded (e.g., "Thank you for listening and taking my request seriously").

BEHAVIORAL EXCESSES

When clients express concern about something that they are doing "too much," they are likely describing behavioral excesses. *Behavioral excesses* are characterized by repeated displays of particular forms of behavior that are excessive in frequency, intensity, or duration and associated with significant distress or impairment in functioning. Behavioral excesses often occur under motivational conditions (or establishing operations) associated with stress, anger, anxiety, or depression and are usually linked to strong and immediate reinforcers that follow such behaviors (Wulfert, Greenway, & Dougher, 1996).

Many of the dysfunctional behavioral excesses that take place in relationship contexts include displays of anger, coercive behaviors and threats, opposition and defiance, aggression, attention seeking, and dependency-related behaviors. These behaviors typically occur at high strength because they produce short-term reinforcing outcomes (e.g., compliance with demands, reduction of acute distress), even though their more distal consequences are often punitive or unpleasant (e.g., relationship discord or dissolution, arrest). In the following sections, we touch on several of these behavioral excesses and the behavioral interventions that have demonstrated efficacy for weakening these behaviors. As will be evident, many interventions for behavioral excesses involve identifying establishing operations and the short-term reinforcers that maintain such behaviors and lessening or eliminating their influence.

Regulating the Expression of Anger

Problems in self-control and emotion dysregulation are often central features of relationship discord or interpersonal ineffectiveness (Benson et al., 2012). High emotional intensity, mood liability, and perceptions of others as rejecting, invalidating, or malevolent are often associated with emotional outbursts dominated by anger and possibly loss of control. The emotion of anger receives special attention in this section because it is perhaps the primary emotion associated with relationship discord, acts of aggression, and rejection by others. Readers are also referred to Chapter 10 for coverage of additional intervention techniques that promote emotion regulation.

Conceptualizing Anger in the Interpersonal Context

Anger is a normal emotional reaction to frustrations, insults, fearful situations, and unfair or unjust treatment. The experience of anger is neither "good" nor "bad." The emotion can convey important information and motivate a course of corrective action. What we become angry about and how we overtly conduct ourselves when angry are, in part, socially constructed scripts that we have learned to perform as a result of our reinforcement history (Kassinove & Tafrate, 2002). Dysfunctional displays of anger that harm relationships can therefore be changed.

Frequent anger episodes often suggest *a skills deficit*, particularly in relation to stress coping, emotion regulation, frustration tolerance, and response inhibition. Other skills deficits might be evident, such as language deficits or deficits in other expressive skills that, in turn, produce frustration related to problems in self-expression. Correspondingly, many of the intervention elements for anger episodes described in this section involve skills training. Anger may also reflect a *natural consequence associated with loss*, such as the death of a loved one, the loss of ability due to a health-related problem, or loss of resources such as money or housing. When loss or impoverished environments are primarily associated with frustration and anger, therapy might also include intervention elements that are focused on grieving, restoring losses, or broadening environmental opportunities for reinforcement (e.g., by strengthening social networks, as discussed in more detail later in the chapter).

Anger is sometimes regarded as a *secondary emotion*, or a reaction to other emotions and the circumstances that occasion them. Often, clients will report the experience of certain intense emotions before the experience of anger, such as anxiety, fear, frustration, loss, shame, worthlessness, or powerlessness. Fear, for example, might be the emotional response associated with the anticipation of some aversive event, with anger being the response to the event's occurrence. Assessments of anger would ideally include an evaluation of possible emotion-related antecedents that, in turn, could be targeted for intervention along with other contextual factors associated with anger-related behaviors. Primary emotions tightly linked to the experience of anger, for example, might be an object of intervention, as progress in dealing effectively with those responses will also likely produce desirable effects with respect to anger.

Chronic or trait-like experiences of anger can also be a sign of additional problem areas, such as a personality disorder (e.g., narcissistic, borderline, antisocial, paranoid), posttraumatic stress disorder, a substance use disorder, chronic pain, or ineffective coping with stress. A careful client assessment around the experience of anger would ideally examine these possibilities because each has relevance for informing decisions about the most efficacious approach for dealing with anger-related issues (e.g., for those with moderate to severe substance abuse, the initial therapeutic focus might be on substance-related interventions or detoxification because progress in these areas might also have beneficial effects on anger expression).

Dodge (1991) also offered a useful distinction between two types of anger-aggression episodes, reactive and proactive. Whereas *reactive aggression* refers to aggressive acts that are associated with high levels of emotional activation, *proactive aggression* refers to aggressive acts that are primarily carried out to produce instrumental outcomes (e.g., to terminate something experienced as aversive or to obtain something that is rewarding). Persons who characteristically exhibit proactive aggression often seek to intimidate through their actions and, correspondingly, have histories of reinforcement for overt displays of anger, aggression, opposition, or coercion. Behaviors that generally fall under Dodge's proactive aggression label are dealt with in later sections of this chapter. Individuals who are more prone to reactive aggression often have difficulty controlling or regulating anger, resulting in escalations of conflict, outbursts of temper, and poorly controlled actions. Persons who exhibit this type of aggression are more inclined to see others as threatening, hostile or dangerous. Anger episodes associated with reactive aggression are more likely to be negatively reinforced than positively reinforced because angry outbursts usually function to ward off perceived threats or to restore balance to a situation. Individuals whose experience falls under this latter category are the primary focus of this section.

Functional Analyses of Anger Episodes

When performing functional analyses of anger episodes, it is often easiest to start with assessments of the relevant *target behaviors* and then move on to the identification of triggers and associated behavioral consequences. The construct of anger consists of a collection of responses that reliably covary, including the following:

- *Physiological and emotional responses:* Sympathetic nervous system activation, heart palpitations, elevated blood pressure, sweating, shaking and trembling, muscle tension, other related emotions (e.g., annoyance, irritation, frustration, rage, resentment).
- *Cognitive and verbal responses:* Use of "angry" words (e.g., profanity, words that convey hatred or threats), arguing, shouting or screaming, hostile verbal statements directed at others, blaming or accusatory statements, sarcasm, thoughts that exaggerate the significance of certain events (e.g., "Since I didn't get admitted to Princeton, my life's going to be a failure!"), appraisals of a situation as threatening, thoughts that externalize the source

of one's difficulties to others, perceived attacks against one's self-worth, distorted thoughts in which others' actions are seen as motivated by a desire to cause harm or pain.

- *Motor behavior:* Agitated movements, harsh facial expressions, leaning toward someone to intimidate, pointing fingers or clinching fists, throwing objects, knocking items over, pushing or shoving others, physically striking someone, acts of deliberate self-harm.

Because not all clients will have the same behavioral profile across anger episodes, it is often useful to take time to develop a detailed behavioral summary of such episodes with reference to the specific behaviors exhibited within the three response domains. Outcomes from such a careful analysis might provide useful information for matching clients to intervention options. Interventions that target physiological arousal (e.g., relaxation training), for example, appear to be more helpful for producing change in state anger rather than trait anger (Del Vecchio & O'Leary, 2004).

When assessing *antecedents* or triggers associated with anger episodes, it is important to focus on both internal and external events related to the anger episode (e.g., recollections of persons or events to which anger is attributed; actions of others that preceded anger episodes). Across persons and cultures, anger episodes tend to occur most commonly in relation to unexpected actions by significant others (Kassinove & Tafrate, 2002), although anger triggered by internal events is also common (e.g., when coming into contact with trauma-related memories, sensations, and emotions).

Anger can also function as an *establishing operation* or trigger for a range of behaviors that are themselves problematic, such as acts of intimidation, retaliation, revenge, or attack. When conducting functional analyses of anger episodes, then, it is also useful to examine whether other dysfunctional behaviors are more likely when the client is in an angry emotional state. When anger is an establishing operation for such behaviors, one might expect that the targeting of anger directly in therapy will result in reductions in these associated behaviors.

The identification of the *consequences* that anger episodes produce can be aided by a consideration of other contextual features within which such episodes are embedded. Anger episodes, for example, might have a primary communication function (e.g., a threat of retaliation in response to an external threat). They are essentially the "fight" or approach response repertoire associated with the familiar fight–flight–freeze response system (Gray & McNaughton, 2000). If anger episodes are successful in warding-off or neutralizing external threats, they become negatively reinforced behaviors that become more probable in the future. Similarly, anger expression might also have a relieving or tension-reduction function. If anger episodes are successful in "blowing off steam" or result in reductions in aversive physiological reactions associated sympathetic nervous system activation, they can be expected to become more frequent in the future given their relieving (negatively reinforcing) associated qualities.

Thus, anger episodes are usually functional behavior in the short term because they can be instrumental in producing relief or removing adversity from the environment. In the long run, however, they can be dysfunctional, as repeated and unpredictable anger episodes often result in the withdrawal of social supports, problems in the workplace and within families, increased risk for physically aggressive acts, and negative health-related consequences (e.g., heart disease).

Elements of Anger Management Interventions

Cognitive behavior therapies for anger have been associated with moderate to large improvements in a variety of client populations (Del Vecchio & O'Leary, 2004; DiGuiseppe & Tafrate, 2003; Sukhodolsky, Kassinove, & Gorman, 2004). These reviews further suggest that benefits derived from therapy are generally maintained over a follow-up period. Several of the interpersonal effectiveness interventions we have described are common components of behavioral interventions for anger, including communication skills training, interpersonal problem solving, and assertiveness training. We now describe other therapy components commonly used to facilitate anger regulation (Kassinove & Tafrate, 2002; Novaco & Jarvis, 2002).

Psychoeducation and Establishing a Motivation to Change. Clients are provided with information about the association between stress and anger, the multifaceted nature of the anger response, and the association between anger and aggression. Although anger is often characterized as a normal and potentially useful emotion, the deleterious effects of angry outbursts and aggression on relationships are emphasized. Because of the short-term reinforcing properties often associated with anger episodes, time is taken to explore whether such episodes comport with longer-term plans or goals, or one's values with respect to relationships.

Self-Monitoring. Components of self-monitoring include the self-recording of contextual elements associated with anger episodes, including antecedents or triggers (e.g., "What happened? What was the triggering event?"), emotion intensity (e.g., "On a scale from 0 to 100, how angry were you?"), the overt expression of anger (e.g., "What did you say? What did you do?"), the outcomes or consequences associated with anger expression (e.g., "Was the way I expressed my anger effective? If so, how? Were there any negative consequences associated with how I showed my anger?"), and ideas for handling similar situations in the future should they arise again (e.g., "If I didn't effectively manage my anger this time, what might I do next time that would be more effective?").

Within-Session Functional Analyses of Anger Episodes. Self-monitoring forms such as those just described can provide insight into the functional aspects of anger episodes, as well as potentially effective alternative behaviors that the client might try on future occasions. Functional analyses might also be conducted within sessions to elicit even greater detail about significant outbursts that occurred between sessions. In addition to the information collected from self-monitoring assessments, within-session functional analyses might also emphasize the following:

- The identification of *anger–behavior links*, which includes action urges when angry even if not acted out (e.g., "I want to punch someone so bad"; "I really, really, want to cut myself when I get mad").
- *Complex behavioral chains*, which include the identification of experiences that precede anger that, in turn, set the occasion for anger episodes. These chain analyses might identify behavior sequences that culminate in anger episodes, in which earlier behaviors in the chain function as discriminative stimuli for later behaviors in the sequence (e.g., primary emotions such as anxiety or shame "trigger" the secondary emotion of anger).
- The identification *"rules" related to the cause or expression of anger* (e.g., "When I get angry, there's nothing I can do to stay in control"; "It's other people's fault when I get angry").
- A *careful and in-depth analysis of consequences*, including those that are reinforcing and punishing and immediate and delayed. In the history of the species, anger has had functional value in promoting survival (Buss, 1990); hence, it is critically important that the therapist attend to possible positive or negative reinforcing consequences that maintain current anger episodes. In particular, it is important to assess the usual actions of others after the client's anger displays (e.g., leave the situation, give into client's demands) as well as changes in the client's internal experiences after such episodes (e.g., a sense of relief or tension reduction, a sense of mastery or control as a result of effecting another's behavior). Ideally, such an examination would also include a weighing of the costs versus benefits of holding onto an angry response style in the future. An exploration of behavioral alternatives that might produce the same reinforcing consequences of anger episodes but without associated harmful consequences might also be undertaken.

Avoidance of or Separation From Anger-Evoking Situations. Cue elimina-tion is a stimulus control technique that behavior therapists often use when problematic behavior reliably occurs in the presence of certain antecedents or triggers. The rationale of this technique is that anger episodes will be less likely when one avoids cues that occasion the emotion's occurrence. Avoid-ing situations that elicit anger or removing oneself from situations in which anger is experienced not only lessen the likelihood of anger episodes but also productively use the informational component that anger provides. If leav-ing a situation when angry is not possible, it is often desirable to insert delays before responding or to walk to another part of a room and return only when the anger has subsided.

Identification and Use of Alternative Behaviors When Angry. Functional analyses or problem-solving exercises can yield ideas for behavioral alterna-tives that can be used when angry. These ideas, in turn, can be listed on "anger options" cards that provide suggestions for alternative behaviors in cer-tain situations, including the use of skills emphasized in recent sessions. The use of *coping self-statements* for preparing or responding to situations that occa-sion anger, for example, are common in anger management programs (e.g., Novaco, 1975; Tafrate & Kassinove, 1998). Self-statements are verbal guides that one can say to oneself, either overtly or covertly, in situations in which anger might be experienced. These self-statements, which can be listed on laminated cards that can be carried in a wallet or purse, include those associ-ated with the preparation for provocation (e.g., "This is going to upset me, but I know how to deal with it"; "I can work out a plan to handle this."), reacting during the confrontation (e.g., "Just roll with the punches and don't get bent out of shape"; "You don't need to prove yourself"), coping with anger-related arousal (e.g., "Slow my breathing down and take deep breaths"; "I can handle this situation calmly"), and reflecting on the experience (e.g., "I was pretty effective in handling the situation"; "I like the way I responded this time").

Perspective Taking. Perspective taking is a particularly useful approach for persons who have a tendency to blame others while minimizing their own responsibilities in conflicts (Day, Howells, Mohr, Schall, & Gerace, 2008). By considering a situation from another's point of view, the oppor-tunity exists to alter perceptions of factors associated with the provocation of anger, thus lessening the subjective experience of anger and increasing opportunities for more adaptive responding. Among the interventions that promote perspective taking is the *empty-chair technique*, initially a Gestalt therapy intervention, which has been adapted to increase self-awareness and expand understanding from another's frame of reference (Day et al., 2008). This method can be adapted to include in the "empty chair" a significant other who is not physically present or conflicting aspects of one's own experi-ences that are difficult to reconcile.

Role-Plays and Exposure-Based Interventions. Within-session role-plays might seek to recreate significant anger episodes, with the therapist assuming the role of an interpersonal anger trigger and the client demonstrating his or her response to the trigger. This is a particularly useful approach for skills assessment and for trying out alternative coping behaviors. Such role-plays can also function as a form of exposure that can aid in the identification of various anger-related responses, including primary emotions that precede anger outbursts. For clients who demonstrate skills deficits, role-reversal role-plays might be attempted in which the therapist assumes role of the client, and the client acts out the interpersonal triggers. This approach facilitates perspective taking and offers the opportunity for observational learning by watching the therapist enact skillful alternatives.

Interventions that emphasize exposure components also appear to hold promise as useful adjuncts to other behavioral techniques in the treatment of anger (Brondolo, DiGiuseppe, & Tafrate, 1997; Tafrate & Kassinove, 1998). The purpose of this approach is to expose individuals to anger triggers under controlled conditions while limiting the range of anger-related expressions and, consequently, accompanying reinforcers for overt displays of anger. With repeated exposures, associations between triggers and anger-related reactions subside, thus allowing for the testing of alternative response options (e.g., coping self-statements; see Tafrate & Kassinove, 1998).

Kassinove and Tafrate's (2002) application of exposure for anger-related problems include the exposure to specific statements referred to as *verbal barbs*. Verbal barbs are specific words or brief verbal statements that are used during exposure sessions as proxies for anger triggers that are relevant to a particular client. In presenting the barbs in an exposure-like context, the initial goal is to reduce the client's reaction (intensity, duration) to the barb statement. When implementing this procedure, it is important that the client understands that the overall purpose of these exercises is to reduce the intensity of the experience of anger and to learn how to respond to trigger events in a more calm and controlled manner. Kassinove and Tafrate stressed caution in using this procedure with clients who have significant histories of assaultive behavior, psychopathy, or antisocial behavior traits.

Letting Go of Anger Tied to Past Events. For many with long-standing anger-related problems, the source of ongoing anger resides in past events. The past events become "current" through the repetitive thoughts about these events and their associated emotions that, in turn, increase vulnerability to acting-out reactions related to the past in one's current environments. Various strategies have been developed for weakening the influence of thoughts about the past on current behavior, including perspective taking (e.g., develop a theory or understanding of another's offensive behavior, and how his or her personal history might have contributed to this behavior), an analysis of pros and cons of holding onto past anger, the cultivation of a "present" or "forward" mind-set over a "backward" mind-set, and radical acceptance (Linehan, 1993a). To let go of grudges also means that one relinquishes the active desire for retribution, revenge, or some attempt at rectification by the source of the anger, and perhaps transitioning from the self-view of oneself as a victim to that of a survivor.

Develop Regular Rhythm. Anger and irritability are sometimes a part of a symptom constellation associated with the bipolar disorders. During the early stages of assessment, it is important to rule out bipolar disorders, as a positive bipolar diagnosis would suggest a different type of intervention. Because people who have difficulties in regulating their anger often have more general problems with self- and emotion-regulation (Benca et al., 2009), some of the techniques used in the treatment of bipolar disorder, primarily those that promote mood stability, may have relevance in the treatment of people with anger control issues. In particular, interventions that work to establish lifestyle balance, regular routines, and consistent rhythms may be particularly pertinent (e.g., Frank et al., 2005). The establishment of balance and regular social routines may, in turn, promote circadian rhythm stability and corresponding reductions in vulnerability to affective episodes.

Coercive, Oppositional, and Defiant Behavior

Coercive, oppositional, and defiant tendencies are common behavioral features associated with the externalizing domain of psychopathology (Farmer, Seeley, Kosty, & Lewinsohn, 2009; Witkiewitz et al., 2013). Although disorders associated with these tendencies are usually first identified in childhood, there is ample evidence that features of these conditions persist into adulthood (e.g., Kimonis & Frick, 2010; Reimherr, Marchant, Olsen, Wender, & Robison, 2013). A social-interactional perspective on the histories of persons with externalizing disorders suggests that ineffective parenting is central to the development of coercive and oppositional tendencies (G. R. Patterson, DeBaryshe, & Ramsey, 1989). Most problematic in the learning histories of persons with these tendencies is the noncontingent awarding of reinforcers and punishers for a broad range of behavior, from prosocial to deviant. A portion of the reinforcement for coercive behavior is in the form of positive reinforcement (e.g., sibling and parental attention). Most of the reinforcement associated with the development and strengthening of coercive behavioral repertoires, however, occurs in the context escape or avoidance contingencies (G. R. Patterson et al., 1989). Disruptive behaviors (e.g., shouting, verbal threats) used by youth in these latter situations function to terminate unwanted intrusions by family members and, when effective, become negatively reinforced behaviors. Over time, coercive family processes escalate in frequency and intensity, often resulting in increasingly more aggressive forms of behavior (e.g., tantrums, throwing objects, physical aggression directed against others). In this process, not only are coercive processes and disruptive behaviors reinforced, prosocial behaviors are either underdeveloped or drop out of the youth's behavioral repertoire as a result of the family's failure to respond consistently to such behaviors with positive reinforcement.

Adults whose social development occurred in a context where coercive family processes were reinforced are likely to apply the same behavioral scripts in current relationships, within which members of a relationship dyad become aversive stimuli for each other over time. Consider, for example, the following exchange between a married couple (based on G. R. Patterson & Hops, 1972):

> Wife: Would you please go to the grocery store today? Can't you see we're just about out of everything?
>
> Husband: (Ignores wife's request, and continues to watch television)
>
> Wife: Do you expect me to do everything around here so you can sit on your ass all day and watch TV?
>
> Husband: Would you please just shut up? I'm trying to watch the damn game!
>
> Wife: All you do is watch TV while I clean up after you. Are you a damn child?
>
> Husband: Fine. I'll go to the store after the game. Give me some peace so I can watch the game!

Each exchange in this scenario includes an element of conflict. Also, it is likely that each element in this exchange reflects previously reinforced behavior. The wife, for example, may have learned over time that insulting and shouting at her husband is the only way to get him to comply with her requests (positive reinforcement for making requests accompanied by hostility). The husband, in turn, has likely learned that vague promises of compliance will cause the aversive insults and shouting from the wife to stop (and is thus negatively reinforced behavior when successful).

Another common form of exchange in coercive relationships, the attack–counterattack reinforcing sequence, also involves negative reinforcement processes associated with escape or avoidance. In this sequence, one member of the dyad demands compliance with an intrusive request (i.e., attack; e.g., "Go fix me some dinner!"). In turn, the other member of the dyad responds with dysfunctional behavior to escape the request (i.e., counterattack; e.g., "Hell no!" followed by a shove to move the other person away), to which the requester responds by supporting (strengthening) the aggressive avoidance behavior of the partner (i.e., a counter to the counterattack; "Fine. I'll make it myself! Your cooking sucks anyway!"). As illustrated in this exchange, the "Hell no!" reply accompanied by shoving are negatively reinforced by the withdrawal of the request to make dinner. The requester's escape behavior (withdrawal of request) is also negatively reinforced, as it results in the de-escalation of the partner's aversive behavior (i.e., yelling and shoving both cease). Because this behavior sequence resulted in termination of aversive behavior of both members of the dyad (i.e., is negatively reinforced for both members), this pattern of exchange is likely to be replicated on future occasions, as well as the escalation of intensity of coercive actions. These modes of interpersonal exchange in conjunction with a host of accompanying aversive verbal behaviors (e.g., put-downs, criticisms, disagreements, disapproval, blaming) and aggressive physical actions (e.g., pushing, shouting, door slamming, object throwing) are common in distressed relationships.

Demonstrations of anger and hostility in social exchanges like those illustrated in the couple's dialogue are often functional because they produce short-term change in another's behavior. Specifically, anger episodes in such instances are instrumental in unblocking obstacles in the way of realizing one's own goals in a given situation. Parents who have tried time-out procedures to reduce the frequency of their child's disruptive behavior have no doubt encountered the *extinction burst*, characterized by tantrums and refusal behavior when reinforcers previously supplied following such behavior are no longer available. In such instances, displays of anger, threats, or intimidation might be used to reinstate the previous reinforcing contingencies (i.e., coercion), in which the implicit (or explicit) message is, "If you do what I want you to do, then I will stop yelling and not carry out my threats." This tactic often works (i.e., is reinforced) because expression of inappropriate anger in this manner is often effective in getting others to comply with demands. Displays of anger consequently become more likely in the future because of their effectiveness in producing rewarding outcomes.

More generally, family environments characterized by high levels of expressed emotion (most importantly, anger and hostility) are risk factors for a variety of psychological disorders and for relapse among persons who have previously recovered (e.g., Butzlaff & Hooley, 1998; Tompson et al., 2010). Intervention effectiveness and a reduced likelihood for future relapse are enhanced when families move from high to low expressed emotion (Butzlaff & Hooley, 1998; Miklowitz et al., 2009).

Following is a list of components of interventions for reducing oppositional and defiant behaviors. Several of the interventions already described, such as communication skills training, assertiveness training, and interpersonal problem solving, have relevance for altering coercive and oppositional behavioral tendencies. Additional interventions that are especially pertinent include the following.

- *Motivational enhancement.* Behavioral excesses are especially difficult to change because several reinforcement processes usually maintain them. As a result, some mental health practitioners have suggested that behavioral problems maintained by reinforcement should be treated, in part, with therapeutic strategies that specifically address a client's ambivalence or a desire to change problematic behaviors (e.g., motivational interviewing; see Chapter 3). Such an exploration might include an analysis of the pros versus cons of ongoing interpersonal conflicts and relationship discord. The pros in this instance would include the noticing of the short-term reinforcing effects that such behavior produces, and the cons would include the identification of behaviors or behavior chains that are experienced as aversive and detrimental to relationships in the long run. Such an analysis highlights the discrepancies between the type of life the client wants and the life the client currently has related to his or her behavior problems. Engaging in such an analysis also increases the client's "change talk," or time devoted to talking about behavior change that, in turn, can be positively reinforced naturally by the therapist. Reinforcement of change talk not only increases statements about behavior change but also orients the client to behavioral alternatives and taking action. The analysis of pros and cons might therefore be followed by an exploration of reasons for change and the possible benefits that might accompany change.
- *Functional analyses.* Research on basic learning processes suggests that attention to or awareness of response consequences is necessary to alter behavior originally established under reinforcement conditions (C. M. Patterson & Newman, 1993; Spielberger & DeNike, 1966). Among those with oppositional tendencies, there is often a mismatch between a behavior's perceived function (i.e., a client's hypotheses concerning the effects of his or her behavior) and the actual consequences of behavior (i.e., how the environment responds). For these reasons, it is often critically important to conduct an in-depth functional analysis of problematic interpersonal behavior that includes an identification of reinforcers and undesirable outcomes that accompany current actions. In addition to the reinforcing consequences noted earlier, therapists might consider the role of other possible positive

reinforcers that maintain coercive and oppositional behavior, including attention from others or a sense of mastery or control that results from seeing others adjust their behavior in response to one's own actions.

■ *Weakening of coercive control practices and strengthening prosocial behavior.* Therapy involving oppositional and coercive relationships, whenever possible, should target the environment that supports such practices. Coercive interpersonal environments are often overly aversive and punitive and likely to shape and maintain behaviors that are characterized by mistrust, anger, fear, avoidance, and caution. If coercion exists within a committed relationship, the focus might be on the behavior of both members of the dyad because each person's behavior constitutes an important component of the larger environment within which coercive processes occur. Family, martial, or couples cognitive behavior therapy has been shown to be effective in reducing relationship distress and enhancing relationship satisfaction (e.g., Carr, 2002; Epstein et al., 2002). Jacobson and colleagues (Jacobson & Christensen, 1998; Jacobson & Margolin, 1979), for example, provided detailed descriptions of behavioral couple therapy techniques, and Benson et al. (2012) reviewed research on the efficacy of these interventions.

In addition to the reinforcing behavior sequences that maintain coercive and oppositional behavior, skills deficits might also be important considerations for some persons. Refusal and defiance might actually indicate the presence of a skills deficit. For some, it is easier to angrily refuse to do something than to acknowledge one does not understand or know how to do it. When self-expression skills are deficit, role-plays coupled with performance feedback might be helpful in teaching clients to appropriately ask for what they want (e.g., "I would appreciate it if . . ."; "Would you be willing to . . . ?"). Abusive communications might similarly signal deficits in basic communication skills that, in turn, could be remedied with skills training in this area as well as assertiveness training and interpersonal problem solving.

High rates of coercion and hostility are often associated with low rates of prosocial behaviors, perhaps because prosocial skills were not consistently supported early in one's development (G. R. Patterson et al., 1989). Prosocial behaviors include those that involve helping, sharing, comforting, and cooperating (Scourfield, John, Martin, & McGuffin, 2004). Coercive relations can be undermined, in part, by the introduction and strengthening of behaviors that promote greater equality in relationships characterized by mutual and equitable long-term reinforcement. At the most basic level, positive reinforcement can be substitute for threat of punishment for carrying out certain behaviors (e.g., one member of the relationship dyad might demonstrate approval and gratitude for the other's behavior of cleaning the dishes in lieu of threats, shaming statements, or yelling as a means to foster compliance).

Finally, it may be that conflicts are resolved to only a limited degree and that therapeutic work might pivot to an examination of whether modest change is acceptable or whether a separation from or dissolution of the relationship might be the most beneficial. In our experience, there is a tendency for persons whose relationships with significant others are characterized by conflict to also have relationships with others that are characterized by discord. Consequently, it would be important to examine the possible reinforcing properties associated with perpetual relationship conflicts as well as underlying skills deficits. History of violence within interpersonal relationships should also be evaluated. When interpersonal violence is a feature of current relationships, interventions designed to enhance the quality of relationships or interpersonal effectiveness are likely contraindicated. In such instances, individual therapy focused on violent behavior is a necessary prerequisite.

The therapeutic environment is a potentially fertile ground for shaping and developing more effective forms of behavior, including interpersonal behaviors. Individuals with histories of externalizing disorders often have had poor social bonding experiences (e.g., harsh and inconsistent parental discipline, little positive involvement by parents early in life, poor monitoring and supervision of the activities when a child) that continue to influence current relationships (Hurtig et al., 2007; G. R. Patterson et al., 1989). Consequently, for some, the function of oppositional behavior might constitute a test of the therapist's commitment to the therapeutic relationship and implicitly convey the questions, "Do you care enough about me to put up with this?" or "Will you ever leave me?" As a result, therapists might anticipate some displays of defiance, opposition, and revolt, including frequent last-minute cancelations, showing up late for sessions, not completing tasks in between sessions, refusal to work cooperatively with the therapist during a session, or introducing crises at the end of a session. Rules for how such situations will be responded to are ideally shared with the client in advance. Whenever possible, the therapist might work to anticipate efforts on the client's part to engage in rule breaking and to take active steps to prevent such attempts from happening (e.g., by noting early in the therapeutic relationship that either party can request an examination of the therapeutic relationship should the behavior of either interfere with the therapeutic process).

In Chapter 11, we detail several strategies for responding to problematic client behavior, and we only touch on a few considerations here when working with oppositional adult clients. Like other behavior therapists (e.g., Linehan, 1993a), we also regard treatment-interfering behaviors as high-priority treatment targets that, when evident, provide opportunities to use interpersonal effectiveness skills with the therapist in vivo and to receive supportive coaching and feedback related to their implementation.

As frequently as is feasible, the therapist should look for and positively respond to instances of prosocial or effective interpersonal behaviors as they occur within the therapeutic setting and naturally reinforce these after they occur (e.g., "I like it when you . . ."). Reinforcing appropriate interpersonal behavior within sessions has at least two functions. First, for those with skills deficits, differential reinforcement of effective interpersonal behavior helps clients learn alternative behaviors that might be more appropriate or effective both within and outside of the therapy setting. Second, for those with histories in which inappropriate interpersonal behavior has been reinforced, differential reinforcement of positive interpersonal behavior coupled with the ignoring of inappropriate behavior can facilitate a behavioral shift to the rewarded alternatives. When using differential reinforcement procedures within sessions, it is important for the therapist to be clear and consistent concerning which target behaviors to reinforce and which to ignore. A smaller set of targets is preferable to a larger set, at least initially. Ideally, reinforcers should be a natural part of the therapist's behavioral repertoire (e.g., warm smiles, nods of approval, statements of support or empathy) and be inserted into the therapeutic context as seamlessly and naturally as possible.

Sometimes resistance is a sign that the therapeutic contract is not clear, explicit, or mutually agreed to or that the client is uncommitted to the therapeutic process. Alternatively, the process of therapy might be too painful or difficult and that resistance provides some relief. If so, the client and therapist might negotiate a less demanding course of therapy or modify the focus of therapy onto less painful or difficult areas. It is important in discussions of these matters not to blame the client for a lack of progress or accept the client's claim that the therapist is solely to blame. Instead, the therapist might try to redirect the client to the problem for which resistance is viewed as a solution and to explore other ways for responding to this problem.

Dependency-Related Behaviors

Dependency is a term often invoked to describe a pattern of interpersonal behavior characterized by passivity, suggestibility, overcompliance to the demands of others, conflict avoidance, subservience, self-doubt, and excessive help or approval seeking (Bornstein, 1993). As with most every other form of clinically significant behavior, dependent behaviors are often instrumental in producing positive or negative reinforcing outcomes in the short term but can result in relationship problems in the long run. In the short term, dependent behavior can function to produce assistance, attention, approval, support, or guidance from others (Livesley, Schroeder, & Jackson, 1990). Similarly, acts of subservience, overcompliance, and conflict avoidance may help maintain relationships in the short run, but often result in frustration and resentment over time. In more extreme instances, dependency-related behaviors compel others to enter into a caretaking role, which others may experience as aversive over time.

Initial assessments of dependency-related behaviors would ideally involve a careful exploration of the social contexts within which such behaviors are usually displayed. A key consideration during such assessments is determining whether maladaptive environmental contingencies, social skills deficits, faulty self-rules related to a low sense of mastery, or related behavioral excesses (e.g., high levels of social anxiety, intense fear of being alone) are primarily associated with such actions because this distinction has important implications for the choice of intervention approaches. Areas to explore that might clarify which of these problem areas is most central to dependency include the following:

- Are significant persons in the client's life controlling, over-protective, or insistent on obedience?
- Do others reinforce helpless behaviors?
- Is the client able to initiate and maintain relationships that are not characterized by overdependence?
- Is the client able to elicit social support through socially appropriate (nondependent) behaviors?
- Does the client endorse being unable to care for himself or herself?
- Does the client express pessimistic views about being able to produce desirable outcomes as a result of his or her decision making and associated actions?
- Is the client highly anxious in social situations?
- Does the client have a phobic-like fear of being alone?

In many instances, each of these contributing factors (maladaptive environmental contingencies, skills deficits, excess anxiety related to interpersonal contexts) will be relevant, and a multicomponent approach to therapy that addresses each of these areas might be indicated (e.g., via couples therapy, skills training, and interventions commonly used to address social anxiety or social phobias). When social skills deficits are noted, therapy might emphasize instruction in skills related to the adaptive expression of interpersonal interests and needs (e.g., conversational and assertiveness skills, appropriate self-disclosure). Skills training in these areas would ideally focus on the strengthening effective and appropriate methods for eliciting support or caring from others, increasing behaviors that are important to the maintenance of intimate relationships, and encouraging actions that facilitate greater autonomy. The client may also benefit from learning skills that promote tolerance of dependency-related emotions to address motivational factors (establishing operations) associated with dependency-related behaviors. Instruction in daily living skills may also be beneficial if such skills are deficit.

When dependent behaviors are carried out as a means to reduce anxiety (e.g., related to possible abandonment or being alone), a combination of anxiety management techniques, skills training, and graded exposure can be used to promote independent decision making and action in relevant social contexts. Situations associated with elevations in anxiety might be addressed through problem-solving procedures, particularly if uncertainty about how to respond contributes to distress.

For those with a low sense of self-mastery or skill independent of actual skill level, therapy might specifically target efficacy-related self-rules as well as additional rules that imply that others must be looked to for protection and support to survive or flourish. To facilitate autonomy and promote mastery experiences, therapeutic tasks such as behavioral experiments could be especially useful (see Chapter 5). Mastery or success resulting from such experiments might alter efficacy and outcome rules related to behavior.

Finally, because dependency-related behaviors are interpersonal behaviors, therapists must be on the watch for compliant, advice-seeking, reassurance-needing, and help-seeking behaviors. Therapists should acknowledge these behaviors when observed, withhold reinforcement for their expression, and instead naturally reward client disclosures that convey initiative, autonomy, or mastery.

ENHANCING THE QUALITY OF RELATIONSHIPS WITH OTHERS

In previous sections, we emphasized building behavioral skills when there are deficits and reducing behavioral excesses that others often find unpleasant or off-putting. In this section, we focus on strategies for enhancing relationship quality and maintaining relationships.

Increasing Psychological Flexibility

Psychological flexibility has been described as "the ability to be mindful of one's thoughts and feelings and to act in the service of one's values even when one's thoughts and feelings discourage taking valued action" (Biglan, Flay, Embry, & Sandler, 2012, p. 257). Increasing levels of psychological flexibility have been associated with decreasing levels of emotional and behavioral difficulties (Biglan et al., 2012) and reductions in negative thoughts about others (Lillis & Hayes, 2007).

On the basis of this conceptualization, there are at least three tasks or skills associated with becoming more psychologically flexible. One task is to identify and make explicit one's values. As observed by Biglan et al. (2012), people rarely value interpersonal conflict; rather, values often include pro-social aspirations, such as having friendships, close relationships, or helping and caring for others.

A second task is to cultivate a perspective in which thoughts and emotions are viewed simply as thoughts and emotions and nothing more—as transient states that repeatedly change in content and intensity. People often become engaged in ongoing struggles with their thoughts and emotions in an effort to change them. An alternative approach is to develop a detachment from them from which one can observe their transience while at the same time recognizing that there are aspects of oneself that are more temporally stable and perhaps more important, including one's values as they relate to others.

A third task is to act consistently and in accordance with one's values, even when the "feeling of the moment" is to act otherwise. Holding on to one's values in the presence of intense and disruptive thoughts or emotions can provide not only a psychological anchor of sorts, it can also provide a sense of direction that might differ from what experiences of the moment might prescribe. Thoughts related to intense acute anxiety in a large social situation involving acquaintances, for example, might emphasize the urgency of leaving the situation to gain a sense of relief. In such instances, contacting values related to the personal importance one attaches to relationships might provide a counter to the anxiety-based thoughts that, in turn, increases the likelihood of remaining in the situation and committing to actions more consistent with valued outcomes. Later in this chapter, we discuss the valuation of relationships as an organizing principle for interpersonal effectiveness. In the next section, we discuss how rigid modes of thought might contribute to psychological inflexibility that results in a style of relating to others that is not always effective or optimal.

Letting Go of Rigid Rules About Others

At times, people regard their thoughts as literal truths. They rigidly and tenaciously hold on to them and while negating information that runs counter to their content. A common effect of rigid rule adherence is inflexible behavior that is insensitive to actual environmental contingencies. Not only is rigid rule adherence associated with behavior that is not optimally effective, it can also contribute to relationship discord, particularly when rules are applied indiscriminately to a broad range of persons and become the primary guide of social interactions.

When referenced to specific persons, rules might be related to *causes of another's behavior* (e.g., whether someone's behavior is the result of an underlying personality trait or situational factors). Other rules might pertain to *the nature of relationships*, including those that guide the roles that persons adopt in their interactions with others (e.g., assumptions about dominance versus equality, entitlement versus subservience, notions of how relationships "should be"). One might hold generalized theories about *the intentions behind others' actions*, including the motives for their behavior or the outcomes they are attempting to produce (e.g., "That waiter spilled coffee on me because I didn't tip him well last time I was here."). Rules may also include *predicted outcomes of another's actions* that, in turn, have implications for one's own actions (e.g., "If I let myself get emotionally close to him, I know he'll eventually hurt me, so I don't let myself get close"). Rigid rule adherence, particularly to faulty rules, may lead not only to ineffective behavior but also to inflexible responding to dynamic situations, resulting in potentially ineffective behavior.

Rules also act as guides for how we view people (e.g., as a source of potential harm, as an object for subjugation, as a judge of our ongoing behavior and worthiness) and how we behave toward them. They are the product of our learning experiences. It is understandable, for example, that a person exposed to severe childhood adversities that include abuse or neglect would develop rules that depict people as sources or harm or pain. Because of earlier life experiences, such persons may have developed and maintained a tendency to interpret others' behavior as hostile in intent which, in turn, increases the risk for displaying aggressive or destructive interpersonal behaviors (Orobio de Castro, Veerman, Koops, Bosch, & Monshouwer, 2002). From a behavioral perspective, unwarranted suspiciousness of others' motives is often the product of faulty overgeneralized rules, inappropriate stimulus control, and, for persons with abuse or neglect histories, response generalization in which suspicious modes of thought were at one time accurate, appropriate, and adaptive but no longer have these beneficial qualities in current environments.

For other people, rigid rule adherence might be carried out with the objective of "being good," "pleasing others," or "avoiding conflict or offense." For such individuals, a rule may have been established that suggests conflict with others is bad (e.g., because it results in relationships ending or in being disliked by others) and one must be passive and compliant to minimize the potential for conflict and the associated bad consequences that follow. Overall, there is no shortage of the types of rules that influence people's behavior, some of which contribute to interpersonal behavior that is not effective or optimal. A general approach for weakening the influence of rigidly held and inaccurate rules is through the promotion of psychological flexibility.

Promoting a Willingness to Think and Act Differently

Willingness sometimes involves doing something different from what maladaptive rules related to thoughts or emotions might suggest (Hayes, Strosahl, & Wilson, 2012). A socially anxious client, for example, might express the view that "I'd really like to go to the dinner party with coworkers on Friday night, but I know I'll get anxious, and I might lose control and do something stupid." The rule in this scenario, "feelings of anxiety" = "high likelihood for bad consequences," will likely result in the client not attending the dinner party if followed. If, however, the client values his coworkers and the relationships he has with them, assisting the client in developing a willingness to experience acute discomfort in the service of his values could make it more likely he will attend rather than avoid the party. Doing so might involve bringing one's anxieties, fears, worries, and doubts into social contexts (vs. fighting them, suppressing them, or avoiding them altogether by not attending). Cheerleading self-statements, (e.g., "I am anxious right now and I'm going to the dinner party anyway)" illustrate ways a person can talk with himself or herself to overcome the escape or avoidance tendencies that accompany anxiety while acknowledging (validating) the experience of these emotions. Cheerleading statements focus on what one wants to do while recognizing the associated challenges and enhancing one's courage to act.

As therapy progresses, intervention approaches described in Chapter 5 for modifying inaccurate rules may be especially relevant. Maladaptive rules, for example, can be examined in terms of their workability within the relationship—that is, in terms of their accuracy in current relationships and whether holding on to such rules enhances or detracts from overall relationship quality. Inaccurate yet firmly held rules might be gently challenged by questions such as "Could there be other explanations for this?" or "How is this view evident in your relationships with others today?" Clients might also be encouraged to notice the full range of potentially disconfirming environmental cues in relevant situations while resisting the urge to focus exclusively on cues consistent with the long-standing rules. By focusing on a greater number of details related to an event or situation, individuals become open to a broader range of possible explanations for events. Similarly, clients can be gently encouraged to explore the factual bases for their conclusions. Disclosures related to uncertainty about others' motives or intentions, in turn, could be a target for natural reinforcement by the therapist as a way to promote the loosening of largely untested rules.

Faulty rules can also be modified through the arrangement of situations that are tests for validity of rule statements (e.g., through behavioral experiments, see Chapter 5, or graded exposure, see Chapter 9). When the natural consequences associated with rules are tested and directly experienced, rule modification may follow, particularly when outcomes conflict with rule content. Of the well-researched behavioral interventions, acceptance and commitment therapy (ACT; Hayes et al., 2012) has the explicit therapeutic goal of undermining the role that maladaptive rules and other verbal functions play in the nonadaptive regulation of behavior. In ACT, emphasis is placed on verbal functions that contribute to the avoidance of private experiences, such as reason giving (e.g., "My depression prevented me from going to the party"), evaluation (e.g., "Anxiety is bad and should be avoided"), and literality (e.g., "I feel worthless so I must be worthless").

Promoting Stability in Interpersonal Relationships

Relationships are dynamic, not static. As such, they need ongoing attention if they are to be maintained and further develop over time. Many of the skills described in this chapter (e.g., communication, problem solving, negotiating conflict, management of anger) are important for the maintenance of relationships over time. Similarly, the ongoing act of valuing relationships can be regarded as an overarching organizing principle for interpersonal effectiveness. The act of valuing relationships can take many forms, one of which is exemplified in the value of *relationship equality*. In cooperative relationships, reinforcement is mutual and equitable, there is no imbalance of power, and there are no discernable "controller–controlee" status distinctions. Equality in a relationship means that both parties have the status of equals and each mutually benefit from the relationship. When the threat of punishment or coercion is absent as means for controlling behavior and when positive reinforcement is routinely delivered for a variety of behaviors, a personal sense of freedom often follows from the wide availability of a variety of reinforcers for a broad range of behavioral alternatives (Baum, 2005).

Other important factors that contribute to relationship maintenance and satisfaction include those that build on positive emotion and behavior (Halford & Bodenmann, 2013; Karney & Bradbury, 1995). In particular, *perceiving oneself as appreciated in relationships* appears to be among the strongest predictors of relationship satisfaction and engagement in positive relationship maintenance behaviors (Gordon, Impett, Kogan, Oveis, & Keltner, 2012; Lambert & Fincham, 2011). Individuals who feel more appreciated by their partners tend to express more appreciation to their partners, are more responsive to their partners' needs, and are more committed to the relationship (Gordon et al., 2012). Examples of behavior that convey appreciation include verbal statements (e.g., offering complements, expressing gratitude, recognizing positive qualities), unsolicited offers of help or assistance (e.g., with household tasks or responsibilities), taking time to understand another's situation or concerns, the provision of validation and respect, demonstrations of a willingness to share aspects of one's life with another, and acts that convey thinking about another when apart (e.g., with texts, e-mails, or through arrangements for the delivery of small gifts).

Valuing *balance among relationship priorities* is an interpersonal effectiveness skill in some behavioral therapies (e.g., Linehan, 1993a) and involves balancing one's own priorities (e.g., doing what one wants versus what needs to get done; participating in activities that are personally important; engaging in pleasurable activities) with demands from others (e.g., doing things that other people want you to do or expect from you). Successful relationships often involve finding a balance between these two relational elements while negotiating the conflicts that inevitably arise without compromising self-respect.

CHANGING THE ENVIRONMENT TO ENHANCE SOCIAL SUPPORT

Another potentially important challenge to interpersonal effectiveness is deficient social environments. Some persons have few or no family members or friends with whom to interact with on a regular basis. Others might have responded to emotional distress through social withdrawal or avoidance. This approach to coping, however, only intensifies distress in the long run and contributes to a downward spiral of increasing avoidance, withdrawal, and distress. Events such as the death of a spouse or close friend, the loss of a job, or relocation to another area are examples of changes in life situations that can alter the availability of reinforcers provided by others with whom life was shared. In each of these examples, the client's environment has changed in important ways, and cues that once signaled reinforcement for certain behaviors are now diminished or gone. Many behavioral repertoires that were influenced by the reinforcers that others previously provided might be affected, resulting in an overall drop in the range of previously reinforced behavior. In the following sections, we describe three approaches for altering the social environment to enhance opportunities for social support and increase the range of reinforcement opportunities: (a) creating supportive social environments, (b) increasing opportunities for reinforcement from the environment, and (c) reducing or eliminating unhealthy social environments.

Creating Supportive Social Environments

Perhaps the most potent reinforcers that influence human behavior are those that signal belonging, companionship, intimacy, alliance, and personal self-worth as reflected in the words and actions of others. The extent to which we experience these relationship qualities depends largely on the quality of our social networks and relationships. Social networks have been described as the "the web of social relationships that surround individuals" (Heaney & Israel, 2008, p. 190), with social support being an important aspect of relationships within the network. Social support and relationship quality varies with respect to several dimensional features (Heaney & Israel, 2008), such as reciprocity (e.g., the extent to which support is both supplied and received), relationship strength (e.g., the degree to which emotional closeness is a defining quality), and relationship complexity (e.g., the variety of functions the relationship serves).

Creating supportive social environments can be an important initial step toward building social networks and supports. Creating such environments requires either strengthening relationships that already exist or entering into situations that offer opportunities for socializing and the formation of new relationships.

- *Strengthening existing social relationships.* Emphasis here is on the strengthening of skills related to providing and receiving social support and in maintaining relationships. Many of the skills or interventions already outlined within this chapter may have relevance for this therapeutic goal.
- *Developing new social supports.* Individuals who are likely to be among the most supportive are those who have had comparable lifetime experiences, who have experienced similar stressors and who have common interests or values. Entry into environments in which such persons are most likely to be found can facilitate initial opportunities for contact. Examples include joining groups where members share similar interests or values (e.g., hobby groups, church groups, political action groups), participating in groups where certain skills are taught (e.g., meditation groups, martial arts groups, dance classes, Toastmasters), or taking part in a relevant self-help group (e.g., Alcoholics Anonymous, Jenny Craig, divorce support group, family bereavement program, Internet-based support groups).
- *Becoming involved in strengthening the community.* Activities associated with this domain involve coming together with other members from the community to address community needs and problems. These activities involve joining others to identify or solve social problems, to provide a service to others in need, or to strengthen relationship ties among members of a commu-

nity. Community-oriented groups (e.g., Kiwanis, United Way, Big Brothers Big Sisters, the Parent–Teacher Association) or community volunteer opportunities (e.g., with high-risk kids, in providing literacy instruction, in aiding sheltered animals) are examples of such groups. Another strategy is to become a mentor by helping others develop skills in areas where one is already skillful.

Increasing Opportunities for Reinforcement From the Social Environment

Participation in social activities is strongly associated with positive moods. Available evidence, reviewed in Watson (2000), suggests bidirectional relationships between positive moods and social activity in which (a) frequent contacts with supportive friends and relatives and regular participation in social activities result in positive moods (e.g., enthusiasm, joy), perhaps because of the rich opportunities for social reinforcement that such occasions afford and (b) increases in positive moods facilitate engagement in prosocial activities and the seeking of opportunities for social contact.

For individuals with a limited range of social reinforcement options, a therapy goal might be to expand the range of reinforcing contexts that supports and maintains desirable social behaviors. This could involve some degree of environmental restructuring, specifically the identification of and participation in social activities that the individual finds rewarding or pleasing. To aid in this process, event schedules such as those developed by Peter Lewinsohn and colleagues (e.g., the Pleasant Events Schedule; MacPhillamy & Lewinsohn, 1982) might be used. Such lists can serve as guides for social behaviors to increase (e.g., "I want to do more outdoor activities with my kids") and perhaps suggest some new skills to learn that could enhance interpersonal effectiveness (e.g., "I want to read up on conversation skills so it will be easier for me to start conversations with people I don't know well"). Such lists can also be used to identify potentially pleasurable social activities that, in turn, could be included in activity-scheduling homework assignments in between sessions. When used for this purpose, the following format might be used (adapted from Lewinsohn et al., 1978):

- *Make a commitment:* Block off time during the day or week that is wholly dedicated to doing something pleasant with someone else. Nothing else is to be done during that time.

- *Identify the activity or activities in which you will participate*: What is it you want to do? What have you done in the past that you enjoyed doing with others that you no longer do? Be specific. Develop a list of potentially pleasant activities that is specific to you. Consider how pleasurable each would be if you were to engage in them. Nothing else is to be done during this time, and the activity identified should be scheduled in advance. If you have a list of potential activities, which are associated with the highest pleasantness ratings?
- *Make plans or arrangements*: Anticipate any obstacles or problems that may arise in carrying out the plan, and develop solutions to these (e.g., make babysitter arrangements, make reservations for the activity if doing so is necessary).
- *Stick to the plan*: Carry out a plan to its completion, particularly a plan that is in the service of your needs or reinforces the idea that you have control over your life, including your social life. You can dictate the direction you take by deciding what you do with your time.
- *After carrying out the plan, reflect on the outcome*: Take some time to reflect on the social activity in which you just participated. Did you enjoy yourself? Did you find it pleasurable? Did you notice a change in your emotions as you participated in the activity?

Reducing or Eliminating Unhealthy Social Environments

When working with a client to alter his or her social environment, it is often useful to consider the possible influence of unhealthy relationships on the client's sense of wellbeing. Does the client report feeling worse when in the presence of specific persons? Is it possible to identify what it is about that person or about the underlying relationship dynamics that contributes to the client's distress? If relationship-based sources of distress are identifiable, is it possible to change these? If change is not possible or feasible, the therapist might work with the client to limit time with such persons while increasing the amount of time spent with others who are enjoyable to be with or whose physical presence is associated with positive emotions.

Some relationships are abusive, and at times beyond repair. In such instances, plans for changing the client's social environment would ideally include consideration of the complete avoidance of individuals who are punitive or abusive, particularly if previous attempts to alter such relationships have not been successful.

SUMMARY

The following considerations apply to interventions used to promote interpersonal effectiveness:

- Interpersonal effectiveness is a culturally defined construct that involves the coordination of several complex social skills and abilities necessary for social interaction, relationship maintenance, and the achievement of social goals across multiple situations and contexts.
- Several quasi-independent factors can influence interpersonal effectiveness, including behavior patterns acquired over one's learning history (e.g., social skills and deficits, behavioral excesses), interpersonally relevant establishing operations (e.g., emotional states, socially relevant rules and values), and characteristics of current social environments (e.g., supportive vs. suppressive environments, availability of reinforcement for social behavior).
- When considering the possibility of a skills deficit, it is important to first establish whether the apparent lack of skills is the primarily result of the behavior's absence from the client's behavioral repertoire, behavioral inhibition related to anxiety, or the product of suppressive environments, as each of these possibilities prescribes a different intervention approach.
- The learning of social skills generally involves skills acquisition (e.g., shaping, direct instruction, modeling), skills strengthening (e.g., behavioral rehearsal, feedback), and skills generalization (e.g., homework assignments to practice skills in relevant situations).
- A common feature of many of the interventions for behavioral excesses (e.g., anger expression, coercive tendencies, dependency-related behaviors) involves identifying the short-term reinforcers that maintain such behaviors and lessening or eliminating their influence.
- Interventions for promoting interpersonal effectiveness include environmental interventions that attempt to strengthen social supports and increase engagement in pleasant activities with others.

8

BEHAVIORAL ACTIVATION

Depression is a common experience among people generally and a frequent concern among persons seeking therapy. A related diagnostic category, major depressive disorder (MDD), has been estimated to have a lifetime risk of approximately 23% based on findings from nationally representative cross-sectional samples (Kessler, Berglund, et al., 2005). Longitudinal research with representative birth cohorts, however, suggests that the actual risk is closer to double this amount (Moffitt et al., 2010; Rohde, Lewinsohn, Klein, Seeley, & Gau, 2013). MDD is also a highly comorbid condition that often co-occurs with other internalizing psychiatric disorders (e.g., Seeley, Kosty, Farmer, & Lewinsohn, 2011; Watson, 2009) and has been projected to be the second leading cause of disease burden worldwide by 2030 (Mathers & Loncar, 2006).

http://dx.doi.org/10.1037/14691-008
Behavioral Interventions in Cognitive Behavior Therapy: Practical Guidance for Putting Theory Into Action,
Second Edition, by R. F. Farmer and A. L. Chapman

Depressed mood and loss of interest and pleasure (anhedonia) are core symptoms in the definition of the MDD diagnostic category. In the current editions of the *Diagnostic and Statistical Manual of Mental Disorders, Fifth Edition* (*DSM–5*; American Psychiatric Association, 2013) and the *International Classification of Diseases, 10th Revision* (World Health Organization, 1991), at least one of these symptoms should be present for a diagnosis of MDD to be considered. Sad mood and anhedonia are not only central features of MDD, they are also frequent concomitants of several other psychiatric conditions (Dichter, 2010; Nestler et al., 2002). Sad mood, for example, is widely regarded as a nonspecific symptom associated with both depressive and anxiety disorders and, correspondingly, an exemplar of a set of symptoms associated with a general negative affect factor (Watson, 2009). Anhedonia is an experience linked to stress exposure (Agrawal et al., 2012; Nikolova, Bogdan, & Pizzagalli, 2012) and is also included as a symptom feature of posttraumatic stress disorder in the *DSM–5*. Whereas general negative affect is frequently associated with avoidance coping (e.g., Borkovec, Alcaine, & Behar, 2004; Dickson, Ciesla, & Reilly, 2012; Kashdan, Breen, Afram, & Terhar, 2010; Trew, 2011), anhedonia is primarily related to a low responsiveness to reward incentives, reduced effort expenditure to obtain rewards, and passivity (e.g., Berton, Hahn, & Thase, 2012; Treadway, Bossaller, Shelton, & Zald, 2012). Although the therapeutic change mechanisms underlying behavioral activation therapies remain speculative (e.g., Hunnicutt-Ferguson, Hoxha, & Gollan, 2012), they are likely tied to the therapy's emphasis on two processes that underlie core symptoms of MDD and other related conditions: avoidance coping and reduced responsiveness to reward incentives.

EFFICACY RESEARCH ON BEHAVIORAL ACTIVATION THERAPY FOR DEPRESSION

Research on the theory underlying contemporary behavioral activation therapy is generally supportive of its basic principles (Dimidjian, Barrera, Martell, Muñoz, & Lewinsohn, 2011; Kanter, Manos, et al., 2010). There is also accumulating evidence that behavioral activation is an effective and economical therapy for reducing depressive symptoms. Two recent meta-analyses that evaluated the efficacy of behavioral activation for the treatment of depression relative to control conditions reported effect sizes between .74 and .87 (Cuijpers, van Straten, & Warmerdam, 2007; Mazzucchelli, Kane, & Rees, 2009). Effect sizes associated with behavioral activation and cognitive therapy interventions for depression are also highly similar (effect size difference = .02; Cuijpers et al., 2007). Although similar in the magnitude of overall effects, commentators have highlighted several advantages of behavioral activation over cognitive therapies (Cuijpers et al., 2007; Kanter, Manos, et al., 2010; Sturmey, 2009). Behavioral activation, for example, does not require clients to have well-developed verbal skills, psychological mindedness, or the ability to differentiate and describe complex internal processes (e.g., the discrimination of thoughts from feelings and their temporal sequencing) and is thus potentially more accessible to a broader range of clients. From a cost-effectiveness perspective, one study demonstrated that the sustained effects of behavioral activation 2 years after treatment discontinuation were as effective in preventing depression relapse as continued antidepressant medication (Dobson et al., 2008).

There are additional suggestions that the "active ingredients" of standard cognitive behavior therapy (CBT) for depression (e.g., A. T. Beck, Rush, Shaw, & Emery, 1979) are primarily related to the behavioral activation component of this treatment approach. Component analyses of treatment effects associated with CBT for depression, for example, reveal that most changes in mood occur within the early stages of therapy, before any formal introduction of cognitive restructuring techniques (Ilardi & Craighead, 1994). These findings suggest that altering schemas or modifying core assumptions—hypothesized to be the main agents of change in some forms of cognitive therapy (e.g., J. E. Young, Rygh, Weinberger, & Beck, 2014)—add little to the overall efficacy of CBT for depression beyond the behavioral interventions instituted early in the therapy process. Additionally, Jacobson et al. (1996) reported that the behavioral components associated with CBT for depression were just as effective in promoting therapeutic change as the entire treatment package that included both behavioral and cognitive interventions. The behavioral components largely involved behavioral activation; the addition of cognitive treatment elements to the behavioral interventions did not result in any additional significant therapeutic benefit. Moreover, 2 years after the discontinuation of active therapy, relapse rates associated with behavioral activation interventions were no greater than those for the full CBT treatment package (Gortner, Gollan, Dobson, & Jacobson, 1998).

Accumulating evidence indicates that contemporary behavioral activation interventions constitute an effective stand-alone treatment approach for depression that is both relatively parsimonious and simple to implement. As we describe subsequently, behavioral activation's two-pronged emphasis on approaching and accessing potential sources of positive reinforcement and reducing avoidance behavior, coupled with comparatively minimal emphasis on skills training or modification of thought content, represents substantial innovations.

APPLICATIONS OF BEHAVIORAL ACTIVATION INTERVENTIONS FOR CONDITIONS OTHER THAN ADULT DEPRESSION

Behavioral activation for depression has been adapted for youth (McCauley, Schloredt, Gudmundsen, Martell, & Dimidjian, 2011; Ritschel, Ramirez, Jones, & Craighead, 2011) and older persons (Lazzari, Egan, & Rees, 2011; Snarski et al., 2011; Yon & Scogin, 2008), as well as for Latinas and Latinos with depression-related concerns (Kanter, Santiago-Rivera, Rusch, Busch, & West, 2010; Santiago-Rivera et al., 2008). Increasingly, behavioral activation therapy has been modified, applied, and evaluated with members from other clinical populations. These applications include interventions that target medication adherence and depressive symptoms among substance abusers (Daughters et al., 2008; Daughters, Magidson, Schuster, & Safren, 2010), suicidal behavior among persons diagnosed with borderline personality disorder (Hopko, Sanchez, Hopko, Dvir, & Lejuez, 2003), posttraumatic stress disorder–related symptoms among veterans or traumatized individuals (Gros et al., 2012; Jakupcak et al., 2006; Wagner, Zatzick, Ghesquiere, & Jurkovich, 2007), relationship distress among couples (Manos et al., 2009), smoking cessation efforts among tobacco users with elevated depressive symptoms (MacPherson et al., 2010), and reductions in weight, caloric intake, sedentary activity, and depressive symptoms among obese persons (Pagoto et al., 2008). Although preliminary data on these extensions of behavioral activation to other problem areas are encouraging, empirical support for this intervention is strongest for MDD or depressive symptoms among adults.

CONTEMPORARY BEHAVIORAL ACTIVATION THERAPY FOR DEPRESSION

Detailed accounts of the theoretical development of contemporary behavioral activation therapies for depression are available (Dimidjian et al., 2011; Kanter, Manos, et al., 2010; Lejuez, Hopko, Acierno, Daughters, & Pagoto, 2011). Briefly, the roots of contemporary behavioral activation therapies can be found in several behavioral theories of depression, most notably those of Peter Lewinsohn (1974; Lewinsohn, Biglan, & Zeiss, 1976; Lewinsohn & Libet, 1972). Lewinsohn's theory, influenced by Charles Ferster's (1973) functional analytic account of depression, emphasized low rates of response contingent positive reinforcement (RCPR) in the development and maintenance of depressive symptoms. Low rates of RCPR were hypothesized to result in low frequencies of a variety of behaviors, thus reducing future opportunities for receiving positive reinforcement. Over time, low RCPR was hypothesized to result in a narrowing of behavioral repertoires, the extinction of some classes of behaviors, and depressive symptoms. Lewinsohn and colleagues subsequently developed a clinical measure for evaluating participation in pleasant or rewarding activities (i.e., the Pleasant Events Schedule; MacPhillamy & Lewinsohn 1982) and a multifaceted therapeutic strategy (i.e., the Coping with Depression Course; Lewinsohn, Antonuccio, Steinmetz-Breckenridge, & Teri, 1984) for promoting alternative behaviors that have a greater potential for producing positively reinforcing consequences from the environment. Since Lewinsohn's seminal work, other groups of researchers have refined the theory and application of behavioral activation for depression (e.g., Jacobson, Martell, & Dimidjian, 2001; Lejuez et al., 2011; Martell, Addis, & Jacobson, 2001; Martell, Dimidjian, & Herman-Dunn, 2010). Our primary emphasis below is on the most recent iterations of behavioral activation interventions.

A central assumption of contemporary behavioral activation theories of depression is that factors that contribute to the development and maintenance of depression reside in the environment, not within the person, and are related to the outcomes of the person's actions. Specifically, depression often arises when an individual's behavior is more frequently responded to with punishment than with positive reinforcement or when a person has reduced access to positive reinforcers because of behavioral avoidance or withdrawal (Martell et al., 2010). When viewed from this perspective, depression is regarded as an experience that results from person–environment interactions. The focus in behavioral activation, then, is on the life context, not inner causes, flaws, or defects.

A related risk factor for depression emphasized in behavioral activation interventions is *contextual change* (Addis & Martell, 2004), which involves increases in situations that place an individual at greater risk for depression. Contextual changes may include life stressors such as a divorce, job change, or physical illness. Sometimes these shifts occur gradually (e.g., increasingly more hours spent on work-related activities and correspondingly less time available for doing enjoyable activities with friends and family), whereas at other times these shifts occur abruptly (e.g., the experience of a job loss and relocation to another city all within a short period of time). In many instances, depression is the cumulative effect of several contextual changes or shifts over time and has resulted in the client's engagement in more activities associated with negative mood and less participation in activities associated with positive moods.

On the basis of these central assumptions, behavioral activation therapy for depression aims to increase activity, counteract avoidance behavior, and increase the individual's access to positive reinforcers (Dimidjian et al., 2011; Martell et al., 2010). These therapeutic aims are accomplished by an emphasis on behavioral assessment, mood and activity monitoring, activity structuring, and the identification of barriers to behavioral activation (e.g., avoidant coping patterns, withdrawal). Although behavioral activation generally includes a common set of interventions for all participants, these interventions are usually tailored on the basis of individualized assessments of contexts within which depression is commonly experienced. A primary goal of behavioral activation is to facilitate engagement in activities or entry into contexts that are reinforcing, mood enhancing, and congruent with an individual's longer term goals or values. Doing so often involves blocking avoidant coping patterns that eliminate opportunities for solving life problems, result in the narrowing of behavioral repertoires, or increase vulnerability to depressed moods.

BEHAVIORAL ACTIVATION APPROACH
TO THERAPY FOR DEPRESSION

Behavioral activation therapy for depression typically lasts between 16 and 24 weeks. In Dimidjian et al.'s (2006) randomized trial, clients participated in two 50-minute sessions each week during the first 8 weeks and one weekly 50-minute session during the following 8 weeks. The therapist primarily serves as a consultant who assists clients in becoming skilled observers of the relationships between behavior and associated consequences. The therapist also acts as a coach by encouraging clients to become active, even when they believe that they cannot engage in life-enhancing actions or derive pleasure from their own actions. Therapists also assist clients in developing routines that function to maintain behavior consistent with long-term goals or values.

In the sections that follow, we summarize the components of behavioral activation therapy for depression based primarily on treatment protocols developed by members of the University of Washington group (e.g., Addis & Martell, 2004; Dimidjian et al., 2006; Jacobson et al., 2001; Martell et al., 2001, 2010). Within this therapeutic framework, therapy components generally follow a sequential format. There is room, however, for the therapist to be flexible in his or her approach, particularly given the idiographic nature of the therapy.

Self-Monitoring Activities and Moods and the Associations Between the Two

In the behavioral activation model, getting to know one's self involves more than noticing what is occurring on the inside. Acquiring self-knowledge also involves detailed and careful analyses of what is taking place on the outside. Noticing how one acts in certain situations is centrally important (e.g., what is going on at work, what one does at home, what one does when confronted with tedious or unpleasant tasks), as are the emotional and environmental consequences associated with one's actions. During initial therapy sessions, primary emphasis is placed on what one does in certain situations because it is often difficult, if not impossible, to change one's personality or genetic endowments. In contrast, it is much easier to change one's activities that, in turn, directly influence how one thinks and feels.

In behavioral activation, the identification of behavioral patterns associated with depressed mood is a precursor to changing those patterns. This process involves the therapist and client working together to identify what to change in a structured and systematic way. To accomplish this, the therapist and client closely examine positive and negative current life events, with special emphasis placed on understanding how the client's life is different when he or she is depressed compared with other occasions when depressed mood is not present. Examples of questions therapists can ask for getting at the latter include, "What is your life like when you are not depressed?" or "Are there things that you are not doing now that you would do if you weren't depressed?"

Detailed *self-monitoring* is also an important part of identifying behavioral patterns associated with depressed mood. A central assessment tool in behavioral activation is the activity monitoring form, a self-monitoring form that involves keeping track of one's activities and associated moods on an hour-to-hour basis each day for at least 1 week. Generally, the more detail a client can provide in relation to his or her activities, the better. It is more informative, for example, to record "ruminated about my day at work while home alone" than simply "home alone" or "ruminated." Information recorded on the activity monitoring form helps reveal the client's current level of activity, connections between his or her activity level and mood, and level of engagement in avoidance behaviors.

After recording activities and associated moods, the next step is to look for patterns. Over the days that the client made recordings, is there an indication that mood fluctuates according to the client's activities? Is there any evidence suggesting that some frequently occurring events are associated with the client's negative moods? Are some events typically associated with the client's positive moods? What about time slots? Are some times of the day characterized by the client's low mood? If so, does this correspond to an activity that often occurs during that time, or is the client's low mood present during these times regardless of the client's activities?

Monitoring one's activities at this level of detail and noticing variable patterns of mood may also help dispel beliefs some depressed persons experience that suggest that they are depressed all of the time. Such monitoring can also reveal *depression loops*, or instances in which efforts to cope with depressed or negative moods actually result in a further worsening of mood. Some people, for example, cope with depressed mood or stressors by drinking alcohol. For many individuals, consumption of alcohol might result in an immediate shift in mood, perhaps from stressed to relaxed or euphoric. When the immediate psychoactive effects wear off, however, the individual's mood can actually end up being worse than it was before drinking. Many clients also report that drinking does not help solve the problems that contributed to their stress in the first place. These examples illustrate how the depression loop can become manifest and might signal that current efforts at coping are actually more unhelpful than helpful.

A Client Illustration: Diane

"Diane" is a 42-year-old, recently divorced mother of two children (ages 7 and 9 years) referred to therapy by a coworker who was concerned about the progressive worsening of her mood. During the clinical interview, Diane reported that she has been "depressed all of the time over the last year," adding that "I cry most days because of how things are." She went on to state that "my life's off track, and I just don't know how to pick up the pieces and go on" and "it seems that I worry all of the time now."

Diane reported that she has become increasingly depressed during the past 3 years. She associated the onset and worsening of her depression with the growing realization that she no longer loved her husband and that "his disinterest in the kids and me was becoming more and more obvious." Diane and her husband agreed to divorce last year, with the divorce finalized 9 months ago. She described the associated process as "generally amicable." Following the finalization of their divorce, Diane's husband of 17 years relocated to another state, leaving her primarily responsible for child care. Diane reported that she and the children frequently talk with each other about the changes that have taken place and the struggle to adapt to their new life circumstances. She added that she maintains an upbeat and optimistic stance when talking with the children, even though she privately views her future with more uncertainty.

Diane reported that her marital difficulties and depressed mood have affected her work as a bank teller. She described difficulty concentrating on her work because her thoughts are often focused on her current life situation and how bad it is. As of last week, Diane reported that she decided to take sick leave because "it was all getting to be too much and I really have to do something about this."

Questionnaire assessments completed after the first session were consistent with Diane's reports. Her responses on the Beck Depression Inventory—II (BDI–II; A. T. Beck, Steer, & Brown, 1996) administered after her first session indicated moderate to severe depressed mood (score = 28). On the Penn State Worry Questionnaire (PSWQ; Meyer, Miller, Metzger, & Borkovec, 1990), her score was 52, a score similar to those often observed among people with anxiety disorders characterized by rumination (Fresco, Mennin, Heimberg, & Turk, 2003). Her score on the short version of the Interpersonal Support Evaluation List (ISEL; Brummett et al., 2006; Cohen, Mermelstein, Kamarck, & Hoberman, 1985) was 21, which is generally regarded as a very low score on this measure.

Other indications of impairment come from Diane's report that her work has been steadily affected by her worsening mood to the point that she has taken sick leave because she felt she could no longer function adequately. She has also become increasingly distant and isolative at work and has adopted the habit during the past few years of having a couple of glasses of wine at night to "wind down" before going to bed. Several other examples suggest that Diane has been coping largely through avoidant coping strategies.

Before discussing possible approaches to therapy for depression, Diane's therapist asked her to participate in daily self-monitoring by listing her activities and associated moods each waking hour on an activity monitoring form. A description of these events would include not only the activity itself but also a brief description of the context within which the activity took place, the days on which the activity occurred, as well as the typical times when the activity was carried out. Activities she participated in between the first and second session, associated moods (1 = *very low or negative*; 10 = *very positive*), and the amount of pleasure derived from activity participation (1 = *very aversive or unpleasant*; 10 = *very pleasant or enjoyable*) are listed in separate columns in Table 8.1.

As Diane and her therapist reviewed this form together, Diane commented that she was surprised to see how much her mood varied over the course of a typical day. This realization contrasted with her previously held view that she was depressed all of the time. Another pattern she and her therapist discussed is that mood and pleasure ratings tended to rise and fall together. Her therapist speculated that engaging in activities that are pleasurable might be mood enhancing, and they agreed that this hypothesis should be further explored as therapy continued. They also noticed that Diane's mood appears to be consistently low in the evening during times that she watches news on television and sips wine. Diane reported that the events of the world are really getting her down and that she perhaps overidentifies with the suffering of others. She also observed that she tends to ruminate a lot about her own life situation during that time of the day and that even though she is watching television, "my thoughts are usually somewhere else."

As the therapist learned more about Diane's history, he shared the view that her current episode of depression appears to be strongly linked with

TABLE 8.1

Diane's Activity Monitoring Form for Days Between First and Second Session

Hour	Monday	Tuesday	Wednesday
7:00 a.m.	Woke, prepared breakfast, ate breakfast with kids *Mood:* 3 *Pleasure:* 4	Woke, prepared breakfast, ate breakfast with kids *Mood:* 4 *Pleasure:* 4	Woke, prepared breakfast, ate breakfast with kids *Mood:* 2 *Pleasure:* 2
8:00 a.m.	Dressed, dropped girls off at school *Mood:* 3 *Pleasure:* 4	Showered, dressed, dropped girls off at school *Mood:* 4 *Pleasure:* 4	Dressed, dropped girls off at school *Mood:* 2 *Pleasure:* 3
9:00 a.m.	Tidied kitchen *Mood:* 3 *Pleasure:* 3	Watched TV (old movie) *Mood:* 3 *Pleasure:* 2	Walked in the park *Mood:* 5 *Pleasure:* 4
10:00 a.m.	Napped *Mood:* (asleep) *Pleasure:* (asleep)	Watched TV (old movie) *Mood:* 3 *Pleasure:* 2	Looked through bills at home (did not pay) *Mood:* 3 *Pleasure:* 1
11:00 a.m.	Cleaned house, laundry *Mood:* 4 *Pleasure:* 2	Watched TV (talk show) *Mood:* 3 *Pleasure:* 2	Read newspaper, drank tea *Mood:* 5 *Pleasure:* 4
12:00 p.m.	Prepared and ate lunch, sat outside and listened to radio *Mood:* 6 *Pleasure:* 7	Ordered a pizza, cleaned house, ate lunch *Mood:* 4 *Pleasure:* 3	Ate lunch (dinner leftovers)/watched TV (news) *Mood:* 3 *Pleasure:* 3
1:00 p.m.	Went grocery shopping *Mood:* 4 *Pleasure:* 4	Napped *Mood:* (asleep) *Pleasure:* (asleep)	Phoned work/read newspaper *Mood:* 5 *Pleasure:* 4
2:00 p.m.	Grocery shopping, returned home and unpacked/put away groceries *Mood:* 4 *Pleasure:* 3	Napped *Mood:* (asleep) *Pleasure:* (asleep)	Played video game on computer (solitaire) *Mood:* 4 *Pleasure:* 3

Time	Activity	Mood	Pleasure
3:00 p.m.	Went to mall with girls	6	6
4:00 p.m.	At mall with girls/shopped	6	7
5:00 p.m.	Dinner at mall	5	5
6:00 p.m.	Drove home/picked up dry cleaning	5	4
7:00 p.m.	Helped girls with homework/ helped girls pick out clothes for tomorrow/packed girls lunch	5	7
8:00 p.m.	Talked with mother on phone	5	6
9:00 p.m.	Watched TV (news)/sipped wine	3	3
10:00 p.m.	Prepare for bed/read in bed/slept	3	3

Activity	Mood	Pleasure
Watched TV (talk show)	3	2
Watched TV (sports)/napped off and on	3	2
Played board game with girls	4	5
Prepared dinner/ate dinner	4	4
Work on computer/helped girls pick out clothes for tomorrow/packed girls lunch	5	3
Watched TV (news)/sipped wine	3	3
Watched TV (news)/sipped wine	3	3
Prepare for bed/slept	2	2

Activity	Mood	Pleasure
Watched girls play in backyard	5	5
Baked cookies with help from girls	7	8
Prepared dinner	5	5
Ate dinner/walked with girls	6	6
Watched TV with girls/helped girls pick out clothes for tomorrow/packed girls lunch	5	3
Watched TV (news)/sipped wine	4	4
Watched TV (news)/sipped wine	2	2
Prepare for bed/slept	3	2

several contextual shifts in her life, including a relocation 10 years ago to a new town and the loss of important relationships after this move. Outside of coworkers, Diane did not establish new friendships, and she developed routines that mostly involved staying at home and caring for her family.

Since moving to her present home 10 years ago, Diane acknowledged that she has not made many friends. Time outside of work had been mostly taken up by child-care responsibilities, and she reported having no energy left over for doing other things. Outside of her coworkers, Diane reported that she really does not regularly associate with anyone other than family members. Although there are a couple of people at work she feels close to, Diane noted that she rarely participates in activities with these people outside of work.

Diane's therapist also suggested that more proximally, her divorce and increased child-care responsibilities signified another contextual shift that further increased her vulnerability to depressed mood. These contextual shifts coupled with her historical overreliance on avoidant coping strategies appear to have maintained her depressed mood while leaving some of her current life problems largely unsolved.

Between her second and third sessions, Diane completed the activity monitoring form for Thursday through Sunday. The patterns for these days were generally consistent with those observed for Monday through Wednesday. On the basis of information derived from the activity monitoring forms, questionnaire assessments, and clinical interviews conducted over the first three sessions, Diane's therapist generated the following problem list:

1. *Sad mood*. Her mood was generally worse in evening, often accompanied by the consumption of wine.
2. *Persistent worry and rumination*. Thought content is generally focused on negative occasions from the past, negative events that might occur in the future, or on negative evaluations concerning current situations. Rumination periods are more concentrated in the evening and appear to have an associated avoidance function.
3. *Restricted social support network*. Her social network largely consists of family and coworkers (at work only), and she rarely engages in leisure activities with persons outside of family.
4. *Nightly wine consumption*. She drinks two to three glasses of wine most nights over the course of 2 to 3 hours while watching TV.
5. *Avoidant patterns*. Patterns include frequent TV watching, frequent naps, rumination, and playing video games to avoid aversive but necessary activities (e.g., paying bills).

Using Problem Solving and Behavioral Experimentation
to Identify Activities Associated With Positive Moods

After a week or more of self-monitoring, the client and therapist work together to identify activities associated with variations in mood. Once activities associated with depressed mood are identified, the therapist might *problem solve* with the client and come up with one or two alternative activities that could be more enjoyable or associated with positive moods.

When problem solving or coming up with alternative behaviors or activities, the first step is to brainstorm. Brainstorming involves writing down whatever comes to mind as a possible alternative, without any censure, editing, or evaluation. Once this process is complete, the next step is to evaluate whether the activity is likely to be associated with positive moods and if it is possible or desirable for the client to do the activity (e.g., some activities might be difficult for the client to do such as going out for an expensive dinner when he or she is financially strapped). These considerations should result in some narrowing of the list. Before choosing among the remaining options, it might be good for the therapist to consider whether some ideas can be combined or integrated. Additionally, when selecting among alternatives, therapists should pay special attention to depression loops. Interrupting these with a substitute activity might lessen the likelihood of deepening one's depression while providing the client with an opportunity for experimenting with an alternative coping behavior. After considering these issues, one or two substitute activities might be selected by the therapist and tested by the client during the day(s) and time(s) that the previous activity took place.

Determining whether new behaviors are indeed more effective (e.g., associated with more positive moods and not with depressed moods) involves *behavioral experimentation*. This process involves trying out a new or substitute behavior in place of the one associated with depressed mood and observing the outcomes associated with this new behavior (see Chapter 5 for a detailed description of behavioral experiments). In conducting experiments, the client's objective is simply to observe what occurs as a result of some event or observing what happens to one's mood when doing some other activity. The overall objective, then, is for the client to learn what happens when y is done instead of x and what effect y has on mood or outcome in comparison to x's effect on mood or outcome. This process involves the client's adoption of an experimenter's attitude, a sense of objectivity in relation to what one finds, and an openness for truth to reveal itself rather than being overly invested in a particular outcome.

This process does not end when the client completes a single behavioral experiment. Rather, experimentation is continuous and ongoing. There is recognition, for example, that changing an activity here or there is not likely to result in a substantial and sustained change in mood. Rather, the goal is to make several contextual changes or shifts in a gradual and systematic fashion and make sustained, if not modest, steps in a valued direction (or in this case, a direction characterized by more favorable moods).

Generating Plans for Testing Ideas From Diane's Activity Monitoring Form

As a result of the self-monitoring process during initial sessions, Diane discovered that watching a 24-hour news channel on TV between 8:00 p.m. and 10:00 p.m. at night while sipping wine is characteristically associated with depressed mood. She also speculated that the wine she has at night results in a less restful sleep and increased tiredness and grogginess the following morning. Perhaps as a result, Diane acknowledged she starts out the day with relatively little energy to do anything.

Diane's therapist suggested that their initial focus might be placed on her evening's activities, as the news watching and wine consumption appear to be not only mood impairing but also a possible depression loop that results in the further lowering of her mood. Diane's therapist subsequently worked up a diagram that illustrated the functional properties of evening TV watching, wine consumption, and rumination to illustrate his point (see Figure 8.1).

In reviewing the diagram with Diane, her therapist observed that these activities generally appeared to help her in a limited way. On the basis of her previous comments, Diane's therapist noted that watching the suffering of others has helped Diane place her own suffering in perspective (i.e., she concluded that her situation is comparatively not that bad) and that this helps her in a limited way by reducing her sense of being overwhelmed by her situation. Because she often worried about her own life while watching the news, Diane initially believed that ruminating helped to solve her problems. In this respect, Diane viewed her worry and rumination as effective coping behavior. Diane's therapist also noted that the wine consumed during TV watching has many immediate reinforcing properties (e.g., stress reduction, mild euphoria). In the aggregate, this pattern of behavior had a number of immediate reinforcing qualities that no doubt contributed to their maintenance over time.

Diane's therapist went on to explore with her the nonimmediate effects of this behavior pattern. When she and her therapist examined her rumination tendencies more closely, Diane concluded that her rumination only increases her depression and does little in the way of solving her life problems. She also demonstrated understanding that frequent exposure to the suffering of others worsened her mood because it contributed to her pessimistic and helpless outlook (e.g., "The world is going to hell, and there's nothing I can do about it") and reduced the amount of time she had to do other

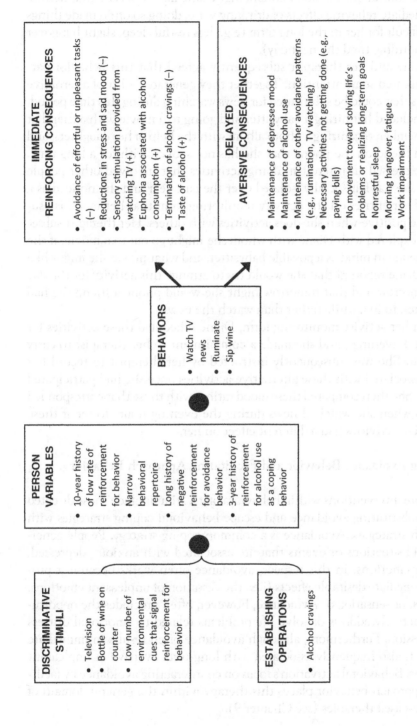

Figure 8.1. Functional analysis of Diane's evening TV watching and wine consumption. Dots between components of the response chain indicate a probability function in which a dot represents a probability that the preceding component will influence the following component. Items listed within the *Immediate Reinforcing Consequences* components followed by (+) indicate positive reinforcing consequences, whereas items followed by (−) indicate negative reinforcing consequences, both of which maintain or strengthen preceding behavior.

activities that might be mood enhancing. Diane also observed that despite the immediate relieving effects of drinking wine, doing so often made things more difficult for her in the long term (e.g., less restful sleep, slight hangover in the morning, tired the next day).

Diane and her therapist subsequently agreed that this behavior pattern warranted some attention. Together they generated a list of alternative activities that could be substituted for news watching during this time period. These included her hiring a babysitter and going to a movie with a friend or family member, organizing a photo album with the help of her daughters, and calling a friend on the phone that she has not spoken with for a long time. Diane expressed an interest in doing activities that involved other people because she has felt socially isolated over the past year and she noticed as a result of her entries on the activity monitoring form that her mood is usually more positive when she does activities with others. Her therapist subsequently explored with Diane with whom she might go out to a movie, if she had someone in mind as a possible babysitter, and what movie she might like to see. Diane reported that she would try to arrange this activity for the day after tomorrow and that tomorrow night she would phone a friend she had not spoken to in a while rather than watch the news.

On her activity monitoring form, Diane scheduled these activities for the next 3 evenings, and she made a commitment to her therapist to carry these out. She was subsequently instructed by her therapist to record her moods associated with these alternative activities once she had participated in them. She then compared these mood ratings with those that corresponded to times when she watched news during the evening hours to see if these alternative activities had a different effect on her.

Blocking Avoidance Behavior and Facilitating Approach Behavior

Core interventions within behavioral activation include those directed toward substituting avoidance and escape behavioral coping strategies with approach strategies. Avoidance is a common coping strategy. People generally avoid situations or events that are associated with anxious, depressed, or angry emotions. In this respect, avoidance often works because it produces immediate desirable effects (i.e., the cessation of unpleasant emotions, thoughts, or sensations). Avoidance, however, often precludes the opportunity to actively address or solve life problems related to emotional distress or depression. Furthermore, although avoidance often results in immediate relief, it is also frequently associated with long-term aversive or unpleasant outcomes. Behavioral activation's focus on counteracting avoidance by facilitating approach behavior places this therapy within the general domain of exposure-based therapies (see Chapter 9).

One acronym used in behavioral activation to help conceptualize avoidance patterns is TRAP, which refers to the following (Martell et al., 2010):

- A *Trigger* is some type of circumstance or event that has an impact on the individual. It may be the start of a series of events and can be internal or external.
- A *Response* is usually an emotional response to the trigger but can also be a thought, a physiological sensation, or an action. Some societal teachings, mores, or values, for example, suggest that negative emotions are "bad" and should be eliminated.
- An *Avoidance Pattern* is the typical avoidance response to the trigger. This may also be a reaction to the emotional response and the accompanying desire to get rid of the unpleasant feelings. Attempts at getting rid of negative emotions often do not work as intended, however, and may cause problems in their own right.

To understand whether people engage in behavior to avoid certain experiences, we must look to the function of the behavior rather than the form of behavior. Watching TV, for example, may or may not be avoidance behavior. To decide, we must understand what the behavior is doing for the individual or the purpose that it serves. An examination of the function of avoidance and escape behaviors also aids in the determination as to whether these are adaptive behaviors that are helpful to the individual or maladaptive behaviors that, in the end, are causing more harm than benefit. Does avoidance reduce the likelihood that an individual will actively address an important problem? Do avoidance or escape behaviors prevent the individual from taking steps toward participating in behavioral alternatives associated with positive moods?

Examples of avoidance in relation to depression might include procrastination, rumination, or low-energy behavior (e.g., excessive sleeping, spending hours sitting on the couch). These activities often do little to solve the situation that is being avoided by the client. Complaining might be another avoidance strategy. For many persons, complaints such as "I feel miserable" have been effective in the histories of people who state them. In the past, persons within the social network of complainers may have removed demands or other aversive conditions in response to such complaints. Perhaps because of such histories, frequent complainers are often not particularly interested in advice, solutions, or suggestions that involve active problem solving. If it were that easy, therapists would be well advised to simply provide advice in response to a client's complaints. But it is not, of course, that easy. Rather, complaining is sometimes an act of avoidance, maintained by its own immediate consequences (even if only intermittently experienced), that does little in the way of helping persons' solve for themselves the problems associated with their complaints. Although complaining may have short-term reinforcing properties similar to other avoidance coping strategies, it is often associated with the loss of social supports over time (Coyne, 1976).

Rumination is a special example of an avoidance strategy that often has a deleterious effect on mood. In Chapter 5, we described some interventions for reducing rumination, including those associated with the expanded behavioral activation treatment package.

Once a TRAP has been identified, the therapist can use a second acronym that represents a model to help the client get back on TRAC (Martell et al., 2010). A therapeutic goal associated with TRAC is the facilitation of an active approach strategy as a means for promoting effective behavior and for blocking avoidance.

- _Trigger_ (same as in TRAP),
- _Response_ (same as in TRAP), and
- _Alternative Coping_ involves an active rather than passive or avoidant response, which might include allowing the emotional reaction and other responses to simply be there while continuing to act in accordance with one's objectives, goals, or values (e.g., sometimes people offer reasons for avoidance through statements such as, "I would have done that, but I didn't because I felt depressed"; statements like these can be modified so that emotions are no longer reasons for avoidance, as in "I feel depressed at the moment, and I'm going to do what I planned to do and bring my depressed mood along").

The overall process of identifying and overcoming avoidance coping is summarized by a third acronym, ACTION (Jacobson, Martell, & Dimidjian, 2001):

- _Assess behavior and mood._ Is current behavior avoidant? How does this behavior serve the client? What emotions does he or she experience when engaging in this behavior?
- _Choose alternative behaviors._ Does the client activate himself or herself and engage in behaviors that could reduce depression over time?
- _Try the alternative behavior selected._ Is the alternative behavior mood enhancing? Is it effective given the purpose for which it was selected?
- _Integrate the alternative behavior into a regular routine._ A goal over time is to eliminate mood-detracting behavior repertoires and substitute these with mood-enhancing activities.

- *Observe the outcome of behavior.* Does it affect mood in a desirable way, result in effective outcomes, or improve some situation?
- *Never give up.* Does the client display recognition that trying a new behavior only once is unlikely to lead to significant change? Does he or she acknowledge that overcoming depression and avoidance takes a lot of hard work and that there will likely be some setbacks along the way? In the face of such setbacks, does the client remain committed to working toward his or her goals?

When changing situations or trying out new behaviors, clients are encouraged to make changes a step at a time rather than all at once. When possible, large activities or event sequences might be broken down into component parts and carried out one component at a time. *Graded task assignments* represent one strategy for taking small yet significant steps toward a goal or overcoming avoidance patterns by approaching avoided activities in small units. In behavioral activation, before actually carrying out tasks, the client is encouraged to imagine and mentally rehearse the activity during a therapy session. This mental rehearsal consists of the client overtly describing the activity that he or she will perform, the setting where the activity will take place, and the actual behaviors that the client will carry out during the task. Cleaning the house, for example, can be broken down into smaller components such as first cleaning one identified area of a room. Similarly, the act of approaching something previously avoided, such as high places for someone with acrophobia, can be decomposed into discrete and graded exposure trials.

With the assistance of the therapist, for example, a client might generate a list of avoided areas and arrange these in terms of their associated level of distress. Distress level might be quantified with subjective units of distress (SUDS) ratings, whereby 0 = *no distress or avoidance at all* and 100 = *most distress ever experienced* or *would not approach under any circumstance*. A first item with the lowest rating for someone with acrophobia might be to climb a three-step stool and to stand on the top and second steps and remain there until he or she is relatively calm and relaxed (SUDS = 35). A midlevel item might be for a client to look over a second-story balcony until he or she is relatively calm and relaxed (SUDS = 55), and a high-level item might be to go to the observation platform on the top of the highest building in town and remain there until he or she is relatively calm and relaxed (SUDS = 90). Once this list is generated, the client might carry out the activity associated with the lowest SUDS rating and proceed to the next item only when the lower level item has been carried out successfully.

Countering mood-dependent behaviors is another general strategy for blocking avoidance. Individuals who experience significant emotional distress, such as frequent anxious or depressed moods, sometimes adopt the view that if it were not for their depression or anxiety, they would do things that they are currently not doing (e.g., "If I weren't so depressed, I'd call my buddy from work to see if he'd want to go to the baseball game tomorrow" or "I wanted to go to that party, but my social anxiety stopped me from going"). Among mood-dependent persons, engagement in desired activities, or moving forward in life, is put on hold until emotions change. In countering mood dependence, a therapeutic goal is to go forward and participate in valued activities despite the presence of negative mood. With experience, clients may come to learn that it is possible to behave independently of acute moods and that the very act of behaving in a valued direction is often a catalyst for bringing about mood change.

Another strategy for countering mood-dependent behavior patterns is *acting "as if."* This strategy involves pursuing a valued course of action "as if" the presumed obstacles for carrying out such an action were absent. A client, for example, might say something like, "If I weren't so socially anxious and if I were more charming, I would go to the party tonight." Acting "as if" in this example would involve going to the party and "acting" as if one was somewhat charming and not socially anxious, and to notice the consequences of behaving in this way. By intentionally acting differently when feeling blocked by negative moods or self-doubts, one might learn that goals are obtainable regardless of emotional states and thoughts and that the very act of pursuing valued goals often changes mood and thinking in desirable directions.

Diane's Ongoing Struggles With Avoidance

Perhaps the greatest potential obstacle to Diane's success in therapy is her frequent use of avoidant coping strategies. This idea, in fact, was shared with Diane during the planning portion of therapy. At the time this was discussed, the therapist noted that it was possible therapy might be challenging at times; that is, difficult topics might be discussed or Diane might find that changing behavior is hard and occasionally frustrating. Her therapist reassured her that they would take small steps toward the realization of her therapeutic goals and that he would work with her to increase the likelihood that lasting benefits are realized from this therapy.

When the issue of avoidance was first discussed, Diane was somewhat unsure if this would emerge as a problem. She did agree, however, to continuously monitor whether avoidance behavior was adversely affecting her progress in therapy, and she agreed to examine this issue with her therapist if he felt that it became a therapy-related issue.

By the 10th therapy session, Diane had made some progress in reducing avoidance. She altered her evening routine by seeking out activities other than news watching and drinking wine, with an extra effort given to incorporating other people into these activities. Although some progress was made, Diane felt somewhat stuck because most of these alternative activities involved her children. She felt that her next step was to branch out and begin to establish friendships in other areas. She reported, however, that she was unable to branch out because of her feelings of being fatigued. Although these feelings were less pronounced as a result of cutting back on her wine consumption, the experience of fatigue kept her from "having the energy to get out there and meet people."

As Diane and her therapist examined this issue further, it also became apparent that Diane had significant social anxiety and negative thoughts about her self-worth and her suitability as a potential friend to someone. She became insistent that she would never have close friendships and expressed significant hopelessness related to her wish to be integrated into a social network and to date once again.

In response to Diane's insistence and accompanying anger, the therapist challenged her to examine what was happening in this moment during their session. After thinking for a while, Diane suggested that she was in a TRAP and that her reactions were largely avoidant. She recognized that if she were to do something different in relation to her social situation, she would likely experience social anxiety and self-doubts. She correctly noted that hanging on to her pessimism and expectations of failure helped her avoid the anxiety and doubt associated with doing anything different.

Having previously worked within the TRAP, TRAC, and ACTION frameworks with her therapist, Diane noted that if she were to get on TRAC, she would need to do something different that would bring her social anxiety and self-doubts to the forefront. She realized that she would need to allow the emotional reaction and negative thoughts to simply be there while taking active steps to realize her objectives and goals, which in this instance was to become more socially connected to people.

The remainder of the session was spent discussing different steps Diane could take to become more socially connected. A number of ideas were generated (e.g., become involved in a hobby group, initiate non–work-related activities with coworkers, join a political action committee). One of these activities (i.e., joining a political organization) was subsequently broken down into a sequence of component parts, and Diane made a commitment to follow through with the first two steps before their next session. She acknowledged that even though taking these steps might be difficult, any acute discomfort would be less unpleasant than the prospect of not realizing the long-term social goals she has for herself.

Decreasing Vulnerability to Future Episodes of Depression

The likelihood of disorder recurrence among formerly depressed clients is high (Rohde et al., 2013). In recognition of this, behavioral activation incorporates elements of relapse prevention into the overall treatment program. One approach for reducing relapse involves therapists encouraging clients to apply principles of behavioral activation to other areas of their lives, particularly those areas associated with an increased vulnerability to future episodes of depression. This approach promotes skills generalization and increases the likelihood that long-standing problem areas will continue to be addressed by the client once active therapy has ended.

As therapy draws to a close, clients are encouraged to consider what they have learned about themselves over the course of therapy. Clients who have received a course of behavioral activation therapy will generally demonstrate a better understanding of the functional aspects of their behavior. That is, they will be better able to identify triggers that are frequently associated with dysphoric mood as well as observe and acknowledge the effects of their behavior on mood and others in their environment. Clients will also likely have learned that avoidance and escape behaviors often provide immediate relief but result in aversive long-term outcomes and are obstacles in the pursuit of goals and valued activities.

In this latter portion of therapy, therapists emphasize the identification of life circumstances, situations, and issues that increase their clients' vulnerability to future episodes of depression. If there are common triggers for depressed mood, for example, clients might be encouraged to avoid these, if possible. Some important life areas also might be singled out for attention. These might include clients working on relationships with others by purposely engaging in more activities that involve other people. In other cases, clients might take stock of their long-term goals or values and make a deliberate decision to bring day-to-day activities more in line with these. For other clients, this might mean making a significant life change, which would involve changing a major life role or responsibility (husband or wife, one's job) for an alternative (divorcee, a new job). Reducing vulnerability to depressed mood might also involve taking steps to overcome past traumas, move beyond them, and shed the perspective of oneself as "damaged" or a "victim" and instead accept and value oneself. Acting differently is one way for a client to reduce the influence of the past, and the client acting in accordance with long-term goals and objectives increases the likelihood that these will eventually be realized.

Establishing regular routines is also often helpful in preventing relapse, particularly if such routines are regarded as pleasing and consistent with the client's long-term goals. The emphasis on developing regular routines is grounded in observations that the disruption of routines is often associated with the maintenance of depression (Jacobson et al., 2001). Regular routines provide a regulation function and, provided that they include behaviors that result in positive reinforcement, keep individuals in regular contact with events that maintain behavior.

Diane's Progress in Shifting Contexts to Reduce Likelihood of Future Depression and to Realize Long-Term Goals

Over the course of 22 sessions, Diane made considerable progress in blocking avoidance patterns and accessing reinforcers from her environment. Her mood has steadily improved over the duration of therapy (BDI–II score from last session = 13), and self-report questionnaires indicated improvement in worry (PSWQ = 32) and perceived social support (ISEL = 30).

In reflecting on her progress, Diane indicated that she was much more aware of the relationships that her activities and mood share. She also described the TRAP associated with some coping strategies and avoidance—that is, their tendency to provide immediate relief but negatively influence mood and overall life satisfaction in the long run.

Although Diane has taken several steps to enhance her life through her own actions, she identified two primary areas that she needed to address to reduce her vulnerability to depression further: (a) her fear and avoidance of romantic relationships and (b) her negative views of herself. As Diane and her therapist examined these two issues, it became apparent that her negative self-view was related to her apprehension around the prospect of dating and establishing intimate relations. Her negative thoughts about herself, however, also had more global effects. Diane noticed that whenever she tried something new, these thoughts would often stop her from going forward, and she would revert back to avoidance patterns.

When her therapist challenged her to consider what she had learned from therapy that she could subsequently apply to these outstanding issues, Diane reported that she just needed to continue to do things that are consistent with what she wants to achieve, adding that the successes she has recently had further weakened the negative views she has of herself. Similarly, she acknowledged that although in some respects it is easier to avoid the possibility of rejection by not dating, she concluded that rejection, if experienced, would hurt for a short period of time, but that not being in a stable and satisfying relationship would likely result in long-term disappointment and further increase her negative self-views and lower her mood. Diane then volunteered that life naturally involves an element of risk and that as a result of therapy, she's discovered that living life is not as threatening as she once viewed it to be.

SUMMARY

When using behavioral activation strategies in the treatment of depression, it is often useful for the therapist to do the following:

- Adopt the view that depression arises from a series of incidents and is not the product of an internal defect or deficit.
- Conduct ideographically based functional analyses of the client's overall activities, with special attention given to circumstances, situations, and events consistently associated with depressed mood.
- Identify harmful behavior patterns that are characteristically associated with depressed mood.
- Institute gradual or small changes in situations associated with depressed mood and compare resultant outcomes with those typically associated with what the client usually does.
- Block avoidant coping patterns that are associated with the maintenance of depressed mood or incompatible with the realization of important life goals or objectives.
- Assist the client in getting back on track or in taking active steps toward reaching his or her long-term goals and objectives.

9

EXPOSURE-BASED INTERVENTIONS

Clients often seek help for difficulties with intense, persistent, and potentially maladaptive fear and anxiety. With a lifetime prevalence of up to one third of the general population, anxiety disorders are among the most common disorders for which people seek clinical assistance (Kessler, Berglund, et al., 2005; Kessler et al., 2006). Anxiety-related disorders also appear to be more severe variants of common experiences. Whereas the lifetime prevalence of panic disorder is approximately 5%, the lifetime prevalence of panic attacks has been found to be 28% (Kessler et al., 2006). Behaviors commonly associated with other anxiety disorders, such as worrying and compulsive checking and ordering, also are common among the general population (Radomsky & Rachman, 2004; Tallis, Eysenck, & Mathews, 1992). Problems with anxiety also predict poorer prognosis and treatment response for other disorders (e.g., major depression; Andreescu et al., 2007; Enns & Cox, 2005). Clinicians, therefore, are likely to encounter clients

http://dx.doi.org/10.1037/14691-009
Behavioral Interventions in Cognitive Behavior Therapy: Practical Guidance for Putting Theory Into Action,
Second Edition, by R. F. Farmer and A. L. Chapman

with anxiety-related difficulties, either as a primary area of concern or as a co-occurring condition associated with other problem areas.

Within contemporary cognitive behavior therapy (CBT), exposure therapy plays a prominent role in the treatment of clinical problems in which fear, anxiety, and avoidance are central features. Exposure-oriented interventions and principles, for example, are core components of treatments for specific phobias (Choy, Fyer, & Lipsitz, 2007), panic disorder with and without agoraphobia (Barlow & Craske, 1994), social phobia (D. M. Clark, 2001; Heimberg & Becker, 2002), posttraumatic stress disorder (PTSD; Foa, Keane, & Friedman, 2004; Foa & Rothbaum, 1998), obsessive–compulsive disorder (OCD; Foa, Yadin, & Lichner, 2012), and generalized anxiety disorder (T. A. Brown, O'Leary, & Barlow, 2001). Exposure-oriented interventions also have been adapted and extended to problems with anger (Brondolo, DiGiuseppe, & Tafrate, 1997; see also Chapter 7, this volume), substance dependence (Conklin & Tiffany, 2002), eating disorders (Toro et al., 2003), compromised immune system functioning (Ader & Cohen, 1985), and complex clinical problems such as borderline personality disorder (Linehan, 1993a).

Given the prominence of exposure interventions among many current evidence-based therapies, this chapter provides practical guidance on how to conceptualize and implement such interventions in CBT. We begin by discussing the history, key features, efficacy, and mechanisms of change associated with exposure-oriented interventions. Subsequently, we discuss ways to use behavioral assessment to guide the use of exposure, considerations regarding different types of exposure strategies, and methods for applying exposure therapies.

KEY FEATURES OF EXPOSURE THERAPY

A review of the history of exposure therapy is beyond the scope of this chapter, but it is important to note that earlier work in this area emphasized the process of counterconditioning as a key feature of treatment for phobias and anxiety-related difficulties. Counter-conditioning, when applied to these difficulties, involves the substitution of an adaptive alternative response (e.g., relaxation) for a maladaptive response (excessive or maladaptive anxiety). One intervention similar to contemporary exposure therapy based on the principles of counterconditioning is *systematic desensitization* (SD; Davison, 1968; Wolpe, 1958). SD involves the presentation of progressively more anxiety-provoking stimuli in imagination while the client is relaxed (the result of participation in progressive muscle relaxation exercises before exposure to anxiety-related stimuli). From a counterconditioning

[handwritten margin note: incompatible responses]

perspective, SD teaches the client to use manifestations of anxiety (e.g., somatic responses such as muscle tension) as cues to substitute replacement behaviors incompatible with anxiety (e.g., those associated with relaxation). Several laboratory-based observations, however, are inconsistent with a counterconditioning explanation of SD for reducing fears (Wilson & Davison, 1971). Several applied studies have also indicated that it is not necessary to pair an incompatible response (e.g., relaxation) with exposure to a feared stimulus to reduce associated anxiety (e.g., Cooke, 1968). Contemporary exposure therapy, which evolved from this earlier work, includes interventions that bring clients into contact with feared events and experiences without necessarily inducing relaxation or other incompatible responses.

One key and defining feature of contemporary exposure therapy is the client's engagement with fear- or emotion-eliciting stimuli in a repeated or prolonged fashion (Abramowitz, 2013). These stimuli might include animate (e.g., spiders, snakes) or inanimate (e.g., toilets, door handles, knives) objects; events, places, or situations (e.g., criticism, public speaking, malls, movie theaters); or internal experiences (e.g., emotions, thoughts, bodily sensations, memories). Over repeated exposures, the probability, frequency, or intensity of the client's emotional response to the stimuli often decline. A client who is afraid of spiders, for example, may eventually encounter spiders at home, work, or other places with greatly diminished fear. Sometimes other emotional reactions to the feared stimulus, such as interest and curiosity, become more dominant over time. The client also may display a broader range of behavior (e.g., gazing at the spider, carefully removing it from the house, allowing it to crawl on her or his hand) in situations previously associated with escape and avoidance.

A second key feature of exposure interventions is the client's engagement in actions that are inconsistent with those commonly associated with the emotional response to feared or emotionally evocative stimuli. Barlow and colleagues (Barlow, 1988; Barlow, Allen, & Choate, 2004) have argued that preventing action tendencies consistent with the emotion (e.g., avoidance or escape in the case of fear) and helping clients engage in action tendencies that are inconsistent with the emotion (e.g., approaching rather than avoiding) are among the most important aspects of treatments for emotional disorders, such as depression and anxiety disorders. For example, for a client who is afraid of public speaking, exposure might involve asking her to give a speech in front of a small group of people (exposure to the feared stimulus) while helping her stay in the situation and engage in behaviors that are inconsistent with anxiety. Such behaviors might involve making eye contact with the audience, adopting a confident posture, or expressing enthusiasm about the topic of the speech. The client also would be encouraged to avoid

until
SUDs ↓

behaviors that are consistent with anxiety, such as looking down, fidgeting, or looking away from the audience. These two key features of exposure interventions are further elaborated and illustrated later in this chapter.

EMPIRICAL BASIS OF EXPOSURE INTERVENTIONS

The application of exposure-based intervention methods is most strongly supported for anxiety and related disorders. Recent meta-analytic reviews have indicated strong empirical support and medium to large effects for interventions that include exposure in the treatment of anxiety and related disorders (Olatunji, Cisler, & Deacon, 2010). CBT-oriented interventions that include exposure, response prevention (ERP), and cognitive restructuring components are among the most effective interventions OCD (Hofmann & Smits, 2008; Olatunji et al., 2010). Additional findings further suggest better recovery rates and lower posttreatment symptom levels for ERP compared with CBT and cognitive therapy. Although studies have yet to examine exposure interventions specifically for youth with OCD, CBT (including ERP) is associated with larger effect sizes (~ 1.45) than pharmacotherapy (~ 0.48) for patients 19 years and younger (Eddy, Dutra, Bradley, & Westen, 2004). The durability of CBT and exposure-oriented interventions for OCD, however, remains unclear given the relatively short follow-up periods across studies (Olatunji et al., 2010).

Exposure and related interventions (e.g., systematic desensitization) have been mainstays of the treatment of various forms of phobia for decades. For specific phobias, in vivo exposure is associated with large effect sizes for pre- to posttreatment symptom reduction, and small to medium effect sizes for symptom reduction, when compared with nonexposure or placebo treatment conditions (Olatunji et al., 2010). For social phobia, CBT treatment packages that include cognitive interventions, exposure, and other behavioral strategies are associated with medium to large effects compared with alternative treatment and wait-list and nontreatment control conditions (Olatunji et al., 2010). Studies examining the relative efficacy of specific interventions for social phobia within these CBT packages (e.g., exposure therapy vs. cognitive restructuring) have not suggested the superiority of one mode of intervention over another. At this time, then, exposure is best considered an important part of a larger treatment package for social anxiety-related problems.

For PTSD, exposure-oriented interventions, which typically include a combination of prolonged imaginal exposure to trauma memories and in vivo exposure to feared situations, have demonstrated large and consistent effects (Olatunji et al., 2010). For prolonged exposure (PE), large effects have been reported for pre- to posttreatment changes in symptoms and in outcome studies in which PE is compared with nonspecific, supportive control treatments

(Olatunji et al., 2010). Effect sizes are similarly large for exposure or exposure plus cognitive restructuring when compared with nonspecific control conditions (Bradley, Greene, Russ, Dutra, & Westen, 2005). In comparisons of CBT with eye movement desensitization and reprocessing (EMDR; a treatment that includes imaginal exposure to trauma memories in conjunction with therapist-guided lateral eye movements), small, nonsignificant effects have favored CBT (Seidler & Wagner, 2006). In addition, findings have suggested that the primary active ingredient in EMDR may be the exposure therapy component of the treatment rather than the facilitation of eye movements (McNally, 1999). Although findings overall support the efficacy of exposure as a stand-alone treatment for trauma-related problems, PE protocols usually include an element of cognitive restructuring (Foa & Rothbaum, 1998), with therapists often helping clients address thoughts about blameworthiness and modify self- or worldviews related to the trauma experience.

CBT interventions for panic disorder often include interoceptive (exposure to feared bodily sensations) and in vivo exposure, along with cognitive interventions and relaxation training. Such interventions have strong empirical support, with findings suggesting success rates of 80% to 100% in the reduction of the frequency of panic attacks (for a review, see Craske & Barlow, 2014). Although exposure therapy is theoretically central to the treatment of panic disorder with and without agoraphobia, it is not clear from the extant research whether the exposure-oriented interventions are the driving force behind the effects of CBT. One review suggested that the full CBT package might be more effective for reducing accompanying depression and improving quality of life, compared with only the behavioral components (e.g., in vivo exposure, interoceptive exposure; Mitte, 2005). Similar to social anxiety disorder, exposure is likely to be an important component of broader treatment for panic-related problems.

Researchers have suggested that generalized anxiety disorder (GAD), characterized by persistent worry, other cognitive symptoms (e.g., difficulty concentrating), and related physiological–emotional symptoms (anxiety, tension), is among the most challenging anxiety disorders to treat (Gould, Safren, Washington, & Otto, 2004). CBT-oriented interventions for GAD typically include behavioral and cognitive strategies (e.g., behavioral experiments; see Chapter 5) that involve an evaluation of the likelihood of worry-related outcomes and an examination of self-efficacy beliefs regarding the client's ability to cope should feared outcomes occur. Other common CBT components often include self-monitoring and relaxation training. Some CBT approaches to GAD emphasize intolerance of uncertainty as an important maintaining factor (Dugas & Koerner, 2005). Interventions based on this model include a variety of cognitive and behavioral strategies addressing worry as well as tolerance of and beliefs about uncertainty (Dugas &

Robichaud, 2007). Exposure tends to be a less prominent component of treatment for GAD (compared with the treatment of other anxiety disorders), sometimes consisting of in vivo exposure to situations associated with worry or exposure to worry thoughts (i.e., worry exposure). As a result, it is difficult to say how efficacious exposure-oriented interventions are for GAD independent of other treatment components. Full CBT treatment packages, however, are generally associated with medium effect sizes for the reduction of anxiety and depression associated with GAD when compared with a variety of control conditions (Olatunji et al., 2010). A recent systematic review found greater reductions in anxiety, worry, and symptoms of depression for GAD patients undergoing CBT compared with wait-list and other control conditions (Hunot, Churchill, Silva de Lima, & Teixeira, 2007). Other findings have suggested that response rates are similar for cognitive therapy (without exposure) versus relaxation training alone (Siev & Chambless, 2007).

Models of GAD emphasizing emotion regulation and experiential avoidance have suggested an important role for exposure in the treatment of GAD. Such models suggest that temporary reductions in anxiety and an increased sense of predictability and control may reinforce and maintain worry (Borkovec, Alcaine, & Behar, 2004; Borkovec & Hu, 1990). Interventions aimed at reducing emotional avoidance and improving the client's understanding, identification, and tolerance of anxiety and other negative emotional states might optimally include a combination of acceptance- and exposure-oriented interventions (Mennin, 2006; Roemer & Orsillo, 2002). Extant data, however, do not clearly indicate whether exposure interventions are necessary or sufficient in the treatment of GAD.

In summary, the evidence supports the use of exposure-oriented interventions for the treatment of a variety of anxiety-related disorders. Among the anxiety disorders, the strongest evidence currently is for the use of ERP in the treatment of OCD. For panic disorder (with or without agoraphobia) social anxiety disorder, and GAD, exposure should be considered as one component of a broader CBT-oriented package given the absence of evidence for exposure as a stand-alone treatment for these disorders. In addition, PE alone and in the context of a broader CBT package has demonstrated efficacy in the treatment of PTSD, even among multidiagnostic, complex clients (Harned, Korslund, & Linehan, 2014).

HOW AND WHY DO EXPOSURE INTERVENTIONS WORK?

Early theoretical accounts for the effects of exposure therapy were based on both classical and operant conditioning principles (Mowrer, 1960, 1974). These principles are highlighted in the following client illustration.

Because of early life experiences of being repeatedly bullied and assaulted by a small group of male teens during high school, a client ("James") in his early adult life has come to have strong emotional, physiological, and behavioral reactions to seeing small groups of male youth in public. James further reported more moderate yet potent reactions to seeing adolescent males by themselves, when overhearing the type of music that the group of bullies from his adolescence frequently played when together, or when seeing others wear some of the distinct clothing items or accessories that the teens who bullied him often wore (e.g., aviator-style sunglasses, large and bulky rings on fingers). A traditional classical conditioning analysis of the client's fear acquisition during high school would suggest that the acquired responses of intense anxiety, accelerated heart rate, and escape behavior (i.e., *conditioned responses*, or CR) to male youth, certain types of music, and aviator-style sunglasses or large finger rings (i.e., *conditioned stimuli*, or CS) came about as a result of the repeated pairing of these previously neutral stimuli with attacks, beatings, and taunts (i.e., *unconditioned stimuli*, or UCS) that elicited intense anxiety, accelerated heart rate, and attempts to behaviorally escape or flee (i.e., *unconditioned response*, or UCR) among other responses when the client was repeatedly exposed to these danger- or threat-related stimuli.

Although the classical conditioning model could explain the conditional properties of these previously neutral cues (male teens, certain styles of music and sunglasses, bulky rings) ensuing from repeated UCS–CS pairings as well as the resultant conditioned responses to conditional stimuli (i.e., the acquisition of the fear response), it could not satisfactorily account for the maintenance of fear responses over time in the absence of the UCS. One account of the maintenance of such responses is Mowrer's (1960, 1974) two-factor model, in which phobic-like fears are acquired through classical conditioning processes and maintained over time through operant conditioning processes. The specific class of operant behavior believed to maintain classically conditioned fears is escape and avoidance behavior. Escape and avoidance are operant behaviors that culminate in the removal of aversive events (e.g., fear stimuli, aversively experienced fear-related responses) and are hence negatively reinforced behaviors that become more probable over time in the presence of such stimuli. Escape and avoidance behavior in the presence of fear-related stimuli, however, do not permit the prolonged presentation of CS in the absence of the UCS and, correspondingly, the weakening of the UCS–CS linkages and the extinction of CRs related to conditioned trauma cues (CS). Rather, escape and avoidance behavior leave the original UCS–CS pairing essentially intact, and, correspondingly, the CRs to CS events are maintained long after the occurrence of the original traumatic events.

Researchers have raised some criticisms about traditional classical conditioning or two-factor learning accounts of fear acquisition and maintenance (e.g., Foa & Rothbaum, 1998). Criticisms include difficulty distinguishing between UCS and CS in naturalistic environments and rejection of automatic associative processes hypothesized to establish CS–UCS linkages and CS–CR pairings. For these reasons, the concept of "habituation" has occasionally been substituted for "extinction" to signify reductions in anxiety in the presence of anxiety-related cues as a result of exposure (e.g., Jaycox, Foa, & Morral, 1998).

As a result of the limitations of earlier theories, alternative accounts of fear acquisition, fear maintenance, and the change mechanisms underlying exposure therapy have been proposed. One such theory includes *emotional processing theory* (EPT; Foa & Kozak, 1986; Foa & McNally, 1996). According to EPT, fear is represented as a memory structure that involves stimuli (e.g., heights, being atop tall buildings or bridges), responses (e.g., avoidance, freezing, shaking), and cognitive "meaning" elements (e.g., "danger" appraisals). Within this framework, this memory structure functions to help people escape danger and includes information indicating that particular stimuli are dangerous. Exposure therapy, according to EPT, must involve the presentation of relevant stimulus elements, the activation of the memory structure, and the incorporation of information that is incompatible with the fear structure to be effective. Through the client's habituation of the emotional response through exposure in contexts that normally elicit fear, the link between the fear stimulus (e.g., the height-related stimuli) and the avoidance or escape response weakens as the client learns that avoidance and escape are not necessary to reduce fear. Lower levels of fear and arousal allow for the client's incorporation of corrective information indicating that the previously feared stimuli are not dangerous. Within the framework of EPT, repeated exposures over time theoretically allow for the client's integration of new, non–fear-related memories, resulting in the meaning elements related to the client's fear becoming divorced from the stimuli that previously elicited them (Foa & Kozak, 1986; Foa & McNally, 1996).

Recent findings on the factors related to outcomes in exposure therapy have further called into question some of the implications of EPT and traditional exposure therapy practices (Craske et al., 2008). One implication of EPT and other accounts of exposure therapy, for example, is that exposure therapy should work best when the client evidences activation of the fear structure (*initial fear activation*) upon presentation of the feared stimulus and subsequently shows a reduction in fear during prolonged exposure to the stimulus (*within-session habituation*). These premises formed the bases for recommendations that clinicians maintain exposure to feared stimuli and situations until the client's fear decreases by at least 50% when referenced to the initial or baseline response (e.g., through prolonged exposure to a spider, the client's subjective units of distress, or SUDs rating, decreases from 90 to 45). Empirical data on exposure interventions, however, call these traditional recommendations into question. Findings, for example, have been mixed regarding whether initial fear activation or within-session habituation predicts treatment outcome, and some research has suggested that exposure therapy is effective even when exposure trials are terminated at peak levels of anxiety (e.g., when the exposure of the client to a spider ends even though no habituation has occurred and SUDS ratings remain at 90; Craske et al., 2008). Moreover, the findings on the importance of habituation of fear between sessions (e.g., a drop in peak fear levels from 90 in one session to 75 in the next session) also have been mixed, with some studies showing that clinical improvement occurs despite lack of reduction in physiological indications of fear responses across sessions (Craske et al., 2008).

Modern learning theory explanations of how exposure therapy works have emphasized inhibitory learning processes and the development of new learned associations with feared stimuli (e.g., Bouton, 2004; Craske et al., 2008). These accounts suggest that exposure does not necessarily weaken or erase previous learning (the CS–UCS link) but rather facilitates the development of new associations of the CS with alternative stimuli through inhibitory learning processes. *Inhibitory learning* involves acquiring competing and nonthreatening associations in which the CS also predicts the nonoccurrence of threatening events and a variety of nonthreatening outcomes. A client who is afraid of nonpoisonous spiders but holds them, looks at them, and spends time with them may learn that such spiders engage in nonthreatening actions (e.g., they simply sit there or crawl around) rather than biting. In the case of nonpoisonous spiders, a client might further experientially learn that a bite from such a spider will not cause illness or otherwise threaten health or well-being. Although such learning may result in less fear of spiders over time, this reduced fear is not the most important gauge of the effects of treatment. Exposure therapy is still successful when the client simply learns and generalizes these new associations to a variety of contexts (e.g., nonpoisonous spiders at home, outside, at work). Fear might still occur despite this new learning, and as such, there is also a greater emphasis within this framework on fear tolerance rather than fear reduction (Craske et al., 2008).

WHEN DO THERAPISTS USE EXPOSURE INTERVENTIONS?

Within this section, we discuss the conditions under which a therapist may choose to use exposure-based interventions. We begin by discussing considerations regarding the application of exposure to problems with fear and anxiety. An important initial consideration regarding the use of exposure therapy is whether the fear is accurate or adaptive in the current context. Fear is generally an accurate and adaptive response in situations in which imminent danger is present, including threats to the individual's life or well-being. In these cases, the physiological (sympathetic nervous system arousal; preparation for flight, fight, or freeze responses) and behavioral tendencies (avoid, escape, protect oneself) associated with fear serve important functions. It would be maladaptive to feel calm and serene when a grizzly bear suddenly walks into the boardroom during a business meeting or when one has unknowingly stepped into the path of oncoming traffic. A first consideration, then, is the accuracy or adaptiveness of the fear response relative to the presence of actual threat stimuli or the probability of harm. Exposure is generally appropriate when fear or anxiety is neither accurate nor adaptive in the current context. A second consideration is that the exposure procedures themselves should not place the client at risk or otherwise strengthen CS–UCS associations. When exposing an acrophobic client to high places, for example, the therapist should ensure that the client is unlikely to slip or fall.

Applications of Exposure-Based Interventions Beyond Maladaptive Fear or Anxiety

When using exposure therapy or any other intervention in this book, behavioral theory will help the clinician determine when and how to apply the interventions effectively. Although there is some evidence for exposure-oriented approaches to problems other than maladaptive anxiety and fear, the theory and proposed mechanisms of change for exposure best fit situations in which the client would benefit from learning new, non-threat associations (inhibitory learning) to current fear-provoking situations (Abramowitz, 2013). As reviewed earlier, the preponderance of the evidence supports the use of exposure for the treatment of clinical problems characterized by maladaptive fear characterized by excessive intensity, associated problematic responses (e.g., avoidance), and resistance to modification (Foa & Kozak, 1986). Extensions of exposure beyond these types of difficulties may be appropriate but should be done with a theoretical rationale that is clearly linked to what is known about how and for what problems exposure works. As Abramowitz (2013) stated, a common error among clinicians is that "when exposure is the hammer, everything is the nail" (p. 551). Some emotions, such as sadness and anger, may not habituate in the same way as fear, nor might they be associated with threat-related conditioned stimuli (Abramowitz, 2013; Abramowitz, Deacon, & Whiteside, 2011). Therefore, exposure is not necessarily the right tool to help clients with all problems with emotions, urges, and aversive states.

We recommend that clinicians seeking to extend exposure beyond its traditional domain conduct a precise and thorough assessment to determine whether the mechanism targeted by exposure (exaggerated threat-related associations, maladaptive anxiety and fear) is relevant to the client's specific clinical problem areas. One area to assess when a client reports excessive anger, for example, is the nature of the potential threat associated with the anger-provoking event(s). Anger often functions to motivate action, encourage attempts to master or control the environment, and to protect or defend against threats or danger (Lewis, Sullivan, Ramsay, & Alessandri, 1992). When anger is related to perceived threat, exposure interventions may be an appropriate part of a broader set of strategies targeting anger. During a thorough assessment, for example, a client who initially reports road rage when someone is driving slowly might subsequently reveal that the "threat" associated with this situation is the resultant late arrival at home or work. In this case, the consequences of arriving late (e.g., disapproval, loss of work time) constitute the threat. Perhaps, though, the client's anger is a secondary emotional reaction to the fear of being late. Exposure therapy could target the feared situation (e.g., arriving late at home) and thus help the client learn that this situation is not dangerous. The client could, for example, start with imaginal exposure, which might include imagining events involving her or his late arrival at home, followed by in vivo exposure. As long as threatening events do not occur, exposure might also help to alter thoughts or rules regarding these events (e.g., "If I come home late, my wife will be furious with me"), much like the behavioral experiments discussed in Chapter 5. If, however, the threat is realistic and potentially damaging (the client will receive a poor performance review at work; the wife will slap him), however, exposure to this situation (i.e., being late) likely would not be advisable or helpful. More appropriate interventions might include arousal reduction and emotion regulation strategies to manage anger more effectively, strategies to enhance empathy and perspective taking, problem-solving strategies to help the client wake earlier or devise alternative routes that would be faster, or approaches that target dysfunctional environments (e.g., the assaultive wife) that contribute to his sense of threat.

Exposure-oriented approaches for other emotions, such as sadness, may be effective, provided that the rationale is clear and based on the principles underlying this treatment approach. "Mandy," for example, had a learning history in which her parents responded to expressions of sadness with harsh criticism ("What's the matter with you? You're so weak and pathetic!"), threats, and physical abuse. She eventually began to respond to physiological signs of sadness (sinking feeling in her chest, heavy limbs), and particularly signs that she may be about to express sadness (sensations in her face, urges to cry, watery eyes), with intense dread, fear, and sometimes panic.

When therapeutic discussions addressed situations eliciting sadness, Mandy often froze, became silent, switched the topic, or expressed anger toward the therapist. She also dissociated periodically in these situations. Her fear of sadness was understandable given her learning history but maladaptive in the present context, in which it was safe (and likely therapeutic) to express sadness. The therapist conceptualized this situation as one in which particular stimuli, such as physical sensations suggesting the impending expression of sadness, had become associated with verbal and physical attacks by others. Exposure therapy, therefore, was a reasonable intervention to consider and might involve exposing Mandy to triggers for sadness while encouraging her to inhibit behaviors that function to block the experience or expression of this emotion.

BEGINNING STEPS: ASSESSMENT AND ORIENTATION

Among the first steps in any of the interventions described in this book are precise behavioral assessment and clear client orientation to the therapeutic approach. Behavioral assessment is important for determining whether exposure strategies are likely to be effective for a particular client's presenting problems and for guiding exactly how exposure should be conducted. Because exposure is often an emotionally taxing intervention, clear orientation of the client to the specifics and rationale for exposure is important. Otherwise, the situation is akin to the therapist taking the client into a burning building without saying why or how they will get through alive. Orientation provides the client with clear expectations regarding how and why this exposure might work. In the sections that follow, we discuss and provide examples of behavioral assessment and orientation as applied to exposure-oriented interventions.

Using Functional Analysis to Guide Exposure Therapy

Because behavioral and functional analysis procedures are thoroughly discussed in Chapter 2, we briefly discuss these assessment strategies here as they pertain to how a therapist proceeds with exposure-oriented interventions. Behavioral assessment generally begins with an understanding of broad problem areas and narrows to precisely specify problematic behaviors (i.e., in terms of topography), followed by the development of a functional understanding of the behaviors of interest. An initial broad-based assessment of clinical problem areas will first reveal whether exposure interventions may be considered as a component of therapy for a particular client and where in the hierarchy of treatment targets such interventions might be most applicable. On the basis of currently available outcome research, clinical problems for

Emphasize rationale

which exposure interventions are likely to be particularly effective include obsessions and compulsive behaviors, phobic anxiety and the avoidance of specific situations or objects, posttraumatic reactions, social anxiety, and recurrent panic with or without agoraphobic avoidance.

As the assessment narrows in focus, an important next step is a precise examination of the client's emotional reactions. Assessment of the intensity, frequency, and duration of the fear response, as well as physiological and cognitive manifestations of anxiety or fear, will help the clinician isolate key treatment targets and understand the client's likely experiences during the exposure process. Assessment of the intensity of the client's emotional responses, in particular, helps to provide guidance regarding where and how to start with exposure therapy. In many therapy approaches, therapists use the SUDS scale, where 0 = *no distress at all* and 100 = *the most distress possible*. Before using exposure, the therapist often asks the client to give SUDS ratings for each situation in which an emotional response occurs. These situations, in turn, might be hierarchically arranged in ascending order of the SUDs rating, with exposure sessions organized according this hierarchy. Exposure sessions might begin with items that do not elicit high SUDS ratings (in the case of graduated exposure). When flooding is used, therapy might be started with the item associated with the highest SUDS rating.

PE is more like flooding

Another important step involves the clarification of avoidance-escape or safety behaviors as well as the potential reinforcers associated with such behaviors (i.e., the short- and long-term reinforcing consequences). As discussed earlier and further later in the chapter, avoidance and safety behaviors or safety signals can hamper the effects of exposure therapy. Clarifying specific avoidance or safety behaviors will help the clinician and client to prevent these from occurring during exposure. Without a precise behavioral assessment, it is easy to overlook a variety of subtle overt (e.g., fidgeting, skin picking, averting the gaze) and covert (e.g., mental distraction, dissociation) avoidance and safety behaviors. When exposure does not seem to be working, one possible explanation is that the client is engaging in avoidance or safety behaviors that the therapist has somehow missed (Abramowitz et al., 2011). Once the therapist and client have isolated these behaviors, they can work together collaboratively to develop plans for preventing their occurrence during within-session exposure interventions and during homework assignments.

Clarifying the specific features of situations in which anxiety, fear (or other targeted emotions), and avoidance occur will help the clinician plan exposure interventions that target the most relevant stimuli. Some socially anxious clients may be able to speak in front of others with little anxiety, for example, when surrounded by friends or while not eating, whereas speaking in front of unfamiliar people or during dinner may be terrifying. Clients with panic disorder generally tend to fear alterations in bodily sensations, but these sensations can be very specific. Some clients might find increases in body temperature or heart rate to be frightening, whereas others' exaggerated fears occur primarily in response to the sensations of dizziness or shortness of breath. Interoceptive exposure to dizziness for a client who has no exaggerated fear of dizziness is unlikely to be productive. For a client with fears of contamination, it is important to know whether she or he is only afraid of touching doorknobs or also fears public toilets, playgrounds, buses, handshakes, or other such situations. Many researchers have emphasized the importance of ensuring that exposure includes as many of the key fear-eliciting stimulus elements as possible (Abramowitz et al., 2011; Foa & Kozak, 1986). If the therapist targets one particular situation and misses out on the plethora of other relevant situations or stimuli, the client's fear may persist in these other situations. Another sign that important stimuli have been excluded is that the client evidences minimal anxiety during exposure (Abramowitz et al., 2011). In these cases, returning to a specific behavioral assessment of key feared situations and stimuli will help to isolate what was missed.

Orienting the Client to Exposure

As mentioned, it is important for a therapist to provide a clear idea of what is involved in exposure therapy and why he or she is recommending this intervention. Key elements of a clear orientation include the therapist (a) providing information on why exposure is the method of choice and giving some detail about any relevant research, (b) describing how exposure works, and (c) outlining the specific tasks involved in exposure. The following is an example of how a therapist might orient a client to exposure methods for fear of speaking in class.

> Therapist: You've said that you really want to work on your fear of speaking in class. From what we can tell, this is what we call a maladaptive fear. Have you heard that expression before?

> Client: No, but I think it makes sense. Is it like fear that's overblown or too much?

> Therapist: It's a lot like that. Maladaptive fears are fears that do not fit the situation. They are sort of like false alarms. Your brain is telling you there's danger when there is little or no danger present. Or maybe there's some mild danger, but your fear is too intense, like you're in a life-or-death situation. What do you think about your fear of speaking in class? Is it a false alarm, too intense for the situation, neither, or both?

Client: I think it's probably both. I mean, I feel so shaky and freaked out when I have something to add to the discussion that I just freeze up.

Therapist: Is there anything in particular that you're afraid of?

Client: I guess, when I think of it, I'm afraid that I might say something stupid, look really nervous, or that kind of thing.

Therapist: You know, those fears are really quite common. Isn't it interesting, though, that your body seems to be going into flight, fight, or freeze mode in your class? Normally, that kind of reaction is most appropriate when your life or safety is in danger. Do you think your life or safety is in danger in class?

Client: No, not really. I mean I might stammer or say something that's not the smartest, but I don't think logically that anyone is going to kill me!

Therapist: I guess that depends on what kind of class you're in! But you're probably right. Have you seen other people appear nervous or say things that weren't perfect?

Client: Yeah, a couple of students do that sometimes. I normally don't think much of it, and the professor is pretty nice.

Therapist: That's good news. That means that your fears (even the less life or death ones) probably don't fit the situation. When that's the case, one of the best ways to overcome fear and become free to speak up when you want is to do something called exposure therapy. Exposure therapy is an important part of treatments that work well for these types of problems. Several studies have shown that treatments including exposure therapy help people to become less afraid of social situations. Have you heard of exposure therapy?

Client: I think so. Like, if you're afraid of heights, you go to high places?

Therapist: Yes, this work involves facing situations that you're afraid of. Think of it this way. You already know logically that you're not really in danger in class, but your brain still goes into alarm mode. Sometimes, the best way to overcome fear is to learn directly from your experience, rather than trying to talk or think your way out of it. Does that make sense?

Client: It does, but it sounds scary. What are you going to get me to do?

Therapist: We can take this at your pace, and you will have a lot of control over how we do it. Exposure therapy basically involves you encountering situations that you're afraid of over and over. We would focus on situations involving speaking in class or in groups of people. We might begin with real-life situations or with situations that you imagine. What you can expect is that when you first go into or imagine these situations, you will feel quite afraid. You sort of feel worse at first to feel better later on. Over time, as your brain learns that there's no real danger, the fear may decline. The thing is, even if it doesn't decline, you will still be better off. You will learn to be free to speak up in class, fear or not. Does that sound like something you'd be willing to try?

TYPES OF EXPOSURE INTERVENTIONS

There are several types of exposure interventions. The key task for the therapist is to apply the most effective type and format of exposure to client's problem areas in the most effective manner, given the unique characteristics of the individual and his or her situation. Commonly used types of exposure interventions include (a) imaginal exposure, (b) in vivo exposure, (c) informal exposure, (d) interoceptive exposure, and (e) cue exposure. Opposite action is another type of intervention based on exposure principles. Table 9.1 provides a decision-making guide for selecting an appropriate exposure intervention for particular clinical problems.

Imaginal Exposure

Imaginal exposure uses the power of the client's imagination to help her or him develop nonthreat associations to feared situations, experiences, or events. This approach is used under a few different conditions: (a) when it is either difficult or impossible to expose the client to relevant stimuli in real life, (b) when the flexibility of the client's (or therapist's) imagination is useful in concocting effective scenarios that trigger emotional responses, or (c) as a precursor for in vivo exposure. Imaginal exposure may also be combined with practice of effective coping strategies in imagination. For a client who fears job interviews, for example, she might imagine being in a job interview and skillfully responding to difficult or challenging questions.

One form of imaginal exposure, called *prolonged exposure* (PE), is frequently used in treatments for PTSD, in which the therapist asks the client to imagine and recount a specific traumatic event in considerable detail (including sights, sounds, smells, and tactile sensations). The rationale for this intervention is that clients with posttraumatic stress responses often fear and avoid the experience of memories of the traumatic event. Although

Great table.

TABLE 9.1
Guidelines for Determining Which Type of Exposure to Use

Clinical problem	Type of exposure to use	Behaviors to prevent
Fear of particular events, people, places, animals, or objects, often related to PTSD, OCD, specific phobias, social anxiety disorder, among other problems	*In vivo exposure* to the feared and avoided events, people, places, animals, or objects, and prevention of the avoidance response	Avoidance, distraction, escape from the situation, object, person, animal, or event
Fear or other emotional responses to situations that are not readily reproducible in "real life" or fear of recollections of trauma (e.g., as in PTSD)	*Imaginal exposure* to the situation or recollections in the client's imagination	Avoidance, distraction, imagery that runs contrary to the exposure stimuli
Suppressing or avoiding an emotional response in session	*Informal exposure* to the emotion or topic that is avoided or suppressed	Any behavior that is consistent with the emotional response, particularly avoidance, distraction, or suppression
Maladaptive emotional responses, including but not limited to fear or anxiety (e.g., shame, envy, anger, irritation, sadness)	*Opposite action,* which involves exposure to the emotion-eliciting stimuli, in combination with acting in a manner opposite to the action urge related to the emotion	Avoidance, distraction, escape, and any behaviors that are consistent with the action urge(s) associated with the problematic emotion
Drug or alcohol use, urges or cravings to use drugs or alcohol	*Cue exposure* to drug or alcohol use cues	Avoidance, distraction, escape, and drug or alcohol use; imagining or fantasizing about drug or alcohol use
Fear and avoidance of specific bodily sensations	*Interoceptive exposure* to the specific bodily sensations, by engaging in activities that produce those sensations (e.g., spinning for fear of dizziness; exercise for elevated heart rate or sweatiness; staring in a mirror for depersonalization; breathing quickly for hyperventilation	Avoidance, distraction, or escape from the feared sensation

Note. OCD = obsessive–compulsive disorder; PTSD = posttraumatic stress disorder.

memories of the trauma will never be positive, they do not pose a material threat to the individuals' safety or well-being. The traumatic event may have been dangerous but the memories are not (Foa & Rothbaum, 1998). The goal of PE, then, is for clients to learn new associations with the experience of the traumatic memory (e.g., that the memory is unpleasant but not threatening or dangerous). Imaginal exposure can be used for a variety of types of fears. "Ann," for example, was a client who experienced intense fear whenever her partner raised his voice. It appeared that this fear was related to a learning history that involved childhood physical abuse. After determining that her current partner was unlikely to engage in physical aggression (he had no history of doing so and was averse to any type of physical confrontation), the therapist conducted imaginal exposure by asking Ann to imagine being in a variety of situations in which her partner raised his voice. The imaginal exposure allowed Ann to use her imagination to increase the partner's voice volume, see him becoming increasingly agitated, and envision the most fear-provoking scenarios involving her partner. Over time, Ann's fear of these specific behaviors of her partner diminished, and she was subsequently more effective in responding to her partner during conflict situations (because she was no longer inhibited by excess fear).

In Vivo Exposure

In vivo exposure involves exposing the client to emotionally evocative stimuli in real life and can occur in a variety of settings, including the client's home, the therapist's office, or various places in the client's natural environment. In vivo exposure with "Maurice" involved the therapist taking him up to high levels of parking garages, dining at the window seat of a fifth-story restaurant, and driving over high bridges and overpasses. In the example of PTSD and PE, although fear of the memory of the trauma is probably maladaptive, an individual's fear in response to an actual traumatic event would be accurate and adaptive; hence, exposure to traumatic events in vivo would make little sense and would be dangerous. The in vivo exposure component of treatment for PTSD, therefore, typically involves exposure to avoided or feared situations associated with the traumatic event (e.g., walking somewhere alone, dark places, men) provided that these situations are characterized by an acceptably low risk of harm or danger. In vivo exposure is often used with clients who have a variety of other difficulties. For instance, some clients with OCD are afraid of engaging in activities that expose them to dirt and germs, even though these activities are unlikely to result in disease. In vivo exposure might involve the therapist asking the client to touch doorknobs, put his or her hands on a well-traveled floor, sit on a public toilet seat, or try other such activities without engaging in compulsive cleaning behavior.

In vivo exposure for someone with problematic social anxiety might involve exposing him or her to social performance situations, such as interacting with other people in a group setting, public speaking, going to parties and "mingling" with people, or other such fear-eliciting activities.

Informal Exposure

Informal exposure involves the therapist exposing the client to stimuli that elicit emotional responses in an ad hoc manner during therapy sessions. Whereas standard in vivo and imaginal exposure interventions are normally conducted formally to a defined set of stimuli in a structured manner, informal exposure is less structured. This form of exposure is often used when the therapist notices that the client is avoiding or suppressing an emotional response, and such avoidance and suppression is likely to create further suffering or reinforce long-standing maladaptive coping patterns (Linehan, 1993a). With informal exposure, the therapist first provides a rationale that explains how informal exposure may be helpful given the client's goals. This is followed by the therapist's description of how and under what circumstances informal exposure might be implemented. During subsequent therapy sessions, if the therapist observes the client avoiding discussions of emotionally difficult material, for example, the therapist might clarify whether, in fact, avoidance is occurring. If the client confirms that he or she is avoiding certain topics or emotions, the therapist might encourage the client to describe in detail the experience or recollection that is being avoided and block any avoidance or escape behaviors while he or she is doing so.

"Sandy," for example, experienced intense anxiety when therapeutic discussions addressed his pursuit of employment. Following a suicide attempt, Sandy had been depressed and on leave from work for several months before entering therapy. One of his goals was to return to work. Because his colleagues were aware of his reasons for the leave, and because this goal seemed insurmountable (he was having difficulty even leaving the house), he felt intense anxiety whenever he and the therapist began to discuss action steps toward his returning to work. Even the small tasks that would help him get closer to this goal, such as getting up at a consistent time in the morning, reestablishing functional daily routines, and engaging in small mastery activities, had become threatening (e.g., associated with unpleasant emotions and the possibility of failure). Early in conversations about these topics, Sandy would begin to fidget, breathe more rapidly and shallowly, look away, and provide one-word answers or noncommittal responses to questions, or change the topic. Once the therapist determined that Sandy was feeling anxious and avoiding topics associated with returning to work, she gradually worked with him to keep him in the conversation, experience his anxiety, and otherwise remain engaged rather than avoid. Following is an example of one exchange involving informal exposure procedures.

Therapist: OK, so we've established that, when you change the topic, you're avoiding stuff to do with returning to work and that this probably helps take the anxiety away, at least temporarily. Does that sound right?

Client: Yeah, I guess that's what I'm doing. I mean, I just feel so overwhelmed when we start talking about the steps I have to take.

Therapist: Understandably so. It was a rough situation when you left work, and getting back on your feet is like climbing a mountain. Even more, it's like climbing a mountain when you have the fear that someone is going to push you off the top once you get there. We can work on your worries and fears about returning to work, but let me ask you this: Do you think you're going to learn to feel less overwhelmed about these small steps if we avoid the topic?

Client: I guess not, if you put it that way. Avoiding the topic feels better, but I'll probably be just as overwhelmed if it comes up again.

Therapist: Right, I would agree. The thing is that, somehow, you perceive our discussions about small steps as threatening or dangerous, and you feel anxious or afraid. In reality, simply discussing small steps is not a dangerous situation. I mean, it's not like you have to do them, right? Discussing these topics actually doesn't threaten your safety or well-being, right?

Client: I guess that makes sense.

Therapist: So, what do you think is one way out of this trap?

Client: I know what you're going to say. The only way to become less afraid of talking about it is to talk about it, right?

Therapist: Exactly, so let's agree to keep that in mind. When I see you avoiding, I'm going to ask you to step back, notice and experience the emotions that come up, and do your best to stay in the conversation. Does that sound like a plan?

Client: OK, I can give it a try.

Interoceptive Exposure

Interoceptive exposure involves the client encountering particular feared bodily sensations. This type of exposure is most often used for panic disorder, in which clients may experience intense fears and catastrophic misinterpretations (e.g., interpreting minor chest pain as an impending heart attack) of small changes in bodily sensations. Interoceptive exposure involves exercises that enhance the salience of bodily sensations that are feared by the client.

It is important to ensure that the most relevant, feared stimulus elements are present during exposure. A precise behavioral assessment will help to determine the types of bodily sensations that the client fears. Some clients (e.g., those with panic disorder) are afraid of the experience of dizziness. In this case, interoceptive exposure might involve the client spinning in circles. Other clients are afraid of the experience of a quickly beating heart; hence, exposure might involve the client engaging in brief periods of vigorous exercise. Interoceptive exposure for a client who fears sensations of derealization might involve the client staring for a prolonged period into a mirror.

Interoceptive exposure most often applies when the client has an intense fear of a particular bodily sensation or set of bodily sensations; however, some clients appear to have a more generalized fear of emotions or are "emotion phobic" (Linehan, 1993a). For this type of client, the therapist may elect to conduct full-on exposure to the entire set of emotions, thoughts, and sensations or may choose to use interoceptive exposure that is focused more specifically on bodily sensations of emotion. One important consideration is that sometimes attending to an emotional response and all of its accompanying experiences may be too challenging or overwhelming for a client. In addition, the thoughts that accompany distressing emotions might distract the client from the exposure experience. For these reasons, it is sometimes more effective to have the client focus specifically on bodily sensations associated with the emotion and to direct his or her attention away from these other experiences, at least initially.

Cue Exposure

Cue exposure (CE) is a behavioral technique that has been applied primarily to therapy for substance use problems, although extensions to other conditions such as bulimia nervosa have been reported (e.g., Toro et al., 2003). When applied to the treatment of substance abuse, CE involves the therapist presenting substance-related cues to the client (e.g., drug paraphernalia, sight and smell of preferred beverage, photographs of illicit drugs). Client consumption of the substance, however, is blocked. Client exposure to drug cues (CS), therefore, is not paired with the UCS (drug use), thus weakening the association that the CS has with the UCS. CE, then, is regarded as an extinction-based approach that results in gradual reductions in clients' conditional emotional and physiological responses (e.g., cravings and urges) to drug-use cues.

CE has been used by therapists in the treatment of persons with dependence on a variety of substances (e.g., tobacco, alcohol, cocaine, opiates) and has been conducted in inpatient and outpatient settings as well as in virtual environments (Lee et al., 2004). Results from this research suggest that CE itself is generally associated with modest treatment effects (Martin, LaRowe, & Malcolm, 2010). Findings have not indicated that CE added to CBT has greater effects on alcohol-related outcomes than CBT alone (Kavanagh et al., 2006). A limited number of studies comparing CBT with CE similarly have found that there are no significant differences in the effects of these approaches on alcohol-related outcomes, such as relapse rates (Loeber, Croissant, Heinz, Mann, & Flor, 2006; Martin et al., 2010), although one investigation found more abstinent days and lower amounts of alcohol consumed daily among CE (vs. CBT) patients (Loeber et al., 2006).

Few studies have examined CE for drugs other than alcohol, generally with small to medium-sized samples ($Ns = 12–110$), and the findings have been mixed (e.g., de Quirós Aragón, Labrador, & de Arce, 2005; Martin et al., 2010). Many of the studies in this area have suffered from limitations pertaining to their methods or procedures (Conklin & Tiffany, 2002; Havermans & Jansen, 2003). Until such limitations are satisfactorily addressed or resolved, CE is best regarded as a component of a larger therapy package rather than a stand-alone treatment (e.g., Rohsenow et al., 2001; Sitharthan, Sitharthan, Hough, & Kavanagh, 1997).

Opposite Action and Reversing Emotion-Linked Action Tendencies

On the basis of the principles of exposure therapy, the skill of *opposite action* involves acting in a manner that is opposite to the urge that accompanies a particular emotion (Linehan, 1993b). As described by Linehan (1993a) and others (Gross, 1998), emotions are often accompanied by urges to engage in particular actions. Fear, for instance, is frequently accompanied by the urge to escape or flee the situation, anger is often accompanied by the urge to yell or fight, and shame is usually accompanied by the urge to hide or withdraw. Opposite action involves exposure to the event that elicited the client's emotion, and the client acts in a manner that is opposite to the action urge that accompanies the emotion. A socially anxious client, for instance, might be afraid (unjustifiably so) of attending his brother's graduation party. His fear is related to his expectation that he will be humiliated and scorned by other attendees. Opposite action in this instance might involve encouraging the client to attend the party and talk to as many people as possible. A client who is angry with and feels the urge to yell or chastise a relative during a dinner party might engage in opposite action by gently avoiding the relative or fostering empathy (a state generally incompatible with anger)

EXHIBIT 9.1
Essential Steps for Performing Opposite Action
to Reduce Unwanted Negative Emotions

1. Identify and label the emotional experience (e.g., is it anxiety, sadness, shame, anger).
2. Determine whether the emotional experience is justified by the situation and whether the client wishes to reduce the emotion.
3. Determine the action urge associated with the emotional experience.
4. If the emotional experience is unjustified, figure out what action would be opposite to the action urge.
5. Ask the client engage in the opposite action thoroughly and repeatedly.

Note. Data from Linehan (1993b, 2015).

by trying to understand the other person's point of view or behavior. Unlike standard exposure procedures, opposite action normally applies more broadly to any potentially maladaptive emotional state (e.g., sadness, shame, anger, envy), not just fear or anxiety (see Exhibit 9.1 for five key steps in conducting opposite action). As with other exposure-based procedures, it is especially important that therapists ensure their clients do not engage in avoidance or safety behaviors when performing opposite action.

Exposure in Virtual Reality Environments

Over the past couple of decades, there has been a growing movement to use computer-assisted approaches to enhance, augment, or even replace standard cognitive–behavioral interventions. In the case of exposure therapy, several investigators have examined the use of virtual reality (VR) technology, ranging from desktop computers alone, to computers combined with head-mounted technologies, to fully immersive environments (Kim, Rosenthal, Zielinski, & Brady, 2014). VR technology would appear to have several advantages, including the ability to present a variety of ecologically valid stimuli that may not be possible without extensive and time-consuming in vivo exposure, the ability to administer exposures without having to leave the office, and precise control over the nature of the stimuli. Several recent reviews and meta-analyses have examined the effects of VR exposure therapy (VRET), primarily for various anxiety-related disorders. Across a variety of anxiety disorders, findings have suggested that VRET outperforms wait-list control conditions in the reduction of anxiety-related symptoms and is associated with the maintenance of treatment effects over follow-up periods (Opriş et al., 2012). Effect sizes for VRET compared with nontreatment control conditions tend to be large (Powers & Emmelkamp, 2008). The largest number of studies of VRET in anxiety disorders has been conducted in clients with PTSD. Although findings for PTSD have been promising, important limitations in the research thus far include small sample sizes, few published randomized controlled trials, very few studies reporting follow-up data, and a lack of measurement of therapist adherence to the treatment protocol (Motraghi, Seim, Meyer, & Morissette, 2014).

Several factors might influence a clinician's decision to use VRET protocols. First, the evidence to date does not suggest the superiority (or inferiority) of VRET compared with standard, empirically supported exposure therapy protocols. Because standard exposure therapy has a large and solid empirical base, questions might arise regarding whether it is necessary to embark on the newer, less well-supported VRET protocols at this time. Second, client preference regarding the use of technology-assisted therapy should be considered. Some findings have suggested that clients (at least those with acrophobia) may prefer VRET to standard in vivo exposure (Coelho, Waters, Hine, & Wallis, 2009). For clients who are less familiar or comfortable with computer technologies, VRET may not fit as well. Third, there are some potential drawbacks to VRET, including the need for clinicians to purchase and become familiar with this technology and related new treatment protocols and procedures, as well as potential concerns regarding the correspondence of what is happening in the office during VRET exposures with the client's practice of exposures in daily life.

IMPORTANT CONSIDERATIONS FOR EXPOSURE THERAPY

Once it is clear that exposure-oriented strategies can be helpful and the client knows how and why these interventions might work, it is important to ensure that exposure is conducted in the most effective manner for the client. Several factors require close attention, including scheduling exposure trials in the most effective and acceptable manner for the individual client, eliminating safety signals, blocking rituals and other safety behaviors, and providing the client with control over the exposure sessions. Within this section, we describe and discuss these considerations (see also Exhibit 9.2 for a list of steps for conducting exposure interventions).

Effective Pacing and Scheduling of Exposure Interventions

There are several important considerations regarding the pacing and scheduling of exposure interventions. One way to think about pacing is whether the client dives into the pool right away or gradually tests the

EXHIBIT 9.2
Ten Essential Steps for Putting Exposure Interventions Into Action

1. Use *functional analysis* to assess emotional reactions, safety signals and avoidance, escape, or ritual behaviors, and to clarify important elements of the stimuli or contexts to include in exposure trials.
2. Provide *clear orientation* to rationale, logistics, and likely outcomes of exposure.
3. Select an appropriate *type of exposure* (e.g., imaginal, in vivo).
4. Select an appropriate *pace, schedule, and duration* for exposure.
5. Before exposure, plan collaboratively with the client to *prevent* the occurrence of safety signals, escape or avoidance behaviors, and any relevant rituals.
6. During exposure, *prevent* the occurrence of safety signals and *prevent or block* escape, avoidance, or ritual behaviors.
7. Before, during, and after exposure, *monitor and assess the client's SUDS ratings* throughout the exposure trials in a nondistracting manner.
8. Provide exposure to *as many relevant stimulus and contextual elements* as possible.
9. Provide the client with *control* over the exposure trial.
10. Provide assignments for the client to *practice exposure* in relevant situations in her or his natural environment.

Note. SUDS = subjective units of distress.

waters, working her or his way up to the dive. *Graduated exposure* would be like gradually testing the waters, and involves exposure to progressively more distressing stimuli. The therapist and client first develop an exposure hierarchy ranging from items that are relatively low in SUDS to items that are the highest in SUDS. An exposure hierarchy for an acrophobic client ("Maurice"), for instance, was as follows: watching television scenes of people rock climbing (SUDS = 20), looking out a second-floor window in a secure building with the window closed (SUDS = 45), driving over a high bridge or overpass (SUDS = 65), walking over a high bridge or overpass (SUDS = 85), and standing at a high level in an open multilevel parking garage and looking down (SUDS = 95). After the therapist and Maurice constructed the exposure hierarchy, Maurice was exposed to items lower on the hierarchy first and then progressively to items higher on the hierarchy. *Flooding*, in contrast, involves diving into the pool right away, or exposing the client to the highest items on the exposure hierarchy first. Many exposure protocols use a combination of flooding and graduated exposure. Prolonged exposure for PTSD, for example, generally involves flooding in the sense that the client begins by recounting distressing memories of traumatic events, which is usually followed by a focus on the most salient and distressing aspects of those memories (Foa & Rothbaum, 1998).

There are a few considerations for a therapist in deciding between graduated exposure and flooding. Perhaps the most important consideration has to do with the effectiveness of these approaches. Generally, findings indicate that flooding is not detrimental or dangerous to clients (Shipley & Boudewyns, 1980). Some studies have suggested that flooding might have better long-term effects than graduated exposure, especially when the flooding is conducted in a massed format (Feigenbaum, 1988). Research and theory have traditionally emphasized the importance of initial fear activation (Kozak, Foa, & Steketee, 1988) or the peak fear-distress response during the first exposure trial, for the outcome of exposure therapy. If initial fear activation is important for outcome, then flooding would appear to be an efficient way to activate high levels of fear during initial exposure trials. Findings are equivocal, however, regarding the association of initial fear activation with outcome (Craske et al., 2008). It may therefore be unnecessary to ensure that clients have a strong fear reaction to stimuli during exposure.

Because research does not suggest a clear advantage of flooding over graduated exposure, a second important consideration is the acceptability of the exposure procedure to the client. Some clients are simply too afraid to agree to undergo flooding (e.g., Horne & Matson, 1977). Other clients, however, will likely react negatively to the suggestion of any type of exposure (whether flooding or graduated) because they are so afraid of encountering feared stimuli. In this case, we have found it useful to reiterate to the client the rationale for exposure and the expectation that distress may be high at first but likely will decline, help the client entertain the pros and cons of embarking on the exposure intervention, and give the client the clear message that he or she may terminate the exposure if need be.

Treatment manuals for particular clinical problems outline the typical schedules for exposure used in those treatments; however, there are a few general considerations. In particular, the therapist (and client) must decide whether to conduct exposure in a *massed format* or a *spaced format*. Exposure formats range anywhere from 3 to 4 hours per day over 5 to 6 days per week (massed format) to 30 to 120 minutes during once-per-week sessions (spaced format). Some research has suggested superior short-term effects for massed exposure (Foa, Jameson, Turner, & Payne, 1980); however, basic research on extinction learning has suggested some potential advantages to long-term learning of spaced exposure trials (Craske et al., 2008). Because the findings do not clearly suggest an advantage of one format over another, however, the scheduling and spacing of exposure trials often depends on the client's willingness and availability.

In terms of session length, therapists who conduct formal exposure interventions might consider scheduling sessions for longer than the standard "50-minute hour." This is because some clients find exposure to be overwhelming and have a difficult time cooling down emotionally by the end of a standard length session. Although it is not necessary for the client's emotional response to habituate by the end of the exposure trial, it is often important to provide time for debriefing and discussion or for practicing emotion coping strategies. Before embarking on exposure interventions, it is also important to ensure that clients with more complex or severe presentations have gone for a period without suicidal or self-injurious behaviors, are able to experience and tolerate aversive emotional states without engaging in harmful escape behaviors or dissociation, and are able to cope with or tolerate distress related to exposure (for additional considerations, see Harned et al., 2014).

Eliminating Safety Signals

Safety signals are stimuli that, when present, signal to the individual that feared outcomes are unlikely to occur. Their presence also interferes with inhibitory learning and reduces the client's emotional engagement with feared stimuli. Examples of safety signals include the presence of a significant other, the provision of reassurance by others, or the possession of a certain inanimate object that somehow neutralizes the threat associated with feared stimuli (e.g., a special pendant or charm, religious writings, medications for reducing anxiety, cell phone).

When safety signals are available in the presence of the actual feared stimuli, the client may associate the nonoccurrence of a threatening or dangerous event to the safety signals and not the actual feared stimuli. If a client wears a spider-proof suit during exposure sessions, for example, the client may learn that it is safe to handle spiders only while wearing a spider-proof suit. This does little to reduce unwarranted fear of spiders in the absence of such a suit. Being in a spider-proof suit may also reduce the client's emotional engagement with the feared stimulus and promote a sense of safety and security. Similarly, a client who repeatedly asks his therapist if touching the insecticide can is safe is likely evoking safety signals from the environment and, in so doing, is less likely to benefit therapeutically from the exposure session.

The elimination of safety signals involves an assessment of signals that are unique to the client, a clear orientation of the client to this process, and collaborative work to reduce or eliminate their presence. When reassurance is a safety signal, for example, the therapist might limit the client to a single reassuring query during an exposure, after which additional demands for reassurance would be ignored. Such ground rules governing safety signals would ideally be discussed in advance with the client, and accompanied by the provision of a rationale and an opportunity for the client to ask questions or express reservations or concerns.

Response (or Ritual) Prevention

Persons who experience ongoing struggles with anxiety or fear often develop behavioral coping strategies to reduce or manage the intensity and frequency of these experiences. As discussed earlier, avoidance and escape behavior are common coping strategies, as are other forms of safety behavior. *Safety behavior* refers to actions carried out by the individual to ward off feared events or to reduce the likelihood of their occurrence (Salkovskis, 1991, 1996). Examples of safety behaviors include repetitive checking (e.g., to determine that the stove is off or the door is locked), repeated verbalizations of religious text or other passages of special significance, or the enactment of rituals to neutralize perceived threats or dangers (e.g., counting, repeatedly touching objects in a certain sequence). *Response (or ritual) prevention* involves blocking behaviors that are associated with the escape from or avoidance of feared stimuli, including the elimination of safety behaviors. Response prevention during exposure sessions is critical if the individual is to discover that the fear response is unwarranted or unjustified and for new associations with fear-related stimuli to be learned.

Response prevention is a central feature of exposure-based therapies for OCD, although response prevention elements are also evident in many CBT-based therapies for mood and anxiety disorders (e.g., Barlow et al., 2011). Individuals with OCD who engage in compulsive behaviors (sometimes referred to as *rituals*) typically do so as a means to reduce anxiety or discomfort associated with unwanted repetitive and intrusive thoughts (i.e., obsessions). Often, compulsive rituals are successful in temporarily reducing discomfort associated with obsessive thoughts and are hence negatively reinforced behaviors. Engagement in compulsions, however, prevents the individual from learning that the obsessive thought, if left alone, will not produce catastrophic outcomes and may instead fade in intensity and frequency over time.

"Candice" had frequent and troubling thoughts about illness, injury, or death befalling her family members. These vivid thoughts were troubling for her not only because they often depicted tragic events happening to loved ones but also because she believed that if she did not "neutralize" the thought through taking action (repeatedly touching a type of container that could "hold" the thought, such as a jewel box), the harmful event involving the family member would actually occur and it would be her fault. Exposure therapy for Candice involved gradually exposing her to the types of thoughts and images she often had about harmful events happening family members, ordered according to the amount of distress associated with the thought or image (i.e., the SUDs rating). Candice and her therapist discussed in advance the importance of response prevention in helping her overcome her obsessions, which meant not touching a box or container when she focused on such thoughts. Although initially quite uncomfortable, Candice engaged in several exposure sessions involving her obsessions, during which she refrained from touching any object while she concentrated on the image or repeated her thought aloud. Ritual prevention in this instance allowed Candice the opportunity to learn that nothing bad happened to family members when she did not touch a container and that her thoughts had no subsequent influence on the health and well-being of others. With this new learning, the frequency and level of discomfort associated with her obsessive thoughts markedly faded over the span of a few weeks. On those occasions when such thoughts or images did come up, they were much less intense, only weakly associated with the urge to touch containers and were much easier to dismiss as she focused on other activities.

For a client who has obsessive thoughts related to contamination and who engages in ritualistic washing, an exposure session might involve the client's touching several "dirty" or "germ-ridden" objects to activate obsessive thoughts. Response prevention in this instance would involve blocking the washing behavior (i.e., the escape response) while the client focuses exclusively on his or her hands and the associated thoughts of being contaminated. By not engaging in the escape or anxiety-reduction response, an opportunity arises for distress associated with contamination-related thoughts to diminish on its own and for new learning to occur (e.g., "I don't instantly get sick when I touch something that's dirty").

Escape, avoidance, or safety behavior in response to troubling thoughts or images can take many forms and does not occur only in the context of OCD. Many clients, for example, cope with distressing thoughts or situations through some type of avoidance or escape strategy, whether through engagement in mental acts (e.g., dissociation, psychogenic amnesia) or overt behaviors (e.g., fleeing a mall at the first signs of panic, engaging in acts of intentional self-injury in response to unpleasant emotional states). Other examples of safety behaviors might include an individual with social anxiety engaging in efforts to prevent people from noticing blushing or other signs of anxiety in social situations (e.g., wearing makeup, standing in dark areas, coming up with alternative explanations for such blushing; D. M. Clark, 2001). The goal of exposure therapy is not to eliminate thoughts, situations, or events that trigger maladaptive anxiety and other responses. Rather, exposure interventions instead endeavor to block avoidance, escape, and safety behaviors while exposing the client to feared objects or situations to promote new learning and reduce distress over time.

Monitoring SUDS Ratings

When conducting exposure-based interventions, it is important for the therapist to know how the client's distress level is fluctuating throughout the exposure trial. To do this, therapists repeatedly ask clients for their SUDS ratings during exposure. It is important, however, to remember that giving SUDS ratings can be distracting for clients. The therapist must gather SUDS ratings frequently enough to know how the client is doing but not frequently enough to distract the client and reduce her or his emotional engagement with key exposure stimuli. There is no solid rule for how many times to do this within a specified period but some researchers suggest that the therapist take SUDS ratings every 5 to 10 minutes (e.g., Steketee, 1993).

Give the Client Control Over Exposure

Although avoiding or escaping the feared or emotionally evocative stimulus may hinder exposure, it also is important for the therapist to let the client know that he or she may stop the exposure at any time. We have found it helpful to tell clients during the orientation how important it is to remain exposed to the stimulus and not engage in avoidance, distraction, or escape. At the same time, it is important to give the client an "out."

SUMMARY

The following guidelines are recommended when exposure therapy is used for reducing unjustified fear or when the therapeutic goal is to develop new–threat-related associations to particular stimuli or situations:

- Because the key mechanism of change in exposure therapy appears to be the client's learning that the feared events (situations, objects, events, or experiences) predict the non-occurrence of the threatening or harmful events and alternative outcomes, design exposure interventions so that new associations to feared stimuli are acquired and acknowledged by the client.
- Ensure that the four key aspects of exposure therapy are in place: (a) exposure to feared stimuli when the probability of a threatening or dangerous outcome is absent or extremely low; (b) elimination of safety signals and behaviors; (c) inclusion of as many feared stimuli as possible during exposure trials (so that

new learning can occur for all relevant stimuli); and (d) application of exposure sessions in multiple contexts, especially those in which previously feared stimuli are likely to be encountered following treatment.

- Orient the client to the purpose of exposure and provide information on how it works. Inform the client that exposure may be distressing at first but that his or her emotional experiences likely will decline in intensity over repeated exposure trials.
- Conduct a precise functional analysis of feared situations, key fear-provoking aspects of these situations, potential avoidance/escape and safety behaviors and signals, and emotional reactions.
- Determine an appropriate type or combination of types of exposure therapy to use.
- Determine an appropriate schedule and format for exposure (i.e., graduated, flooding, variable, massed vs. spaced).
- Allow the client to terminate the exposure session if needed.

10

ENHANCING EMOTION REGULATION

Problems with emotions and the desire to feel better emotionally are among the most common reasons for which people seek therapy. Clients often hope to find ways to understand what they are feeling and to experience comfortable or pleasant emotions more often and uncomfortable or aversive emotions less often. Common reasons to enter therapy, for example, include the desire to reduce depressive mood and its impact on life functioning, to deal effectively with feared situations, to reduce or manage anger more effectively, or simply to better anticipate and manage life stress. The motivation to feel better is ubiquitous across clinical and nonclinical populations, with therapy often viewed as a means to achieve the goals of emotional stability, balance, and peace. One way to help clients attain these goals is to assist them in enhancing their understanding, awareness, and effective regulation of emotions.

Drawing from treatment development in the area of emotion regulation and from contemporary emotion science, this chapter emphasizes ways

http://dx.doi.org/10.1037/14691-010
Behavioral Interventions in Cognitive Behavior Therapy: Practical Guidance for Putting Theory Into Action,
Second Edition, by R. F. Farmer and A. L. Chapman

to help clients enhance emotion regulation. The scientific field of emotion regulation has grown considerably over the past two decades (Gross, 2013). Researchers are using a variety of methods to clarify how people regulate their emotions, and this research has influenced, and in some cases has formed the backbone of, existing empirically supported treatments (e.g., Barlow, Farchione, et al., 2011; Gratz & Gunderson, 2006; Linehan, 1993a, 1993b, 2015). In this chapter, we synthesize some of this work, provide a framework for understanding emotion regulation, and describe and discuss practical strategies to help clients more effectively regulate emotions.

PROBLEMS WITH EMOTION REGULATION

Difficulty with excesses or deficits in emotional states are common across many problems that come to clinical attention. Some clients seem to have a deficit in normative emotional responses, such as the lack of empathy or remorse often observed among people with serious antisocial or psychopathic traits. Others experience an excess of particular emotions, such euphoria or irritability among clients with bipolar disorder, intense and fluctuating emotional states among people with borderline personality disorder, chronic anxiety and fear among those with anxiety disorders, and feelings of sadness and emptiness among people with major depressive disorder. In addition, people with posttraumatic stress disorder often experience chronic or episodic hyperarousal (American Psychiatric Association, 2013), including agitation, irritability, and other such emotional experiences.

Many of these and other clinical problems also have in common associated difficulties in the regulation or management of emotional states. Many disorders, notably anxiety and mood disorders, have emotional avoidance behaviors as either defining or associated features. Self-destructive behaviors and substance use disorders, which are ubiquitous client problems in most clinical settings, also often function to reduce or avoid unwanted emotions. Some researchers have argued that *experiential avoidance*, including behaviors functioning to alter the form or frequency of emotional experiences, constitutes a common feature across many clinical problems (Hayes, Wilson, Gifford, Follette, & Strosahl, 1996). In addition, emotional excesses, deficits, and problems regulating emotions (e.g., as manifested in angry outbursts) can pose challenges during therapy sessions.

Commonalities in etiology, symptom presentation, and latent structure across various clinical problem areas characterized by emotional excesses have sparked the development of transdiagnostic treatment protocols focused on emotion regulation (Barlow, Allen, & Choate, 2004; Ehrenreich, Goldstein, Wright, & Barlow, 2009). One example of treatment development emerging from this work is the Unified Protocol for the Treatment of Emotional Disorders (the UP; Barlow et al., 2004; Barlow, Farchione, et al., 2011), consisting of interventions that specifically target emotion regulation (by modifying cognitive appraisals, reducing emotional avoidance, and encouraging emotion-inconsistent action). Other treatments similarly include systematic protocols to develop and improve emotion regulation (e.g., dialectical behavior therapy [DBT; Linehan, 1993a]; emotion-regulation group therapy [ERGT; Gratz & Gunderson, 2006; Gratz & Tull, 2011]).

UNDERSTANDING EMOTIONS AND EMOTION REGULATION

From a behavioral perspective, emotions are important links in the chain of events involved in maintaining both life-enhancing and life-detracting behavior, and they play a critical role in life satisfaction and well-being. We discuss in this section definitions and helpful ways to think about emotions and emotion regulation.

Characteristics of Emotions

Emotions are multifaceted and have many parts or components (Gross, 2013). Emotions consist of changes in subjective experience, behavior, physiology, and brain activity (Mauss, Levenson, McCarter, Wilhelm, & Gross, 2005). These components of emotion are difficult to separate and tend to occur close in time. The physiological and subjective aspects of emotion, although considered part of the same emotional response, are often not highly correlated; thus, researchers often refer to emotions as a "loosely coupled" collection of cognitive, physiological, and brain activities (Gross, 2013). Rather than constituting a single form of behavior, subjectively experienced emotions are the emergent property of the activities of multiple aggregated response systems within a brief span of time.

Subjective sensations associated with changes in physiological activity are often among the most salient aspects of an emotional response. Examples include increased heart rate, muscle tension, increased body temperature and perspiration, sensations of tingling, among others. These types of sensations are perhaps what people commonly associate with emotions and are often referred to as "feelings." Although it may be possible to infer and label an emotional state based on hallmark physical sensations, different emotions sometimes share similar constellations of physiological sensations. An individual who is angry might experience facial flushing, rapid heartbeat, and perspiration, and another person who is afraid might have similar experiences. To understand and effectively label emotional experiences, it is therefore important for the individual to understand the range of common features of emotional responses and not just physiological sensations.

Emotions Occur in Motivationally Relevant Contexts

Although there has been much debate about the nature of emotions, a common thread across theories is that emotions are evolutionarily linked responses that serve important social and behavioral functions (Cosmides & Tooby, 2000; Gross, 2013; Lynch, in press; Lynch et al., 2013; Panksepp, 2005). Within these frameworks, emotions typically occur in *motivationally relevant* contexts—situations in which events are experienced as relevant to the individual's goals, including those associated with basic survival, social bonding or affiliation, or other such pursuits.

Goals from a behavioral perspective refer to the reinforcer that typically follows a given activity (Baum, 2005). Witnessing a bear charging toward you, for example, would likely produce a number of emotional reactions and other behaviors that serve the goal of survival (e.g., running, hiding, playing dead, or engaging in strategies known to minimize the likelihood of bear attacks). Emotions experienced such a situation help facilitate or mobilize adaptive behavior, which may be carried out on the basis of rules previously imparted by others ("If a bear is running after you, do these things . . .") or shaped as a result of earlier experiences. Overall, emotional responses help prepare the individual to take actions that increase the likelihood of realizing particular goals (or reinforcers), such as receiving comfort or support (in the case of sadness), the removal of threat or danger (in the case of fear), or the reparation of reinforcing relationships (in the case of guilt).

Emotions Are Time-Limited Responses

In contrast to moods, which occur over longer periods and fluctuate less in response to changing circumstances, emotions tend to last seconds to minutes at most (Ekman & Davidson, 1994) and vary considerably throughout the day. In this way, moods are like the climate of a city, whereas emotions are like the weather on a particular day or week. Climate occurs over long periods in response to slow-acting forces, whereas the weather can fluctuate widely during a particular day or week in response to changing wind direction, low and high pressure systems, and so on.

Moods, like depression, often change with consistent effort over time, whereas emotions can change quickly in response to events, thoughts, and physiological activity. Consider behavioral activation for depression (reviewed in Chapter 8). A client's engagement in pleasurable or mastery activities might affect her emotional state in the moment, while she is engaging in these activities. It takes more time and consistent effort, however, for behavioral activation to reduce her more enduring depressed mood. The time-limited and reactive nature of emotional states are often what make emotions both so challenging to manage and tolerate and so amenable to practical coping strategies and skills.

Emotions Can Be Primary or Secondary Responses

Within some therapeutic frameworks, emotions are categorized as *primary* or *secondary* (Gratz & Gunderson, 2006; Greenberg & Watson, 2005; Linehan, 1993a, 1993b, 2015). Primary emotional responses are those that occur in direct response to particular stimuli. A father witnessing his son being bullied by a larger child might feel the primary emotion of anger, which then increases his likelihood of intervening to protect his son. The father, however, might experience anger as a secondary emotion, whereas the primary (or initial) emotional response might be fear for his son's safety or well-being. A client who is angry with her therapist for being unavailable to speak during a vacation might experience anger as a primary emotion, in that her goal to receive help is blocked (anger or frustration are common responses to situations in which the pursuit of reinforcement is hampered; Kassinove, 1995). Alternatively, anger could be a secondary emotion, with the primary emotions including hurt or sadness. Understanding which emotions are primary versus secondary can open up important avenues for therapeutic intervention (Greenberg & Watson, 2005).

Emotions Contribute to Response Tendencies

From an evolutionary perspective, emotions are linked with behavioral *response tendencies* (e.g., Gross, 1998) that evolved over millennia to serve humans in their quest for survival (LeDoux, 2002). Often, the subjective experience of emotions involves the inclination to engage in a particular type of action, such as the urge to yell when angry, to flee when afraid, or to withdraw when sad or ashamed. In the framework of DBT, these inclinations are referred to as *action urges* (Linehan, 1993b, 2015). Emotion-related response tendencies often fall within the broader categories of approach or avoidance behavior in response to particular stimuli or situations. Anger, for example, is often associated with behavioral approach tendencies—to move toward, attack, or remove an anger provoking event or person. When driving, this may manifest as road-rage behaviors, such as dodging around slow-moving cars, yelling, and gesticulating. Fear, in contrast, often involves behavioral tendencies of escape or avoidance of situations experienced as threatening or dangerous.

Emotions Serve a Communication Function

Another important behavioral response associated with emotions is that of communication. Research and theory suggest that emotions evolved in part to facilitate social bonds and group survival via communication of intentions and needs, ongoing experiences (e.g., pain, pleasure, excitement, fear in reaction to danger), and observations about the world. Emotional communication also appears to be bidirectional. Emotional expression, particularly including facial expressions, are associated with brain activity relating to similar emotional reactions in interaction partners (Montgomery & Haxby, 2008; van der Gaag, Minderaa, & Keysers, 2007), and some research suggests that humans mimic the facial expressions of those with whom they are interacting (Hess & Blairy, 2001). Beyond simply communicating that something needs attending to (e.g., "Yikes, there's a bear on the trail ahead of us!"), emotional communication has the potential to serve important social functions, including eliciting of empathy, support, altruism, and the deepening of social bonds (Lynch, in press).

Emotions Can Alter the Reinforcing Properties of Consequences

Emotions also can function as *establishing operations* (EOs; see Chapter 2). Establishing operations refer to the influence that events, operations, or conditions have on behavior by temporarily altering reinforcing or punishing properties of consequences (Michael, 1982; Miltenberger, 2005). Intense anger, for example, can be an EO that enhances the reinforcing consequences of yelling or aggressive behavior. Escape behaviors might be particularly reinforcing in the presence of intense anxiety or fear because the subsequent avoidance of aversive stimuli can lead to a greater decrease in uncomfortable feelings when compared with avoidance occurring during a calm state. When deprivation from social contact leads to feelings of loneliness and sadness, the potentially reinforcing outcomes of affiliative and support-seeking behaviors (both adaptive and maladaptive) might be magnified.

Emotions Can Function as Consequences for Preceding Behavior

Changes in emotional states also can serve as *consequences* for preceding behavior. Within the *four-function model* of nonsuicidal self-injury (Nock & Prinstein, 2004), for example, the consequences of self-injury are separated into *social* and *automatic reinforcers* as well as *positive* or *negative reinforcers*. *Automatic reinforcers* include changes in internal states that might reinforce preceding behaviors, such as self-injury. Within this framework, a change in emotional states following an act of self-injury could be considered an *automatic positive reinforcer* (e.g., when self-injury results in an increase in particular emotional states, such as feelings of excitement or a "rush") or an *automatic negative reinforcer* (e.g., when self-injury results in reductions in aversive emotional states, such as tension, anxiety, anger, or sadness), provided that these emotional consequences are associated with increases in the future likelihood of self-injury in similar contexts.

Emotion Regulation

For this chapter, we base our conceptualization of emotion regulation on work by James Gross, who defined emotion regulation as "the processes by which individuals influence which emotions they have, when they have them, and how they experience and express these emotions" (Gross, 1998, p. 275). The term *emotion regulation* refers to a variety of actions that people might take to influence their experience and expression of emotions. Defined in this way, effective emotion regulation clearly plays an important role both in clinical problem areas and in daily life. It would be difficult to maintain employment if we were unable to modulate our occasional frustration or annoyance at coworkers or employers. Difficulties in the ability to modulate panic symptoms during a final exam could result in disastrous consequences. Adaptive and fulfilling social relationships, including romantic relationships, friendships, and relationships with children, often require the regulation of a variety of emotions (anger, frustration, irritation, sadness, embarrassment, and so forth) as well as our expression of these emotions. Indeed, facial and other nonverbal emotional expression can have a strong influence on social interactions, such as by signaling cooperation, affiliation, or threat, and eliciting varying reactions from others (Lynch, in press). Research on the suppression of emotional expression, for example, has shown that people interacting with those who are suppressing their negative emotions feel less affiliative and show higher psychophysiological arousal compared with those interacting with people who are not suppressing (Butler et al., 2003; Gross, 2013).

Difficulties With Emotion Regulation

Difficulties with emotion regulation can take several forms. Such difficulties may be evident in problems understanding, identifying, or labeling emotions; overreliance on particular types of emotion regulation strategies (e.g., emotional avoidance); or the over- or underregulation of emotional experience or expression. Gratz and Roemer (2004), for example, defined difficulties in emotion regulation as consisting of the following: poor emotional clarity and awareness, nonacceptance of emotional responses, difficulty persisting in goal-directed behavior or inhibiting impulsive actions when upset, and skill deficits associated with the up- or down-regulation of emotional states.

Other models have emphasized the problems associated with the *over-regulation* of emotions and behavior. Lynch (in press), for example, defined a key component of psychological well-being as *flexible control*, including the flexible use of self- and emotion-regulation in response to changing environmental conditions. Within this model, the overcontrol or regulation of emotions and behavior contributes to and maintains social alienation, loneliness, and particular mental health problems.

Key Features of Emotion Regulation

Within Gross's (1998, 2013) framework, there are three key features of emotion regulation, including (a) the activation of emotion regulation goals, (b) altering the emotion trajectory, and (c) emotion regulation outcomes. The first feature, *emotion regulation goals*, includes the individual's goal to change the emotional reaction or experience. When conceptualized within a behavioral perspective, this would suggest that individuals adjust their emotional reactions and expression to increase the likelihood of obtaining reinforcement or decrease the likelihood of receiving punishment. In many instances, emotion regulation goals center on the *down-regulation* of certain emotional states. An individual preparing for an important lecture, for example, might have the goal of performing well and experiencing validation or appreciation from colleagues. Related emotion regulation goals might be to reduce the likelihood of panic or the intensity of anxiety, as such emotional reactions would likely reduce the probability of reinforcement for lecturing. A person experiencing intense waves of sadness or grief at work the day after a death in the family might have the goal to at least limit the duration of the waves of sadness so that she or he can function effectively at work. Other times, regulation goals might include the *up-regulation* of certain states. Someone who is tired and feeling emotionally blunted might have the goal of increasing feelings of happiness or enthusiasm during his best friend's surprise birthday party as a way to maintain or strengthen that important and reinforcing relationship. Additionally, people sometimes report that they self-injure to "feel something" (M. Z. Brown, Comtois, & Linehan, 2002; Kleindienst et al., 2008; Turner, Chapman, & Layden, 2012).

Altering the emotion trajectory involves strategies to modify the likelihood, duration, or intensity of emotional responses. Gross (1998, 2013) has highlighted several points in the emotion generative process in which strategies might be used to regulate emotions. These strategies include (a) situation selection, (b) situation modification, (c) attentional deployment, (d) cognitive change, and (e) response modulation. Individuals often suppress or attenuate the expression of emotion because doing so makes reinforcing outcomes more likely or punishing outcomes less likely. We expand on some of these approaches in the later section on strategies targeting emotion regulation.

Finally, *emotion regulation outcomes* refer to the effect of emotion regulation behaviors or strategies on different aspects of emotional responding. These strategies can influence the *likelihood* of an emotional response. A socially anxious client, for example, might experience anticipatory anxiety before a party and subsequently avoid the party, both reducing the anticipatory anxiety and eliminating the possibility for any anxiety experienced during the party. Emotion regulation strategies also might influence *latency*, or how long an emotional response takes to occur. Someone who is repeatedly teased by his sister might use the strategy of *attentional deployment* to ignore the teasing (e.g., distracting himself by playing a game on his iPhone), and this might increase the time between the onset of the teasing and the onset of intense frustration. In addition, emotion regulation strategies also can influence the magnitude, rise time, and physiological sensations associated with an emotional state (Gross, 2013).

EMOTION REGULATION INTERVENTIONS WITHIN CONTEMPORARY CBT APPROACHES

Many contemporary CBTs that emphasize emotion regulation tend to target several core processes. Almost all existing emotion-focused CBT approaches, for example, include psychoeducation about emotions, interventions to enhance the ability to recognize and label emotions, and strategies to facilitate the regulation of emotions. Some of these approaches also include strategies to accept emotional states or engage in mindfulness around the experience of emotions; others target behaviors related to intense emotions (e.g., escape or avoidance behavior) or the overregulation of emotions.

A couple of examples of contemporary emotion-focused CBT approaches include the UP (Barlow et al., 2004; Barlow, Farchione, et al., 2011) and DBT (Linehan, 1993a). The UP includes emotional awareness training and emphasizes strategies to reappraise emotionally evocative situations, reduce emotional avoidance, and reverse emotion-related action tendencies (Barlow et al., 2004; Barlow, Farchione, et al., 2011). In the emotion regulation skills module of DBT, clients are first educated on the nature of emotions and then taught to recognize and label emotions. Subsequently, the skills module addresses a variety of emotion regulation strategies, including problem-solving strategies to modify emotionally evocative situations, mindfulness strategies to reduce emotional avoidance, cognitive skills to modify appraisals and interpretations, and behavioral skills to reverse emotion-related action tendencies. Other skills involve engaging in pleasurable or mastery activities (much like behavioral activation, discussed in Chapter 8) and enhancing self-care in the areas of sleeping, eating, medication, drug and alcohol use, and exercise, to reduce vulnerability to stress and accompanying negative emotions. Although not included in the emotion regulation module specifically, DBT also includes attentional deployment strategies, including distraction, as well as other strategies for modulating emotional responses, such as self-soothing, relaxation skills, and other approaches for modifying physiological arousal (e.g., by modifying body temperature or engaging in intense physical exercise; Linehan, 1993b, 2015).

Some emotion regulation–oriented therapies also have incorporated *value- and goal-oriented* interventions. ERGT (Gratz & Gunderson, 2006), for example, was developed to treat nonsuicidal self-injury primarily among people with borderline personality disorder. Although this treatment includes some strategies to directly regulate emotions that overlap with those in DBT or the UP, ERGT more strongly emphasizes acceptance of emotions as well as the clarification of client values and goals. In addition, the revised version of DBT emotion regulation skills includes skills for clients to clarify their values and develop specific goals and action plans to bring their behavior in line with these values. The rationale is that engaging in behavior that is consistent with one's values will, over time, reduce vulnerability to stressful or emotionally evocative situations (Linehan, 2015).

At least two contemporary cognitive behavioral approaches specifically target overregulation. One of these, acceptance and commitment therapy (ACT; Hayes, Strosahl, & Wilson, 2012), is based on the assumption that many clinical problems are related to the tendency to engage in avoidance- or escape-oriented attempts to manage emotions or other unwanted private events, such as thoughts or bodily sensations (Hayes et al., 1996, 2012). This treatment uses a variety of strategies to help clients understand the problems with chronic experiential avoidance, to clarify their values and goals, and to move forward in valued life directions without having to modify or regulate their thoughts or feelings. Based in part on the assumption that human language and cognition (including verbal rules) promote and maintain experiential avoidance, some interventions in ACT aim to reduce the grip of language and cognition on behavior through the use of cognitive defusion strategies (Hayes et al., 2012).

Radically open DBT (RO-DBT; Lynch, in press), a new adaptation of DBT, focuses on clients who are overcontrolled. Within this framework, overcontrolled individuals have a constellation of personality features (e.g., high behavioral inhibition, interpersonal constraint, perfectionism, and threat sensitivity) that are associated with heightened self-regulation and constricted emotional expression. The tendency of such individuals to overregulate emotional expression, gestures and body language, and emotional experience can interfere with their interpersonal functioning, social bonding, and emotional intimacy in relationships. Similar to ACT, interventions within this framework aim to help the client develop psychological and behavioral flexibility. Some strategies emphasize skills to modify emotional expression and social signaling, for example, by teaching skills in the area of social gestures, the use of voice tone to convey emotional states, and strategies to genuinely express emotions. Other skills aim to enhance emotional intimacy through effective self-disclosure or to assist the individual in adopting a self-reflective stance while improving openness to novelty, new learning, and negative or disconfirmatory feedback (Lynch, in press).

HELPING CLIENTS TO UNDERSTAND AND LABEL EMOTIONS

Often an important starting point in helping clients learn to effectively regulate their emotions is to help them better understand their emotions. Strategies to help clients understand emotions more generally as well as their own emotions specifically include (a) psychoeducation about emotions, (b) strategies to help clients understand their patterns of emotional reactions, and (c) approaches to assist clients in recognizing and accurately labeling emotions. Next, we describe and provide examples of these strategies.

Providing Psychoeducation on Emotions

One important component of interventions that address emotional regulation involves providing information to the client about emotions and emotion regulation. Just as it is helpful to have a roadmap when traveling in unfamiliar territory, understanding the terrain, features, and nature of emotions can help clients more effectively regulate their emotions in ways that bring them closer to their desired destinations or goals. Some clients find emotions to be confusing, overwhelming, and mystifying. For such clients, clarifying and demystifying the nature of emotions may help them feel more capable of managing their emotions.

There are several important points to make when teaching clients about emotions. First, it can be helpful to emphasize that emotions are temporary states. Emotions wax and wane and rarely last longer than a few minutes. This is an especially useful point to make with clients who experience their emotions as overwhelming and intolerable. Ideally, a combination of psychoeducation and practice with emotion regulation skills will help these clients understand that even the most painful emotions are temporary.

Second, emotions serve important social and behavioral functions. As mentioned earlier in this chapter, emotions evolved over millennia to facilitate survival and social bonding. As such, emotions serve important communicative functions. When emotions are used effectively to communicate needs, preferences, desires, and reactions, they can further facilitate intimacy and deeper relationships. Emotions, when attended to, can also promote effective action in a variety of situations. When crossing the street, if we had to work out logically that the big truck heading toward us probably appears larger and larger because it is getting closer, we would probably be much less likely to get out of the way in time than if we simply let our immediate fear response guide our behavior. Some researchers have suggested that emotions are part of an important *perceptual valuation system* that helps us to automatically evaluate situations as helpful or dangerous, and assist us in taking appropriate actions without the need to engage higher order cognitive processing (Ochsner & Gross, 2013).

Third, emotions have many components or parts. When an emotion fires, activity in the brain changes, as does physiological activity, thinking patterns, desires, wishes, and urges to engage in particular actions. Because of the multifaceted, dynamic and systemic nature of emotions, there are many ways to change the activity of the emotion system. When talking with clients about emotion regulation strategies, it is useful to emphasize is that there are many roads to Rome, so to speak. Changes in one aspect of the emotion system can modify the entire system. Following is an example of how a therapist might make some of these key points when discussing emotions with a client:

Therapist: Remember how you mentioned that one of your therapy goals is to better understand and manage your emotions?

Client: Yes, definitely.

Therapist: Well, I thought we might spend a little bit of time today talking about what emotions are. I was thinking it would be important for you to start off with an understanding of emotions before we try to figure out what to do about them. What do you think about that?

Client: That sounds like a great plan. My emotions often seem really confusing, and I don't even know what the point is of all these really unpleasant feelings I have all the time, like sadness and emptiness.

Therapist: That makes a lot of sense to me. I can see why you would wonder why you're having these emotions when all they seem to do is make you miserable. One important point about emotions is that they are temporary. Even though they might seem like they last way longer than you want them to at times, from what we can tell, an emotional reaction usually tends to last less than a minute. Some recent research suggests that all of the chemical and hormonal changes that go along with emotions are pretty much flushed out of the system within 45 to 90 seconds after emotions are first experienced.

Client: That's interesting. My feelings seem like they last a lot longer than that.

Therapist: Well, that's probably because there's an important difference between emotions and moods. Mood is a lot like the climate. It's sort of how the weather is in general rather than how the weather is on a particular day. So you can think of moods like depression as being like the climate of the city that you live in. Emotions, in contrast, would be a lot like the rainy day on Tuesday. So while your moods, such as being in an irritable or depressed mood, might last for a few days to a couple of weeks, and emotional state tends to flare up and die down much more quickly.

Client: OK, that makes sense. Maybe it's just that I'm having a lot of flare-ups!

Therapist: I think that's probably true. The good news about emotions being temporary is that, as uncomfortable as they sometimes are, they will not last forever. You might feel a wave of sadness, for example, and if you manage it effectively and don't do anything to keep it around or increase it, it will probably die down of its own accord.

Client: I think I've noticed that sometimes. There are times when my kids are really annoying me, and I feel really irritated, but as long as I don't yell or do anything, it passes pretty quickly.

Therapist: Great example! So that brings us to another important point about emotions. Remember when you mentioned that you thought your emotions were sort of pointless?

Client: Absolutely.

Therapist: Well, imagine for a moment what it would be like if you had no physical pain. You've probably heard of people who have little or no experience of physical pain and how much trouble they end up getting into, with serious injuries and bruises and broken bones.

Client: Yes, I've heard of those people. It might seem nice not to have any pain, but when you really think about it, it seems kind of dangerous.

Therapist: Exactly. In some ways, you can think of emotions as being a lot like physical pain. One of the most important things that emotions do for us is that they give a signal that something important is going on. If you were in a meeting at your office, and all the sudden you heard a loud growl from right outside the door, how do you think you would feel?

Client: I would probably feel afraid, like my heart would start pounding.

Therapist: Same here. That fear is probably telling you something important. It might be telling you at least to be aware that there could be danger. Does that make sense?

Client: Definitely. I can understand how fear might be helpful in that way.

Therapist: We think the other emotions work this way as well. They give us important information about what is going on around us. The other thing that emotions do for us is that they prepare us to take action in particular ways. If you felt fear when you heard that growl, your emotion system is probably already preparing you to escape to safety, freeze and scan the environment for danger, or possibly fight to ensure your survival.

Although not illustrating all of the main points about emotions, this example highlights some approaches for effectively conveying them to the client. Notice how the therapist uses analogies, metaphors, and examples to illustrate the main points in an engaging and accessible manner. The therapist also periodically asks questions, queries the client's understanding of the main points, and asks for her or his input and examples. When providing psychoeducation on emotions or other topics in the context of CBT, using an interactive teaching style and avoiding jargon can help the client to maintain interest, better understand the content, and remember key points (see also Chapter 6 for further suggestions on effective teaching methods).

Helping Clients Understand Their Own Patterns of Emotional Reactions

In addition to helping clients understand the concept of emotions more generally, it can also be helpful to assist clients in understanding their own specific patterns of emotional reactions. Through understanding these patterns, clients might be better equipped to predict, proactively plan, and cope with emotionally challenging situations. Understanding patterns of emotional reactions also can be one step toward helping clients more effectively recognize and label their emotional experiences.

There are several ways to assist clients in understanding their patterns of emotional reactions. One method is to conduct regular functional analyses of emotionally evocative situations. For a client struggling with anger problems, for example, the therapist and client could regularly conduct functional analyses of anger-related episodes. Such episodes might include times when the client engaged in dysfunctional behavior while angry or might simply include times when she or he experienced particularly intense or troubling anger. Such an analysis would also emphasize the consequences associated with the experience of the emotion or its expression.

The client might also self-monitor emotional reactions by recording the contextual features associated with such instances as a means for understanding how the emotion came about (i.e., the antecedents), how it was expressed (e.g., verbally, overt motor behaviors), what other behaviors accompanied the emotions (e.g., thoughts, physiological sensations, other overt actions), and the consequences of the emotional reaction and its expression. In setting up a self-monitoring system, it is helpful to delineate the target emotion or set of target emotions to monitor. In some cases, these target emotions might be unclear, or the client might have yet to develop the skills to label such emotions. In these cases, the client might be encouraged to simply make her or his best guess about the emotion or to start by simply keeping track of general emotional distress. The therapist and client can subsequently review the self-monitoring activity and work together to help the client understand what emotional reactions she or he was experiencing in the documented situations.

Helping Clients Learn to Label Their Emotions

Several clinical problems are defined, in part, by difficulties in accurately discriminating among and labeling private events, including emotions. The accurate labeling of emotions can facilitate effective emotion regulation because different emotion regulation strategies might be appropriate for different emotional states. Strategies to regulate intense sadness, for example, might include self-soothing or active engagement in pleasurable or stimulating activities. In contrast, anger management strategies often emphasize approaches for reducing emotional arousal (see Chapter 7). Some studies have found that the act of labeling emotions itself (without any other instructed emotion regulation strategies) can attenuate activity in areas of the limbic system involved in emotional responding (Lieberman et al., 2007). In addition, when clients improve their understanding and labeling of emotional states, they are better able to decipher their own unique patterns of emotional responding, determine which situations are associated with particular emotional reactions, and engage in proactive coping.

Behavioral interventions for problems with emotion labeling include discrimination training and training in the accurate application of feeling-state words to various emotional experiences. *Self-labeling training*, for example, involves teaching the client skills that assist him or her in accurately identifying and labeling emotional experiences. Components of this form of discrimination training include (a) an identification of the events that occasioned the emotional experience; (b) a description of the nature of the emotion, such as quality, intensity, and the physical sensations or thoughts that accompany it; (c) a delineation of types of behaviors that might be used to express the emotion; and (d) the types of other behaviors that the emotion might occasion (Linehan, 1993a). Reinforcing the accurate application of labels to private events such as emotions is considerably more difficult than it is for overt behaviors, and requires attentiveness and empathy on the part of the therapist.

The aforementioned self-monitoring approach also can facilitate the discrimination and labeling of different emotional states. If a client monitors various aspects of the emotional experience, the context surrounding it, and related thoughts and action tendencies, the resulting data can provide clues about the client's specific emotional state. A client, for example, who reported muscle tension, a feeling of heat, and the experience of perspiration might want to determine whether these experiences were indicative of anger or another arousing emotion, such as anxiety or fear. Clues about this distinction may be found in the client's pattern of thinking. Thoughts about revenge, injustice, inconvenience, or frustration might suggest the presence of anger. In contrast, worries, catastrophic thinking, or interpretations of a situation as threatening to the client's well-being might suggest anxiety or fear. Action tendencies or urges, such as the desire to harm someone else, yell, scream, or engage in aggressive behavior, are suggestive of anger, whereas the urge to avoid, freeze, or escape might suggest fear.

Associated events, cues, or context can also provide hypotheses about the specific emotional state. Being stuck in traffic behind a car that is moving excessively slowly, being criticized or verbally (or physically) attacked, experiencing some kind of serious inconvenience or roadblock to goal-directed actions (e.g., computer breakdown in the middle of writing a term paper), would be common situations associated with anger or frustration. In contrast, situations such as the client accidentally handing in the wrong term paper, being late for an important meeting, having to give an impromptu (or scheduled) speech, or encountering a large animal on a wilderness trail might be more consistent with fear.

Other approaches to emotion labeling involve assisting the client in the matching of emotion labels with particular facial expressions, situations, or actions. A therapist, for example, might use standardized photographs or drawings of facial expressions and ask the client to match emotion words with particular expressions. Over time and with practice, the client will ideally improve her or his accuracy in emotion identification, after which steps can be taken to generalize this skill to more natural environments and stimuli.

Mindfulness strategies also can be helpful in facilitating emotional awareness and labeling. When emotions arise during therapy sessions, the therapist might help guide the client's attention to various aspects of the emotional experiences, including physiological sensations, thoughts, and urges to engage in actions. Simply paying attention mindfully to emotional states as they arise can be both an effective emotion regulation strategy and a method to help clients label and describe their ongoing emotional experience (variations of this approach are presented in Barlow, Farchione, et al., 2011; Linehan, 1993a). Additional reading and worksheets designed to assist clients in the labeling of emotions can be found in Linehan (2015).

CORE EMOTION REGULATION STRATEGIES

Several core strategies to regulate emotions have been examined extensively in laboratory and field research and incorporated into contemporary CBTs. Many of the strategies tend to fit within a few key categories: (a) modifying or selecting alternative situations, (b) regulating attention and modifying cognitive appraisals, and (c) modifying emotional responses and emotion-related action tendencies. We next discuss some of these specific emotion regulation strategies and provide clinical examples.

Modifying and Selecting Alternative Situations

One way to assist clients with emotion regulation is to help them develop strategies either to avoid or to change situations that occasion particular emotional states. The premise is that if unwanted emotional states typically occur in particular situations, then changing those situations or entering alternative situations should reduce the frequency of those states. These approaches fit within the category of strategies discussed in Chapter 4 involving the modification of behavior antecedents (i.e., cue elimination and the modification of antecedents to problem behaviors). Therapies for anger, for example, often involve at least temporary avoidance of anger-provoking situations, at least until skills are established for effectively navigating those situations. Other approaches emphasize the modification of emotion-eliciting situations. The latest version of DBT skills training (Linehan, 2015), for example, includes *problem solving* as a core emotion regulation skill (see also Chapter 7 on enhancing interpersonal effectiveness).

A functional analysis of situations associated with particular emotional states is needed to effectively use these strategies. Repeated self-monitoring, discussed earlier, in combination with in-session or self-directed functional analyses of emotion-eliciting situations, can help to clarify which types of antecedents to modify or avoid (in the sense of entering alternative situations not associated with the target emotional response). Once these are clarified, the therapist and client can devise a plan to modify or eliminate particular antecedents. This approach can be taken with regard to particular target emotions (e.g., anger, sadness) or to stress in life more generally.

Following are several examples of strategies to alter, avoid, or select alternative situations. We emphasize, however, that these strategies should be determined idiographically with the client, on the basis of a functional analysis.

- In couples therapy, taking a time out when anger or irritation become intense temporarily removes clients from cues for anger and allows them to use coping and emotion regulation skills before reentering the problem discussion or conflict.

- In the treatment of anger problems, clients may be asked to identify anger-provoking situations and temporarily avoid them, resulting in more time in situations that do not elicit anger.
- Clients who have difficulty with road rage might avoid particular driving routes, use alternative forms of transportation, minimize driving in some way, or restructure their commuting routine to reduce the likelihood of being in a rush.
- A client who is grieving and having difficulty with sadness might temporarily avoid reminders of a lost loved one, including objects, photographs, and other items, and spend time instead talking with support persons about topics other than a deceased loved one.
- A client who experiences intense anxiety and fear during public speaking might either minimize his engagement in this activity or take steps to increase the chances that he will feel confident and less anxious, such as by preparing well ahead of time, practicing self-soothing or anxiety management strategies, limiting the number of audience members present, engaging in practice sessions, and so on (ultimately, exposure therapy, discussed in Chapter 9, may be most helpful).
- A client who feels hurt when her partner provides harsh criticism of her cleanliness around the house might use interpersonal skills to ask the partner to modulate the way this criticism is conveyed, or alternatively improve her housework regimen (within reason) so that the criticism does not occur in the first place.
- A client who feels anxious and embarrassed about going to work, because his clothing is tattered and out of style, might decide to invest in a new wardrobe.
- A woman who feels afraid of going home, because her partner is physically and emotionally abusive, might work to extricate herself from the relationship safely.

Regulating Attention and Modifying Cognitive Appraisals

Regulating attention and modifying cognitive appraisals fit with another category of emotion regulation strategies that largely target early links in a chain of behaviors that culminate in emotional responses and the consequences they produce. These interventions target the initial behaviors in a sequence in an effort to alter the trajectory of emotional responding and include (a) engaging in distracting activities that divert attention away from emotional stimuli and (b) attending to nondistressing aspects of a distressing situation. A common goal to both of these strategies is to bring behavior under the influence of cues that are less emotionally evocative.

Distracting activities can help to temporarily divert the client's attention to nonemotional material or stimuli. One advantage to distraction is that it is a fairly easy skill to use and master in a variety of circumstances. "Miranda," for example, was having difficulty tolerating the sound of another client's voice during her therapy group. She stated that the voice grated on her nerves, leaving her feeling frustrated, and made it difficult to focus on the group. She successfully used distraction by surreptitiously drawing scenes on her papers, conjuring imagery of a recent vacation, and reading through handouts in her group binder when the other client was talking.

"Alfonse's" father had just passed away 2 weeks ago, and he was having great difficulty imagining how he could go back and function at work. Before returning to work, he practiced periodically distracting himself from the sadness and grief related to his loss by doing crossword and Sudoku puzzles, playing games on his iPhone, and talking with other people. He gave himself time to process his sadness and grieve each day, but at other times he practiced diverting his attention to these distracting tasks. By the time he returned to work, he was better able to perform at his job than he had expected, and during breaks, he gave himself a few moments to experience his emotions.

Another approach for facilitating emotion regulation is to attend to nondistressing aspects of a distressing situation. To use this strategy effectively, it is helpful to identify as many stimulus elements of the emotion-eliciting situation as possible and then to determine which elements are most and least strongly associated with the target emotion. Subsequently, the client and therapist can work together to determine which aspects of the situation, if attended to, would be associated with alternative emotional responses, or the same emotional response at a lower level of intensity. Following are a few examples of this strategy.

- "Ted," a new father, was stressed out by the sound of his baby crying several times per day. When his baby started crying and screaming, he began to attend to his baby's facial features more so than the piercing sound of the screaming and found that his irritation and frustration reduced, and he was more able to effectively assist in child care.
- "Sandy" felt tense and anxious while taking public transportation. She discovered, however, that her anxiety and tension reduced to more manageable levels when she focused her attention on the scenery and buildings, the other patrons' clothing

and interesting behaviors, and the sensations of the breeze coming in through the bus window.

- "Alexis" was intensely afraid of spiders, particularly large spiders with thick bodies. During autumn, these spiders would weave large, intricate webs on the patio outside. Realizing that she would never be able to completely avoid spiders, Alexis decided one day to sit on the patio and simply watch a spider in its web. She attended to the shape and patterns of the web, the color variations of the spider, and the gracefulness with which it moved. Although initially quite anxious, she found that the longer she remained on the patio and attended to these aspects of the spider, the less threatening it became and the lower her fear was.

In contrast to approaches that divert attention away from emotionally evocative cues, *cognitive reappraisal* largely involves (a) modifying appraisals of the magnitude or possible outcomes of the stressor or emotionally evocative situation (i.e., appraising the situation as being less catastrophic or threatening and as more manageable), (b) modifying appraisals of one's ability to cope with or manage the situation (i.e., self-efficacy beliefs), or combining these two approaches. While distraction reduces the individual's contact with emotion-eliciting stimuli, cognitive reappraisal introduces alternative thoughts or modifies rules about situations as a way to alter emotional responding.

Because cognitive reappraisal strategies are mainstays of various forms of contemporary CBT (e.g., J. S. Beck, 2011) and core strategies from a functional behavioral perspective are covered in Chapter 5, we discuss these here only briefly. One example of a cognitive reappraisal strategy as applied to emotion regulation skills in DBT is *checking the facts* (Linehan, 2015). This skill involves a few key steps: (a) identifying and describing the situation eliciting the emotional state, (b) describing interpretations and appraisals of the situation, (c) considering alternative interpretations and appraisals, (d) thinking about what type of threat is associated with the situation and evaluating the probability that the threat will occur, and (e) thinking through the worst case scenario (i.e., the catastrophe) and the probability that this will occur.

Modifying Emotional States and Action Tendencies

The modification of emotional states and action tendencies, often referred to as *response modulation*, takes place after the emotion-eliciting processes have occurred and emotion-related response tendencies are well underway (Gross, 2013). These are response-focused strategies that aim to reduce or modify the emotional response in some way. Response-focused emotion regulation sometimes involves relaxation practices, such as breathing or muscle relaxation, intense exercise, or the modification of body temperature to change physiological arousal associated with the emotion (Linehan, 2015), or engagement in self-soothing strategies.

Alternative response-focused approaches include engagement in behaviors that are inconsistent with the emotional response. One example of this from DBT is *opposite action*, discussed in Chapter 9, in which the client engages in behaviors that are opposite to the action tendencies associated with particular emotional states. When the client is sad and feels like withdrawing, for example, opposite action might involve activating behavior, engaging in energetic activities, or socializing. When the client is afraid of something that is not harmful, opposite action is similar to exposure therapy, in which the client approaches the situation of which he or she is afraid. For anger, opposite action might involve going against the behavioral approach tendencies that often accompany anger, such as by gently avoiding the situation or countering aggressive tendencies by generating empathy or compassion for the target of one's anger (Linehan, 2015). Reversing emotion-related action tendencies also is a core component of the UP for emotional disorders. Within the UP, clients are encouraged to engage in actions that are contrary to emotion-related behaviors, particularly those that involve actively approaching feared situations (Barlow et al., 2004, 2011).

FACILITATING EFFECTIVE EMOTION REGULATION IN SESSION

Emotion regulation problems do not occur only in situations outside of the therapy room. Clients who struggle to regulate their emotions often evidence these problems within therapy sessions. Clients with anger management problems sometimes feel angry during therapy sessions, either while discussing other anger-provoking events or in response to the therapist's actions. Clients who struggle with depression might also evidence strong sadness, emptiness, and associated depressive behaviors during therapy sessions (e.g., eyes focused downward, slumped posture, slow rate of speech, lack of talking, nonresponsiveness). When emotion regulation problems arise during therapy sessions, including instances when emotional displays interfere with therapy, an opportunity exists for helping the client learn and put new emotion regulation strategies into action. There are two key ways in which therapists can make use of this opportunity: (a) attend to the client's emotional expression and behavior in session and (b) facilitate the client's use of effective emotion regulation strategies in the moment.

Attending to the Client's Emotional Expression and Behavior in Session

Some therapy approaches are founded on the premise that therapeutic change results from the processing of ongoing emotional experiences in session (Greenberg & Watson, 2005). Although CBT principles are not entirely consistent with this premise, client displays of excessive emotions during sessions can provide unique opportunities for facilitating therapeutic change.

Emotional experiences are often conveyed through facial expressions and changes in eye contact, changes in the pace, rate, and intonation of speech, the use of particular words or phrases, body language, and so on. Keen observation of shifts in such emotional expressive behavior or of the divergence between content discussed (e.g., horrifying or upsetting events) and emotional expression (e.g., laughter or lack of emotional expression) can help to generate hypotheses about the client's current emotional experiences. Such hypotheses might help illuminate the connection between key topics, events, or thoughts, and the client's emotional reactions. Cognitive therapists, for example, attend closely to *hot* cognitions, or thoughts occurring in the context of intense emotional expression, as these thoughts may be particularly relevant to the client's general well-being or core cognitive schemas (J. S. Beck, 2011).

Once an apparent emotional shift or change has occurred, the therapist might inquire about the client's current emotional state. One way to do this is for the therapist to describe what she or he observed, for example, by stating, "I noticed that you just looked down, your voice changed, and your eyes appeared a little moist. I'm wondering what you're experiencing right now." Another example might be, "When you said that, you raised your voice, and you were staring really intently at me. I'm wondering if there's a chance that you were feeling annoyed just then." Attending to and inquiring about the client's ongoing emotional experience can help both the client and the therapist better understand and label the client's emotional reactions.

Facilitating the Client's Effective Use of Emotion Regulation Strategies in Session

Once the therapist and client have a common understanding of the client's current emotional experience, the therapist might consider his or her role as a coach, assisting the client in the use of various behavioral skills to tolerate, accept, or regulate emotional reactions. One effective starting point is for the client is simply to experience, mindfully observe, and describe the physiological sensations, thoughts, and action urges associated with the current emotional state. This strategy can help the client become "unstuck" from the habitual behavioral tendencies (e.g., to avoid, escape, switch topics, yell, leave) associated with the emotion. In addition, mindful attention to and verbal descriptions of emotional states might help the client learn to ride out and tolerate overwhelming emotions without acting on them.

Another strategy is to introduce an emotional stimulus on purpose and then have the client practice an emotion regulation strategy in session. In an example of this strategy, Otto, Safren, and Pollack (2004) intentionally exposed clients to internal emotional states and bodily sensations that often function as cues for drug use. Once these internal states were successfully produced, clients practiced adaptive, non–drug-related emotion regulation strategies. The steps in this approach are as follows: (a) identification of internal and external cues or antecedents for drug use over the past week, (b) determination of alternative responses to these cues, (c) induction of the most relevant internal (emotional) cues, (d) practice in labeling and accepting the emotional states and cues, and (e) rehearsal of adaptive coping strategies. Such coping strategies could include any of the above emotion regulation strategies, coping self-statements, or any of a number of other adaptive coping skills. Such an approach could also be used with clients struggling with problem behaviors other than drug use and a variety of alternative emotional states. In such an extension of this approach, the therapist and client would first determine appropriate emotion-eliciting strategies, such as imagery, exposure to emotionally evocative films, the recounting of distressing events, and so on. Subsequently, there should be a plan for the client to engage in adaptive emotion regulation in the presence of the target emotional state and to avoid any dysfunctional or potentially harmful behaviors. As with exposure therapy, clear orientation to the rationale, purpose and potential benefits of this approach as well as what the client might expect (i.e., to feel a significant degree of emotional distress, and feel worse before feeling better) is important.

Some examples of different ways to apply this approach are the following:

- The therapist might expose a client who has difficulty regulating anger to "anger barbs" or cues that routinely elicit anger, and then coach her or him in adaptive anger management strategies that can be applied in the presence of these anger-evoking cues (see Chapter 7).
- For a depressed client who responds to feelings of sadness and fatigue with behavioral withdrawal, therapy might expose the client to cues for sadness and provide active practice in behaviors that are inconsistent with sadness and depression. Such behaviors might involve modifying body posture and positioning (assuming an upright, alert posture), becoming actively engaged in an activity, physical exercise, or in a conversation with the therapist.

- A client who struggles with shame or embarrassment about some aspect of herself or her behavior might be asked to talk at length about shame-inducing topics and practice opposite action for shame (e.g., appearing confident, making eye contact, and avoiding the "hiding" behaviors that often accompany shame or embarrassment; Rizvi & Linehan, 2005).
- A client is exposed to internal emotional cues associated with self-injury and prompted to engage in alternative skills to tolerate distress or regulate emotions.

SUMMARY

When helping clients effectively regulate their emotions, several considerations and strategies are useful:

- Provide a clear understanding of contemporary views and theories of emotion and emotion regulation, as well as applications of emotion-based frameworks to CBT.
- Assist clients in developing greater awareness of their patterns of emotional responding.
- Help clients learn to label their emotional experiences effectively and accurately.
- Use key strategies for targeting antecedents to emotional responses, including approaches for modifying and selecting alternative situations and cognitive reappraisal strategies.
- Facilitate a shift away from emotionally evocative cues through distraction or by attending to aspects of the situation that occasion alternative emotional responses.
- Provide instruction in response-focused emotion regulation strategies that involve engaging in actions that are inconsistent with the behavioral tendencies that normally accompany the emotional state, as well as those that involve the direct modification of the emotional response through physiological means, relaxation, or self-soothing.
- Approach the strong expression of emotions in session as opportunities to help clients regulate their emotions, which might involve (a) helping the client observe and describe his or her emotional states, (b) coaching the client on how to use effective emotion regulation strategies in the moment, (c) providing emotional cues and helping the client use effective emotion regulation strategies in session, and (d) discussing the applicability of in-session emotion regulation practice to situations in everyday life.

11

NAVIGATING THERAPEUTIC CHALLENGES

In the context of any therapeutic approach, challenges will arise from time to time. It can be difficult for clients to change their behavior and remain squarely on a path toward their goals. In fact, it can be easier to go astray than to stay on that path. Consider how difficult it is to make and sustain basic lifestyle changes, such as improving sleep and eating patterns, regularly engaging in exercise, and so on. Many of the behavioral changes that we ask of clients are even harder, more emotionally evocative, and more difficult to begin or sustain. In the context of exposure therapy, for example, we ask clients to confront their greatest fears not only during the session but also repeatedly between sessions. When we help clients to manage anger more effectively, we often ask them to experience, notice, and respond differently to the emotion of anger and to find different ways to react to anger-provoking situations. Similarly, clients who struggle with depression might find getting out of bed

http://dx.doi.org/10.1037/14691-011
Behavioral Interventions in Cognitive Behavior Therapy: Practical Guidance for Putting Theory Into Action,
Second Edition, by R. F. Farmer and A. L. Chapman

and becoming more behaviorally active to be much like climbing a mountain without proper equipment. Behavior change is challenging work.

Not surprisingly, given the many challenges that therapy presents, clients (and therapists) may engage in a variety of behaviors that hamper therapeutic progress. Examples include session absences; lateness; repeated failures to complete homework; angry behavior toward the therapist, avoidance of emotions, thoughts, and problems; and so on. Therapists may also engage in behavior that takes treatment off course, and we discuss examples of this later in the chapter. It is important, therefore, to be mindful of and effectively address therapy-interfering behaviors (TIB) on the part of both the client and the therapist.

This chapter addresses challenges and factors that make it difficult to implement therapy or that compromise therapy effectiveness. We use many of the behavioral principles discussed in previous chapters to provide guidance on how to conceptualize, assess, and manage these difficulties on an ongoing basis throughout treatment. In a single chapter, it is not possible to discuss all the ways to put behavioral theory into action to solve all potential problems, but we can provide a framework that will point therapists in useful directions, even when therapy appears to be veering completely off course or is headed for a cliff. We begin with some key principles to keep in mind, and following this, we discuss preventative strategies that clinicians can use to set the stage for work on TIB and to reduce the likelihood of future problems. Subsequently, we outline some assessment and treatment strategies that are applicable across many forms of treatment-interfering difficulties. Although therapeutic challenges can be disheartening, they nearly always present opportunities for growth and learning (on the part of both the therapist and the client).

APPLYING A BEHAVIORAL FRAMEWORK
TO THERAPY-INTERFERING OBSTACLES

In this section, we emphasize the use of a behavioral conceptualization for addressing TIB. Like any behavior, TIB are learned behavior, governed by the same learning principles as any other behavior. Consequently, the therapeutic management of TIB follows the same general framework as the management of any other behavior of clinical interest. Another assumption is that relationship challenges in therapy result from, and are often maintained by, *transactions* between the client and therapist; these TIB are rarely due to either the client's or the therapist's actions alone. The therapist's behavior can shape, influence, and elicit the client's behavior, and vice versa. Solutions to TIB must involve changes in the therapeutic system and context, not just the behavior of one individual within this system. We further describe these principles in this section and illustrate how therapists might put them into action.

Perhaps the first guiding principle for addressing TIB from a behavioral perspective is that such behavior should be conceptualized *functionally*. From a behavioral viewpoint, we do not define a TIB on the basis of its topography, surface features, or form. TIB are instead conceptualized in terms of the behavior's influence on the therapy or the therapeutic relationship (i.e., how the behavior functions in the context of therapy). Indeed, behavior that might appear on the surface to be problematic may not hamper therapy. A client with anger management problems, for example, may yell at his therapist on occasion. This behavior may appear to be therapy interfering, aversive, and contrary to what most of us expect or want to experience in our clinical work. Whether such yelling has therapy-interfering consequences, however, depends on the therapist's personal limits and preferences, whether the therapist and client are able to use instances of this behavior as opportunities to work effectively on anger management in the heat of the moment, and whether the therapist is willing or able to tolerate the yelling without becoming personally affected. Other actions, such as missing appointments, arriving late, and so on, may seem by default to be therapy interfering. Even in these instances, however, it is often useful to think about why and how these actions interfere with therapy. Periodic absences from sessions make therapy difficult to conduct, can reduce the "dose" and effectiveness of therapy, and can result in the therapist feeling demoralized and discouraged (Sledge, Moras, Hartley, & Levine, 1990). Therefore, from a behavioral perspective, it is useful to conceptualize instances of TIB as any action on the part of the therapist or client that makes it difficult to achieve therapeutic goals, hampers therapeutic progress, or negatively affects the therapeutic relationship (Chapman & Rosenthal, in press; Linehan, 1993a).

To develop a functional perspective on TIB, a therapist works collaboratively with the client to better assess and understand the factors that control, maintain, or otherwise influence this behavior. It is, for example, useful to conceptualize TIB as part of a chain of behavior, including antecedents (discriminative stimuli, establishing operations), the behavior itself (e.g., instances of TIB, such as arriving late, failing to show up for sessions), and consequences (positive and negative reinforcement, punishment). Once the client and therapist better understand this chain, the therapist can piece together a useful formulation of TIB and generate behavioral alternatives.

A second principle associated with a behavioral approach to TIB is that any behavior is understandable in the context of the client's (or therapist's) learning history, current contexts and contingencies, and the therapeutic relationship. Even behaviors that appear outrageous, such as the client physically attacking or insulting the therapist, ultimately are understandable in the context of the client's life, current level of skills, and the therapeutic environment. The adoption of a behavioral perspective from which all TIB is understandable can help to reduce therapist judgment of client's challenging behaviors. Everything is exactly as it should be, given the causes and effects operating in the client's (and therapist's) life (Linehan, 1993a).

In many cases, TIB fall within functional classes of behavior that were effective in previous contexts but do not serve a similarly useful function in the therapy context (Chapman & Rosenthal, in press). Avoidance of discussions of topics associated with sadness, for example, makes sense in the context of a learning history involving severe invalidation or emotional abuse, where stoicism was reinforced and vulnerability was punished or ignored. The problem, of course, is that extreme stoicism, guardedness, and avoidance of emotional topics are generally ineffective in many forms of therapy. Understanding these functional classes of behavior can help illuminate directions for effective intervention.

The therapist who adopts the viewpoint that all behavior is understandable, including TIB, is in a better position to accurately validate the client's experience. Accurate validation can strengthen the therapeutic relationship, help the client feel understood, model effective self-validation (Linehan, 1997), and realign the therapeutic dyad when challenges make working collaboratively difficult. Accurate validation, however, requires a clear understanding of the antecedents, behaviors, and consequences involved in the chain of events associated with TIB, and how these constituents, in combination, have historically "worked" for the client.

PREVENTATIVE STRATEGIES

Within this section, we discuss two strategies that can help to establish an effective framework for addressing challenges or roadblocks that may also minimize their likelihood. First, it is usually helpful for the therapist and client to begin with a clear strategy for how they might both understand, identify, and address TIB. This requires clear *orientation* of the client to the topic of TIB and the therapist's approach to it. Second, it is helpful for the therapist to have clear ideas of how to address client behavior that stretches her or his own personal or professional boundaries, or how the therapist might help the client *observe therapeutic limits*. Indeed, some of the factors that interfere the most with therapy involve demands that the therapist is unable or unwilling to meet, or behaviors that stress the therapeutic relationship, contribute to burnout, or reduce the therapist's motivation to treat the client. In this section, we discuss approaches for effectively orienting clients to a collaborative, behaviorally oriented approach to TIB, as well as strategies that clients can use for observing and monitoring therapeutic limits.

Orientation

Orientation, as defined here, occurs when the therapist provides information on the logistics and rationale for therapeutic procedures and activities. Orientation is among the most important strategies in the beginning phases of any treatment and includes a discussion with the client about the specific procedures and goals of the initial assessment, the focus and rationale for particular interventions, and actions required of the client (e.g., homework). Orientation provides the client with an invaluable roadmap to therapy, making the therapeutic journey smoother and more efficient. Orientation also can help set the stage for the effective management of obstacles in therapy and ensure that the client and therapist are approaching these obstacles with a similar mind-set.

Clearly Define and Explain TIB

During orientation, among the first topics to address regarding therapeutic obstacles is how the therapist conceptualizes TIB. A clear and shared definition of TIB can help ensure that the client and therapist are on the same page and recognize TIB when it occurs. Generally, it is helpful to convey that TIB is any action on the part of the client or therapist that interferes with therapeutic progress or makes it difficult for the therapist and client to work effectively together (Chapman & Rosenthal, in press; Linehan, 1993a). In this way, the definition conveyed to the client is broader than simply logistical factors that limit therapeutic progress, such as lateness, lack of homework compliance, or absence from therapy. Therapy involves a professional relationship between two (or more) people, and either party may engage in behavior that reduces the quality or effectiveness of that relationship. When the therapeutic relationship suffers, the therapy suffers, and the client is less likely to attain her or his goals.

It is important for therapists to discuss TIB early in therapy, particularly given that many clients may approach treatment with the mind-set that the therapist is a professional constricted to a role and thereby unlike a regular human being in some ways. One of our colleagues, for example, saw a client who was upset after a session and subsequently e-mailed the therapist a long list of harsh complaints and criticisms. The therapist tried to learn what she could from the complaints but was also quite hurt by many of the client's disparaging and unjustified statements. When she brought up this issue during the next session, and the client responded, "I had no idea that anything I said could affect you." This was a turning point in treatment; the client began to perceive the therapist as a human being with emotional responses and the therapeutic relationship as one that provides learning opportunities that could be transferred to other relationships. The following is an example of how a therapist might talk about TIB.

Therapist: I'd like to spend a little time talking about our work together and how we might get around some barriers that could come up in therapy.

Client: OK, that sounds like a good idea. What do you mean by barriers?

Therapist: Well, as you may know, therapy is sometimes not easy. As we've discussed, you'll be working on addressing really uncomfortable feelings, changing patterns that have been around for a long time, and learning new things. It's a lot of work, and it's difficult work.

Client: I know, I've done therapy before, and it was helpful, but I had a hard time sticking with it.

Therapist: Exactly, that's one of the things I'm talking about: having a hard time sticking with therapy, not showing up for sessions, being late, or not doing some of the homework activities in between sessions. These are all things that could get in the way of your achieving your goals. I call these therapy-interfering behaviors. Can you imagine some of these therapy-interfering behaviors popping up?

Client: That makes sense, and yes, some of these. I can't see myself being late a lot, as I'm a person who really gets anxious about being on time, but the homework stuff is going to be hard for me.

Therapist: That's good to know, and we'll definitely want to talk about that ahead of time and do some troubleshooting to increase the chances that you'll be successful with homework. So the thing about therapy-interfering behaviors is that either of us might do them. Despite my best efforts, for example, I might agree to do something and then not follow through, I could show up late myself, be unprepared, and so on. Of course, I try my best to avoid these problems, but they are possibilities. Does that make sense?

Client: Sure, of course. Other therapists haven't said that before, but they have definitely done some of those things, and it was frustrating, because they didn't seem to want to talk about it and got all defensive.

Therapist: Well, I'm going to do my best to avoid being defensive. Here's the other thing about therapy-interfering behavior. It doesn't just have to do with the things we both need to do to make therapy work, but it also has to do with how we are working together—our relationship. If we're really working well together as a team, your therapy will probably go well, but if we're having problems in our working relationship, you may not get what you want out of therapy. Does that make sense?

Client: Yeah, I mean if I can't stand working with you, therapy obviously isn't going to work. I don't think that's going to happen, but you never know . . .

Therapist: True, you never know. This might be a really important thing for us to both keep in mind. I know one of your goals is to get more connected with other people and to improve your relationships. If stuff comes up in our relationship, that might be a great opportunity to learn new things and get you closer to your goals. So we really have to pay attention to things that make it hard for you to work with me, or things that make it hard for me to work with you. If I'm doing something like that, I'd like you to bring it up. The same thing goes for me— I'll bring it up if I'm having a hard time working with you.

Client: I get what you're saying, but that might be really hard for me to do . . .

Therapist: Well, let's spend a little time talking about how that might work.

As illustrated in this example, orientation ideally would acknowledge that the client is not the only one who may engage in TIB. Examples might include arriving late; being inattentive to the client or her or his needs; not providing a clear orientation regarding therapeutic interventions, goals, or directions; avoiding discussions of (or confrontation about) certain topics so as to not hurt the client's feelings (or to challenge the client's perceived fragility); missing appointments; ineffectively managing frustration or irritation; making ineffective treatment decisions; conveying disdain or failing to convey the importance of issues that are critically important to the client; deviating from the treatment manual; following the treatment manual too closely without regard to the client's uniqueness or to the detriment of the relationship; and so on (see further examples in Chapman & Rosenthal, in press). Although the therapist might drive the client right out of therapy if she or he described all of these possibilities, some concrete examples can help to illustrate this important point. Therapists are, despite their best intentions, fallible.

Continued Orientation Throughout Therapy

The process of orienting the client to therapy need not stop after the first few sessions. Obstacles may occur at various points throughout therapy, and ongoing discussions of how these obstacles will be collaboratively approached can be helpful. Compared with orientation at the beginning of treatment, ongoing orientation may be briefer, ad hoc, and focused on the particular topic at hand (e.g., lateness, angry behavior, attendance problems). A therapist addressing problems with attendance, for example, might state,

> I've noticed that you have missed two of our last four sessions, and I'm concerned that you're only going to get what you need out of therapy if you attend more consistently. I'd like us to spend a little time talking through what might be getting in the way of your attendance and how we might work together to solve this problem.

In this example, the therapist highlights the problem behavior (missing sessions), describes the rationale for addressing this (client may not benefit as much if she or he keeps missing sessions), and then provides brief orientation to the ensuing discussion about attendance. If the therapist is using a well-defined assessment strategy to better understand the client's attendance problems, such as *functional analysis* (described in Chapter 2), she or he may provide a brief orientation as follows:

> One way to address your missing sessions is for us to investigate together what led you to miss last week's session. This is called a functional analysis—a blow-by-blow account of the chain of events that led up to your missing the session, including what you were thinking, feeling and doing and what happened afterward. If we really understand this chain of events, maybe we can find a way to break the chain in the future.

Ideally, TIB orientation is reintroduced throughout treatment in small doses as indicated, thus providing the client with regular instructions and direction regarding the therapeutic journey.

Observing Therapeutic Limits

Another way to prevent and manage therapeutic obstacles is for the therapist to monitor, observe, and address her or his therapeutic limits. We define limits here similarly to Linehan (1993a), in that limits have to do with what the therapist is willing to do or tolerate (see also Chapman & Rosenthal, in press). Common limits have to do with demands or requests from the client, such as for between-session contact (e-mail, phone, text) and extra assistance, or requests to read material (e.g., journal entries) or carry out other activities between sessions. Other limits may be imposed on the client's inquiries about the therapist's personal life, challenging in-session behavior (e.g., angry outbursts, lack of talking), hygiene practices, and explorations of differences in values or worldviews (e.g., the acceptance of racial prejudice). Therapists who attend to their own limits may find that they are able to prevent problems before they escalate, maintain an effective working relationship with the client, and reduce the likelihood of burnout.

It is important to remember that therapeutic limits are often idiosyncratic. Different therapists have different limits around client behavior. Some therapists, for example, are willing to be available between sessions for numerous phone calls, are comfortable with their clients texting them for help, and happy to spend extra time engaging in a variety of case management activities. Other therapists are uncomfortable with and unwilling to accept phone calls for help in between sessions, do not wish to e-mail or text message with their clients, and prefer to keep the therapeutic work to the therapy hour. Some therapists also have a wide tolerance for client behaviors (e.g., yelling, angry outbursts, harsh criticism) that may burn out other therapists fairly quickly. There is no one set of effective therapeutic limits that all must adopt (excepting those that conform to ethical guidelines); therapists should become familiar with and monitor their own individual limits.

Monitoring and observing limits involve a variety of tasks. At the beginning of therapy, if the therapist sets clear limits to begin with, she or he may solve problems ahead of time by orienting the client to these limits. A therapist who does not wish to accept e-mails from clients might say, for example,

> I am happy to take phone calls from you in between sessions if you have questions or need help, but I prefer not to e-mail with my clients. I find that I am much more helpful in person or on the phone.

Orienting ideally addresses the specific therapeutic limit in a clear manner and involves a rationale for why the limit exists.

During therapy, the therapist may discover limits that were not clearly delineated at the beginning. A therapist working with a client who repeatedly criticizes her approach, is nonresponsive in session, repeatedly misses appointments, and so on might realize that these behaviors push her or his limits. Often, the first step in the observation of such limits on an ongoing basis is for the therapist to observe and describe her or his emotions and thoughts in reaction to the client's actions. When the client misses a second appointment in a row, for example, the therapist might attend to her or his own emotional reactions and thoughts about this. Common reactions might be worry that the client is not going to benefit from treatment, frustration regarding this unexpected alteration in the therapist's schedule, irritation about the therapist having prepared for a session that did not occur, and so on. These reactions are often the first sign that the client is engaging in behaviors that, if ongoing, may stress the therapeutic relationship. In addition, some useful questions the therapist might ask himself or herself include the following:

- How does this behavior affect me and our therapy right now?
- What emotional reactions and thoughts am I having?
- What is it about this behavior that bothers me?
- Could this behavior, if it were to continue, contribute to burnout?
- Can I tolerate this for the next 10 sessions?

Once a therapist has observed that her or his limits are being stretched, several additional steps can be helpful. One step is to develop a plan for addressing these limits with the client. It is often effective for the therapist to proactively think through ways to bring up or highlight the problem with the client, specifically describe the behavior that is pushing her or his limits (and why), provide a rationale for why it is important for the client to change her or his behavior, and then engage in collaborative problem solving around this behavior (as discussed in detail in a following section). A therapist receiving many personal questions from a client, for example, might state the following:

> I have noticed that you often ask me some fairly personal questions about my past romantic partners. I should let you know that I'm not comfortable sharing this type of information with my clients. It's nothing to do with you specifically; this is just one of my limits with my clients. I don't believe it's professional or reasonable for me to discuss my sex life in therapy. I hope this makes sense to you. Maybe we could discuss what you hope to get by asking these questions and ways to avoid this in the future.

Some limits, and some clients, require more planning and assistance than do others. If the client is missing sessions or is repeatedly late, the therapist may be able to address this pattern fairly easily using some of the strategies we discuss in the next section. With clients who are especially sensitive emotionally or who engage in behaviors that are more difficult to address (such as frequent crisis calls in between sessions, angry outbursts in session, repeated "quitting" therapy, sexual remarks, and so on), therapists may also consider consulting with colleagues about the situation. One of our colleagues recently started to notice that her client was pushing her limits in a particularly challenging manner. The client, "Sally," was in a physically abusive relationship with another woman, and therapy focused on helping the client find a safe place to live and initiate appropriate legal action (e.g., seek a restraining order).

When the therapist brought up these topics, Sally stated that she was unwilling to work on this because she was afraid the therapist would not be sufficiently available and supportive of her while she underwent these stressful legal proceedings and life changes. Instead of talking about these goals, Sally criticized (in person, by phone, and via e-mail) the therapist for her choice of words, voice tone, and demeanor, as well as for the amount of time she took to return calls, among other issues. The therapist noticed that she had begun to dread her sessions with Sally, her repeated criticisms, as well as with the protracted discussions of the therapeutic relationship that rarely ended with any resolution. Observing that she was too deep into frustration and possible burnout to work out an effective approach on her own, she consulted with her treatment team, which provided her with support, validation, opportunities to practice new ways to respond to the client, and suggestions for how to bring up and address this pattern with the client.

STRATEGIES FOR UNDERSTANDING AND MANAGING TIB

Now that we have discussed key principles and strategies for establishing a therapeutic frame vis-à-vis TIB and methods for proactively managing problems that may arise in therapy, we go on to describe approaches for assessing and addressing TIB when it occurs. A behavioral approach involves directly targeting problematic behaviors, and as such, the first step is often to observe and bring the TIB to the client's attention (highlight the problem). Second, to effectively address TIB, the therapist needs to understand why the behavior is occurring, and as such, an important next step is to assess the functional aspects of the problem behavior. Third, once the therapist and client have a common understanding of the problem, the next step is often to work collaboratively to devise solutions to the problem. Finally, because TIB is often difficult to change, it is important to establish that the client is adequately motivated and committed to behavioral change (ensuring adequate commitment) and that potential obstacles that could interfere with possible solutions to problem behavior are discussed or circumvented (troubleshooting).

Highlighting the Problem

Highlighting involves the therapist raising the topic of TIB in a behaviorally specific manner and bringing to the client's attention his or her specific TIB-related behaviors. When a client has been late for the past few sessions, for example, the therapist might state, "I've noticed that you have arrived about 15 to 20 minutes late the last three sessions in a row." For a client who

appears irritated and is harshly criticizing the therapist, the therapist highlighting the problem might say,

> Did you notice, just now, that you were yelling at me? You seem to be
> frowning a fair bit, talking in an abrupt manner, and saying that I don't
> know what I'm doing. Would you be willing to spend some time talking
> about this?

Highlighting can open the door to a collaborative discussion that
models clear, open, and nonjudgmental descriptions of events and behavior. Effective highlighting also includes a rationale for why the therapist is
broaching the topic. We recommend that the therapist avoid adding interpretations or assumptions when initially highlighting TIB, which is often
incompatible with a collaborative and unbiased exploration of the issue.
When highlighting, the therapist may also clarify contingencies, such as the
effect of the behavior on the therapist or the therapeutic process, including
the client's attainment of important goals. In the case of the client arriving
late, for example, the therapist might add, "I'm concerned that when you
come late, we have a lot less time to really work on your goal of learning how
to better connect with other people."

Assessing the Problem

Following the highlighting of the behavior or problem, the therapist
and client may proceed to assess the problem collaboratively. It is important
to first understand the terrain (the factors triggering and maintaining TIB, or
the behavior's context) before embarking on the journey (intervention). In
previous chapters, we have discussed various behavioral assessment strategies,
including functional analysis. *Functional analysis*, often used in DBT (Linehan,
1993a) and discussed earlier in Chapter 2, is a common and useful approach
to assessment of TIB. To use this strategy effectively, the therapists must be
alert to a variety of clinically relevant behavior.

Although some of the most common behaviors emphasized in a functional analysis of TIB include lateness, absence, and lack of homework completion, any clinically relevant behavior can be the object of analysis. At
times, the therapist also may conduct a functional analysis of actions occurring in the moment-to-moment therapeutic process. One of us was seeing a
client, "Antonio," who frequently stated, "I don't know," "I don't remember,"
abruptly changed the topic, or gave terse, one-word answers to questions
about therapeutic topics (e.g., relationship with her mother, looking for volunteer work, anger management). After this pattern occurred several times,
it was clear that therapy would have limited effects if this were to continue.
During one of their discussions, the therapist highlighted that Antonio had

just said, "I don't know." He explained that he has noticed Antonio saying this frequently during therapy and that he was concerned that he wasn't getting enough information from Antonio to be helpful. He then asked whether he might be willing to explore what is happening when he says, "I don't know." Antonio agreed, and through a detailed analysis of the "I don't know" that had just occurred, the therapist and client discovered that the problem was not that Antonio did not know the answer to the question but rather that he experienced tremendous fear of the emerging sadness when he discussed the problem they had been discussing (a recent conflict with his partner). The fear spiked quickly, and he experienced mild dissociation, became confused, and then said, "I don't know" to the therapist's question. This functional analysis was tremendously helpful in that an important treatment goal emerged from the discussion—learning to experience and tolerate sadness.

A functional analysis is most effective when the therapist attends to specific details surrounding the client's actions as well as the functions that these actions serve. The main anchor points in the analysis include (a) antecedents, (b) person variables, (c) the specific TIB, and (d) the consequences or events occurring after these actions. The *antecedents* include the triggering event and establishing operations that, in turn, set the occasion for the TIB. In the case of Antonio, one antecedent was the therapist asking a question about a recent conflict with his partner. Associated establishing operations included Antonio's current emotional state at the beginning of sessions. He felt anxious about using public transportation to get to the therapist's office and often arrived feeling agitated and stressed. Antonio's learning history with respect to stress-coping and self-soothing (*person variable*) was deficient, as he earlier demonstrated some difficulty in coming up with coping strategies for stressful events that involved anything other than escape or avoidance coping strategies. The *specific TIB* included his pausing for 30 seconds or more, looking away, and stating "I don't know" in an abrupt voice tone. In terms of *consequences*, his stating "I don't know" was often followed by a reduction in fear of experiencing sadness, avoidance of discussions of topics eliciting sadness, and a lessening of anxiety related to being on the spot and answering questions.

As a further illustration, the following is an exchange between a client and his therapist after the client arrived late for his session.

Therapist: Hi Barry, nice to see you today.

Client: Nice to see you, too.

Therapist: I'm noticing that you're about 20 minutes late, and I believe you were late for our last session as well. I'm thinking it would be helpful for us to talk about that, so that we can find a way for you to have a full session more consistently. If we have more time, we'll really be able to make more progress on your social anxiety.

Client: I know, I'm sorry I've been late. I'm not really sure what's going wrong.

Therapist: Well, we can figure that out together. Let's spend some time going through step-by-step of what led up to your being late, and figure out together how we can make things go differently next time. This is called a behavior analysis. Do you remember when we did this before around times when you were having a hard time doing your homework?

Client: Yes, I remember. It was pretty helpful.

Therapist: OK, good. Well, let's start with what happened today. When did the thought of your therapy session first enter your mind today?

Client: Oh, when I first woke up this morning, it was on my mind. I knew I'd have to come in at 2 p.m. I was so tired when I woke up, though . . .

Therapist: Good news that it was on your mind. What time did you wake up?

Client: My alarm went off around 8 a.m., but I had been up so late last night that I just kept pressing snooze until it was about noon.

Therapist: Sounds like you were pretty exhausted and maybe feeling sleep deprived. What thoughts were going through your mind, and how were you feeling, when your alarm went off?

Client: I felt sluggish, like I couldn't move, and I was thinking, "I know I should get up, but I really need more sleep." I guess I was feeling tired but also kind of agitated and worried that I wasn't going to be able to function today.

Therapist: I see, and a lot of people in your shoes would probably feel that way if they didn't get a very good sleep. It's normal to be a little worried about how you'll get through the day. So you were thinking that if you just got a little more sleep, you'd be better off today?

Client: Yeah, that's about right. I knew I'd have to come in here, and it's pretty tough, what we're working on these days. Sometimes, I just kind of want to not think about it.

Therapist: Was that thought in your mind, that if you went back to sleep, you wouldn't have to worry about therapy?

Client: Yeah, just before I pressed snooze!

Therapist: OK, well, we may need to work on that your anxiety about coming to therapy. But for now, let's figure out what else happened. Now, waking up at noon should technically have given you enough time to get here on time, so I'm wondering what happened when you finally got up.

Client: I guess I kind of dragged my feet a bit. I did shower, and I felt pretty good about that, and then I sat down to eat.

Therapist: What happened next?

Client: I looked at the clock and realized I had to start getting ready to come in. Then, I decided to spend just a few more minutes reading stuff on my iPad, and I kind of got absorbed.

Therapist: Were you thinking of coming in here while you were reading?

Client: I had a nagging thought that I'm reading for too long and might end up late or missing our appointment, but then I just kept reading.

Therapist: Interesting, so maybe even some more therapy avoidance going on here, huh? What was it like to read instead of get ready for therapy?

Client: I guess I felt absorbed in what I was reading, and I wasn't thinking about therapy. So maybe a little less anxiety.

Therapist: Totally understandable. You got absorbed in a distracting activity, and you got to avoid thoughts, feelings, or anything to do with therapy. Does that sound right?

Client: Yes, true. It's not like I don't find therapy helpful, it's just that I felt so tired and crappy and didn't really want to deal with it.

Therapist: How long was it before you ended up getting ready to come in?

Client: I really left it to the very last minute, and even then, I knew I should rush, but I was just dragging my feet.

Therapist: At that point, how were you feeling, and what kinds of thoughts were going through your mind?

Client: I guess, by that point, I was already feeling nervous about coming in, but I was also dreading the fact that I'd be coming late again. I was thinking you'd be disappointed or inconvenienced, that it was too late to cancel, and it was all just a big mess.

Therapist: Alright, well, that does sound really stressful, and I can see how leaving it to the last minute would heap even more stress and anxiety onto the situation. Let's spend some time figuring out how to make things go better next time. I'm thinking the place to start might be with your anxiety about coming in. What do you think?

This exchange has provided several potentially useful pieces of information with which to build a conceptualization of Barry's TIB. When conducting a functional analysis of a deficit in desired behavior (i.e., Barry not arriving on time), it is helpful to pay attention to the presence of alternative, less desirable behaviors. In Barry's case, these alternative behaviors included pressing the snooze button repeatedly instead of getting up and ready for the day. Closer in time to the therapy session, the alternative behaviors included spending time on his iPad. The antecedents for the latter appear to include the time of day (noon, when the time for the therapy session was approaching), the presence of the iPad, and negative thoughts and anxiety about therapy. The person variables are not clear from this example, but let us say that Barry is a highly anxious person who suffers from agoraphobia and has an extensive history of negative reinforcement for avoidance of appointments and other anxiety-provoking activities. In terms of consequences, Barry's reading his iPad seems to have resulted in short-term negative reinforcement in the form of avoidance of thoughts and anxiety about therapy, avoidance of the work involved in getting ready for therapy, and avoidance of therapy itself. There may also have been some positive reinforcers for his spending time on the iPad, in that the activity itself may have been pleasurable, exciting, or interesting.

Solving the Problem: Moving From Assessment to Intervention

Understanding precisely how the TIB functions, with an emphasis on factors currently maintaining TIB, can suggest useful intervention strategies. In the following sections, we have organized common contributing factors to client TIB into the following categories: (a) motivational deficits, (b) skill deficits, (c) environmental contingencies (within and outside the therapeutic relationship), (d) avoidance coping related to excess fear and anxiety, (e) problematic thinking patterns, and (f) problematic environments and life stressors. Once the client and therapist have identified which of these factors are especially relevant, directions for effective intervention are clearer. We include some examples of intervention strategies for each of these areas, and the reader may also match these problem areas with interventions that we have described in the other chapters in this book. Many of the interventions described next have been earlier discussed as methods for helping clients achieve their therapeutic goals. In the following sections, these methods are modified specifically for addressing TIB within the therapy setting.

Addressing Motivational Problems Related to TIB

At times, problems that interfere with therapy are related to *motivational deficits*. The client may not be sufficiently motivated to change her or his behavior in ways that support ongoing therapy goals. We are using a behavioral perspective regarding motivation, conceptualizing motivation as being strongly related to the balance of potential reinforcing versus punishing consequences of engaging in a particular behavior. As such, we do not conceptualize motivation as an autonomous force within the client that initiates or directs action. Rather, from a behavioral perspective, motivation to alter behavior is evident by the client's actions; for example, when the client speaks about change ("change talk"; Miller & Rollnick, 2012), takes observable steps toward change, and behaviorally exhibits a sustained commitment to change. Many factors can reduce or increase a client's engagement in change-oriented talk or behavior, with motivation regarded as distinctly different from how much a person "wants" to change. Similar to the perspective in DBT, therefore, we assume that clients want to change and also need to become more motivated to change if behavior change is to occur (Linehan, 1993a).

A common therapeutic error involves the therapist assuming that a skill deficit is a motivational problem. For example, it is common for therapists to assume that clients are being "resistant" or simply do not want to change when they fail to show up to therapy, do not complete their homework assignments, or make slower progress than desired or expected. As discussed further later, a client who lacks the skills necessary to change TIB may appear unmotivated to change, but this "lack of motivation" would be much like the lack of motivation that any of us would experience at the bottom of a huge rock face if we have absolutely no rock-climbing skills. As such, we assume that motivation to change TIB may be limited due to deficits in the skills or abilities that are necessary for change, difficulties with awareness of one's TIB, beliefs associated with the inability to change the TIB, or misunderstandings about the context of treatment, among other factors. What appears to be a lack of motivation may also, in fact, be a lack of clarity around one's values or a disconnect between one's values and actions. We find that this action-oriented view of motivation is pragmatic, particularly in dealing with TIB.

Despite his chronic and impairing social anxiety and obsessive–compulsive disorder, "Bob" was going to receive an award for his volunteer work with children. He had to go and accept this award in front of a large crowd and then mingle with people during a cocktail party afterward. This was his worst nightmare. He said, "I just can't do this," and he often avoided even less anxiety-provoking social situations, such as by not paying his landlord in person, declining friends' invitations to go for coffee, and avoiding interactions with his family. Some of these activities were homework assignments—ones that he did not complete. It may seem clear that this client's intense social anxiety would make it hard for him to attend an award ceremony (or do some of the other avoided tasks) and might reduce his motivation to do so; thus, this might appear to be a good situation for standard exposure-oriented intervention. What might be less clear, however, was that the client had serious skill deficits that if unaddressed would likely result in his fears coming true in a variety of social situations. He tended to talk tangentially and in an unfocused manner, stare at his feet while talking, avoid eye contact, mumble, and make socially inappropriate utterances, even when his anxiety level was medium to low. Indeed, he had been let go from jobs before due to odd social behavior. The problem was not his lack of wanting to engage in the world; he desperately wanted to live what he would consider a more "normal" life. Rather, a skills deficit made these valued goals difficult to achieve, and the balance of potential reinforcers (moving toward goals, connecting more frequently with others, experiencing desired behavioral outcomes) and punishers (experiencing negative reactions from others, rejection) did not support social engagement.

Strategies to enhance motivation and commitment to change are detailed extensively elsewhere (e.g., Linehan, 1993a; Miller & Rollnick, 2012), but we will comment on a few of such strategies here. When motivation is the focus, it can be useful to start by helping the client clarify her or his goals and values. Once values and goals are clearer, the therapist and client can discuss how therapy broadly and the therapeutic tasks specifically might fit with the client's goals. A client who has difficulty starting a behavioral activation homework activity might benefit from discussions of how monitoring and increasing her engagement in reinforcing activities relate to her therapy goals, such as reducing depression, increasing social connections, working toward goals at school, and so on. When a client's behavior is discrepant with her or his goals, the therapist can help increase the saliency of the discrepancy by asking how the behavior fits within the life that the client wants to live (Miller & Rollnick, 2012).

Another useful strategy is to help the client think through the pros and cons of changing versus not changing her or his behavior. A client who has angry outbursts in session, for example, might think through the costs and benefits of continuing to engage in such outbursts versus the costs and benefits of learning new anger management and communication strategies. Other strategies involve rolling with resistance by maintaining an empathetic and client-centered therapeutic stance, arguing against change to elicit arguments from the client in favor of change (the "devil's advocate" strategy; Linehan, 1993a), and highlighting the client's ambivalence about change (Miller & Rollnick, 2012). Finally, another approach, drawn from DBT, involves the therapist explicitly stating that the client has the freedom to choose not to change, and that, if the client wants to improve her or his life, there is really no alternative but to change ("freedom to choose and absence of alternatives"; Linehan, 1993a). For a client whose TIB involves arriving intoxicated for therapy, the therapist might state the following:

> Well, here's the thing: I am not going to say you can't come in if you're high, mainly because I'm concerned I would never see you again if I did that! And, you can choose to keep coming in high; as you know, it's really up to you. If you do, though, I'm thinking you're going to keep wasting your time, understand and remember very little of what we talk about, and your life is pretty much going to stay the same as it is right now, or maybe even get worse.

Addressing Skill Deficits Related to TIB

Skill deficits often contribute to TIB. If the TIB appears to be primarily related to a *skill deficit*, helpful interventions might involve improving skills. It is first important to determine that an actual skill deficit is present. We refer the reader to Chapter 2 on initial assessment strategies and to Chapter 3 on skills training for strategies to determine the presence of a skill deficit. There are several examples of skill deficits that might interfere with therapy. Some clients, for example, have tremendous difficulty organizing themselves, regulating their behavior, and arriving on time to appointments. If poor self-management skills appear to be the primary difficulty contributing to lack of therapy attendance or lateness, then the therapist might help the client improve organizational and self-management strategies. Examples include the appropriate use of stimulus control strategies (e.g., setting an alarm, effectively using a to-do list, organizing or scheduling activities throughout the day, establishing regular routines and rhythms), learning how to manage and prioritize competing demands, or strengthening skills that help the client focus on the task at hand (training in attentional focus or mindfulness skills). Clients who struggle with anger management problems may have deficits in their awareness of cues that trigger anger, difficulty recognizing or labeling anger, and few tools to regulate emotional arousal. These deficits can contribute to frustration, which can become therapy interfering quickly when transformed into displays of overt hostility. Skills training in these cases might address anger management skills, emotion recognition and labeling, and strategies to reduce physiological arousal (some of these strategies are discussed in Chapters 6, 7, and 10). One of us saw a client who, when she wished to make requests of the therapist (e.g., a change in appointment time), would do so in a loud, aggressive, yelling fashion (e.g., "I need to change my appointment time to 6 p.m., and you'd better be there!"). She came from a family characterized by hostile, coercive interaction patterns, and she had little practice in effective assertiveness skills. She tended to oscillate between angry, demanding behavior and passive avoidance of making requests. Therapy began to target interpersonal skills, and through repeated practice, she learned to make effective requests, both with the therapist and in other important contexts (e.g., with her boss and partner). We discuss extensively in Chapter 6 the use of skills training strategies, so we refer the reader to this chapter for more information.

Managing Contingencies Related to TIB

When TIB appears related to *contingencies* operating within or outside of the therapeutic relationship, the modification of those contingencies (the focus of Chapter 4) may remove supports for such behavior. With respect to TIB, problems related to contingencies often take the form that an adaptive or desired behavior (e.g., showing up on time for therapy) is punished or not reinforced, or a maladaptive or undesired behavior (e.g., yelling at the therapist, switching topics) is reinforced. A client with problems with attendance may experience more immediate and powerful reinforcers for behavior other than therapy attendance (e.g., staying at home, in bed; watching television; visiting friends; exercising; using drugs or alcohol). Some clients may be fully committed to self-monitoring and engaging in behavioral activation assignments, but the immediate consequences of sitting down and reviewing their actions, thoughts, feelings, and behaviors on a particular day (e.g., the work involved in doing the self-monitoring assignment, intense anxiety or shame, avoidance of fatigue) might be sufficiently aversive so as to override rules that connote eventual benefits associated with such monitoring (e.g., the therapist's suggestion that the simple act self-monitoring often produces behavior change in desirable directions). Clients who call the therapist repeatedly in a crisis might experience more reinforcement (e.g., in the form of reassurance, reduction in loneliness, help with problem solving) from contact with the therapist than from the use of behavioral coping skills on her or his own.

As discussed in Chapter 4, when using contingency management strategies, it is important to clearly specify the behaviors to decrease and increase. Take the example of a client who is having difficulty with therapy attendance. The client has missed three of the last six therapy sessions. Increasing the client's attendance rate might intuitively seem to be the most obvious behavior to increase. Less obvious, however, is that to accomplish this goal, behavioral targets to increase necessarily involve those that make the client's attendance at sessions more likely. To actually attend therapy, the client may need to increase several other behaviors, such as setting an alarm or reminder, arranging for social activities outside of therapy time, planning ahead for traffic, managing anxiety or other emotions related to therapy, and so on. In terms of behaviors to decrease, the therapist might assess what the client is doing instead of coming to therapy, such as staying home and gaming, watching television, talking with or seeing friends, surfing the Internet, sleeping, using drugs or alcohol, or other such actions. These are the behaviors to decrease (or at least to schedule for times other than when therapy appointments are scheduled). Changes in the rate of TIB is much more likely when it is clear which supporting behaviors the client needs to increase and which interfering behaviors should be targeted for weakening or elimination. Simply focusing on the deficit or absence of a behavior rather than on the strengthening of alternative behaviors will limit the utility of contingency management strategies.

The therapist might also pay particularly close attention to contingencies operating in the therapeutic relationship. Many therapists, for example, learn their way out of effective therapy through punishment or lack of reinforcement from clients. A therapist whose attempts at problem solving are met with contempt, angry outbursts, or repeated statements of "I don't know" or "yes, but" may learn that it is more reinforcing simply to talk about what the client wants to talk about, change topics, or avoid altogether problem solving or confronting the client even when confrontation is potentially effective or necessary. In these cases, it can be effective for the therapist to address these contingencies directly, orient the client to the nature of the problem, and work collaboratively with the client to modify the contingencies, as shown in the example below.

> We seem to be in a bind here. I really think that talking about work is important and critical to you getting closer to your goals, but I've noticed that I'm backing off of these topics a lot these days. I think this is because it's easier to back off; when I move in, you get angry at me. So I've been doing you a disservice and avoiding these topics altogether. Can you see how this might be a problem?

When Fear, Escape, or Emotional Avoidance Is Involved in TIB

When *excessive fear* or *anxiety* and related *escape* or *avoidance* underlie a client's TIB, interventions might focus on exposure, mindfulness, or acceptance-based strategies to help the client reduce avoidance and fear. As an example, first described in Chapman and Rosenthal (in press), one of us saw a client, "Harry," who became attached to therapy and the therapist and had difficulty contemplating termination. Harry had been thoroughly oriented at the beginning of treatment to the notion that, within about a year or so, therapy will end, ideally once he has met his goals and benefited from treatment. Approximately two thirds of the way through treatment, the therapist briefly broached the topic of when Harry might know that he is finished with therapy. Although the therapist framed the termination process as a collaborative decision-making endeavor, Harry became extremely angry. His face turned red, his muscles tightened up, and he raised his voice, saying, "Why are you talking about this?!" followed by a string of criticisms leveled at the therapist. He was so angry that it took some time before he was able to reflect and take the time to better understand his own reactions.

The therapist and client worked together to assess the situation, and at that point, it became clear that Harry's initial reaction was not anger; rather, it was intense fear. Harry was afraid of how he would do without the therapist's support, and his bringing up termination posed, in his mind, a tremendous threat. Harry panicked and then became extremely angry. Under these conditions, with termination not being imminent, it would be easy for any therapist or client to simply avoid discussing termination. The therapist, however, viewed this situation as an opportunity to help Harry reduce his fear of termination. This work, in turn, could have potentially beneficial long-term effects by helping him better navigate termination effectively when the time came. For the therapist, the solution related to the problem posed by TIB, was to use the principles of exposure therapy. The therapist first discussed the problems with avoidance and oriented the client to the purposes and procedures of exposure therapy. The therapist and client purposely had the discussion about termination, several times, over the next couple of sessions. After a few sessions, during which approximately 10 to 15 minutes were dedicated to an exposure-oriented intervention, Harry concluded that he was bored of the discussion. His fear had reduced to 15 out of 100 on the subjective units of distress scale, and he stated that he was "OK" with termination and did not need to keep working on this issue. Several months later, Harry brought up termination on his own. He indicated that he had met many of his goals and was ready to start tapering the session.

Addressing Problematic Thinking Patterns Related to TIB

Problematic cognitions influencing TIB may be addressed via interventions to address thinking patterns, including some of those discussed in Chapter 5. We have already discussed extensively the use of such strategies to address thinking patterns on the part of clients. In this section, we instead focus on how the *therapist* might address her or his own therapy-interfering thinking patterns. Indeed, therapists often have problematic cognitions that may reduce effectiveness. Some examples of these include unrealistic expectations of the client, negative judgments, and distorted assumptions or inferences regarding the client's intentions. When confronted with challenging behavior in session, it may be common for therapists to assume that such behavior represents "resistance," an unwillingness to change, a lack of motivation, or manipulativeness (Freeman & McCloskey, 2003). These types of assumptions can reduce the therapist's empathy and willingness to work with the client or can result in frustration or irritation. One of us, when managing particularly challenging client behavior, was discussing the situation with a colleague, who suggested, "That sounds really stressful. And isn't it true that you mainly work with a lot of people with borderline personality disorder?" The therapist was annoyed at first but, after thinking this through, realized that he had a number of expectations regarding his client that were causing problems for him. In essence, he had temporarily forgotten that he works with challenging clients who do challenging things and realized that he was actually expecting the client to be different (e.g., "easier," more "reasonable," already knowledgeable that it was inappropriate to ask personal questions).

We would suggest that therapists, when having thoughts that may play a negative role in therapy, consider using some of the same strategies with themselves as they would use with their clients. The therapist might, for example, first identify her or his thinking (e.g., "I'm having the thought that the client is intentionally making things difficult or is unmotivated to change"), emotional reactions (e.g., irritation, frustration, annoyance, demoralization), related behaviors (e.g., pushing the client harder to change, reducing or avoiding validation), and consequences (e.g., negative effects on therapy sessions). Another step might be to describe the situation in a behaviorally specific manner, removing assumptions, inferences, or judgments. A therapist who infers manipulativeness when a client speaks about suicide, for example, might instead describe the situation as follows: "When I asked the client whether she has had a chance to do her homework, she sighs, looks down, and starts talking about how she has been thinking of killing herself." In addition, it can be effective to frame thoughts as hypotheses to be tested through behavioral experiments. If the therapist's thought is that the client is unmotivated, she may test this by discussing with the client his motivation to change, the pros and cons of changing, and by assessing whether anything might be interfering with motivation to change.

Problematic Environments and Life Stressors

Other factors that may influence TIB are problematic environments or acute or chronic stressors. The client, for example, may be experiencing an overwhelming amount of stress at home or at work, may be in an abusive or otherwise toxic relationship, may have financial or occupational problems, or may have few social contacts or support. Any of these factors is likely to interfere with the client's quality of life and ability to function effectively in therapy. As a result, the therapist and client may need to work together to find solutions to problems in everyday living. The therapist also may be experiencing problematic environments, may have personal problems that interfere with treatment, may not be engaging in adequate self-care or receiving enough social support, or may be working in a difficult or stressful environment, among other problems. If these factors contribute to the therapist engaging in TIB or are leading the therapist down the path to professional burnout, then problem-solving strategies can effectively surmount these obstacles, ideally with the help of a supportive personal and professional network.

Problem-solving strategies can help reduce stressors and environmental barriers to treatment. Such strategies have been discussed in another chapter of this book (Chapter 7) and in other volumes (Linehan, 2015; Nezu, Nezu, & D'Zurilla, 2013), but the basic steps generally involve (a) clearly specifying and describing the problem; (b) specifying goals, objectives, or needs; (c) generating possible solutions (often through brainstorming); (d) selecting a few promising solutions for further consideration and evaluation (e.g., through reviewing the pros and cons of each or considering likely outcomes); (e) implementing the solution(s); (f) evaluating the results; and (g) deciding whether more problem solving is needed. Following is an example of the use of problem solving to address therapy attendance problems of a client.

- *Clearly specify and describe the problem:* "June" has missed approximately every third therapy session. At times, her nanny became ill and had to go home early or had to take time off, requiring June to cancel therapy sessions so that she could take care of her two small children. June really wants to be in therapy and is frustrated and having hopeless thoughts about the situation (e.g., "There's really no way around this. Maybe this isn't the right time for me to be in therapy.").
- *Specify goals and needs:* June wants to come to therapy to address her anxiety and her alcohol problems. She is worried that her alcohol use, if unaddressed, will get worse and start affecting her parenting. She also is anxious, socially withdrawn, and has difficulty functioning at work. Her goal is to learn ways to better manage anxiety and reduce alcohol use, and she would like to be able to come to therapy every week. Longer term goals are to advance in her job and to be a caring and conscientious mother.
- *Generate solutions:* June and her therapist set a timer for 5 minutes and separately wrote out as many possible solutions to this problem as they could, without evaluating, judging, or getting rid of any of the solutions generated. They then discussed together their solutions. In combination, they had come up with about 15 possible solutions.
- *Evaluate potential solutions:* June and her therapist selected a couple of the most promising solutions to evaluate: (a) asking her mother if she would be willing to be a backup for child care and (b) bringing her children to the therapy office when needed (the therapy office provided some child-care services and supervision). As they reviewed the pros and cons of these solutions,

it became clear that the primary cons to solution (a) is that the mother may not always be available on such short notice and that it would be hard for June to ask this of her mother. The primary cons of (b) were that June may be distracted during her session and that she might feel like she is imposing by bringing the children. Ultimately, they decided on a combination of both options, with the first step being to contact her mother, and then, if unavailable, to bring the children to her session.

- *Evaluate the results*: After putting this plan into action, June ended up attending five of the next six sessions, with one missed because her children were ill. This, of course, was another problem to solve, albeit a more challenging one.

Commitment and Troubleshooting Strategies

Once the client and therapist have discovered the essence of the problem contributing to TIB and collaboratively devised possible solutions (e.g., involving strategies to address motivation, skill deficits, cognitions, fear and avoidance, or problems and barriers that need to be solved), a useful next step is for the therapist to elicit a commitment from the client to put these solutions into action. The strategies that a therapist might use to elicit a commitment are similar to those discussed earlier in the section on addressing motivational issues, and essentially, the goal is for the client to agree to implement behavioral changes. Obtaining a commitment may be as simple as the therapist asking the client, "OK, so this is our plan, right? Are you on board with and willing to do this?" Or it might be more complicated, involving motivational enhancement strategies, such as reviewing the pros and cons of changing or implementing the solutions, the devil's advocate strategy, or other such motivational or commitment strategies (Linehan, 1993a; Miller & Rollnick, 2012). Some therapists may also use behavioral contracting to increase the likelihood that a client will follow through with the plan.

Following an agreement or commitment from the client, another useful step is to troubleshoot, or discuss and proactively solve problems that might interfere with the successful implementation of the devised interventions or solutions. As the quote from Robert Burns goes, "The best laid plans of mice and men often go awry." Troubleshooting can help the therapist and client to avoid this problem. If the client, for example, has difficulty with anger management and has been engaging in outbursts in sessions and has committed to practice anger management skills in between sessions, it can be helpful to discuss and plan for obstacles to such practice. Common obstacles may include the client forgetting the plan; not fully understanding the task, skills, or solution; becoming unwilling to enact the plan; or experiencing other problems, life stressors, or obstacles that make it difficult to do what has been planned. The therapist might say, for example,

> So our plan is for you to practice diaphragmatic breathing each day so that you'll be more ready to use this skill when you get angry during our sessions and in other situations. Can you think of anything that might get in the way of our plan? Is there anything that might make it hard for you to pull this off?

A discussion of these potential obstacles and barriers ahead of time can not only help to prevent them but may also reveal new and useful information about the client. Consider, for example, the client who responds to the foregoing questions with, "I don't know, I really just don't see how this is going to help. I mean, the anger just goes from zero to one hundred like that. How is breathing supposed to help me?" Given this response, the therapist is aware that the client is either not fully on board with the rationale for the skill or that perhaps other skills or strategies are needed (i.e., breathing may actually be inadequate, as the client suggests). The therapist also might encourage the client to consider a behavioral experiment, testing out her thoughts about whether the breathing will work.

WHEN THERAPISTS ENGAGE IN TIB

We have thus far focused more on client TIB than on therapist TIB. In this section, we briefly discuss ways in which therapists might engage in TIB and some strategies to address this. Even therapists with extensive training, expertise, and experience can get in the way of effective treatment just as much (or more so) as clients can. Therapists are human and are subject to the same influences on their behavior as are clients' behavior. Reinforcement contingencies can shape ineffective therapist behaviors; therapists may lack skills in important areas; they may become overwhelmed by their emotional responses, fears, worries, or burnout; or they may have dysfunctional thoughts that negatively affect their approach to treatment. Across various forms of psychotherapy, there are several common examples of therapist TIB (Chapman & Rosenthal, in press; Freeman & McCloskey, 2003), including the following:

- talking too long, or being long-winded;
- being silent or passive for too long, particularly when the client is seeking direct suggestions, advice, or intervention;
- using too much therapeutic jargon or wording that does not resonate with the client;
- assuming the client knows what the therapist is talking about;

- expressing frustration intensely and ineffectively;
- not genuinely showing emotions or appearing aloof, distant, or uninterested;
- expressing unrealistic confidence in the likelihood of treatment working;
- minimizing the magnitude of a client's problems, or invalidating the client by suggesting simple solutions for complex, overwhelming problems;
- changing the subject or otherwise avoiding uncomfortable discussions;
- rejecting, criticizing, or punishing client behavior;
- avoiding confrontation when needed or effective;
- failing to attend to standard professional behavior, such as missing sessions, showing up late, forgetting or failing to do agreed-on tasks, and so on;
- adhering rigidly to an agenda without regard for the client's current state or wishes;
- failing to adhere to professional and ethical standards;
- providing unclear or vague treatment plans, case conceptualization, assessment findings; and/or
- providing unorganized or haphazard interventions or session structure.

Several strategies can help to minimize the likelihood of therapist TIB. First, therapists can prevent and identify problems by reflecting on their work. There are many ways to do this, including taking time after a session to think through how it went, what was effective or ineffective, and how the client responded to the interventions occurring during the session. The therapist also may record her or his sessions, review them at a later time, and critique her or his own work. When we supervise trainees, we often encourage them to record their own work, listen to or watch these recordings, and take note of what they are doing that is effective or ineffective. We also asked them to take the additional step of considering constructive feedback that they would give themselves. After reflecting on the session, it can be helpful to take note of a brief plan to continue effective actions and reduce ineffective interventions for next time.

Second, it can be helpful to consult with and elicit feedback from others. Perhaps the first person from whom to elicit feedback might be the client. Therapists could, for example, take time at the end of each session to inquire about how the client experienced the session, what was most helpful and least helpful, and what she or he would like to focus on next time. This strategy can enhance the collaborative therapeutic alliance, provide the client an opportunity to bring up problems before they become more chronic and frustrating, and allow the therapist to model effective and nondefensive responses to constructive criticism.

Another way to receive feedback is to engage a regular network of peers, supervisors, or consultants about one's work. In DBT, for example, therapists meet weekly for a consultation team meeting in which the focus is on enhancing the therapist's skills, motivation, and competence, as well as providing support for therapists engaged in challenging clinical work (Linehan, 1993a). Even if a formal team is not possible, it can be invaluable to consult with and receive feedback and support from colleagues with relevant expertise. Such individuals, usually from a more objective perspective, can highlight ways in which the therapist is going astray. Having session recordings available for such consultation can be valuable; otherwise, consultation relies solely on the therapist's potentially limited and biased memories of events. Even when problems are not apparent from the session recordings or from the therapist's description of what is happening, others may sometimes notice potential problems in the ways in which the therapist describes the client or her or his work. We have noticed in our treatment teams that therapists may not be aware that they are heading for burnout until someone on the team highlights the fact that the therapist appeared frustrated, was expressing hopeless thoughts, or was describing her or his client in judgmental terms.

Third, therapists can apply the same principles and strategies discussed earlier in this chapter when they engage in TIB. Not all problems can be avoided or fixed beforehand. Therapists sometimes make mistakes. One of our colleagues recently agreed, upon a client's request, to provide a brief, gentle reminder about the day therapy group meetings are held each week. This client was struggling with major depression, recently separated from her partner, and was having a hard time getting motivated to attend group. The therapist agreed to help in this way, but on one week when she was away, she completely forgot to provide the reminder. Upon her return, she apologized to the client, told the client how she would schedule a reminder on her iPhone, and agreed to be sure to follow through next week. Next week came, and the therapist again failed to send the reminder. It turns out that iPhone reminders only work when therapists remember to look at their iPhones! The therapist apologized again, and then decided to use the principle of *overcorrection*. Overcorrection involves the individual engaging in an effortful response that more than corrects the effects of some undesired behavior. In this case, the undesired behavior was the therapist failing to provide the reminder. To correct the effects of the behavior, she told the client how she would solve this problem, remember to view the reminder, and so on. Overcorrection involved offering the client an extra, free, 30-minute session to discuss and get extra help with what she was learning in group sessions. The client expressed appreciation for this, and the therapist diligently provided these reminders until they were no longer needed.

SUMMARY

The following guidelines, when applied, can reduce the likelihood of TIB or suggest means for addressing such behavior when it arises:

- Recognize and accept that clients and therapists are fallible human beings, that behavior change is difficult, and that road-blocks and obstacles to therapy are inevitable.
- Establish a frame for effective management of therapy obstacles and roadblocks by (a) conceptualizing TIB within a behavioral framework, (b) orienting the client ahead of time to TIB and to the therapist's approach to the management of therapeutic obstacles, and (c) remembering to observe and monitor her or his own therapeutic limits.
- Use orientation throughout therapy, and, as TIB occurs, use it to establish a therapeutic frame in which the client and thera-pist can work collaboratively to solve problems that may other-wise interfere with effective therapy.
- When TIB is ongoing during therapy, first highlight the problem or bring the TIB to the client's attention, then join with the client to collaboratively conduct a behavioral analysis of the TIB.
- Once clear hypotheses about the controlling variables maintain-ing TIB can be offered, consider additional intervention strategies such as motivational strategies, skills training, exposure-oriented interventions, cognitive strategies, contingency management, problem solving, or other core cognitive-behavioral approaches.
- Elicit a clear commitment from the client to participate in new, desired behavior and to engage in troubleshooting to pro-actively circumvent obstacles to the new plan.
- Be aware that therapists may also engage in TIB, and when this happens, effective strategies for reducing therapist TIB include reflecting on one's work, consulting and seeking feedback and suggestions, and applying the same principles and strategies that would be used for addressing the client's TIB.

12

BRINGING THERAPY TO A CLOSE AND AFTERCARE

Therapy is frequently about helping people break free from unhelpful behavior patterns and assisting them in making their behavior more consistent with personal goals and values. When considered from these perspectives, the conclusion of therapy is not so much an end unto itself but rather a big step—or a big leap—squarely onto a path that has the potential to produce a more satisfying and rewarding life. In this chapter, we discuss several issues related to ending therapy. Topics include deciding when it is appropriate to end therapy, the process of ending therapy, and planning for aftercare. Within these areas we also touch on several other topics, such as strategies for reducing the likelihood of relapse or recurrence, methods for facilitating the client's ongoing generalization of learning and the maintenance of gains that have taken place during therapy, and approaches for establishing a client commitment for continual growth in directions consistent with personal goals and values.

http://dx.doi.org/10.1037/14691-012
Behavioral Interventions in Cognitive Behavior Therapy: Practical Guidance for Putting Theory Into Action,
Second Edition, by R. F. Farmer and A. L. Chapman

DECIDING WHEN TO END THERAPY

Decisions involving therapy discontinuation are ideally the result of a collaborative process between the client and therapist that started during the earliest stages of therapy and periodically revisited throughout the active treatment phase. In most instances, initial discussions about the course of therapy will take place early in the process (e.g., the informed consent or treatment formulation stages), during which time specific therapeutic goals are discussed as well as ideas about what a successful therapy might look like in terms of the type and degree of behavior change that is possible or probable.

Orienting the Client to the Process of Therapy Discontinuation

Factors that inform decisions about therapy discontinuation are often included in the informed consent form, the therapy contract, or some other notice that the client has the opportunity to review and agree to before receiving services or shortly after initial therapy assessments have been concluded. Therapy discontinuation could, for example, be discussed in terms of a fixed number of sessions that is reasonable given the objectives of therapy, an estimate of the number of sessions or amount of time needed to accomplish a therapeutic goal (which might be revised as therapy progresses), or the degree of change observed in the target behaviors identified at the therapy's outset. The informed consent form or therapy contract might also include passages that specify possible reasons for therapy discontinuation (D. D. Davis, 2008). These could include reasons based on client discretion (e.g., client believes he or she cannot work productively with the therapist), therapist discretion (e.g., therapist views therapy as unhelpful due to the client's refusal to participate in the therapy process), mutual agreement (e.g., consensus that therapy goals have been met), or clinic rules (e.g., two consecutive no-show appointments, failure to reschedule psychotherapy sessions within 60 days of the last session).

Just as it is important at the outset of therapy for the therapist to orient the client to what to expect from therapy, it is also helpful to provide the client with some clear expectations regarding therapy discontinuation. Such information might include the following:

- how the therapist and client will work together to increase the likelihood that the client will maintain therapy gains following discontinuation;
- whether discontinuation will involve ending therapy abruptly or some kind of tapering schedule;
- the availability of "booster sessions" after the active phase of therapy (discussed later in this chapter);

- how the client might access services in an emergency, if the therapist has been the primary emergency care provider; and
- how the relationship with the therapist will change after discontinuation.

Providing the client with clear information about topics such as these can help dispel any misconceptions and alleviate some of the concerns that a client might have about discontinuation. "Jill," for example, was asked if she had thoughts or concerns about therapy eventually coming to a close. Jill replied, "Well, I'm a little worried about it, but I can still call you from time to time for help if I'm suicidal, right?" The therapist realized that this was a good time to talk further with Jill about therapy discontinuation and clarify that she will not be available to provide her with assistance in the event of a crisis once therapy concludes.

> Actually, I'm really glad that you brought this up. When we stop seeing each other for therapy, things will change in several ways, and it is important for you to know how this will happen. For instance, when I am no longer your therapist, I will not be available for phone calls or to help you if you are suicidal or in a crisis. I am happy to be available, however, if you need a referral, if you want to meet to discuss the resumption of therapy, or if you are having trouble figuring out how to get help from someone else. Let's talk a little bit about a plan for therapy discontinuation.

Judging the Length of Therapy

Weiner (1975) suggested that the length of therapy is likely to be influenced by several factors, including the orientation of the therapist, the depth and intensity of therapy, and the severity and complexity of the client's problem areas. Although cognitive behavior therapies (CBTs) are often time limited, the duration of therapy can range between a few sessions to 1 to 2 years, depending on several factors, including the severity and pervasiveness of the client's problem areas. Although many research studies that evaluated CBT therapies have had fixed durations, therapists in applied settings usually considers a number of factors with respect to therapy discontinuation, including whether ending therapy on a particular date would be premature, clinically contraindicated, or likely to result in the client's problematic behaviors reemerging (Barnett & Sanzone, 1997).

There are no clear and specific criteria for deciding when to end therapy; rather, there are often several considerations that vary in relevance across clients. Ideally, by the time therapy closes, the client has made progress toward the fulfillment of his or her therapy goals and has acquired and practiced skills that can, in turn, benefit him or her when challenging situations arise in the future (Weiner, 1975). Skills acquired during therapy may also help the client develop behavior patterns that are consistent with how he or she would ideally like to be, or are more in harmony with his or her personal goals and values.

Unplanned or Premature Discontinuation of Therapy

On occasion, therapy might end before reaching a natural or optimal conclusion. About one of five clients, for example, drops out of therapy early (Swift & Greenberg, 2012). The client, for example, might unexpectedly indicate a desire to end therapy and may do so with little notice and a sense of urgency. At times, such client-initiated terminations might be in response to life events such as a job change or relocation. On other occasions, however, the client may terminate therapy for unforeseen reasons. When unexpected requests for therapy termination arise, a therapist might explore with the client not only the reasons behind the request but also the associated functional context. Examples of questions for exploring this latter area might include the following:

- Is this something that you recently thought about?
- Is there something happening now that has influenced your thinking about this?
- Do you recall when you first thought about ending therapy?
- Is there something happening in therapy that is related to your decision?
- Are you thinking that up until now therapy hasn't been all that helpful to you?
- I thought that therapy was beginning to help in some ways. Would you agree?
- What are the pros versus cons of ending therapy now?
- Do you think ending therapy now will help you more than continuing with it?
- If we continued with therapy and it helped to resolve some of the problems we've been addressing, would something be lost?

When the client's decision to terminate therapy appears to be somewhat impulsive or in response to some unspecified current situation, it is often useful for the therapist to suggest at least one more meeting, perhaps after a 2- to 3-week break. A brief vacation from therapy might allow enough time for any the acute situation that influenced the client's decision to pass, or provide the client with opportunities to consider the pros versus cons of therapy discontinuation or alternatives to therapy closure. When a meeting eventually occurs, the therapist might further explore the reasons why the client is proposing a discontinuation of therapy and remind the client about any problem areas that remain. If the therapist believes that the potential harms associated with discontinuation outweigh the benefits, he or she can express this to the client in clear terms. The therapist might also consider a phone call to the client during the therapy break to assess the client's welfare should this be a potential concern.

Although therapists may make some modest efforts to encourage a client to reexamine his or her decision to end therapy prematurely, it is often not productive for a therapist to repeatedly cajole or plead with a client to continue. When premature termination appears unavoidable, the therapist might elect to end therapy as gracefully as possible. If the client has made a clear decision to terminate therapy and the therapist has helped him or her think this decision through, it can be helpful for the therapist to express encouragement and support in relation to this decision. The therapist also might provide referrals to other mental health care professionals as well as an invitation to return to therapy at a later date. The therapist might also initiate a follow-up telephone contact to inquire whether the client has sought out additional therapy or to offer assistance if indicated (Barnett & Sanzone, 1997).

Sometimes therapists need to end or suspend therapy prematurely or transfer the client's care to another therapist. This might occur for several reasons, such as job relocation or illness or in response to threats or intimidation from the client. The American Psychological Association (APA; 2010) *Ethical Principles of Psychologists and Code of Conduct* (hereafter referred to as the APA Ethics Code) holds that "psychologists make reasonable efforts to provide for orderly and appropriate resolution of responsibility for client/patient care" in such instances, "with paramount consideration given to the welfare of the client/patient" (Standard 10.09, Interruption of Therapy). D. D. Davis (2008) and Younggren and Gottlieb (2008) have provided additional guidance for negotiating such situations when they occur. On other occasions, the discontinuation of therapy might be considered if there is an unexpected lack of treatment response or if the client's condition worsens. According to the APA's Ethics Code (2010), psychologists should "terminate therapy when it becomes reasonably clear that the client/patient no longer needs the service, is not likely to benefit, or is being harmed by continued service" (Standard 10.10, Terminating Therapy). In such instances, the therapist will usually provide the client with a list of appropriate referrals who are qualified to assist the client with his or her problem areas.

THE PROCESS OF DISCONTINUING THERAPY

Ending therapy is not so much a singular event as it is a multistage process. In this section, we describe some of the processes associated with therapy termination and steps that therapists can take at each stage to increase the likelihood that discontinuation will be a productive transition for the client.

Anticipating Problems That May Arise Around Therapy Discontinuation

Therapy discontinuation can be a difficult transition for clients who are overly sensitive or reactive to disruptions in interpersonal relations. For some clients, the end of therapy can represent the end of an important relationship. For others, the end of the therapeutic relationship might have some functional similarity to previous separations or losses and can be an occasion for marked anxiety, hopelessness, and sadness. Some clients might exhibit varieties of avoidance behavior (e.g., the development of new problems, the reemergence of behaviors targeted in therapy) that are efforts to cope with or delay the experience of loss (Strupp & Binder, 1984).

Whenever possible, a therapist should try to anticipate a client's adverse reactions associated with therapy discontinuation before their occurrence, perhaps as early as the case formulation phase when considering potential obstacles to effective therapy provision (see Chapter 3). Periodically throughout therapy, and as tapering or discontinuation approaches, the therapist might discuss with the client the issue of eventual therapy closure. Discussions around these issues could involve informal problem solving in which the therapist and client identify possible future problems and promising solutions. For other clients, examining the meaning associated with separation from the therapist or the loss of therapy could be helpful. Explorations such as these might reveal, for example, the presence of several rules related to loss forged from the client's earlier life experiences that have been generalized to the therapeutic context. If such rules are evident and appear to be inaccurate or biased in relation to this circumstance, the therapist could address them like other faulty rules that incorrectly represent actual antecedent–behavior or behavior–consequence relations (see Chapter 5). "Mandy," for example, had a history of rejection from caregivers. When she was distressed or upset, her family members would often ignore or dismiss her, or, when she was older, cut off contact with her altogether (e.g., by telling her to stop calling them). As therapy discontinuation approached, she thought: "If he is ending therapy, it must mean that he does not care about me. If I stop seeing him, I will be left with nobody." In this case, the therapist might discuss these issues with Mandy and perhaps use the strategies highlighted in Chapter 5 to target rules or thoughts about discontinuation.

Therapists, too, might have ideas about therapy discontinuation that draw him or her away from a more professional course of action (e.g., "Therapy should not be discontinued so long as the client wants to continue"; "Clients should initiate therapy discontinuation, not the therapist"; "My client depends on me"; see D. D. Davis, 2008). According to contemporary best practices and ethical standards of care, therapists should consistently monitor a client's progress and consider therapy discontinuation once therapy goals have been realized, when the prospect for ongoing benefit diminishes, or if continued work is potentially harmful. Professionally, ongoing discussions about therapy discontinuation with the client can be productive. Such discussions, for example, can provide a metric for assessing client progress, an occasion for integrating and consolidating the experience of therapy, and an opportunity for decreasing the likelihood of lapses or relapse.

Consolidating and Extending the Experience of Therapy

As therapy begins to wind down, it is often useful for the therapist to help the client reflect on his or her time in treatment. The therapist might give particular consideration to what has been learned and achieved during therapy, what aspects of therapy the client can apply to future challenges that are likely to arise (i.e., generalization of skills), and what lifestyle changes should be retained or further cultivated to preserve psychological health and well-being (i.e., maintenance of therapeutic gains).

Evaluating the Outcomes of Therapy

Before concluding the active phase of therapy, it is often useful for the therapist and client to reflect on the outcomes of their work together. Successful therapies will often produce meaningful change in behavior and overall well-being. In addition to symptomatic relief, by the end of therapy, clients often demonstrate greater flexibility in behavior, display more effective coping resources, and realign behavioral repertoires with important values and goals. It is also useful for clients to consider what they have learned about themselves during therapy and comment on any skills that they have found to be useful in responding to or coping with difficult challenges. By the end of therapy, for example, clients will often be better able to differentiate themselves from their experiences or to be a witness to their experience rather than be their experience (e.g., "I'm aware that I feel more anxious when I go into the shopping mall and that my level of anxiety rises and falls depending on the presence of certain features when I'm in the mall" vs. "I'm anxious when I go into the mall"). Clients who have undergone behavioral assessment and interventions will also likely be able to demonstrate a functional understanding of their behavior, as evident in their knowledge of the common antecedents of problematic behaviors or the usual effects that their actions have on situations and those around them. They may, for example, have an understanding that maladaptive avoidance and escape behaviors provide temporary or immediate relief but often pose additional problems (e.g., obstacles to personal goals or valued activities, aversive delayed outcomes).

It can be helpful for the therapist and the client to come up with a list of some of the important points that the client has learned throughout therapy. Such a list, for example, might include reminders of the relationship between certain behaviors and positive or negative consequences. A client who has struggled with depression and previously avoided activities and people might write down, "Avoiding makes me feel better in the short term, but in the long term, avoidance is my enemy." A client who has learned about the effects of her aggressive interpersonal behavior on others might write, "When I yell and push people to do things, they might do what I want, but my relationships suffer. It works much better when I use my new assertiveness skills."

The therapist and the client might consider together areas from the client's problem list (see Chapter 3) and discuss the progress that has been made and additional areas where future attention and work might be directed (Ledley, Marx, & Heimberg, 2010). The therapist, for example, might review with the client graphs of data collected during self-monitoring (e.g., the frequency of target behaviors) or scores on questionnaire measures that were administered repeatedly. The therapist and the client could also discuss the client's previously stated short- and long-term goals for therapy and whether these goals were achieved. In some cases, therapy might not result in the reduction or elimination of, for example, experiences related to depression, periodic emotional turmoil or distress, unrealistic fears, or other such problems. Even if the client still struggles with these problems to some degree, therapy might have helped him or her act in a way that is more consistent with important values. If this is the case, it is important to point out that, in some essential ways, the work the client did in therapy was helpful.

The therapist might also assess, acknowledge, and validate a client's concerns about backsliding once therapy has concluded. When used therapeutically and strategically, the validation of these concerns might include an acknowledgment that the problem behaviors will likely resurface. The framework for such a discussion might be based on the relapse prevention model, which we describe later in this chapter. When therapy gains have been relatively modest for certain problem areas, the therapist might conceptualize these as future goals that the client might continue to work toward after therapy comes to a close.

Helping the Client Extend Therapy Learning to Future Challenges: Promoting the Generalization and Maintenance of Therapeutic Change

Behavioral interventions based on operant or Pavlovian learning principles, when effective, do not destroy past learning but instead promote new learning (Bouton, 2000). New learning that occurs during the course of therapy is likely to transfer to situations or contexts most similar to those emphasized in therapy. The likelihood that this new learning, however, will transfer to contexts not explicitly targeted is comparatively small (Bouton, 2000). Lapses and relapse, then, might be particularly common given that new learning is often context dependent and that harmful behaviors that have persisted for some time have likely occurred and been reinforced in a multitude of contexts not explicitly targeted in therapy. To enhance the transfer of new learning acquired through therapy participation, therapists might consider including interventions that facilitate the generalization and maintenance of skills. *Generalization* refers to the transfer of new learning to environments beyond the therapeutic environment, and *maintenance* refers to the durability of treatment effects over time (W. M. Nelson & Politano, 1993).

Therapists, for example, could provide clients with reminders of therapy and therapeutic strategies that they can bring into new situations that represent heightened risks for lapse or relapse. Such reminders might include *coping cards* that promote the retrieval of skills or strategies learned in therapy, periodic telephone calls from the therapist, or materials that summarize the skills learned over the course of therapy (Bouton, 2000). One may develop coping cards, for example, that list high-risk situations or triggers (e.g., certain environments, emotions, thoughts, cravings) and coping responses that can be used in those situations (J. S. Beck, 2011). These cards can be carried in the client's wallet or purse, and he or she can take them out and review them whenever high-risk situations are anticipated or present. Such cards also act as a reminder of therapy, with these reminders thus available in situations in which therapy may not have explicitly occurred.

To promote therapy generalization and maintenance, it is also sometimes useful to anticipate or allow some limited exposure to signals associated with problem behavior (e.g., sensibly incorporate occasional desserts into one's eating habits in the case of someone who received therapy for binge eating, watch a sad movie for someone who has made good progress in overcoming a depressive episode). This could consist of controlled exposure to relapse cues (or controlled lapses). In the case of cigarette smoking, for example, relapse-prevention strategies might seek to weaken or extinguish the connection between smoking a few cigarettes and smoking many of them (Bouton, 2000). Alternatively, therapists might encourage clients to avoid certain contexts that represent high-risk situations for lapse or relapse. This approach, known as *cue elimination*, involves the removal of as many cues as possible that signal the availability of reward for engagement in harmful behavior. In some extreme circumstances, such as might be the case with a client with a long-standing and severe substance abuse problem, cue elimination might involve physically relocating to another city in and effort to eliminate the variety of cues that have become associated with drug use and intoxication (Cunningham, 1998).

Clients frequently attribute progress during therapy to the therapy itself, and often deemphasize their own role in bringing about behavior change. When reviewing areas in which significant gains have been made, it is often useful for therapists to highlight what the client did to help facilitate those changes. Doing so helps the client develop a sense of self-efficacy and mastery and perhaps lessens any anxieties about his or her ability to maintain or build on gains experienced in therapy. In reviewing factual information concerning accomplishments in therapy and the effects of behaving in different ways, the therapist also assists the client in developing new rules related to what he or she can do, and the consequences that behavior can produce.

Toward the end of a successful therapy, clients will often show indications that they overestimate the stability of behavior change and the ease with which change is maintained while underestimating the need for ongoing work and committed action (D. D. Davis, 2008). To counter such tendencies, therapists will often facilitate a shift in perspective as therapy draws to a close in which they teach clients to be their own therapist (J. S. Beck, 2011; Ledley et al., 2010). Such instruction might include perspective-taking exercises in which the client is asked to describe what the therapist might suggest for responding to a specific challenging situation. An outcome from such an exercise might be that the client, particularly during periods of challenge or crisis, learns to relate to himself or herself much in the same way the therapist responded to him or her under similar scenarios in the past. The therapist might also explore with the client his or her plans for posttherapy self-care. What strategies, for example, might the client use for producing and maintaining positive behavioral change or for incorporating effective behaviors into his or her daily life (e.g., daily scheduling of activities that preserves lifestyle balance; ongoing behavioral practice [e.g., mindfulness practice, regular exercise, healthy eating, frequent initiation of social contact])?

As therapy comes to a close, Hayes, Strosahl, and Wilson (2012) recommended that the therapist evaluate the client's commitment to build on therapeutic gains. A therapist might ask the client, for example, to provide a rating (e.g., on a 1–10 scale) of how committed he or she is to aligning future behavior with longer term goals or values. Provided there is a commitment from the client, the therapist might take time to identify what it means to act in accordance with this valued direction by identifying specific actions or behavior patterns that would be consistent with this commitment. Acting in a manner that is consistent with long-term goals or objectives simultaneously decreases the influence of the past and increases the likelihood that the client will continue to act in accordance his or her future-oriented goals and objectives.

As discontinuation approaches, another useful strategy for the therapist is to troubleshoot future problems that might arise, or anticipate and proactively solve problems that might occur following termination. In the previous section, we noted that most clients would have learned some important facts about their patterns of behavior during the active phase of therapy. For clients who have acquired such knowledge, it is often useful for the therapist to present future scenarios that represent a challenge and have a good chance of occurring. The therapist might first ask the client to describe his or her typical way of responding to a situation and have him or her comment on the typical consequences associated with such responding, both pro and con. The therapist might subsequently ask the client to reflect on what he or she has learned in therapy and what could be done differently that is both effective and relatively free of aversive outcomes should this challenging situation arise. If the client is able to describe potentially effective alternatives, the therapist might ask him or her about potential obstacles that would make it difficult to behave in this new way. If potential obstacles are identified, the therapist might ask the client about how he or she might work through or around these, and so on. The following are some examples of this strategy:

- "So, you've made lots of progress in terms of reducing your depression and increasing your activity level and social contacts. When we are finished working together, what are you going to do if, say, you wake up one morning and feel too lethargic and sad to do anything?"
- "You have really made some changes. You no longer avoid high places, and even when you are in a high place, you feel a minimal amount of fear. We may not have conquered all of the situations in which you are afraid of heights, though. What will you do if you find yourself sitting in a restaurant on the sixth floor of a building and you start to feel panicky?"
- "You haven't cut yourself for 4 months, and you have coped really well with some incredibly stressful situations, like being fired. I know, however, that going through a breakup is a big trigger for shame and thoughts about self-harm. What would you do to cope if your girlfriend were to break up with you after we are finished with therapy?"

Tapering the Frequency of Therapy Sessions

In many situations, the therapist and client will not end therapy abruptly but will instead taper the frequency of sessions. Discussions concerning tapering the acute therapy phase would ideally take place several weeks before the implementation of this approach (J. S. Beck, 2011), perhaps even before therapy is actively initiated. Tapering might involve the therapist increasing the spacing between visits (e.g., from weekly to biweekly to monthly sessions), or scheduling "booster sessions" or follow-up sessions, or some combination of these strategies. These contacts might consist of face-to-face meetings, perhaps for reduced periods of time (e.g., 30 minutes). Alternatively, they might be carried out over the telephone.

J. S. Beck (2011) suggested that both the client and the therapist regard the tapering phase as a type of experiment. Questions that could be tested during the tapering phase include the following: "Have I gotten anything useful out of therapy?" "Will I be able to handle difficult situations when they come up?" and "Will I be able to tolerate not being in therapy?" The maintaining of therapeutic gains during the tapering process might help the client answer many of these questions for himself or herself. In the event that the client has sustained losses in treatment gains or a significant relapse, the therapist might suspend the tapering and reinstitute regular therapy. If this were to occur, it would be important for the therapist to clarify what association, if any, the thinning of therapy had with the loss of therapy gains. When there is evidence that tapering set the occasion for the worsening of the client's behavior, the therapist might consider whether the client is ready to end therapy or whether the therapist is inadvertently reinforcing the client's harmful behaviors by offering more frequent therapy contingent on their occurrence.

Correspondingly, therapists might perform posttreatment assessments of behavior patterns targeted in therapy immediately after the conclusion of therapy and at spaced intervals thereafter (e.g., 1, 3, 6, and 12 months posttreatment). The main purpose for these assessments is for the therapist to evaluate the maintenance of therapy gains over time and detect instances when targeted behavior patterns recur or regain strength that, if evident, might suggest the need for additional therapy or booster sessions.

Identifying Signs That Suggest a Return to Therapy

During the preparation for discontinuation, the therapist and client might clarify signs that would indicate the usefulness of a return to therapy, with the same therapist or with someone else. It can, for example, be beneficial for the therapist and the client to come up with a plan to implement if certain problems return. This plan might include the client contacting the therapist to reenter therapy, even for a relatively brief period, until reemergence of the problem area subsides. The plan might also include accessing other mental health resources, speaking with a primary care physician, or other such activities that would connect the client to the type of help that he or she might need.

Signs that indicate the need for help will vary according to the client and the problem areas addressed during his or her therapy. For any former client, however, the emergence of self-harm urges, suicidal ideation, ideation or urges to harm others, or an inability to care for oneself in several basic life areas are signs to return to therapy or seek immediate help. For other clients, signs might be more specific to the problem areas targeted in treatment. An individual who pursued a course of therapy for alcohol-related problems, for example, should consider returning to therapy if sustained patterns of binge drinking reemerge. For a client who received therapy for bulimia, the sustained recurrence of binge-eating episodes would be a sign to return to therapy. Similarly, for a client who received CBT interventions for bipolar disorder in addition to pharmacotherapy, any sudden changes in sleep patterns, mood, and activity levels suggest the possible emergence of a manic episode, which should be addressed as soon as possible. When such signs are evident, the therapist might schedule booster sessions, particularly if the client believes that he or she is not responding effectively to emerging problem areas.

RELAPSE AND RECURRENCE PREVENTION

High rates of relapse and recurrence of problems targeted in therapy are common for many clinical conditions (Marlatt & Donovan, 2005; Rohde, Lewinsohn, Klein, Seeley, & Gau, 2013; Simons, Rohde, Kennard, & Robins, 2005). Because of this, many contemporary approaches to therapy include additional intervention components after the completion of the active phase of therapy that are geared toward reducing the likelihood that problematic behavior patterns will reoccur. These intervention components include the incorporation of (a) relapse prevention intervention strategies into the treatment program, (b) a therapy continuation phase geared toward the prevention of relapse following remission and the promotion of full recovery, and (c) a maintenance phase directed at lessening the likelihood of the recurrence of problem areas and behaviors targeted in therapy, or (d) some combination of these approaches.

In the following sections, terms such as remission, relapse, recovery, and recurrence are informed by earlier conceptualizations of these concepts (Chung & Maisto, 2006; Frank et al., 1991). *Remission* as used here refers to sustained cessation of a target behavior or disorder for a minimal period of time (e.g., 1 full month) extended over a period during which the reemergence of the behavior or disorder is most probable (e.g., within 12 months following the discontinuation of the target behavior or offset of the disorder). The prolonged resolution of the target behavior or disorder episode (e.g., a period of sustained remission lasting 12 months or longer) is regarded as a *recovery*. A *relapse* is regarded as a return of the target behavior or disorder episode rather than a new episode and is often defined as the sustained reemergence of the behavior or disorder after a period of remission (e.g., more than 1 month but less than 12 months after initial behavior or disorder offset). A *recurrence* is regarded as the emergence of a new behavior or episode after a period of sustained recovery (e.g., more than 12 months following sustained discontinuation of a target behavior or disorder offset).

Relapse Prevention

Relapse prevention has been characterized as a tertiary intervention approach for decreasing the probability and severity of relapse following the diminution or successful discontinuation of a problem behavior (Hendershot, Marlatt, & George, 2009). To a large extent, the therapeutic goals associated with relapse prevention are generally realized when the therapist helps the client anticipate and effectively cope with future situations within which he or she might be particularly vulnerable. If vulnerability factors can be decreased or eliminated and if skills learned during therapy can be transferred and applied to future challenging situations as they arise, then the therapeutic benefits realized during the acute phase of therapy are more likely to endure (Simons et al., 2005). Although originally developed as part of an intervention package for substance abuse problems, relapse prevention procedures have been introduced into therapies for a wide variety of psychological and physiological health-related concerns (Barlow, Farchione, et al., 2011; Hendershot et al., 2009).

Distinguishing Lapse From Relapse

Central components of relapse prevention include discussions with the client concerning distinctions between a lapse and relapse and the collaborative development of a plan for preventing or responding to a lapse or relapse (Marlatt & Witkiewitz, 2005). A *lapse* is a recurrence of a previously ceased behavior or behavior pattern targeted for elimination, whereas a *relapse* is a sustained return to near pretreatment levels of a problematic behavior pattern (Marlatt & Witkiewitz, 2005). It is not uncommon for a client who has made substantial changes in the frequency or intensity of a behavior to have a lapse following the discontinuation of the acute phase of therapy. These lapses, in turn, can demoralize the client, a sign that "I'm back where I was before" and "No matter what I do, things just never get better." Feelings of guilt, shame, and hopelessness might also accompany a lapse. As a result, a lapse often sets the occasion for a full-blown relapse.

Research by Marlatt and others (reviewed in Hendershot et al., 2009; Marlatt & Witkiewitz, 2005) suggests that interpretations of lapses, when they occur, often influence whether clients will progress to a full relapse. Individuals, for example, who interpret a lapse (e.g., an episode of excessive drinking for an otherwise abstinent former alcohol abuser) as a result of internal, global, and uncontrollable factors (e.g., a disease, a personality defect) are more likely to progress to a relapse than others who view a lapse as a result of external, unstable, and controllable factors (e.g., an isolated occurrence in response to a set of unique circumstances, a transitional learning experience). Whereas the former type of individual might regard a lapse as an inevitable outcome and feel hopeless (e.g., "I'll never be anything more than an alcoholic"), individuals like the latter type might instead strive to anticipate similar future circumstances that occasioned the lapse and develop alternative coping strategies for responding to such situations should they again occur.

In working with clients around these issues, the therapist conveys the message that lapses can be anticipated and regarded as natural part of the behavior change process. Clients are encouraged to exercise a level of acceptance when a lapse has occurred and view a lapse as an opportunity for new learning and for adjusting coping responses. The therapist might, for example, use a metaphor to illustrate some of these points:

> Therapy and learning new things in life are a lot like taking a road trip. So far, in therapy, you have driven quite a long way. You have stopped using drugs, gotten a job, and are in a relationship with a woman whom you love. You have driven away from "Hell" and are now many miles closer to where you want to be. It is always possible, though, that you might decide to exit the freeway that you are on. You might see a sign that says, "heroin—this way." Let's say that you take the exit and use heroin. This is a lapse, not a relapse. It's a lapse, because you have already made many gains in treatment, and you slipped up and took the wrong exit. You can always get back to the freeway that you were on. You just need to stop using heroin and find a good map. If this happens, see it as a learning opportunity. It's your chance to learn how to get back on track when you fall off track. And we all fall off track from time to time. A relapse is more like deciding to turn around completely and drive all the way back to "Hell" again.

Anticipating High-Risk Situations

Relapse prevention interventions include the identification of *high-risk situations*, or contexts that increase vulnerability or set the occasion for engagement in the problem behavior, including specific situations or persons, emotional states, physiological events such as withdrawal, or the accumulated impact of lifestyle factors (e.g., exposure to high rates of stressful life events, low rates of participation in pleasurable activities; see Hendershot et al.,

2009). Psychosocial and lifestyle factors associated with the recurrence of depressed mood, for example, include family environments characterized by high expressed emotion, frequent family conflicts and discord, unpleasant or stressful life events, and cognitive factors such as attributional style and dysfunctional attitudes (Lewinsohn & Gotlib, 1995; Simons et al., 2005). The client's awareness of high-risk situations, particularly when in the midst of them, can serve as a cue to engage in coping responses that have been previously learned and practiced as a way to reduce the likelihood of a subsequent lapse (Hendershot et al., 2009).

In the chain of behaviors that eventuate into a full-blown relapse, an *abstinence violation effect* (Curry, Marlatt, & Gordon, 1987) often occurs somewhere near the beginning. The abstinence violation effect occurs when a lapse sets the occasion for a full-blown relapse. Abstinence violation involves a breach of a self-imposed rule or standard that specifies how things should be. When applied to problematic or harmful behaviors that have been eliminated, these rules or standards might involve prohibitions against any future recurrence of the targeted behaviors. In such instances, the client who struggles with binge eating, for example, might think, "I've had one piece of chocolate cake, so I've blown it. I might as well eat the whole cake, because it doesn't really matter anymore. I'm back to being a binge eater again!" A person who has struggled with depression and behavioral inertia might think, "Well, I've messed up this behavioral activation stuff, so I might as well just stay in bed for the rest of the week!" Some individuals regard recurrences of clinically relevant behaviors as a sign of a full return to pretreatment levels of functioning. As a result, a wholesale loss in self-regulation (a relapse) sometimes occurs in response to a mild self-regulation loss (a lapse). In relapse prevention, therapists anticipate possible lapses such as these, reframe them as a natural part of the behavior change process, and view them as an opportunity to test out relapse prevention plans.

When lapses occur, the frequently ensuing emotions of self-blame and guilt and the associated sense of loss of control sometimes obscure values that had been instrumental in the earlier behavior change process. As suggested by Hayes et al. (2012), the occurrence of a lapse might be an occasion to reconnect the individual with these important guides (e.g., "Which of your values changed as a result of this lapse?"). An analysis of the client's subsequent response will likely reveal that values are unchanged, although confidence in aligning one's behavior with them might have been shaken (e.g., "I might as well give up"; "I'm a failure, always have been, and always will be"). Such client statements could be an occasion to revisit the notion of thoughts as thoughts (not literal truths; see Chapter 5), to reflect on the past consequences associated with lapse-related behaviors, and to return to values as a way to navigate out of unproductive modes of thinking. When successful, the client comes to regard a lapse as a setback (rather than a wholesale return to baseline), with the problem behavior corrected by reinstating the desired alternative behavior.

Developing New Behavior Patterns

In addition to identifying high-risk situations, the therapist might also evaluate the range of the client's coping skills and resources that can be used in such situations should they occur. Where indicated, the therapist may use additional skills training (e.g., drink-refusal skills, stress-management techniques, inactive-coping strategies [e.g., noticing and observing but not otherwise responding to an urge to drink]), cognitive interventions (e.g., directed at enhancing self-efficacy, reducing positive outcome expectations associated with substance use), and psychoeducation to aid the client in responding differently in high-risk situations, thus reducing the likelihood of future relapse (Marlatt & Witkiewitz, 2005). Positive social supports can also be helpful in supporting gains made through therapy. Other persons can provide support and encouragement, and offer reminders of what to do in the face of uncertainty (e.g., what skills to use). Positive social supports are also sources of reinforcement for prosocial behavior and offer validation or convey respect, which further strengthen a sense of mastery and skill.

Establishing Sustained Patterns of Behavior

Once the client has identified, anticipated, and learned coping responses for high-risk situations, the therapist emphasizes relapse prevention steps that the client can take to achieve *lifestyle balance* (Marlatt & Gordon, 1985). A lifestyle is imbalanced, for example, if the ratio of external demands, or "shoulds," outweighs participation in enjoyable activities, or "wants." Imbalance tends to be associated with stress that, in turn, is often an establishing operation for lapses or relapses. Conversely, balance is typically associated with lower levels of stress and hence critically important for the maintenance of treatment gains and for reducing the likelihood of future relapse (Marlatt & Witkiewitz, 2005). Achieving balance might also involve the client avoiding high-risk situations as well as making concerted efforts to engage in valued or pleasurable activities or improving social networks.

The therapist might also develop *relapse road maps* in collaboration with the client (Marlatt & Witkiewitz, 2005). In this case, the client and therapist consider possible outcomes associated with various ways of responding in high-risk situations and map these out in such a way that they can serve as guides to help clients navigate difficult situations that might arise in the future. Such road maps would show where the client would be headed if he or she were to take certain courses of action. If, for example, the client just suffered a breakup with a partner and noticed the exit to his drug dealer's house up ahead, the relapse road map might involve the therapist showing the client how taking this exit might propel him down the road to using drugs.

Regular routines, particularly those that promote well-being and are consistent with life goals, can serve a regulating function and, consequently, lessen the likelihood of relapse. The maintenance of routines is often a protective factor against the recurrence of mood disturbance or problematic behavior patterns (e.g., Jacobson, Martell, & Dimidjian, 2001). Similarly, if routines result in beneficial outcomes that are pleasing and rewarding, or maintained by positive (rather than negative) reinforcement, they also keep persons in contact with influences that will maintain their behavior over time.

One strategy for developing and sustaining routines is social *rhythm metric self-monitoring* (Monk, Kupfer, Frank, & Ritenour, 1991). This self-monitoring approach is used to keep track of habits that if disrupted, could result in an increased vulnerability to returning to old and harmful behavior patterns. Areas that might be monitored with this method include eating and sleeping habits, exercise, mood patterns, and engagement in social activities. Goals of such monitoring include (a) reducing certain establishing operations that might occasion problematic behavior (e.g., by targeting factors that are associated with sleep deprivation, oversleeping, erratic sleeping habits, skipping meals, unhealthy snacking on junk foods), (b) increasing engagement in social activities, and (c) linking mood and behavior variations to adherence to or deviations from routines. If regular routines are disrupted, for example, a client who self-monitors these areas is in an excellent position to evaluate effects that such disruptions cause. Similarly, daily monitoring of these areas might reveal that engagement in regular routines contributes to stability in mood and behavior patterns. Daily social rhythmic monitoring increases the likelihood that a person will spot progressions that signal change, for the worse or better, thus creating opportunities for reestablishing routines before further deterioration occurs.

Addressing Ambivalence About Permanent Behavior Change

Therapists can also facilitate a *sustained motivation for change* by talking with clients about any remaining ambivalence related to making permanent changes in their behavior (Marlatt & Witkiewitz, 2005). This might involve a discussion of the pros versus cons of continuing with such change or on whether continued engagement in harmful behavior is consistent with or in opposition to the client's values or life objectives. This process also involves taking active steps to reduce the harm associated with problematic behaviors, particularly during a lapse episode.

The Continuation Phase: Promoting Generalization and Maintenance of Skills

Whereas the acute phase of therapy is generally focused on behavior change or symptomatic improvement, the *continuation phase* includes interventions that are primarily geared toward reducing the likelihood of relapse and recurrence and the promotion generalization and maintenance of skills across settings and over time. The addition of a continuation phase (e.g., scheduled monthly meetings over a 9-month interval) after the discontinuation of the acute phase has been shown, for example, to decrease episode recurrence of major depressive disorder (Beshai, Dobson, Bockting, & Quigley, 2011; Kennard et al., 2008; Vittengl, Clark, Dunn, & Jarrett, 2007).

An example of the goals and structure of a continuation phase of therapy is nicely illustrated in the Treatment for Adolescents With Depression Study (TADS; Rohde, Feeny, & Robins, 2005; Simons et al., 2005). Stage I of this three-stage treatment approach consists of 12 weeks of acute CBT. Stages II and III are primarily focused on continuation and maintenance, respectively. The 6-week continuation phase was tailored according to the client's needs and progress, with the primary goals being the consolidation, generalization, and integration of skills into the client's daily life. Within this phase, therapy work included distinguishing between lapses and relapses, anticipating challenging situations that could arise, and identifying and using skills or coping strategies for such situations. An additional goal of this stage was to transfer skills from the therapist to the client or to assist the client in becoming his or her own therapist. The number of sessions a client received during this 6-week period, either two or four, was influenced by how well the client responded to the acute phase, with those who demonstrated only a partial response receiving more therapy sessions (nonresponders to the acute phase in this study were referred for an alternative therapy; Simons et al., 2005).

The Maintenance Phase: Reducing the Likelihood of Behavior Recurrence

The *maintenance phase* is primarily directed at reducing the recurrence of problem areas or behaviors targeted in therapy. The inclusion of a maintenance component to therapy is especially indicated for problem areas that have a high rate of recurrence following successful therapy (e.g., substance abuse, depression, obesity) and would typically involve the systematic monitoring of the client's progress via infrequent follow-up visits. In TADS (Rohde et al., 2005; Simons et al., 2005), for example, the maintenance phase (Stage III) consisted of three sessions stretched out in regular intervals over 18 weeks, with the overall focus on relapse prevention. Within this stage, therapists generally do not teach clients new skills. Rather, emphasis is placed on the use and generalization of skills clients already learned.

The maintenance phase concept has some similarity to the idea of booster sessions or, as described in the medical literature, *continuous care* (Thorpe, McMillan, Owings, & Dawson, 2008). In traditional CBT, therapists use booster sessions to facilitate the use of coping skills as difficulties emerge, thus providing opportunities for clients to further solidify or consolidate previous learning. Booster sessions are frequently problem focused. The goal of these sessions is to challenge the client to reflect on what he or she has learned in therapy and evaluate whether skills or insights gained from therapy can be applied to current circumstances.

SUMMARY

Before ending the acute phase of therapy, it is often useful for therapists to do the following:

- Consider the amount of progress made in therapy and whether discontinuation is indicated, while taking into account any agreements reached with the client concerning the duration and course of therapy.
- Explore the client's perceptions as to whether he or she is approaching a suitable stopping point or a point at which therapy might be tapered before being brought to full closure.
- Anticipate any problems that may arise around therapy tapering or discontinuation and discuss these periodically with the client, particularly before reducing or ending therapy.
- Thoroughly examine any client requests for premature therapy termination not only the reasons the client offers but also the functional context surrounding the request.
- Review with the client his or her progress toward the realization of therapy-related goals and highlight the client's role in bringing about behavior change.
- Encourage the client to discuss what he or she has learned during therapy, including specific skills associated with effective responding.
- Anticipate lapses as part of the normal behavior-change process and collaboratively develop plans with the client for responding to high-risk situations should they arise.

- Work with the client to develop regular routines, lifestyle balance, and environments that will reinforce and maintain therapeutic gains.
- Consider the use of booster sessions periodically in the months after completion of the acute or continuation phases of therapy as a means of reducing the recurrence of problematic behavior patterns.
- Develop with the client a list of signs that, if present, suggest a need to contact the therapist and explore whether a return to therapy is indicated.

REFERENCES

Abramowitz, J. S. (2013). The practice of exposure therapy: Relevance of cognitive-behavioral theory and extinction theory. *Behavior Therapy, 44,* 548–558. http://dx.doi.org/10.1016/j.beth.2013.03.003

Abramowitz, J. S., Deacon, B. J., & Whiteside, S. H. (2011). *Exposure therapy for anxiety: Principles and practice.* New York, NY: Guilford Press.

Achenbach, T. M., & Rescorla, L. A. (2001). *Manual for the ASEBA School-Age Forms & Profiles.* Burlington: University of Vermont, Research Center for Children, Youth, and Families.

Adams, A. N., Adams, M. A., & Miltenberger, R. G. (2003). Habit reversal. In W. T. O'Donohue, J. E. Fisher, & S. C. Hayes (Eds.), *Cognitive behavior therapy: Applying empirically supported techniques in your practice* (pp. 189–195). New York, NY: Wiley.

Addis, M. E., & Carpenter, K. M. (2000). The treatment rationale in cognitive behavioral therapy: Psychological mechanisms and clinical guidelines. *Cognitive and Behavioral Practice, 7,* 147–156. http://dx.doi.org/10.1016/S1077-7229(00)80025-5

Addis, M. E., & Martell, C. R. (2004). *Overcoming depression one step at a time: The new behavioral activation approach to getting your life back.* Oakland, CA: New Harbinger.

Ader, R., & Cohen, N. (1985). CNS–immune system interactions: Conditioning phenomena. *Behavioral and Brain Sciences, 8,* 379–426. http://dx.doi.org/10.1017/S0140525X00000765

Agrawal, A., Nelson, E. C., Littlefield, A. K., Bucholz, K. K., Degenhardt, L., Henders, A. K., . . . Lynskey, M. T. (2012). Cannabinoid receptor genotype moderation of the effects of childhood physical abuse on anhedonia and depression. *Archives of General Psychiatry, 69,* 732–740. http://dx.doi.org/10.1001/archgenpsychiatry.2011.2273

Aguilera, A., & Muñoz, R. F. (2011). Text messaging as an adjunct to CBT in low-income populations: A usability and feasibility pilot study. *Professional Psychology: Research and Practice, 42,* 472–478. http://dx.doi.org/10.1037/a0025499

Alberti, R., & Emmons, M. (1990). *Your perfect right: A guide to assertive living* (6th ed., rev.). San Luis Obispo, CA: Impact.

Alessi, G. (1992). Models of proximate and ultimate causation in psychology. *American Psychologist, 47,* 1359–1370. http://dx.doi.org/10.1037/0003-066X.47.11.1359

American Psychiatric Association. (1980). *Diagnostic and statistical manual of mental disorders* (3rd ed.). Washington, DC: Author.

American Psychiatric Association. (2013). *Diagnostic and statistical manual of mental disorders* (5th ed.). Washington, DC: Author.

American Psychological Association. (2010). *Ethical principles of psychologists and code of conduct (2002, Amended June 1, 2010)*. Retrieved from http://www.apa.org/ethics/code/index.aspx

Anderson, C. M., Hawkins, R. P., Freeman, K. A., & Scotti, J. R. (2000). Private events: Do they belong in a science of human behavior? *The Behavior Analyst, 23,* 1–10.

Andreescu, C., Lenze, E. J., Dew, M. A., Begley, A. E., Mulsant, B. H., Dombrovski, A. Y., . . . Reynolds, C. F. (2007). Effect of comorbid anxiety on treatment response and relapse risk in late-life depression: Controlled study. *The British Journal of Psychiatry, 190,* 344–349. http://dx.doi.org/10.1192/bjp.bp.106.027169

Arkowitz, H., Westra, H. A., Miller, W. R., & Rollnick, S. (Eds.). (2008). *Motivational interviewing in the treatment of psychological problems*. New York, NY: Guilford Press.

Ayllon, T. (1963). Intensive treatment of psychotic behavior by stimulus satiation and food reinforcement. *Behaviour Research and Therapy, 1,* 53–61. http://dx.doi.org/10.1016/0005-7967(63)90008-1

Ayllon, T., & Michael, J. (1959). The psychiatric nurse as a behavioral engineer. *Journal of the Experimental Analysis of Behavior, 2,* 323–334. http://dx.doi.org/10.1901/jeab.1959.2-323

Bandura, A. (1977). *Social learning theory*. Englewood Cliffs, NJ: Prentice Hall.

Bandura, A. (1986). *Social foundations of thought and action: A social cognitive theory*. Englewood Cliffs, NJ: Prentice Hall.

Bandura, A. (1997). *Self-efficacy: The exercise of control*. New York, NY: W. H. Freeman.

Barkley, R. A. (1997). Behavioral inhibition, sustained attention, and executive functions: Constructing a unifying theory of ADHD. *Psychological Bulletin, 121,* 65–94. http://dx.doi.org/10.1037/0033-2909.121.1.65

Barlow, D. H. (1988). *Anxiety and its disorders: The nature and treatment of anxiety and panic*. New York, NY: Guilford Press.

Barlow, D. H. (Ed.). (2014). *Clinical handbook of psychological disorders: A step-by-step treatment manual* (5th ed.). http://dx.doi.org/10.1093/oxfordhb/9780199328710.001.0001

Barlow, D. H., Allen, L. B., & Choate, M. L. (2004). Toward a unified treatment for emotional disorders. *Behavior Therapy, 35,* 205–230. http://dx.doi.org/10.1016/S0005-7894(04)80036-4

Barlow, D. H., & Craske, M. G. (1994). *Mastery of your anxiety and panic* (2nd ed.). San Antonio, TX: Harcourt Brace.

Barlow, D. H., Farchione, T. J., Fairholme, C. P., Ellard, K. K., Boisseau, C. L., Allen, L. B., & Ehrenreich-May, J. (2011). *Unified protocol for transdiagnostic treatment of emotional disorders: Therapist guide*. New York, NY: Oxford University Press.

Barnes-Holmes, D., O'Hora, D., Roche, B., Hayes, S. C., Bissett, R. T., & Lyddy, F. (2001). Understanding and verbal regulation. In S. C. Hayes, D. Barnes-Holmes, & B. Roche (Eds.), *Relational frame theory: A post-Skinnerian account of human language and cognition* (pp. 103–117). New York, NY: Kluwer Academic/Plenum.

Barnett, J. E., & Sanzone, M. (1997). Termination: Ethical and legal issues. *Clinical Psychologist, 50,* 9–13.

Baucom, D. H., Hahlweg, K., Atkins, D. C., Engl, J., & Thurmaier, F. (2006). Long-term prediction of marital quality following a relationship education program: Being positive in a constructive way. *Journal of Family Psychology, 20,* 448–455. http://dx.doi.org/10.1037/0893-3200.20.3.448

Baum, W. H. (2005). *Understanding behaviorism: Behavior, culture, and evolution* (2nd ed.). Malden, MA: Blackwell.

Bechdolf, A., Knost, B., Kuntermann, C., Schiller, S., Klosterkötter, J., Hambrecht, M., & Pukrop, R. (2004). A randomized comparison of group cognitive-behavioural therapy and group psychoeducation in patients with schizophrenia. *Acta Psychiatrica Scandinavica, 110,* 21–28. http://dx.doi.org/10.1111/j.1600-0447.2004.00300.x

Beck, A. T. (1963). Thinking and depression: Idiosyncratic content and cognitive distortions. *Archives of General Psychiatry, 9,* 324–333. http://dx.doi.org/10.1001/archpsyc.1963.01720160014002

Beck, A. T. (1976). *Cognitive therapy and the emotional disorders.* New York, NY: International Universities Press.

Beck, A. T., & Dozois, D. J. (2011). Cognitive therapy: Current status and future directions. *Annual Review of Medicine, 62,* 397–409. http://dx.doi.org/10.1146/annurev-med-052209-100032

Beck, A. T., Freeman, A., & Associates. (1990). *Cognitive therapy for personality disorders.* New York, NY: Guilford Press.

Beck, A. T., Rush, A. J., Shaw, B. F., & Emery, G. (1979). *Cognitive therapy of depression.* New York, NY: Guilford Press.

Beck, A. T., Steer, R. A., & Brown, G. K. (1996). *Beck Depression Inventory–II manual.* San Antonio, TX: The Psychological Corporation.

Beck, J. S. (2005). *Cognitive therapy for challenging problems: What to do when the basics don't work.* New York, NY: Guilford Press.

Beck, J. S. (2011). *Cognitive behavior therapy: Basics and beyond* (2nd ed.). New York, NY: Guilford Press.

Becker, R. E., Heimberg, R. G., & Bellack, A. S. (1987). *Social skills training treatment for depression.* Elmsford, NY: Pergamon Press.

Bell, A. C., & D'Zurilla, T. J. (2009). Problem-solving therapy for depression: A meta-analysis. *Clinical Psychology Review, 29,* 348–353. http://dx.doi.org/10.1016/j.cpr.2009.02.003

Bellack, A. S. (2004). Skills training for people with severe mental illness. *Psychiatric Rehabilitation Journal, 27,* 375–391. http://dx.doi.org/10.2975/27.2004.375.391

Bellack, A. S., Hersen, M., & Turner, S. M. (1979). Relationship of role playing and knowledge of appropriate behavior to assertion in the natural environment. *Journal of Consulting and Clinical Psychology, 47,* 670–678. http://dx.doi.org/10.1037/0022-006X.47.4.670

Benca, R., Duncan, M. J., Frank, E., McClung, C., Nelson, R. J., & Vicentic, A. (2009). Biological rhythms, higher brain function, and behavior: Gaps, opportunities, and challenges. *Brain Research Reviews, 62,* 57–70. http://dx.doi.org/10.1016/j.brainresrev.2009.09.005

Bennett-Levy, J., Westbrook, D., Fennell, M., Cooper, M., Rouf, K., & Hackmann, A. (2004). Behavioural experiments: Historical and cultural underpinnings. In J. Bennett-Levy, G. Butler, M. Fennell, A. Hackmann, M. Mueller, & D. Westbrook (Eds.), *Oxford guide to behavioural experiments in cognitive therapy* (pp. 1–20). http://dx.doi.org/10.1093/med/9780198529163.001.0001

Benson, L. A., McGinn, M. M., & Christensen, A. (2012). Common principles of couple therapy. *Behavior Therapy, 43,* 25–35. http://dx.doi.org/10.1016/j.beth.2010.12.009

Benton, M. K., & Schroeder, H. E. (1990). Social skills training with schizophrenics: A meta-analytic evaluation. *Journal of Consulting and Clinical Psychology, 58,* 741–747. http://dx.doi.org/10.1037/0022-006X.58.6.741

Berkman, L. F., Glass, T., Brissette, I., & Seeman, T. E. (2000). From social integration to health: Durkheim in the new millennium. *Social Science & Medicine, 51,* 843–857. http://dx.doi.org/10.1016/S0277-9536(00)00065-4

Berton, O., Hahn, C.-G., & Thase, M. E. (2012). Are we getting closer to valid translational models for major depression? *Science, 338,* 75–79. http://dx.doi.org/10.1126/science.1222940

Beshai, S., Dobson, K. S., Bockting, C. L. H., & Quigley, L. (2011). Relapse and recurrence prevention in depression: Current research and future prospects. *Clinical Psychology Review, 31,* 1349–1360. http://dx.doi.org/10.1016/j.cpr.2011.09.003

Biglan, A. (2003). Selection by consequences: One unifying principle for a transdisciplinary science of prevention. *Prevention Science, 4,* 213–232. http://dx.doi.org/10.1023/A:1026064014562

Biglan, A., Flay, B. R., Embry, D. D., & Sandler, I. N. (2012). The critical role of nurturing environments for promoting human well-being. *American Psychologist, 67,* 257–271. http://dx.doi.org/10.1037/a0026796

Biglan, A., & Hayes, S. C. (1996). Should the behavioral sciences become more pragmatic? The case for functional contextualism in research on human behavior. *Applied & Preventive Psychology, 5,* 47–57. http://dx.doi.org/10.1016/S0962-1849(96)80026-6

Bijou, S. W., & Baer, D. M. (1966). Operant methods in child behavior and development. In W. K. Honig (Ed.), *Operant behavior: Areas of research and application* (pp. 718–789). New York, NY: Appleton-Century-Crofts.

Borkovec, T. D. (1994). The nature, functions, and origins of worry. In G. Davey & F. Tallis (Eds.), *Worrying: Perspectives on theory, assessment, and treatment* (pp. 5–33). New York, NY: Wiley.

Borkovec, T. D., Alcaine, O. M., & Behar, E. (2004). Avoidance theory of worry and generalized anxiety disorder. In R. G. Heimberg, C. L. Turk, D. S. Mennin, R. G. Heimberg, C. L. Turk, & D. S. Mennin (Eds.), *Generalized anxiety disorder: Advances in research and practice* (pp. 77–108). New York, NY: Guilford Press.

Borkovec, T. D., & Hu, S. (1990). The effect of worry on cardiovascular response to phobic imagery. *Behaviour Research and Therapy, 28*, 69–73. http://dx.doi.org/10.1016/0005-7967(90)90056-O

Borkovec, T. D., Weerts, T. C., & Bernstein, D. A. (1977). Behavioral assessment of anxiety. In A. Ciminero, K. Calhoun, & H. E. Adams (Eds.), *Handbook of behavioral assessment* (pp. 367–428). New York, NY: Wiley.

Bornstein, R. F. (1993). *The dependent personality.* New York, NY: Guilford Press.

Bouton, M. E. (2000). A learning theory perspective on lapse, relapse, and the maintenance of behavior change. *Health Psychology, 19*(Suppl.), 57–63. http://dx.doi.org/10.1037/0278-6133.19.Suppl1.57

Bouton, M. E. (2004). Context and behavioral processes in extinction. *Learning & Memory, 11*, 485–494. http://dx.doi.org/10.1101/lm.78804

Bowers, A. H. (2003). Satiation therapy. In W. T. O'Donohue, J. E. Fisher, & S. C. Hayes (Eds.), *Cognitive behavior therapy: Applying empirically supported techniques in your practice* (pp. 349–353). Hoboken, NJ: Wiley.

Bradley, R., Greene, J., Russ, E., Dutra, L., & Westen, D. (2005). A multidimensional meta-analysis of psychotherapy for PTSD. *The American Journal of Psychiatry, 162*, 214–227. http://dx.doi.org/10.1176/appi.ajp.162.2.214

Brondolo, E., DiGiuseppe, R., & Tafrate, R. C. (1997). Exposure-based treatment for anger problems: Focus on the feeling. *Cognitive and Behavioral Practice, 4*, 75–98. http://dx.doi.org/10.1016/S1077-7229(97)80013-2

Brown, M. Z., Comtois, K. A., & Linehan, M. M. (2002). Reasons for suicide attempts and nonsuicidal self-injury in women with borderline personality disorder. *Journal of Abnormal Psychology, 111*, 198–202. http://dx.doi.org/10.1037/0021-843X.111.1.198

Brown, T. A., O'Leary, T. A., & Barlow, D. H. (2001). Generalized anxiety disorder. In D. H. Barlow (Ed.), *Clinical handbook of psychological disorders: A step-by-step treatment manual* (3rd ed., pp. 154–208). New York, NY: Guilford Press.

Brummett, B. H., Babyak, M. A., Siegler, I. C., Vitaliano, P. P., Ballard, E. L., Gwyther, L. P., & Williams, R. B. (2006). Associations among perceptions of social support, negative affect, and quality of sleep in caregivers and noncaregivers. *Health Psychology, 25*, 220–225. http://dx.doi.org/10.1037/0278-6133.25.2.220

Bryant, M. J., Simons, A. D., & Thase, M. E. (1999). Therapist skill and patient variables in homework compliance: Controlling an uncontrolled variable in cognitive therapy outcome research. *Cognitive Therapy and Research, 23*, 381–399. http://dx.doi.org/10.1023/A:1018703901116

Burns, D. D. (1980). *Feeling good: The new mood therapy.* New York, NY: Signet.

Buss, D. M. (1990). *Evolutionary psychology: The new science of the mind.* Boston, MA: Allyn and Bacon.

Butler, E. A., Egloff, B., Wilhelm, F. H., Smith, N. C., Erickson, E. A., & Gross, J. J. (2003). The social consequences of expressive suppression. *Emotion, 3,* 48–67. http://dx.doi.org/10.1037/1528-3542.3.1.48

Butzlaff, R. L., & Hooley, J. M. (1998). Expressed emotion and psychiatric relapse: A meta-analysis. *Archives of General Psychiatry, 55,* 547–552. http://dx.doi.org/10.1001/archpsyc.55.6.547

Campbell, C., Hansen, D. J., & Nangle, D. W. (2010). Social skills and psychological adjustment. In D. W. Nangle, D. J. Hansen, C. A. Erdley, & P. J. Norton (Eds.), *Practitioner's guide to empirically based measures of social skills* (pp. 51–67). http://dx.doi.org/10.1007/978-1-4419-0609-0_4

Carr, A. (2002). Child and adolescence problems. In F. W. Bond & W. Dryden (Eds.), *Handbook for brief cognitive-behaviour therapy* (pp. 207–238). West Sussex, England: Wiley.

Catania, A. C. (2013). *Learning* (5th ed.). Cornwall-on-Hudson, NY: Sloan.

Chapman, A. L., & Rosenthal, M. Z. (in press). *Overcoming therapeutic challenges: Using dialectical behavior therapy principles and strategies.* Washington, DC: American Psychological Association.

Charney, D. S., Sklar, P., Buxbaum, J. D., Nestler, E. J. (Eds.). (2013). *Neurobiology of mental illness* (4th ed.). http://dx.doi.org/10.1093/med/9780199934959.001.0001

Chiles, J. A., & Strosahl, K. D. (1995). *The suicidal patient: Principles of assessment, treatment, and case management.* Arlington, VA: American Psychiatric Association.

Chiles, J. A., & Strosahl, K. D. (2004). *Clinical manual for assessment and treatment of suicidal patients.* Washington, DC: American Psychiatric Association.

Chorpita, B. F., Weisz, J. R., Daleiden, E. L., Schoenwald, S. K., Palinkas, L. A., Miranda, J., . . . Gibbons, R. D., & the Research Network on Youth Mental Health. (2013). Long-term outcomes for the Child STEPs randomized effectiveness trial: A comparison of modular and standard treatment designs with usual care. *Journal of Consulting and Clinical Psychology, 81,* 999–1009. http://dx.doi.org/10.1037/a0034200

Choy, Y., Fyer, A. J., & Lipsitz, J. D. (2007). Treatment of specific phobia in adults. *Clinical Psychology Review, 27,* 266–286. http://dx.doi.org/10.1016/j.cpr.2006.10.002

Chueire, V. B., Romaldini, J. H., & Ward, L. S. (2007). Subclinical hypothyroidism increases the risk for depression in the elderly. *Archives of Gerontology and Geriatrics, 44,* 21–28. http://dx.doi.org/10.1016/j.archger.2006.02.001

Chung, T., & Maisto, S. A. (2006). Relapse to alcohol and other drug use in treated adolescents: Review and reconsideration of relapse as a change point in clinical course. *Clinical Psychology Review, 26,* 149–161. http://dx.doi.org/10.1016/j.cpr.2005.11.004

Ciminero, A. R., Calhoun, K. S., & Adams, H. E. (Eds.). (1977). *Handbook of behavioral assessment*. New York, NY: Wiley.

Clark, D. A., & Beck, A. T. (2010). Cognitive theory and therapy of anxiety and depression: Convergence with neurobiological findings. *Trends in Cognitive Sciences, 14,* 418–424. http://dx.doi.org/10.1016/j.tics.2010.06.007

Clark, D. M. (2001). A cognitive perspective on social phobia. In W. R. Crozier & L. E. Alden (Eds.), *International handbook of social anxiety: Concepts, research and interventions relating to the self and shyness* (pp. 405–430). New York, NY: Wiley.

Coelho, C. M., Waters, A. M., Hine, T. J., & Wallis, G. (2009). The use of virtual reality in acrophobia research and treatment. *Journal of Anxiety Disorders, 23,* 563–574. http://dx.doi.org/10.1016/j.janxdis.2009.01.014

Cohen, S., Mermelstein, R., Kamarck, T., & Hoberman, H. (1985). Measuring the functional components of social support. In I. G. Sarason & B. R. Sarason (Eds.), *Social support: Theory, research and application* (pp. 73–94). http://dx.doi.org/10.1007/978-94-009-5115-0_5

Conklin, C. A., & Tiffany, S. T. (2002). Applying extinction research and theory to cue-exposure addiction treatments. *Addiction, 97,* 155–167. http://dx.doi.org/10.1046/j.1360-0443.2002.00014.x

Conners, C. K. (2008). *The Conners 3rd Edition (Conners 3)*. North Tonawanda, NJ: Multi-Health System.

Cooke, G. (1968). Evaluation of the efficacy of the components of reciprocal inhibition psychotherapy. *Journal of Abnormal Psychology, 73,* 464–467. http://dx.doi.org/10.1037/h0026202

Corr, P. J. (Ed.). (2008). *The reinforcement sensitivity theory of personality*. http://dx.doi.org/10.1017/CBO9780511819384

Corrigan, P. W. (1991). Social skills training in adult psychiatric populations: A meta-analysis. *Journal of Behavior Therapy and Experimental Psychiatry, 22,* 203–210. http://dx.doi.org/10.1016/0005-7916(91)90017-Y

Cosmides, L., & Tooby, J. (2000). Evolutionary psychology and the emotions. In M. Lewis & J. M. Haviland-Jones (Eds.), *Handbook of emotions* (2nd ed., pp. 91–115). New York, NY: Guilford Press.

Coyne, J. C. (1976). Toward an interactional description of depression. *Psychiatry: Journal for the Study of Interpersonal Processes, 39,* 28–40.

Craske, M. G., & Barlow, D. H. (2014). Panic disorder and agoraphobia. In D. H. Barlow (Ed.), *Clinical handbook of psychological disorders* (5th ed., pp. 1–61). New York, NY: Guilford Press.

Craske, M. G., Kircanski, K., Zelikowsky, M., Mystkowski, J., Chowdhury, N., & Baker, A. (2008). Optimizing inhibitory learning during exposure therapy. *Behaviour Research and Therapy, 46,* 5–27. http://dx.doi.org/10.1016/j.brat.2007.10.003

Cross-Disorder Group of the Psychiatric Genomics Consortium. (2013). Identification of risk loci with shared effects on five major psychiatric disorders: A genome-wide analysis. *The Lancet, 381,* 1371–1379. http://dx.doi.org/10.1016/S0140-6736(12)62129-1

Cui, Y., Yang, W., & Weng, Y. (2004). Effectiveness of social skills training in patients with chronic schizophrenia. *Chinese Mental Health Journal, 18,* 799–805.

Cuijpers, P., Muñoz, R. F., Clarke, G. N., & Lewinsohn, P. M. (2009). Psychoeducational treatment and prevention of depression: The "Coping With Depression" course thirty years later. *Clinical Psychology Review, 29,* 449–458. http://dx.doi.org/10.1016/j.cpr.2009.04.005

Cuijpers, P., van Straten, A., Andersson, G., & van Oppen, P. (2008). Psychotherapy for depression in adults: A meta-analysis of comparative outcome studies. *Journal of Consulting and Clinical Psychology, 76,* 909–922. http://dx.doi.org/10.1037/a0013075

Cuijpers, P., van Straten, A., & Warmerdam, L. (2007). Behavioral activation treatments of depression: A meta-analysis. *Clinical Psychology Review, 27,* 318–326. http://dx.doi.org/10.1016/j.cpr.2006.11.001

Cunningham, C. L. (1998). Drug conditioning and drug-seeking behavior. In W. O'Donohue (Ed.), *Learning and behavior therapy* (pp. 518–544). Boston, MA: Allyn and Bacon.

Curry, S., Marlatt, G. A., & Gordon, J. R. (1987). Abstinence violation effect: Validation of an attributional construct with smoking cessation. *Journal of Consulting and Clinical Psychology, 55,* 145–149. http://dx.doi.org/10.1037/0022-006X.55.2.145

Daughters, S. B., Braun, A. R., Sargeant, M. N., Reynolds, E. K., Hopko, D. R., Blanco, C., & Lejuez, C. W. (2008). Effectiveness of a brief behavioral treatment for inner-city illicit drug users with elevated depressive symptoms: The life enhancement treatment for substance use (LETS Act!). *Journal of Clinical Psychiatry, 69,* 122–129. http://dx.doi.org/10.4088/JCP.v69n0116

Daughters, S. B., Magidson, J. F., Schuster, R. M., & Safren, S. A. (2010). ACT HEALTHY: A combined cognitive-behavioral depression and medication adherence treatment for HIV-infected substance users. *Cognitive and Behavioral Practice, 17,* 309–321. http://dx.doi.org/10.1016/j.cbpra.2009.12.003

David, D., & Szentagotai, A. (2006). Cognitions in cognitive-behavioral psychotherapies; toward an integrative model. *Clinical Psychology Review, 26,* 284–298. http://dx.doi.org/10.1016/j.cpr.2005.09.003

Davis, D. D. (2008). *Terminating therapy: A professional guide to ending on a positive note.* Hoboken, NJ: Wiley.

Davis, M., Eshelman, E. R., & McKay, M. (2000). *The relaxation & stress reduction workbook* (5th ed.). Oakland, CA: New Harbinger.

Davison, G. C. (1968). Systematic desensitization as a counter-conditioning process. *Journal of Abnormal Psychology, 73,* 91–99. http://dx.doi.org/10.1037/h0025501

Day, A., Howells, K., Mohr, P., Schall, E., & Gerace, A. (2008). The development of CBT programmes for anger: The role of interventions to promote perspective-taking skills. *Behavioural and Cognitive Psychotherapy, 36,* 299–312. http://dx.doi. org/10.1017/S135246580800430X

de Quirós Aragón, M. B., Labrador, F. J., & de Arce, F. (2005). Evaluation of a group cue-exposure treatment for opiate addicts. *The Spanish Journal of Psychology, 8,* 229–237. http://dx.doi.org/10.1017/S1138741600005114

Del Vecchio, T., & O'Leary, K. D. (2004). Effectiveness of anger treatments for specific anger problems: A meta-analytic review. *Clinical Psychology Review, 24,* 15–34. http://dx.doi.org/10.1016/j.cpr.2003.09.006

Derogatis, L. R. (1992). *Brief Symptom Inventory (BSI).* Minneapolis, MN: National Computer Systems.

Dichter, G. S. (2010). Anhedonia in unipolar major depressive disorder: A review. *The Open Psychiatry Journal, 4,* 1–9. http://dx.doi.org/10.2174/187435440100 4010001

Dickson, K. S., Ciesla, J. A., & Reilly, L. C. (2012). Rumination, worry, cognitive avoidance, and behavioral avoidance: Examination of temporal effects. *Behavior Therapy, 43,* 629–640. http://dx.doi.org/10.1016/j.beth.2011.11.002

DiGuiseppe, R., & Tafrate, R. C. (2003). Anger treatments for adults: A meta-analytic review. *Clinical Psychology: Science and Practice, 10,* 70–84. http://dx.doi.org/10.1093/ clipsy.10.1.70

Dimeff, L., Rizvi, S. L., Brown, M., & Linehan, M. M. (2000). Dialectical behavior therapy for substance abuse: A pilot application to methamphetamine-dependent women with borderline personality disorder. *Cognitive and Behavioral Practice, 7,* 457–468. http://dx.doi.org/10.1016/S1077-7229(00)80057-7

Dimidjian, S., Barrera, M., Jr., Martell, C., Muñoz, R. F., & Lewinsohn, P. M. (2011). The origins and current status of behavioral activation treatments for depression. *Annual Review of Clinical Psychology, 7,* 1–38. http://dx.doi.org/10.1146/ annurev-clinpsy-032210-104535

Dimidjian, S., Hollon, S. D., Dobson, K. S., Schmaling, K. B., Kohlenberg, R. J., Addis, M. E., . . . Jacobson, N. S. (2006). Randomized trial of behavioral activation, cognitive therapy, and antidepressant medication in the acute treatment of adults with major depression. *Journal of Consulting and Clinical Psychology, 74,* 658–670. http://dx.doi.org/10.1037/0022-006X.74.4.658

Dixon-Gordon, K. L., Chapman, A. L., & Turner, B. J. (in press). Specificity of the effects of DBT emotion regulation skills training among women with borderline personality disorder. *Journal of Experimental Psychopathology.*

Dobson, K. S. (Ed.). (2010). *Handbook of cognitive-behavioral therapies* (3rd ed.). New York, NY: Guilford Press.

Dobson, K. S., & Dozois, D. J. A. (2001). Historical and philosophical bases of the cognitive behavioral therapies. In K. S. Dobson (Ed.), *Handbook of cognitive-behavioral therapies* (2nd ed., pp. 3–39). New York, NY: Guilford Press.

Dobson, K. S., Hollon, S. D., Dimidjian, S., Schmaling, K. B., Kohlenberg, R. J., Gallop, R. J., . . . Jacobson, N. S. (2008). Randomized trial of behavioral activation, cognitive therapy, and antidepressant medication in the prevention of relapse and recurrence in major depression. *Journal of Consulting and Clinical Psychology, 76,* 468–477. http://dx.doi.org/10.1037/0022-006X.76.3.468

Dobson, K. S., & Khatri, N. (2000). Cognitive therapy: Looking backward, looking forward. *Journal of Clinical Psychology, 56,* 907–923. http://dx.doi.org/10.1002/1097-4679(200007)56:7{907::AID-JCLP9}3.0.CO;2-I

Dodge, K. A. (1991). The structure and function of reactive and proactive aggression. In D. J. Pepler & K. H. Rubin (Eds.), *Development and treatment of childhood aggression* (pp. 201–218). Hillsdale, NJ: Erlbaum.

Dow, M. G. (1985). Peer validation and idiographic analysis of social skill deficits. *Behavior Therapy, 16,* 76–86. http://dx.doi.org/10.1016/S0005-7894(85)80057-5

Dow, M. G. (1994). Social inadequacy and social skill. In L. W. Craighead, W. E. Craighead, A. E. Kazdin, & M. J. Mahoney (Eds.), *Cognitive and behavioral interventions: An empirical approach to mental health problems* (pp. 123–140). Boston, MA: Allyn and Bacon.

Duckworth, M. P. (2003). Assertiveness skills and the management of related factors. In W. O'Donohue, J. E. Fisher, & S. C. Hayes (Eds.), *Cognitive behavior therapy: Applying empirically supported techniques in your practice* (pp. 16–22). Hoboken, NJ: Wiley.

Dugas, M. J., & Koerner, N. (2005). Cognitive-behavioural treatment for generalized anxiety disorder: Current status and future directions. *Journal of Cognitive Psychotherapy, 19,* 61–81. http://dx.doi.org/10.1891/jcop.19.1.61.66326

Dugas, M. J., & Robichaud, M. (2007). *Cognitive-behavioral treatment for generalized anxiety disorder: From science to practice.* New York, NY: Routledge.

Eddy, K. T., Dutra, L., Bradley, R., & Westen, D. (2004). A multidimensional meta-analysis of psychotherapy and pharmacotherapy for obsessive-compulsive disorder. *Clinical Psychology Review, 24,* 1011–1030. http://dx.doi.org/10.1016/j.cpr.2004.08.004

Eells, T. D. (1997). Psychotherapy case formulation: History and current status. In T. D. Eells (Ed.), *Handbook of psychotherapy case formulation* (pp. 1–25). New York, NY: Guilford Press.

Eells, T. D. (2007). History and current status of psychotherapy case formulation. In T. D. Eells (Ed.), *Handbook of psychotherapy case formulation* (2nd ed., pp. 3–32). New York, NY: Guilford Press.

Ehrenreich, J. T., Goldstein, C. M., Wright, L. R., & Barlow, D. H. (2009). Development of a unified protocol for the treatment of emotional disorders in youth. *Child & Family Behavior Therapy, 31,* 20–37. http://dx.doi.org/10.1080/07317100802701228

Eifert, G. H., Schulte, D., Zvolensky, M. J., Lejuez, C. W., & Lau, A. W. (1997). Manualized behavior therapy: Merits and challenges. *Behavior Therapy, 28,* 499–509. http://dx.doi.org/10.1016/S0005-7894(97)80005-6

Ekman, P., & Davidson, R. J. (1994). *The nature of emotion: Fundamental questions.* New York, NY: Oxford University Press.

Ellis, A. (1957). Rational psychotherapy and individual psychology. *Journal of Individual Psychology, 13*, 38–44.

Endicott, J., & Spitzer, R. L. (1978). A diagnostic interview: The schedule for affective disorders and schizophrenia. *Archives of General Psychiatry, 35*, 837–844. http://dx.doi.org/10.1001/archpsyc.1978.01770310043002

Enns, M. W., & Cox, B. J. (2005). Psychosocial and clinical predictors of symptom persistence vs. remission in major depressive disorder. *Canadian Journal of Psychiatry, 50*, 769–777.

Epstein, N. B., Baucom, D. H., Hunt, W., & La Taillade, J. J. (2002). Brief cognitive-behavioral therapy with couples. In F. W. Bond & W. Dryden (Eds.), *Handbook for brief cognitive-behaviour therapy* (pp. 187–205). West Sussex, England: Wiley.

Etkin, A., Pittinger, C., Polan, J., & Kandel, E. R. (2005). Toward a neurobiology of psychotherapy: Basic science and clinical applications. *Journal of Neuropsychiatry and Clinical Neurosciences, 17*, 145–158.

Eysenck, H. J. (1959). Learning theory and behaviour therapy. *Journal of Mental Science, 105*, 61–75.

Eysenck, H. J. (Ed.). (1960). *Behavior therapy and the neuroses.* New York, NY: Pergamon Press.

Falloon, I. R., Boyd, J. L., McGill, C. W., Williamson, M., Razani, J., Moss, H. B., . . . Simpson, G. M. (1985). Family management in the prevention of morbidity of schizophrenia. Clinical outcome of a two-year longitudinal study. *Archives of General Psychiatry, 42*, 887–896. http://dx.doi.org/10.1001/archpsyc.1985.01790320059008

Farmer, R. F. (2000). Issues in the assessment and conceptualization of personality disorders. *Clinical Psychology Review, 20*, 823–851. http://dx.doi.org/10.1016/S0272-7358(99)00014-8

Farmer, R. F., Kosty, D. B., Seeley, J. R., Olino, T. M., & Lewinsohn, P. M. (2013). Aggregation of lifetime Axis I psychiatric disorders through age 30: Incidence, predictors, and associated psychosocial outcomes. *Journal of Abnormal Psychology, 122*, 573–586. http://dx.doi.org/10.1037/a0031429

Farmer, R. F., & Latner, J. L. (2007). Eating disorders. In P. Sturmey (Ed.), *The handbook of functional analysis and clinical psychology* (pp. 379–402). Boston, MA: Academic Press.

Farmer, R. F., & Nelson-Gray, R. O. (2005). *Personality-guided behavior therapy.* http://dx.doi.org/10.1037/11197-000

Farmer, R. F., & Rucklidge, J. J. (2006). An evaluation of the response modulation hypothesis in relation to attention-deficit/hyperactivity disorder. *Journal of Abnormal Child Psychology, 34*, 545–557. http://dx.doi.org/10.1007/s10802-006-9034-y

Farmer, R. F., Seeley, J. R., Kosty, D. B., & Lewinsohn, P. M. (2009). Refinements in the hierarchical structure of externalizing psychiatric disorders: Patterns of lifetime liability from mid-adolescence through early adulthood. *Journal of Abnormal Psychology, 118*, 699–710. http://dx.doi.org/10.1037/a0017205

Farmer, R. F., Seeley, J. R., Kosty, D. B., Olino, T. M., & Lewinsohn, P. M. (2013). Hierarchical organization of Axis I psychiatric disorder comorbidity through age 30. *Comprehensive Psychiatry*, *54*, 523–532. http://dx.doi.org/10.1016/j.comppsych.2012.12.007

Feigenbaum, W. (1988). Long-term efficacy of ungraded versus graded massed exposure in agoraphobics. In I. Hand & H. Wittchen (Eds.), *Panic and phobias: Treatments and variables affecting course and outcome* (pp. 149–158). http://dx.doi.org/10.1007/978-3-642-73543-1_8

Fenigstein, A. (1996). Paranoia. In C. G. Costello (Ed.), *Personality characteristics of the personality disordered* (pp. 242–275). New York, NY: Wiley.

Ferguson, K. E., & Christiansen, K. (2008). Shaping. In W. T. O'Donohue & J. E. Fisher (Eds.), *Cognitive behavior therapy: Applying empirically supported techniques in your practice* (2nd ed., pp. 493–501). Hoboken, NJ: Wiley.

Ferster, C. B. (1973). A functional analysis of depression. *American Psychologist*, *28*, 857–870. http://dx.doi.org/10.1037/h0035605

Fiester, A. R., & Rudestam, K. E. (1975). A multivariate analysis of the early dropout process. *Journal of Consulting and Clinical Psychology*, *43*, 528–535.

First, M. B., Spitzer, R. L., Gibbon, M., & Williams, J. B. W. (1997). *Structured Clinical Interview for DSM–IV Axis I Disorders (SCID–I), Clinician Version*. Arlington, VA: American Psychiatric Press.

Foa, E. B., Jameson, J. S., Turner, R. M., & Payne, L. L. (1980). Massed vs. spaced exposure sessions in the treatment of agoraphobia. *Behaviour Research and Therapy*, *18*, 333–338. http://dx.doi.org/10.1016/0005-7967(80)90092-3

Foa, E. B., Keane, T. M., & Friedman, M. J. (2004). *Effective treatments for PTSD: Practice guidelines from the International Society for Traumatic Stress Studies*. New York, NY: Guilford Press.

Foa, E. B., & Kozak, M. J. (1986). Emotional processing of fear: Exposure to corrective information. *Psychological Bulletin*, *99*, 20–35. http://dx.doi.org/10.1037/0033-2909.99.1.20

Foa, E. B., & McNally, R. J. (1996). Mechanisms of change in exposure therapy. In M. Rapee (Ed.), *Current controversies in the anxiety disorders* (pp. 329–343). New York, NY: Guilford Press.

Foa, E. B., & Rothbaum, B. (1998). *Treating the trauma of rape: Cognitive-behavioral therapy for PTSD*. New York, NY: Guilford Press.

Foa, E. B., Yadin, E., & Lichner, T. K. (2012). *Exposure and response (ritual) prevention for obsessive compulsive disorder: Therapist guide*. New York, NY: Oxford University Press.

Follette, W. C., & Callaghan, G. M. (1995). Do as I do, not as I say: A behavior-analytic approach to supervision. *Professional Psychology: Research and Practice*, *26*, 413–421. http://dx.doi.org/10.1037/0735-7028.26.4.413

Follette, W. C., & Hayes, S. C. (2000). Contemporary behavior therapy. In C. R. Snyder & R. E. Ingram (Eds.), *Handbook of psychological change: Psychotherapy processes & practices for the 21st century* (pp. 381–408). Hoboken, NJ: Wiley.

Follette, W. C., Naugle, A. E., & Linnerooth, P. J. N. (2000). Functional alternatives to traditional assessment and diagnosis. In M. J. Dougher (Ed.), *Clinical behavior analysis* (pp. 99–125). Reno, NV: Context Press.

Forman, E. M., Chapman, J. E., Herbert, J. D., Goetter, E. M., Yuen, E. K., & Moitra, E. (2012). Using session-by-session measurement to compare mechanisms of action for acceptance and commitment therapy and cognitive therapy. *Behavior Therapy, 43,* 341–354. http://dx.doi.org/10.1016/j.beth.2011.07.004

Forman, E. M., & Herbert, J. D. (2009). New directions in cognitive behavior therapy: Acceptance-based therapies. In W. O'Donohue & J. E. Fisher (Eds.), *General principles and empirically supported techniques of cognitive behavior therapy* (pp. 102–114). Hoboken, NJ: Wiley.

Forsyth, J. P., & Eifert, G. H. (1998). Phobic anxiety and panic: An integrative behavioral account of their origin and treatment. In J. J. Plaud & G. H. Eifert (Eds.), *From behavior theory to behavior therapy* (pp. 38–67). Boston, MA: Allyn and Bacon.

Fowler, L., Blackwell, A., Jaffa, A., Palmer, R., Robbins, T. W., Sahakian, B. J., & Dowson, J. H. (2006). Profile of neurocognitive impairments associated with female in-patients with anorexia nervosa. *Psychological Medicine, 36,* 517–527. http://dx.doi.org/10.1017/S0033291705006379

Fowles, D. C. (2001). Biological variables in psychopathology: A psychobiological perspective. In P. B. Sutker & H. E. Adams (Eds.), *Comprehensive handbook of psychopathology* (3rd ed., pp. 85–104). New York, NY: Kluwer/Plenum.

Frank, E., Kupfer, D. J., Thase, M. E., Mallinger, A. G., Swartz, H. A., Fagiolini, A. M., . . . Monk, T. (2005). Two-year outcomes for interpersonal and social rhythm therapy in individuals with bipolar I disorder. *Archives of General Psychiatry, 62,* 996–1004. http://dx.doi.org/10.1001/archpsyc.62.9.996

Frank, E., Prien, R. F., Jarrett, R. B., Keller, M. B., Kupfer, D. J., Lavori, P. W., . . . Weissman, M. M. (1991). Conceptualization and rationale for consensus definitions of terms in major depressive disorder. Remission, recovery, relapse, and recurrence. *Archives of General Psychiatry, 48,* 851–855. http://dx.doi.org/10.1001/archpsyc.1991.01810330075011

Freeman, A., & McCloskey, R. (2003). Impediments to effective psychotherapy. In R. L. Leahy (Ed.), *Roadblocks in cognitive-behavioral therapy: Transforming challenges into opportunities for change* (pp. 24–48). New York, NY: Guilford Press.

Fresco, D. M., Mennin, D. S., Heimberg, R. G., & Turk, C. L. (2003). Using the Penn State Worry Questionnaire to identify individuals with generalized anxiety disorder: A receiver operating characteristic analysis. *Journal of Behavior Therapy and Experimental Psychiatry, 34,* 283–291. http://dx.doi.org/10.1016/j.jbtep.2003.09.001

Friman, P. C., & Finney, J. W. (2003). Time-out (and time-in). In W. O'Donohue, J. E. Fisher, & S. C. Hayes (Eds.), *Cognitive behavior therapy: Applying empirically supported techniques in your practice* (pp. 429–435). Hoboken, NJ: Wiley.

Goldfried, M. R., & Davison, G. R. (1976). *Clinical behavior therapy.* New York, NY: Holt, Rinehart, & Winston.

Goldfried, M. R., & Kent, R. N. (1972). Traditional versus behavioral personality assessment: A comparison of methodological and theoretical assumptions. *Psychological Bulletin, 77,* 409–420. http://dx.doi.org/10.1037/h0032714

Goldfried, M. R., & Sprafkin, J. N. (1976). Behavioral personality assessment. In J. T. Spence, R. C., Carson, & J. W. Thibaut (Eds.), *Behavioral approaches to therapy* (pp. 295–321). Morristown, NJ: General Learning Press.

Goldiamond, I. (1974). Toward a constructional approach to social problems: Ethical and constitutional issues raised by applied behavior analysis. *Behaviorism, 2,* 1–84.

Gordon, A. M., Impett, E. A., Kogan, A., Oveis, C., & Keltner, D. (2012). To have and to hold: Gratitude promotes relationship maintenance in intimate bonds. *Journal of Personality and Social Psychology, 103,* 257–274. http://dx.doi.org/10.1037/a0028723

Gortner, E. T., Gollan, J. K., Dobson, K. S., & Jacobson, N. S. (1998). Cognitive-behavioral treatment for depression: Relapse prevention. *Journal of Consulting and Clinical Psychology, 66,* 377–384. http://dx.doi.org/10.1037/0022-006X.66.2.377

Gould, R. A., Safren, S. A., Washington, D. O., & Otto, M. W. (2004). A meta-analytic review of cognitive-behavioral treatments. In R. G. Heimberg, C. L. Turk, & D. S. Mennin (Eds.), *Generalized anxiety disorder: Advances in research and practice* (pp. 248–264). New York, NY: Guilford Press.

Granholm, E., Holden, J., Link, P. C., & McQuaid, J. R. (2014). Randomized clinical trial of cognitive behavioral social skills training for schizophrenia: Improvement in functioning and experiential negative symptoms. *Journal of Consulting and Clinical Psychology, 82,* 1173–1185. http://dx.doi.org/10.1037/a0037098

Gratz, K. L., & Gunderson, J. G. (2006). Preliminary data on an acceptance-based emotion regulation group intervention for deliberate self-harm among women with borderline personality disorder. *Behavior Therapy, 37,* 25–35. http://dx.doi.org/10.1016/j.beth.2005.03.002

Gratz, K. L., & Roemer, L. (2004). Multidimensional assessment of emotion regulation and dysregulation: Development, factor structure, and initial validation of the difficulties in emotion regulation scale. *Journal of Psychopathology and Behavioral Assessment, 26,* 41–54. http://dx.doi.org/10.1023/B:JOBA.0000007455.08539.94

Gratz, K. L., & Tull, M. T. (2011). Extending research on the utility of an adjunctive emotion regulation group therapy for deliberate self-harm among women with borderline personality pathology. *Personality Disorders: Theory, Research, and Treatment, 2,* 316–326. http://dx.doi.org/10.1037/a0022144

Gray, J. A., & McNaughton, N. (2000). *The neuropsychology of anxiety* (2nd ed.). London, England: Oxford University Press.

Greenberg, L. S., & Watson, J. C. (2005). *Emotion-focused therapy for depression.* Washington, DC: American Psychological Association.

Greenberger, D., & Padesky, C. A. (1995). *Mind over mood: Change how you feel by changing the way you think.* New York, NY: Guilford Press.

Gros, D. F., Price, M., Strachan, M., Yuen, E. K., Milanak, M. E., & Acierno, R. (2012). Behavioral activation and therapeutic exposure: An investigation of relative symptom changes in PTSD and depression during the course of integrated behavioral activation, situational exposure, and imaginal exposure techniques. *Behavior Modification, 36,* 580–599. http://dx.doi.org/10.1177/014544 5512448097

Gross, J. J. (1998). The emerging field of emotion regulation: An integrative review. *Review of General Psychology, 2,* 271–299. http://dx.doi.org/10.1037/1089-2680.2.3.271

Gross, J. J. (2013). Emotion regulation: Taking stock and moving forward. *Emotion, 13,* 359–365. http://dx.doi.org/10.1037/a0032135

Grusec, J., & Mischel, W. (1966). Model's characteristics as determinants of social learning. *Journal of Personality and Social Psychology, 4,* 211–215. http://dx.doi.org/10.1037/h0023561

Halford, W. K., & Bodenmann, G. (2013). Effects of relationship education on maintenance of couple relationship satisfaction. *Clinical Psychology Review, 33,* 512–525. http://dx.doi.org/10.1016/j.cpr.2013.02.001

Hallam, R. S. (2013). *Individual case formulation.* Waltham, MA: Academic Press.

Hammen, C. (2003). Interpersonal stress and depression in women. *Journal of Affective Disorders, 74,* 49–57. http://dx.doi.org/10.1016/S0165-0327(02)00430-5

Harned, M. S., Korslund, K. E., & Linehan, M. M. (2014). A pilot randomized controlled trial of dialectical behavior therapy with and without the dialectical behavior therapy prolonged exposure protocol for suicidal and self-injuring women with borderline personality disorder and PTSD. *Behaviour Research and Therapy, 55,* 7–17. http://dx.doi.org/10.1016/j.brat.2014.01.008

Havermans, R. C., & Jansen, A. T. (2003). Increasing the efficacy of cue exposure treatment in preventing relapse of addictive behavior. *Addictive Behaviors, 28,* 989–994. http://dx.doi.org/10.1016/S0306-4603(01)00289-1

Hawkins, J. D., Catalano, R. F., Jr., & Wells, E. A. (1986). Measuring effects of a skills training intervention for drug abusers. *Journal of Consulting and Clinical Psychology, 54,* 661–664. http://dx.doi.org/10.1037/0022-006X.54.5.661

Hawkins, R. P. (1986). Selection of target behaviors. In R. O. Nelson & S. C. Hayes (Eds.), *Conceptual foundations of behavioral assessment* (pp. 331–385). New York, NY: Guilford Press.

Hayes, S. C. (2004a). Acceptance and commitment therapy and the new behavior therapies. In S. C. Hayes, V. M. Follette, & M. M. Linehan (Eds.), *Mindfulness and acceptance: Expanding the cognitive-behavioral tradition* (pp. 1–29). New York, NY: Guilford Press.

Hayes, S. C. (2004b). Acceptance and commitment therapy, relational frame theory, and the third wave of behavioral and cognitive therapies. *Behavior Therapy, 35,* 639–665. http://dx.doi.org/10.1016/S0005-7894(04)80013-3

Hayes, S. C., Barlow, D. H., & Nelson-Gray, R. O. (1999). *The scientist-practitioner: Research and accountability in the age of managed care* (2nd ed.). Boston, MA: Allyn and Bacon.

Hayes, S. C., Barnes-Holmes, D., & Roche, B. (Eds.). (2001). *Relational frame theory: A post-Skinnerian account of human language and cognition.* New York, NY: Kluwer Academic/Plenum.

Hayes, S. C., Brownstein, A. J., Zettle, R. D., Rosenfarb, I., & Korn, Z. (1986). Rule-governed behavior and sensitivity to changing consequences of responding. *Journal of the Experimental Analysis of Behavior, 45,* 237–256. http://dx.doi.org/10.1901/jeab.1986.45-237

Hayes, S. C., Follette, V. M., & Linehan, M. M. (Eds.). (2004). *Mindfulness and acceptance: Expanding the cognitive-behavioral tradition.* New York, NY: Guilford Press.

Hayes, S. C., & Follette, W. C. (1992). Can functional analysis provide a substitute for syndromal classification? *Behavioral Assessment, 14,* 345–365.

Hayes, S. C., Hayes, L. J., Reese, H. W., & Sarbin, T. R. (Eds.). (1993). *Varieties of scientific contextualism.* Reno, NV: Context Press.

Hayes, S. C., Nelson, R. O., & Jarrett, R. B. (1986). Evaluating the quality of behavioral assessment. In R. O. Nelson & S. C. Hayes (Eds.), *Conceptual foundations of behavioral assessment* (pp. 463–503). New York, NY: Guilford Press.

Hayes, S. C., & Smith, S. (2005). *Get out of your mind and into your life: The new acceptance and commitment therapy.* Oakland, CA: New Harbinger.

Hayes, S. C., & Strosahl, K. D. (Eds.). (2004). *A practical guide to acceptance and commitment therapy.* http://dx.doi.org/10.1007/978-0-387-23369-7

Hayes, S. C., Strosahl, K. D., Bunting, K., Twohig, M., & Wilson, K. G. (2004). What is acceptance and commitment therapy? In S. C. Hayes & K. D. Strosahl (Eds.), *A practical guide to acceptance and commitment therapy* (pp. 3–29). http://dx.doi.org/10.1007/978-0-387-23369-7_1

Hayes, S. C., Strosahl, K. D., & Wilson, K. G. (2012). *Acceptance and commitment therapy: The process and practice of mindful change.* New York, NY: Guilford Press.

Hayes, S. C., Wilson, K. G., Gifford, E. V., Follette, V. M., & Strosahl, K. (1996). Experimental avoidance and behavioral disorders: A functional dimensional approach to diagnosis and treatment. *Journal of Consulting and Clinical Psychology, 64,* 1152–1168. http://dx.doi.org/10.1037/0022-006X.64.6.1152

Haynes, S. N. (1986). The design of intervention programs. In R. O. Nelson & S. Hayes (Eds.), *Conceptual foundations of behavioral assessment* (pp. 386–429). New York, NY: Guilford Press.

Haynes, S. N., O'Brien, W. H., & Kaholokula, J. K. (2011). *Behavioral assessment and case formulation*. Hoboken, NJ: Wiley.

Heaney, C. A., & Israel, B. A. (2008). Social networks and social support. In K. Glanz, B. K. Rimer, & K. Viswanath (Eds.), *Health behavior and health education: Theory, research, and practice* (4th ed., pp. 189–210). San Francisco, CA: Jossey-Bass.

Heatherton, T. F., & Baumeister, R. F. (1991). Binge eating as escape from self-awareness. *Psychological Bulletin, 110*, 86–108. http://dx.doi.org/10.1037/0033-2909.110.1.86

Heimberg, R. G., & Becker, R. E. (2002). *Cognitive-behavioral group therapy for social phobia: Basic mechanisms and clinical strategies*. New York, NY: Guilford Press.

Heinssen, R. K., Levendusky, P. G., & Hunter, R. H. (1995). Client as colleague. Therapeutic contracting with the seriously mentally ill. *American Psychologist, 50*, 522–532. http://dx.doi.org/10.1037/0003-066X.50.7.522

Hendershot, C. S., Marlatt, G. A., & George, W. H. (2009). Relapse prevention and the maintenance of optimal health. In S. A. Shumaker, J. K. Ockene, & K. A. Riekert (Eds.), *The handbook of health behavior change* (3rd ed., pp. 127–149). New York, NY: Springer.

Henin, A., Otto, M. W., & Reilly-Harrington, N. A. (2001). Introducing flexibility in manualized treatments: Application of recommended strategies to the cognitive-behavioral treatment of bipolar disorder. *Cognitive and Behavioral Practice, 8*, 317–328. http://dx.doi.org/10.1016/S1077-7229(01)80004-3

Herbert, J. D., Gaudiano, B. A., Rheingold, A. A., Myers, V. H., Dalrymple, K., & Nolan, E. M. (2005). Social skills training augments the effectiveness of cognitive behavioral group therapy for social anxiety disorder. *Behavior Therapy, 36*, 125–138. http://dx.doi.org/10.1016/S0005-7894(05)80061-9

Herbert, J. D., Rheingold, A., & Brandsma, L. L. (2010). Assessment of social anxiety and social phobia. In S. Hoffman & P. DiBartolo (Eds.), *Social anxiety: Clinical, developmental, and social perspectives* (2nd ed., pp. 24–64). http://dx.doi.org/10.1016/B978-0-12-375096-9.00002-X

Herrnstein, R. J. (1961). Relative and absolute strength of response as a function of frequency of reinforcement. *Journal of the Experimental Analysis of Behavior, 4*, 267–272. http://dx.doi.org/10.1901/jeab.1961.4-267

Hersen, M., Himmelhoch, J. M., Thase, M. E., & Bellack, A. S. (1984). Effects of social skill training, amitriptyline, and psychotherapy in unipolar depressed women. *Behavior Therapy, 15*, 21–40. http://dx.doi.org/10.1016/S0005-7894(84)80039-8

Hess, U., & Blairy, S. (2001). Facial mimicry and emotional contagion to dynamic emotional facial expressions and their influence on decoding accuracy. *International Journal of Psychophysiology, 40*, 129–141. http://dx.doi.org/10.1016/S0167-8760(00)00161-6

Higgins, S. T., Budney, A. J., Bickel, W. K., Hughes, J. R., Foerg, F., & Badger, G. (1993). Achieving cocaine abstinence with a behavioral approach. *The American Journal of Psychiatry, 150*, 763–769. http://dx.doi.org/10.1176/ajp.150.5.763

Higgins, S. T., Delaney, D. D., Budney, A. J., Bickel, W. K., Hughes, J. R., Foerg, F., & Fenwick, J. W. (1991). A behavioral approach to achieving initial cocaine abstinence. *The American Journal of Psychiatry, 148*, 1218–1224. http://dx.doi.org/10.1176/ajp.148.9.1218

Higgins, S. T., Sigmon, S. C., & Heil, S. H. (2014). Drug use disorders. In D. H. Barlow (Ed.), *Clinical handbook of psychological disorders* (5th ed., pp. 588–616). New York, NY: Guilford Press.

Hofmann, S. G., Asnaani, A., Vonk, I. J., Sawyer, A. T., & Fang, A. (2012). The efficacy of cognitive behavioral therapy: A review of meta-analyses. *Cognitive Therapy and Research, 36*, 427–440. [Erratum appears in *Cognitive Therapy and Research* (2014), 38, 386.] http://dx.doi.org/10.1007/s10608-012-9476-1

Hofmann, S. G., & Smits, J. A. (2008). Cognitive-behavioral therapy for adult anxiety disorders: A meta-analysis of randomized placebo-controlled trials. *Journal of Clinical Psychiatry, 69*, 621–632. http://dx.doi.org/10.4088/JCP.v69n0415

Hopko, D. R., Lejuez, C. W., Ruggiero, K. J., & Eifert, G. H. (2003). Contemporary behavioral activation treatments for depression: Procedures, principles, and progress. *Clinical Psychology Review, 23*, 699–717. http://dx.doi.org/10.1016/S0272-7358(03)00070-9

Hopko, D. R., Sanchez, L., Hopko, S. D., Dvir, S., & Lejuez, C. W. (2003). Behavioral activation and the prevention of suicidal behaviors in patients with borderline personality disorder. *Journal of Personality Disorders, 17*, 460–478. http://dx.doi.org/10.1521/pedi.17.5.460.22970

Horne, A. M., & Matson, J. L. (1977). A comparison of modeling, desensitization, flooding, study skills and control groups for reducing test anxiety. *Behavior Therapy, 8*, 1–8. http://dx.doi.org/10.1016/S0005-7894(77)80114-7

Houmanfar, R., Maglieri, K. A., & Roman, H. R. (2003). Behavioral contracting. In W. O'Donohue, J. E. Fisher, & S. C. Hayes (Eds.), *Cognitive behavior therapy* (pp. 40–45). Hoboken, NJ: Wiley.

Hull, D. L., Langman, R. E., & Glenn, S. S. (2001). A general account of selection: Biology, immunology, and behavior. *Behavioral and Brain Sciences, 24*, 511–528.

Hunnicutt-Ferguson, K., Hoxha, D., & Gollan, J. (2012). Exploring sudden gains in behavioral activation therapy for major depressive disorder. *Behaviour Research and Therapy, 50*, 223–230. http://dx.doi.org/10.1016/j.brat.2012.01.005

Hunot, V., Churchill, R., Silva de Lima, M., & Teixeira, V. (2007). Psychological therapies for generalised anxiety disorder. *Cochrane Database of Systematic Reviews, 1*, CD001848.

Hurtig, T., Ebeling, H., Taanila, A., Miettunen, J., Smalley, S., McGough, J., . . . Moilanen, I. (2007). ADHD and comorbid disorders in relation to family environment and symptom severity. *European Child & Adolescent Psychiatry, 16*, 362–369. http://dx.doi.org/10.1007/s00787-007-0607-2

Ilardi, S. S., & Craighead, W. E. (1994). The role of non-specific factors in cognitive-behavior therapy for depression. *Clinical Psychology: Science and Practice, 1*, 138–156. http://dx.doi.org/10.1111/j.1468-2850.1994.tb00016.x

Jacobson, N. S. (1982). Communication skills training for married couples. In J. P. Curran & P. M. Monti (Eds.), *Social skills training: A practical handbook for assessment and treatment* (pp. 224–252). New York, NY: Guilford Press.

Jacobson, N. S., & Christensen, A. (1996). *Integrative couple therapy*. New York, NY: Norton.

Jacobson, N. S., & Christensen, A. (1998). *Acceptance and change in couple therapy: A therapist's guide to transforming relationships*. New York, NY: Norton.

Jacobson, N. S., Dobson, K. S., Truax, P. A., Addis, M. E., Koerner, K., Gollan, J. K., . . . Prince, S. E. (1996). A component analysis of cognitive-behavioral treatment for depression. *Journal of Consulting and Clinical Psychology, 64,* 295–304. http://dx.doi.org/10.1037/0022-006X.64.2.295

Jacobson, N. S., & Margolin, G. (1979). *Marital therapy: Strategies based on social learning and behavioral exchange principles*. New York, NY: Brunner/Mazel.

Jacobson, N. S., Martell, C. R., & Dimidjian, S. (2001). Behavioral activation treatment for depression: Returning to contextual roots. *Clinical Psychology: Science and Practice, 8,* 255–270. http://dx.doi.org/10.1093/clipsy.8.3.255

Jakupcak, M., Roberts, L. J., Martell, C., Mulick, P., Michael, S., Reed, R., . . . McFall, M. (2006). A pilot study of behavioral activation for veterans with posttraumatic stress disorder. *Journal of Traumatic Stress, 19,* 387–391. http://dx.doi.org/10.1002/jts.20125

Jaycox, L. H., Foa, E. B., & Morral, A. R. (1998). Influence of emotional engagement and habituation on exposure therapy for PTSD. *Journal of Consulting and Clinical Psychology, 66,* 185–192. http://dx.doi.org/10.1037/0022-006X.66.1.185

Johansen, E. B., Aase, H., Meyer, A., & Sagvolden, T. (2002). Attention-deficit/hyperactivity disorder (ADHD) behaviour explained by dysfunctioning reinforcement and extinction processes. *Behavioural Brain Research, 130,* 37–45. http://dx.doi.org/10.1016/S0166-4328(01)00434-X

Johnson, W. G., Schlundt, D. G., Barclay, D. R., Carr-Nangle, R. E., & Engler, L. B. (1995). A naturalistic functional analysis of binge eating. *Behavior Therapy, 26,* 101–118. http://dx.doi.org/10.1016/S0005-7894(05)80085-1

Jones, M. C. (1924). A laboratory study of fear: The case of Peter. *Pedagogical Seminary, 31,* 308–315. http://dx.doi.org/10.1080/08856559.1924.9944851

Kaminer, Y., Burleson, J. A., & Goldberger, R. (2002). Cognitive-behavioral coping skills and psychoeducation therapies for adolescent substance abuse. *Journal of Nervous and Mental Disease, 190,* 737–745. http://dx.doi.org/10.1097/00005053-200211000-00003

Kanfer, F. H., & Busemeyer, J. R. (1982). The use of problem solving and decision making in behavior therapy. *Clinical Psychology Review, 2,* 239–266. http://dx.doi.org/10.1016/0272-7358(82)90014-9

Kanfer, F. H., & Saslow, G. (1969). Behavioral diagnosis. In C. M. Franks (Ed.), *Behavior therapy: Appraisal and status* (pp. 417–444). New York, NY: McGraw-Hill.

Kanter, J. W., Manos, R. C., Bowe, W. M., Baruch, D. E., Busch, A. M., & Rusch, L. C. (2010). What is behavioral activation? A review of the empirical literature. *Clinical Psychology Review, 30*, 608–620. http://dx.doi.org/10.1016/j.cpr.2010.04.001

Kanter, J. W., Santiago-Rivera, A. L., Rusch, L. C., Busch, A. M., & West, P. (2010). Initial outcomes of a culturally adapted behavioral activation for Latinas diagnosed with depression at a community clinic. *Behavior Modification, 34*, 120–144. http://dx.doi.org/10.1177/0145445509359682

Karney, B. R., & Bradbury, T. N. (1995). The longitudinal course of marital quality and stability: A review of theory, method, and research. *Psychological Bulletin, 118*, 3–34. http://dx.doi.org/10.1037/0033-2909.118.1.3

Kashdan, T. B., Breen, W. E., Afram, A., & Terhar, D. (2010). Experiential avoidance in idiographic, autobiographical memories: Construct validity and links to social anxiety, depressive, and anger symptoms. *Journal of Anxiety Disorders, 24*, 528–534. http://dx.doi.org/10.1016/j.janxdis.2010.03.010

Kassinove, H. (1995). *Anger disorders: Definition, diagnosis, and treatment.* Philadelphia, PA: Taylor & Francis.

Kassinove, H., & Tafrate, R. C. (2002). *Anger management: The complete treatment guidebook for practitioners.* Atascadero, CA: Impact.

Kavanagh, D. J., Sitharthan, G., Young, R. M., Sitharthan, T., Saunders, J. B., Shockley, N., & Giannopoulos, V. (2006). Addition of cue exposure to cognitive-behaviour therapy for alcohol misuse: A randomized trial with dysphoric drinkers. *Addiction, 101*, 1106–1116. http://dx.doi.org/10.1111/j.1360-0443.2006.01488.x

Kazantzis, N., Whittington, C., & Dattilio, F. (2010). Meta-analysis of homework effects in cognitive and behavioral therapy: A replication and extension. *Clinical Psychology: Science and Practice, 17*, 144–156. http://dx.doi.org/10.1111/j.1468-2850.2010.01204.x

Kazdin, A. E. (1978). *History of behavior modification: Experimental foundations of contemporary research.* Baltimore, MD: University Park Press.

Kazdin, A. E. (2001). *Behavior modification in applied settings* (6th ed.). Belmont, CA: Wadsworth/Thomson Learning.

Kazdin, A. E. (2012). *Behavior modification in applied settings* (7th ed.). Long Grove, IL: Waveland Press.

Kazdin, A. E., & Krouse, R. (1983). The impact of variations in treatment rationales on expectancies for therapeutic change. *Behavior Therapy, 14*, 657–671. http://dx.doi.org/10.1016/S0005-7894(83)80088-4

Kearney, A. J. (2006). A primer of covert sensitization. *Cognitive and Behavioral Practice, 13*, 167–175. http://dx.doi.org/10.1016/j.cbpra.2006.02.002

Kellam, S. G., Brown, C. H., Poduska, J. M., Ialongo, N. S., Wang, W., Toyinbo, P., . . . Wilcox, H. C. (2008). Effects of a universal classroom behavior management program in first and second grades on young adult behavioral, psychiatric, and social outcomes. *Drug and Alcohol Dependence, 95*(Suppl. 1), S5–S28. http://dx.doi.org/10.1016/j.drugalcdep.2008.01.004

Kelly, G. (1955). *The psychology of personal constructs.* New York, NY: Norton.

Kennard, B. D., Emslie, G. J., Mayes, T. L., Nightingale-Teresi, J., Nakonezny, P. A., Hughes, J. L., . . . Jarrett, R. B. (2008). Cognitive-behavioral therapy to prevent relapse in pediatric responders to pharmacotherapy for major depressive disorder. *Journal of the American Academy of Child & Adolescent Psychiatry, 47,* 1395–1404. http://dx.doi.org/10.1097/CHI.0b013e31818914a1

Kernberg, O. F., Selzer, M. A., Koenigsberg, H. W., Carr, A. C., & Appelbaum, A. H. (1989). *Psychodynamic psychotherapy of borderline patients.* New York, NY: Basic Books.

Kessler, R. C., Berglund, P., Demler, O., Jin, R., Merikangas, K. R., & Walters, E. E. (2005). Lifetime prevalence and age-of-onset distributions of *DSM–IV* disorders in the National Comorbidity Survey Replication. *Archives of General Psychiatry, 62,* 593–602. http://dx.doi.org/10.1001/archpsyc.62.6.593

Kessler, R. C., Chiu, W. T., Jin, R., Ruscio, A. M., Shear, K., & Walters, E. E. (2006). The epidemiology of panic attacks, panic disorder, and agoraphobia in the National Comorbidity Survey Replication. *Archives of General Psychiatry, 63,* 415–424. http://dx.doi.org/10.1001/archpsyc.63.4.415

Kim, K., Rosenthal, M. Z., Zielinski, D. J., & Brady, R. (2014). Effects of virtual environment platforms on emotional responses. *Computer Methods and Programs in Biomedicine, 113,* 882–893. http://dx.doi.org/10.1016/j.cmpb.2013.12.024

Kimonis, E. R., & Frick, P. J. (2010). Oppositional defiant disorder and conduct disorder grown-up. *Journal of Developmental and Behavioral Pediatrics, 31,* 244–254. http://dx.doi.org/10.1097/DBP.0b013e3181d3d320

Kleim, B., Grey, N., Wild, J., Nussbeck, F. W., Stott, R., Hackmann, A., . . . Ehlers, A. (2013). Cognitive change predicts symptom reduction with cognitive therapy for posttraumatic stress disorder. *Journal of Consulting and Clinical Psychology, 81,* 383–393. http://dx.doi.org/10.1037/a0031290

Kleindienst, N., Bohus, M., Ludäscher, P., Limberger, M. F., Kuenkele, K., Ebner-Priemer, U. W., . . . Schmahl, C. (2008). Motives for nonsuicidal self-injury among women with borderline personality disorder. *Journal of Nervous and Mental Disease, 196,* 230–236. http://dx.doi.org/10.1097/NMD.0b013e3181663026

Klerman, G. L., Weissman, M. M., Rounsaville, B. J., & Chevron, E. S. (1984). *Interpersonal psychotherapy of depression.* New York, NY: Basic Books.

Kohlenberg, R. J., & Tsai, M. (1991). *Functional analytic psychotherapy: Creating intense and curative therapeutic relationships.* http://dx.doi.org/10.1007/978-0-387-70855-3

Korotitsch, W. J., & Nelson-Gray, R. O. (1999). An overview of self-monitoring research in assessment and treatment. *Psychological Assessment, 11,* 415–425. http://dx.doi.org/10.1037/1040-3590.11.4.415

Kozak, M. J., Foa, E. B., & Steketee, G. (1988). Process and outcome of exposure treatment with obsessive-compulsives: Psychophysiological indicators of emotional processing. *Behavior Therapy, 19,* 157–169. http://dx.doi.org/10.1016/S0005-7894(88)80039-X

Krasner, L., & Ullmann, L. P. (1965). *Research in behavior modification—new developments and implications.* New York, NY: Holt, Rinehart and Winston.

Kuppens, P., Allen, N. B., & Sheeber, L. B. (2010). Emotional inertia and psychological maladjustment. *Psychological Science, 21,* 984–991. http://dx.doi.org/10.1177/0956797610372634

Kurtz, M. M., & Mueser, K. T. (2008). A meta-analysis of controlled research on social skills training for schizophrenia. *Journal of Consulting and Clinical Psychology, 76,* 491–504. http://dx.doi.org/10.1037/0022-006X.76.3.491

Lambert, N. M., & Fincham, F. D. (2011). Expressing gratitude to a partner leads to more relationship maintenance behavior. *Emotion, 11,* 52–60. http://dx.doi.org/10.1037/a0021557

Laraway, S., Snycerski, S., Michael, J., & Poling, A. (2003). Motivating operations and terms to describe them: Some further refinements. *Journal of Applied Behavior Analysis, 36,* 407–414. http://dx.doi.org/10.1901/jaba.2003.36-407

Latner, J. D., & Wilson, G. T. (2000). Cognitive-behavioral therapy and nutritional counseling in the treatment of bulimia nervosa and binge eating. *Eating Behaviors, 1,* 3–21. http://dx.doi.org/10.1016/S1471-0153(00)00008-8

Lazarus, A. A. (1958). New methods in psychotherapy: A case study. *South African Medical Journal, 32,* 660–663.

Lazzari, C., Egan, S. J., & Rees, C. S. (2011). Behavioral activation treatment for depression in older adults delivered via videoconferencing: A pilot study. *Cognitive and Behavioral Practice, 18,* 555–565. http://dx.doi.org/10.1016/j.cbpra.2010.11.009

Leahy, R. L. (2003). *Cognitive therapy techniques: A practitioner's guide.* New York, NY: Guilford Press.

Ledley, D. R., Marx, B. P., & Heimberg, R. G. (2010). *Making cognitive behavioral therapy work* (2nd ed.). New York, NY: Guilford Press.

LeDoux, J. (2002). *Synaptic self: How our brains become who we are.* New York, NY: Viking.

Lee, J., Lim, Y., Graham, S. J., Kim, G., Wiederhold, B. K., Wiederhold, M. D., . . . Kim, S. I. (2004). Nicotine craving and cue exposure therapy by using virtual environments. *CyberPsychology & Behavior, 7,* 705–713. http://dx.doi.org/10.1089/cpb.2004.7.705

Lejuez, C. W., Hopko, D. R., Acierno, R., Daughters, S. B., & Pagoto, S. L. (2011). Ten year revision of the brief behavioral activation treatment for depression: Revised treatment manual. *Behavior Modification, 35,* 111–161. http://dx.doi.org/10.1177/0145445510390929

Lejuez, C. W., Hopko, D. R., & Hopko, S. D. (2001). A brief behavioral activation treatment for depression. Treatment manual. *Behavior Modification, 25,* 255–286. http://dx.doi.org/10.1177/0145445501252005

Lejuez, C. W., Hopko, D. R., & Hopko, S. D. (2002). *The brief behavioral activation treatment for depression (BATD): A comprehensive patient guide.* Boston, MA: Pearson Custom.

Lewinsohn, P. M. (1974). A behavioral approach to depression. In R. M. Friedman & M. M. Katz (Eds.), *The psychology of depression: Contemporary theory and research* (pp. 157–185). New York, NY: Wiley.

Lewinsohn, P. M., Antonuccio, D. O., Steinmetz-Breckenridge, J., & Teri, L. (1984). *The coping with depression course.* Eugene, OR: Castalia.

Lewinsohn, P. M., Biglan, A., & Zeiss, A. S. (1976). Behavioral treatment of depression. In P. O. Davidson (Ed.), *The behavioral management of anxiety, depression, and pain* (pp. 91–146). New York, NY: Brunner/Mazel.

Lewinsohn, P. M., & Gotlib, I. H. (1995). Behavioral theory and treatment of depression. In E. E. Beckham & W. R. Leber (Eds.), *Handbook of depression* (2nd ed., pp. 352–375). New York, NY: Guilford Press.

Lewinsohn, P. M., & Libet, J. (1972). Pleasant events, activity schedules, and depressions. *Journal of Abnormal Psychology, 79,* 291–295. http://dx.doi.org/10.1037/h0033207

Lewinsohn, P. M., Muñoz, R. F., Youngren, M. A., & Zeiss, A. M. (1978). *Control your depression.* Englewood Cliffs, NJ: Prentice Hall.

Lewinsohn, P. M., Steinmetz, J. L., Antonuccio, D., & Teri, L. (1984). Group therapy for depression: The Coping With Depression course. *International Journal of Mental Health, 13,* 8–33.

Lewis, M., Sullivan, M. W., Ramsay, D. S., & Alessandri, S. M. (1992). Individual differences in anger and sad expressions during extinction: Antecedents and consequences. *Infant Behavior & Development, 15,* 443–452. http://dx.doi.org/10.1016/0163-6383(92)80012-J

Lieberman, M. D., Eisenberger, N. I., Crockett, M. J., Tom, S. M., Pfeifer, J. H., & Way, B. M. (2007). Putting feelings into words: Affect labeling disrupts amygdala activity in response to affective stimuli. *Psychological Science, 18,* 421–428. http://dx.doi.org/10.1111/j.1467-9280.2007.01916.x

Lillis, J., & Hayes, S. C. (2007). Applying acceptance, mindfulness, and values to the reduction of prejudice: A pilot study. *Behavior Modification, 31,* 389–411. http://dx.doi.org/10.1177/0145445506298413

Lindenboim, N., Chapman, A. L., & Linehan, M. M. (2006). Homework use in dialectical behavior therapy for borderline personality disorder. In N. Kazantzis & L. L'Abate (Eds.), *Handbook of homework assignments in psychotherapy: Research, practice, and prevention* (pp. 227–245). New York, NY: Springer.

Lindsley, O. R., Skinner, B. F., & Solomon, H. C. (1953). *Studies on behavior therapy: Status report 1.* Waltham, MA: Metropolitan State Hospital.

Linehan, M. M. (1993a). *Cognitive-behavioral treatment of borderline personality disorder*. New York, NY: Guilford Press.

Linehan, M. M. (1993b). *Skills training manual for treating borderline personality disorder*. New York, NY: Guilford Press.

Linehan, M. M. (1997). Validation and psychotherapy. In A. C. Bohart & L. S. Greenberg (Eds.), *Empathy reconsidered: New directions in psychotherapy* (pp. 353–392). http://dx.doi.org/10.1037/10226-016

Linehan, M. M. (2011). Dialectical behavior therapy and telephone coaching. *Cognitive and Behavioral Practice, 18*, 207–208. http://dx.doi.org/10.1016/j.cbpra.2010.06.003

Linehan, M. M. (2015). *DBT skills training manual* (2nd ed.). New York, NY: Guilford Press.

Linehan, M. M., Dimeff, L. A., Reynolds, S. K., Comtois, K. A., Welch, S. S., Heagerty, P., & Kivlahan, D. R. (2002). Dialectical behavior therapy versus comprehensive validation therapy plus 12-step for the treatment of opioid dependent women meeting criteria for borderline personality disorder. *Drug and Alcohol Dependence, 67*, 13–26. http://dx.doi.org/10.1016/S0376-8716(02)00011-X

Linehan, M. M., Schmidt, H., III, Dimeff, L. A., Craft, J. C., Kanter, J., & Comtois, K. A. (1999). Dialectical behavior therapy for patients with borderline personality disorder and drug-dependence. *The American Journal on Addictions, 8*, 279–292. http://dx.doi.org/10.1080/105504999305686

Livesley, W. J. (2001). A framework for an integrated approach to treatment. In W. J. Livesley (Ed.), *Handbook of personality disorders: Theory, research, and treatment* (pp. 570–600). New York, NY: Guilford Press.

Livesley, W. J., Schroeder, M. L., & Jackson, D. N. (1990). Dependent personality disorder and attachment problems. *Journal of Personality Disorders, 4*, 131–140. http://dx.doi.org/10.1521/pedi.1990.4.2.131

Loeber, S., Croissant, B., Heinz, A., Mann, K., & Flor, H. (2006). Cue exposure in the treatment of alcohol dependence: Effects on drinking outcome, craving and self-efficacy. *British Journal of Clinical Psychology, 45*, 515–529. http://dx.doi.org/10.1348/014466505X82586

Logue, A. W. (1998). Laboratory research on self-control: Applications to administration. *Review of General Psychology, 2*, 221–238. http://dx.doi.org/10.1037/1089-2680.2.2.221

Longmore, R. J., & Worrell, M. (2007). Do we need to challenge thoughts in cognitive behavior therapy? *Clinical Psychology Review, 27*, 173–187. http://dx.doi.org/10.1016/j.cpr.2006.08.001

Lovaas, O. I., Freitag, G., Gold, V. J., & Kassorla, I. C. (1965). Experimental studies in childhood schizophrenia. I. Analysis of self-destructive behavior. *Journal of Experimental Child Psychology, 2*, 67–84. http://dx.doi.org/10.1016/0022-0965(65)90016-0

Lynch, T. R. (in press). *Radically open DBT: Treating the overcontrolled client.* New York, NY: Guilford Press.

Lynch, T. R., Gray, K. H., Hempel, R. J., Titley, M., Chen, E. Y., & O'Mahen, H. A. (2013). Radically open-dialectical behavior therapy for adult anorexia nervosa: Feasibility and outcomes from an inpatient program. *BMC Psychiatry, 13,* 293. http://dx.doi.org/10.1186/1471-244X-13-293

MacPherson, L., Tull, M. T., Matusiewicz, A. K., Rodman, S., Strong, D. R., Kahler, C. W., . . . Lejuez, C. W. (2010). Randomized controlled trial of behavioral activation smoking cessation treatment for smokers with elevated depressive symptoms. *Journal of Consulting and Clinical Psychology, 78,* 55–61. http://dx.doi.org/10.1037/a0017939

MacPhillamy, D. J., & Lewinsohn, P. M. (1974). Depression as a function of levels of desired and obtained pleasure. *Journal of Abnormal Psychology, 83,* 651–657. http://dx.doi.org/10.1037/h0037467

MacPhillamy, D. J., & Lewinsohn, P. M. (1982). The Pleasant Events Schedule: Studies on reliability, validity, and scale intercorrelation. *Journal of Consulting and Clinical Psychology, 50,* 363–380. http://dx.doi.org/10.1037/0022-006X.50.3.363

Mahoney, M. J. (1974). *Cognition and behavior modification.* Cambridge, MA: Ballinger.

Mahoney, M. J. (1991). *Human change processes: The scientific foundations of psychotherapy.* New York, NY: Basic Books.

Malott, R. W. (1989). The achievement of evasive goals: Control by rules describing contingencies that are not direct acting. In S. C. Hayes (Ed.), *Rule-governed behavior: Cognition, contingencies, and instructional control* (pp. 269–322). http://dx.doi.org/10.1007/978-1-4757-0447-1_8

Malott, R. W., Malott, M. E., & Trojan, E. A. (2000). *Elementary principles of behavior* (4th ed.). Upper Saddle River, NJ: Prentice Hall.

Manning, S. Y. (2011). Common errors made by therapists providing telephone consultation in dialectical behavior therapy. *Cognitive and Behavioral Practice, 18,* 178–185. http://dx.doi.org/10.1016/j.cbpra.2010.06.002

Manos, R. C., Kanter, J. W., Rusch, L. C., Turner, L. B., Roberts, N. A., & Busch, A. M. (2009). Integrating functional analytic psychotherapy and behavioral activation for the treatment of relationship distress. *Clinical Case Studies, 8,* 122–138. http://dx.doi.org/10.1177/1534650109332484

Marlatt, G. A., & Donovan, D. M. (Eds.). (2005). *Relapse prevention: Maintenance strategies in the treatment of addictive behaviors* (2nd ed.). New York, NY: Guilford Press.

Marlatt, G. A., & Gordon, J. R. (Eds.). (1985). *Relapse prevention: Maintenance strategies in the treatment of addictive behaviors.* New York, NY: Guilford Press.

Marlatt, G. A., & Witkiewitz, K. (2005). Relapse prevention for alcohol and drug problems. In G. A. Marlatt & D. M. Donovan (Eds.), *Relapse prevention:*

Maintenance strategies in the treatment of addictive behaviors (2nd ed., pp. 1–44). New York, NY: Guilford Press.

Martell, C. R., Addis, M. E., & Jacobson, N. S. (2001). *Depression in context: Strategies for guided action*. New York, NY: Norton.

Martell, C. R., Dimidjian, S., & Herman-Dunn, R. (2010). *Behavioral activation for depression: A clinician's guide*. New York, NY: Guilford Press.

Martin, T., LaRowe, S., & Malcolm, R. J. (2010). Progress in cue exposure therapy for the treatment of addictive disorders: A review update. *Open Addiction Journal, 3*, 92–101. http://dx.doi.org/10.2174/1874941001003020092

Mathers, C. D., & Loncar, D. (2006). Projections of global mortality and burden of disease from 2002 to 2030. *PLoS Medicine, 3*(11), e442.

Mattick, R. P., Breen, C., Kimber, J., & Davoli, M. (2009). Methadone maintenance therapy versus no opioid replacement therapy for opioid dependence. *Cochrane Database of Systematic Reviews, 3*, CD002209.

Mauss, I. B., Levenson, R. W., McCarter, L., Wilhelm, F. H., & Gross, J. J. (2005). The tie that binds? Coherence among emotion experience, behavior, and physiology. *Emotion, 5*, 175–190. http://dx.doi.org/10.1037/1528-3542.5.2.175

Maxwell, B., & Tappolet, C. (2012). Rethinking cognitive mediation: Cognitive-behavioral therapy and the perceptual theory of emotion. *Philosophy, Psychiatry, & Psychology, 19*, 1–12. http://dx.doi.org/10.1353/ppp.2012.0001

Mazzucchelli, T., Kane, R., & Rees, C. (2009). Behavioral activation treatments for depression in adults: A meta-analysis and review. *Clinical Psychology: Science and Practice, 16*, 383–411. http://dx.doi.org/10.1111/j.1468-2850.2009.01178.x

McCauley, E., Schloredt, K., Gudmundsen, G., Martell, C., & Dimidjian, S. (2011). Expanding behavioral activation to depressed adolescents: Lessons learned in treatment development. *Cognitive and Behavioral Practice, 18*, 371–383. http://dx.doi.org/10.1016/j.cbpra.2010.07.006

McCrady, B. S. (2014). Alcohol use disorders. In D. H. Barlow (Ed.), *Clinical handbook of psychological disorders: A step-by-step treatment manual* (5th ed., pp. 533–587). New York, NY: Guilford Press.

McCrady, B. S., & Epstein, E. E. (2013). *Addictions: A comprehensive guidebook* (2nd ed.). New York, NY: Oxford University Press.

McHugh, R. K., Murray, H. W., & Barlow, D. H. (2009). Balancing fidelity and adaptation in the dissemination of empirically-supported treatments: The promise of transdiagnostic interventions. *Behaviour Research and Therapy, 47*, 946–953. http://dx.doi.org/10.1016/j.brat.2009.07.005

McMillan, D., & Lee, R. (2010). A systematic review of behavioral experiments vs. exposure alone in the treatment of anxiety disorders: A case of exposure while wearing the emperor's new clothes? *Clinical Psychology Review, 30*, 467–478. http://dx.doi.org/10.1016/j.cpr.2010.01.003

McNally, R. J. (1999). EMDR and Mesmerism: A comparative historical analysis. *Journal of Anxiety Disorders*, *13*, 225–236. http://dx.doi.org/10.1016/S0887-6185(98)00049-8

Meichenbaum, D. H. (1977). *Cognitive-behavior modification: An integrative approach.* http://dx.doi.org/10.1007/978-1-4757-9739-8

Meichenbaum, D. H. (1996). Stress inoculation training for coping with stressors. *The Clinical Psychologist*, *49*, 4–7.

Meichenbaum, D. H., & Goodman, J. (1971). Training impulsive children to talk to themselves: A means of developing self-control. *Journal of Abnormal Psychology*, *77*, 115–126. http://dx.doi.org/10.1037/h0030773

Mennin, D. S. (2006). Emotion regulation therapy: An integrative approach to treatment resistant anxiety disorders. *Journal of Contemporary Psychotherapy*, *36*, 95–105. http://dx.doi.org/10.1007/s10879-006-9012-2

Merckelbach, H., Arntz, A., & de Jong, P. (1991). Conditioning experiences in spider phobics. *Behaviour Research and Therapy*, *29*, 333–335. http://dx.doi.org/10.1016/0005-7967(91)90068-E

Meyer, T. J., Miller, M. L., Metzger, R. L., & Borkovec, T. D. (1990). Development and validation of the Penn State Worry Questionnaire. *Behaviour Research and Therapy*, *28*, 487–495. http://dx.doi.org/10.1016/0005-7967(90)90135-6

Michael, J. (1982). Distinguishing between discriminative and motivational functions of stimuli. *Journal of the Experimental Analysis of Behavior*, *37*, 149–155. http://dx.doi.org/10.1901/jeab.1982.37-149

Michael, J. (2000). Implications and refinements of the establishing operation concept. *Journal of Applied Behavior Analysis*, *33*, 401–410. http://dx.doi.org/10.1901/jaba.2000.33-401

Miklowitz, D. J. (2014). Bipolar disorder. In D. H. Barlow (Ed.), *Clinical handbook of psychological disorders: A step-by-step treatment manual* (5th ed., pp. 462–501). New York, NY: Guilford Press.

Miklowitz, D. J., Axelson, D. A., George, E. L., Taylor, D. O., Schneck, C. D., Sullivan, A. E., . . . Birmaher, B. (2009). Expressed emotion moderates the effects of family-focused treatment for bipolar adolescents. *Journal of the American Academy of Child & Adolescent Psychiatry*, *48*, 643–651. http://dx.doi.org/10.1097/CHI.0b013e3181a0ab9d

Miller, W. R., Forcehimes, A. A., & Zweben, A. (2011). *Treating addiction: A guide for professionals*. New York, NY: Guildford Press.

Miller, W. R., & Rollnick, S. (2012). Meeting in the middle: Motivational interviewing and self-determination theory. *The International Journal of Behavioral Nutrition and Physical Activity*, *9*, 25. http://dx.doi.org/10.1186/1479-5868-9-25

Miller, W. R., & Rollnick, S. (2013). *Motivational interviewing: Helping people change* (3rd ed.). New York, NY: Guilford Press.

Miller, W. R., Zweben, A., DiClemente, C. C., & Rychtarik, R. G. (1995). *Motivational enhancement therapy manual: A clinical research guide for therapists treating individuals with alcohol abuse and dependence*. Rockville, MD: U.S. Department of Health and Human Services.

Miltenberger, R. G. (2004). *Behavior modification: Principles and procedures* (3rd ed.). Belmont, CA: Wadsworth/Thomson Learning.

Miltenberger, R. G. (2005). The role of automatic negative reinforcement in clinical problems. *International Journal of Behavioral Consultation and Therapy, 1*, 1–11. http://dx.doi.org/10.1037/h0100729

Mitchell, J. E., Mussell, M. P., Peterson, C. B., Crow, S., Wonderlich, S. A., Crosby, R. D., . . . Weller, C. (1999). Hedonics of binge eating in women with bulimia nervosa and binge eating disorder. *International Journal of Eating Disorders, 26*, 165–170. http://dx.doi.org/10.1002/(SICI)1098-108X(199909)26:2{165::AID-EAT5}3.0.CO;2-H

Mitte, K. (2005). A meta-analysis of the efficacy of psycho- and pharmacotherapy in panic disorder with and without agoraphobia. *Journal of Affective Disorders, 88*, 27–45. http://dx.doi.org/10.1016/j.jad.2005.05.003

Moak, Z. B., & Agrawal, A. (2010). The association between perceived interpersonal social support and physical and mental health: Results from the National Epidemiological Survey on Alcohol and Related Conditions. *Journal of Public Health, 32*, 191–201. http://dx.doi.org/10.1093/pubmed/fdp093

Moffitt, T. E., Caspi, A., Taylor, A., Kokaua, J., Milne, B. J., Polanczyk, G., & Poulton, R. (2010). How common are common mental disorders? Evidence that lifetime prevalence rates are doubled by prospective versus retrospective ascertainment. *Psychological Medicine, 40*, 899–909. http://dx.doi.org/10.1017/S0033291709991036

Monk, T. H., Kupfer, D. J., Frank, E., & Ritenour, A. M. (1991). The Social Rhythm Metric (SRM): Measuring daily social rhythms over 12 weeks. *Psychiatry Research, 36*, 195–207. http://dx.doi.org/10.1016/0165-1781(91)90131-8

Montgomery, K. J., & Haxby, J. V. (2008). Mirror neuron system differentially activated by facial expressions and social hand gestures: A functional magnetic resonance imaging study. *Journal of Cognitive Neuroscience, 20*, 1866–1877. http://dx.doi.org/10.1162/jocn.2008.20127

Monti, P. M., Abrams, D. B., Binkoff, J. A., Zwick, W. R., Liepman, M. R., Nirenberg, T. D., & Rohsenow, D. J. (1990). Communication skills training, communication skills training with family and cognitive behavioral mood management training for alcoholics. *Journal of Studies on Alcohol, 51*, 263–270.

Morganstern, K. P., & Tevlin, H. E. (1981). Behavioral interviewing. In M. Hersen & A. S. Bellack (Eds.), *Behavioral assessment: A practical handbook* (2nd ed., pp. 71–100). New York, NY: Pergamon Press.

Morin, C. M. (2004). Cognitive-behavioral approaches to the treatment of insomnia. *Journal of Clinical Psychiatry, 65*(Suppl. 16), 33–40.

Morin, S. F., & Rothblum, E. D. (1991). Removing the stigma: Fifteen years of progress. *American Psychologist, 46*, 947–949. http://dx.doi.org/10.1037/0003-066X.46.9.947

Morrison, J. (1995). *The first interview: Revised for DSM–IV*. New York, NY: Guilford Press.

Motraghi, T. E., Seim, R. W., Meyer, E. C., & Morissette, S. B. (2014). Virtual reality exposure therapy for the treatment of posttraumatic stress disorder: A methodological review using CONSORT guidelines. *Journal of Clinical Psychology, 70*, 197–208. http://dx.doi.org/10.1002/jclp.22051

Mowrer, O. H. (1960). *Learning theory and behavior*. http://dx.doi.org/10.1037/10802-000

Mowrer, O. H. (1974). O. Hobart Mowrer. In G. Lindzey (Ed.), *A history of psychology in autobiography* (Vol. VI, pp. 329–364). http://dx.doi.org/10.1037/11553-011

Mowrer, O. H., & Mowrer, W. M. (1938). Enuresis—a method for its study and treatment. *American Journal of Orthopsychiatry, 8*, 436–459. http://dx.doi.org/10.1111/j.1939-0025.1938.tb06395.x

Mueser, K. T., Levine, S., Bellack, A. S., Douglas, M. S., & Brady, E. U. (1990). Social skills training for acute psychiatric inpatients. *Hospital & Community Psychiatry, 41*, 1249–1251.

Nangle, D. W., Hansen, D. J., Erdley, C. A., & Norton, P. J. (Eds.). (2010). *Practitioner's guide to empirically based measures of social skills*. http://dx.doi.org/10.1007/978-1-4419-0609-0

Naugle, A. E., & Follette, W. C. (1998). A functional analysis of trauma symptoms. In V. M. Follette, J. I. Ruzek, & F. R. Abueg (Eds.), *Cognitive-behavioral therapies for trauma* (pp. 48–73). New York, NY: Guilford Press.

Naugle, A. E., & O'Donohue, W. (1998). The future direction of behavior therapy: Some applied implications of contemporary learning research. In W. O'Donohue (Ed.), *Learning and behavior therapy* (pp. 545–558). Needham Heights, MA: Allyn & Bacon.

Nelson, R. O. (1977). Assessment and therapeutic functions of self-monitoring. In M. Hersen, R. Eisler, & P. Miller (Eds.), *Progress in behavior modification* (Vol. 5, pp. 236–308). New York, NY: Academic Press.

Nelson, R. O., & Hayes, S. C. (Eds.). (1986a). *Conceptual foundations of behavioral assessment*. New York, NY: Guilford Press.

Nelson, R. O., & Hayes, S. C. (1986b). Nature of behavioral assessment. In R. O. Nelson & S. C. Hayes (Eds.), *Conceptual foundations of behavioral assessment* (pp. 3–41). New York, NY: Guilford Press.

Nelson, W. M., III, & Politano, P. M. (1993). The goal is to say "goodbye" and have the treatment effects generalize and maintain: A cognitive-behavioral view of termination. *Journal of Cognitive Psychotherapy, 4*, 251–263.

Nelson-Gray, R. O., & Farmer, R. F. (1999). Behavioral assessment of personality disorders. *Behaviour Research and Therapy, 37*, 347–368. http://dx.doi.org/10.1016/S0005-7967(98)00142-9

Nelson-Gray, R. O., & Paulson, J. F. (2003). Behavioral assessment and the DSM system. In S. N. Haynes & E. M. Heiby (Eds.), *Behavioral assessment* (pp. 470–486). New York, NY: Wiley.

Nestler, E. J., Barrot, M., DiLeone, R. J., Eisch, A. J., Gold, S. J., & Monteggia, L. M. (2002). Neurobiology of depression. *Neuron, 34,* 13–25. http://dx.doi.org/10.1016/S0896-6273(02)00653-0

Newman, M. G., & Llera, S. J. (2011). A novel theory of experiential avoidance in generalized anxiety disorder: A review and synthesis of research supporting a contrast avoidance model of worry. *Clinical Psychology Review, 31,* 371–382. http://dx.doi.org/10.1016/j.cpr.2011.01.008

Nezu, A. M., Nezu, C. M., & D'Zurilla, T. J. (2013). *Problem solving therapy: A treatment manual.* New York, NY: Springer.

Nezu, A. M., Nezu, C. M., & Perri, M. G. (1989). *Problem-solving therapy for depression: Therapy, research, and clinical guidelines.* New York, NY: Wiley.

Nikolova, Y., Bogdan, R., & Pizzagalli, D. A. (2012). Perception of a naturalistic stressor interacts with 5-HTTLPR/rs25531 genotype and gender to impact reward responsiveness. *Neuropsychobiology, 65,* 45–54. http://dx.doi.org/10.1159/000329105

Nisbett, R. E., & Wilson, T. D. (1977). The halo effect: Evidence for unconscious alteration of judgments. *Journal of Personality and Social Psychology, 35,* 250–256. http://dx.doi.org/10.1037/0022-3514.35.4.250

Nock, M. K., & Mendes, W. B. (2008). Physiological arousal, distress tolerance, and social problem-solving deficits among adolescent self-injurers. *Journal of Consulting and Clinical Psychology, 76,* 28–38. http://dx.doi.org/10.1037/0022-006X.76.1.28

Nock, M. K., & Prinstein, M. J. (2004). A functional approach to the assessment of self-mutilative behavior. *Journal of Consulting and Clinical Psychology, 72,* 885–890. http://dx.doi.org/10.1037/0022-006X.72.5.885

Nolen-Hoeksema, S., Wisco, B. E., & Lyubomirsky, S. (2008). Rethinking rumination. *Perspectives on Psychological Science, 3,* 400–424. http://dx.doi.org/10.1111/j.1745-6924.2008.00088.x

Novaco, R. W. (1975). *Anger control: The development and evaluation of an experimental treatment.* Lexington, MA: D. C. Heath.

Novaco, R. W., & Jarvis, K. L. (2002). Brief cognitive behavioral intervention for anger. In F. W. Bond & W. Dryden (Eds.), *Handbook for brief cognitive-behaviour therapy* (pp. 77–100). West Sussex, England: Wiley.

Ochsner, K. N., & Gross, J. J. (2013). The neural bases of emotion and emotion regulation: A valuation perspective. In J. J. Gross (Ed.), *Handbook of Emotion Regulation* (2nd ed., pp. 23–42). New York, NY: Guilford Press.

O'Donohue, W. (1998). Conditioning and third-generation behavior therapy. In W. O'Donohue (Ed.), *Learning and behavior therapy* (pp. 1–14). Boston, MA: Allyn and Bacon.

O'Donohue, W., & Krasner, L. (1995). *Handbook of psychological skills training: Clinical techniques and applications.* Needham Heights, MA: Allyn & Bacon.

Olatunji, B. O., Cisler, J. M., & Deacon, B. J. (2010). Efficacy of cognitive behavioral therapy for anxiety disorders: A review of meta-analytic findings. *Psychiatric*

Clinics of North America, 33, 557–577. http://dx.doi.org/10.1016/j.psc. 2010.04.002

O'Leary, K. D., & Wilson, G. T. (1987). *Behavior therapy: Application and outcome* (2nd ed.). Englewood Cliffs, NJ: Prentice Hall.

Olino, T. M., Klein, D. N., Dyson, M. W., Rose, S. A., & Durbin, C. E. (2010). Temperamental emotionality in preschool-aged children and depressive disorders in parents: Associations in a large community sample. *Journal of Abnormal Psychology, 119,* 468–478. http://dx.doi.org/10.1037/a0020112

Oliver, P. H., & Margolin, G. (2003). Communication/problem-solving skills training. In W. O'Donohue, J. E. Fisher, & S. C. Hayes (Eds.), *Cognitive behavior therapy: Applying empirically supported techniques in your practice* (pp. 96–102). Hoboken, NJ: Wiley.

Opriş, D., Pintea, S., García-Palacios, A., Botella, C., Szamosközi, Ş., & David, D. (2012). Virtual reality exposure therapy in anxiety disorders: A quantitative meta-analysis. *Depression and Anxiety, 29,* 85–93. http://dx.doi.org/10.1002/da.20910

Orobio de Castro, B., Veerman, J. W., Koops, W., Bosch, J. D., & Monshouwer, H. J. (2002). Hostile attribution of intent and aggressive behavior: A meta-analysis. *Child Development, 73,* 916–934. http://dx.doi.org/10.1111/1467-8624.00447

Otto, M. W., Reilly-Harrington, N. A., Kogan, J., & Winett, C. A. (2003). Treatment contracting in cognitive-behavior therapy. *Cognitive and Behavioral Practice, 10,* 199–203. http://dx.doi.org/10.1016/S1077-7229(03)80031-7

Otto, M. W., Safren, S. A., & Pollack, M. H. (2004). Internal cue exposure and the treatment of substance use disorders: Lessons from the treatment of panic disorder. *Journal of Anxiety Disorders, 18,* 69–87. http://dx.doi.org/10.1016/j. janxdis.2003.07.007

Pagoto, S., Bodenlos, J. S., Schneider, K. L., Olendzki, B., Spates, C. R., & Ma, Y. (2008). Initial investigation of behavioral activation therapy for co-morbid major depressive disorder and obesity. *Psychotherapy: Theory, Research, Practice, Training, 45,* 410–415. http://dx.doi.org/10.1037/a0013313

Panksepp, J. (2005). Affective consciousness: Core emotional feelings in animals and humans. *Consciousness and Cognition: An International Journal, 14,* 30–80. http:// dx.doi.org/10.1016/j.concog.2004.10.004

Paradise, L. V., Conway, B. S., & Zweig, J. (1986). Effects of expert and referent influence, physical attractiveness, and gender on perceptions of counselor attributes. *Journal of Counseling Psychology, 33,* 16–22. http://dx.doi.org/10.1037/0022-0167.33.1.16

Patterson, C. M., & Newman, J. P. (1993). Reflectivity and learning from aversive events: Toward a psychological mechanism for the syndromes of disinhibition. *Psychological Review, 100,* 716–736. http://dx.doi.org/10.1037/0033-295X.100.4.716

Patterson, G. R., DeBaryshe, B. D., & Ramsey, E. (1989). A developmental perspective on antisocial behavior. *American Psychologist, 44,* 329–335. http://dx.doi. org/10.1037/0003-066X.44.2.329

Patterson, G. R., & Hops, H. (1972). Coercion, a game for two: Intervention techniques for marital conflict. In R. Ulrich & P. Mountjoy (Eds.), *The experimental analysis of social behavior* (pp. 424–440). New York, NY: Appleton-Century-Crofts.

Pavlov, I. P. (1927). *Conditioned reflexes* (G. V. Anrep, Trans.). London, England: Oxford University Press.

Persons, J. B. (1989). *Cognitive therapy in practice: A case formulation approach*. New York, NY: Norton.

Persons, J. B., Roberts, N. A., Zalecki, C. A., & Brechwald, W. A. (2006). Naturalistic outcome of case formulation-driven cognitive-behavior therapy for anxious depressed outpatients. *Behaviour Research and Therapy, 44*, 1041–1051. http://dx.doi.org/10.1016/j.brat.2005.08.005

Persons, J. B., & Tompkins, M. A. (2007). Cognitive-behavioral case formulation. In T. D. Eells (Ed.), *Handbook of psychotherapy case formulation* (2nd ed., pp. 290–316). New York, NY: Guilford Press.

Petry, N. M., Alessi, S. M., & Rash, C. J. (2013). Contingency management treatments decrease psychiatric symptoms. *Journal of Consulting and Clinical Psychology, 81*, 926–931. http://dx.doi.org/10.1037/a0032499

Petry, N. M., Petrakis, I., Trevisan, L., Wiredu, G., Boutros, N. N., Martin, B., & Kosten, T. R. (2001). Contingency management interventions: From research to practice. *The American Journal of Psychiatry, 158*, 694–702. http://dx.doi.org/10.1176/appi.ajp.158.5.694

Phillips, L., & Zigler, E. (1961). Social competence: The action-thought parameter and vicariousness in normal and pathological behaviors. *The Journal of Abnormal and Social Psychology, 63*, 137–146. http://dx.doi.org/10.1037/h0040685

Poling, A., & Gaynor, S. (2003). Stimulus control. In W. O'Donohue, J. E. Fisher, & S. C. Hayes (Eds.), *Cognitive behavior therapy: Applying empirically supported techniques in your practice* (pp. 396–401). New York, NY: Wiley.

Powers, M. B., & Emmelkamp, P. M. G. (2008). Virtual reality exposure therapy for anxiety disorders: A meta-analysis. *Journal of Anxiety Disorders, 22*, 561–569. http://dx.doi.org/10.1016/j.janxdis.2007.04.006

Pratt, S., & Mueser, K. T. (2002). Social skills training for schizophrenia. In S. G. Hofmann & M. C. Tompson (Eds.), *Treating chronic and severe mental disorders: A handbook of empirically supported interventions* (pp. 18–52). New York, NY: Guilford Press.

Premack, D. (1959). Toward empirical behavior laws. I. Positive reinforcement. *Psychological Review, 66*, 219–233. http://dx.doi.org/10.1037/h0040891

Rachlin, H. (1976). *Introduction to modern behaviorism* (2nd ed.). San Francisco, CA: Freeman.

Radomsky, A. S., & Rachman, S. (2004). Symmetry, ordering and arranging compulsive behaviour. *Behaviour Research and Therapy, 42*, 893–913. http://dx.doi.org/10.1016/j.brat.2003.07.001

Rakos, R. F. (1991). *Assertive behavior: Theory, research, and training.* New York, NY: Routledge.

Rehm, L. P. (1979). A comparison of self-control and assertion skills treatments of depression. *Behavior Therapy, 10,* 429–442.

Reimherr, F. W., Marchant, B. K., Olsen, J. L., Wender, P. H., & Robison, R. J. (2013). Oppositional defiant disorder in adults with ADHD. *Journal of Attention Disorders, 17,* 102–113. http://dx.doi.org/10.1177/1087054711425774

Resick, P. A., & Schnicke, M. K. (1993). *Cognitive processing therapy for rape victims: A treatment manual.* Thousand Oaks, CA: Sage.

Rhee, S. H., Feigon, S. A., Bar, J. L., Hadeishi, Y., & Waldman, I. D. (2001). Behavior genetic approaches to the study of psychopathology. In P. B. Sutker & H. E. Adams (Eds.), *Comprehensive handbook of psychopathology* (3rd ed., pp. 53–84). New York, NY: Kluwer/Plenum.

Ritschel, L. A., Ramirez, C. L., Jones, M., & Craighead, W. E. (2011). Behavioral activation for depressed teens: A pilot study. *Cognitive and Behavioral Practice, 18,* 281–299. http://dx.doi.org/10.1016/j.cbpra.2010.07.002

Rizvi, S. L., & Linehan, M. M. (2005). The treatment of maladaptive shame in borderline personality disorder: A pilot study of "opposite action." *Cognitive and Behavioral Practice, 12,* 437–447. http://dx.doi.org/10.1016/S1077-7229 (05)80071-9

Robins, C. J., Schmidt, H., III, & Linehan, M. M. (2004). Dialectical behavior therapy: Synthesizing radical acceptance with skillful means. In S. C. Hayes, V. M. Follette, & M. M. Linehan (Eds.), *Mindfulness and acceptance: Expanding the cognitive-behavioral tradition* (pp. 30–44). New York, NY: Guilford Press.

Roemer, L., & Orsillo, S. M. (2002). Expanding our conceptualization of and treatment for generalized anxiety disorder: Integrating mindfulness/acceptance-based approaches with existing cognitive-behavioral models. *Clinical Psychology: Science and Practice, 9,* 54–68. http://dx.doi.org/10.1093/clipsy.9.1.54

Rohde, P., Feeny, N. C., & Robins, M. (2005). Characteristics and components of the TADS CBT approach. *Cognitive and Behavioral Practice, 12,* 186–197. http://dx.doi.org/10.1016/S1077-7229(05)80024-0

Rohde, P., Lewinsohn, P. M., Klein, D. N., Seeley, J. R., & Gau, J. M. (2013). Key characteristics of major depressive disorder occurring in childhood, adolescence, emerging adulthood, and adulthood. *Clinical Psychological Science, 1,* 41–53. http://dx.doi.org/10.1177/2167702612457599

Rohsenow, D. J., Monti, P. M., Rubonis, A. V., Gulliver, S. B., Colby, S. M., Binkoff, J. A., & Abrams, D. B. (2001). Cue exposure with coping skills training and communication skills training for alcohol dependence: 6- and 12-month outcomes. *Addiction, 96,* 1161–1174. http://dx.doi.org/10.1046/j.1360-0443.2001.96811619.x

Roth, T. L., & Sweatt, J. D. (2011). Annual research review: Epigenetic mechanisms and environmental shaping of the brain during sensitive periods of development.

Journal of Child Psychology and Psychiatry, 52, 398–408. http://dx.doi.org/10.1111/j.1469-7610.2010.02282.x

Rouf, K., Fennell, M., Westbrook, D., Cooper, M., & Bennett-Levy, J. (2004). Devising effective behavioural experiments. In J. Bennett-Levy, G. Butler, M. Fennell, A. Hackmann, M. Mueller, & D. Westbrook (Eds.), *Oxford guide to behavioural experiments in cognitive therapy* (pp. 21–58). Oxford, England: Oxford University Press.

Røysamb, E., Kendler, K. S., Tambs, K., Orstavik, R. E., Neale, M. C., Aggen, S. H., . . . Reichborn-Kjennerud, T. (2011). The joint structure of DSM–IV Axis I and Axis II disorders. *Journal of Abnormal Psychology, 120,* 198–209. http://dx.doi.org/10.1037/a0021660

Rusby, J. C., Westling, E., Crowley, R., & Light, J. M. (2013). Concurrent and predictive associations between early adolescent perceptions of peer affiliates and mood states collected in real time via ecological momentary assessment methodology. *Psychological Assessment, 25,* 47–60. http://dx.doi.org/10.1037/a0030393

Sacco, W. P., & Beck, A. T. (1995). Cognitive theory and therapy. In E. E. Beckham & W. R. Leber (Eds.), *Handbook of depression* (2nd ed., pp. 329–351). New York, NY: Guilford Press.

Saini, M. (2009). A meta-analysis of the psychological treatment of anger: Developing guidelines for evidence-based practice. *Journal of the American Academy of Psychiatry and the Law, 37,* 473–488.

Salkovskis, P. (1991). The importance of behaviour in the maintenance of anxiety and panic: A cognitive account. *Behavioural Psychotherapy, 19,* 6–19. http://dx.doi.org/10.1017/S0141347300011472

Salkovskis, P. M. (1996). The cognitive approach to anxiety: Threat beliefs, safety-seeking behavior and the special case of health anxiety and obsessions. In P. M. Salkovskis (Ed.), *Frontiers of cognitive therapy* (pp. 48–74). New York, NY: Guilford Press.

Salter, A. (1949). *Conditioned reflex therapy.* New York, NY: Creative Age Press.

Sanchez, V., & Lewinsohn, P. M. (1980). Assertive behavior and depression. *Journal of Consulting and Clinical Psychology, 48,* 119–120. http://dx.doi.org/10.1037/0022-006X.48.1.119

Santiago-Rivera, A., Kanter, J., Benson, G., Derose, T., Illes, R., & Reyes, W. (2008). Behavioral activation as an alternative treatment approach for Latinos with depression. *Psychotherapy: Theory, Research, Practice, Training, 45,* 173–185. http://dx.doi.org/10.1037/0033-3204.45.2.173

Schlinger, H. D., Jr. (1993). Separating discriminative and function-altering effects of verbal stimuli. *The Behavior Analyst, 16,* 9–23.

Schneider, S. M. (2012). *The science of consequences.* Amherst, NY: Prometheus Books.

Schunk, D. H., & Hanson, A. R. (1985). Peer models: Influence on children's self-efficacy and achievement. *Journal of Educational Psychology, 77,* 313–322. http://dx.doi.org/10.1037/0022-0663.77.3.313

Scourfield, J., John, B., Martin, N., & McGuffin, P. (2004). The development of prosocial behaviour in children and adolescents: A twin study. *Journal of Child Psychology and Psychiatry, 45*, 927–935. http://dx.doi.org/10.1111/j.1469-7610.2004.t01-1-00286.x

Seeley, J. R., Kosty, D. B., Farmer, R. F., & Lewinsohn, P. M. (2011). The modeling of internalizing disorders on the basis of patterns of lifetime comorbidity: Associations with psychosocial functioning and psychiatric disorders among first-degree relatives. *Journal of Abnormal Psychology, 120*, 308–321. http://dx.doi.org/10.1037/a0022621

Segal, Z. V., Williams, J. M. G., & Teasdale, J. D. (2002). *Mindfulness based cognitive therapy for depression: A new approach to preventing relapse*. New York, NY: Guilford Press.

Seidler, G. H., & Wagner, F. E. (2006). Comparing the efficacy of EMDR and trauma-focused cognitive-behavioral therapy in the treatment of PTSD: A meta-analytic study. *Psychological Medicine, 36*, 1515–1522. http://dx.doi.org/10.1017/S0033291706007963

Sheeber, L., Hops, H., Alpert, A., Davis, B., & Andrews, J. (1997). Family support and conflict: Prospective relations to adolescent depression. *Journal of Abnormal Child Psychology, 25*, 333–344. http://dx.doi.org/10.1023/A:1025768504415

Shipley, R. H., & Boudewyns, P. A. (1980). Flooding and implosive therapy: Are they harmful? *Behavior Therapy, 11*, 503–508. http://dx.doi.org/10.1016/S0005-7894(80)80066-9

Siev, J., & Chambless, D. L. (2007). Specificity of treatment effects: Cognitive therapy and relaxation for generalized anxiety and panic disorders. *Journal of Consulting and Clinical Psychology, 75*, 513–522. http://dx.doi.org/10.1037/0022-006X.75.4.513

Simon, N. M., Blacker, D., Korbly, N. B., Sharma, S. G., Worthington, J. J., Otto, M. W., & Pollack, M. H. (2002). Hypothyroidism and hyperthyroidism in anxiety disorders revisited: New data and literature review. *Journal of Affective Disorders, 69*, 209–217. http://dx.doi.org/10.1016/S0165-0327(01)00378-0

Simons, A. D., Rohde, P., Kennard, B. D., & Robins, M. (2005). Relapse and recurrence prevention in the Treatment of Adolescents with Depression Study. *Cognitive and Behavioral Practice, 12*, 240–251. http://dx.doi.org/10.1016/S1077-7229(05)80029-X

Sitharthan, T., Sitharthan, G., Hough, M. J., & Kavanagh, D. J. (1997). Cue exposure in moderation drinking: A comparison with cognitive-behavior therapy. *Journal of Consulting and Clinical Psychology, 65*, 878–882. http://dx.doi.org/10.1037/0022-006X.65.5.878

Skinner, B. F. (1938). *The behavior of organisms: An experimental analysis*. New York, NY: Appleton-Century-Crofts.

Skinner, B. F. (1969). *Contingencies of reinforcement: A theoretical analysis*. New York, NY: Appleton-Century-Crofts.

Skinner, B. F. (1971). *Beyond freedom and dignity*. New York, NY: Knopf.

Skinner, B. F. (1981). Selection by consequences. *Science, 213*, 501–504. http://dx.doi.org/10.1126/science.7244649

Skinner, B. F. (1989). *Recent issues in the analysis of behavior*. Columbus, OH: Merrill.

Sledge, W. H., Moras, K., Hartley, D., & Levine, M. (1990). Effect of time-limited psychotherapy on patient dropout rates. *The American Journal of Psychiatry, 147*, 1341–1347. http://dx.doi.org/10.1176/ajp.147.10.1341

Smits, J. A. J., Rosenfield, D., McDonald, R., & Telch, M. J. (2006). Cognitive mechanisms of social anxiety reduction: An examination of specificity and temporality. *Journal of Consulting and Clinical Psychology, 74*, 1203–1212. http://dx.doi.org/10.1037/0022-006X.74.6.1203

Snarski, M., Scogin, F., DiNapoli, E., Presnell, A., McAlpine, J., & Marcinak, J. (2011). The effects of behavioral activation therapy with inpatient geriatric psychiatry patients. *Behavior Therapy, 42*, 100–108. http://dx.doi.org/10.1016/j.beth.2010.05.001

Sobell, L. C., & Sobell, M. B. (2003). Using motivational interviewing techniques to talk with clients about their alcohol use. *Cognitive and Behavioral Practice, 10*, 214–221. http://dx.doi.org/10.1016/S1077-7229(03)80033-0

Spanier, G. B. (1976). Measuring dyadic adjustment: New scales for assessing quality of marriage and similar dyads. *Journal of Marriage and Family, 38*, 15–28. http://dx.doi.org/10.2307/350547

Spiegler, M. D., & Guevremont, D. C. (2010). *Contemporary behavior therapy* (5th ed.). Belmont, CA: Wadsworth.

Spielberger, C. D., & DeNike, L. D. (1966). Descriptive behaviorism versus cognitive theory in verbal operant conditioning. *Psychological Review, 73*, 306–326. http://dx.doi.org/10.1037/h0023454

Spielberger, C. D., Gorsuch, R. L., Lushene, R., Vagg, P., & Jacobs, G. (1983). *Manual for the State-Trait Anxiety Inventory (Form Y)*. Palo Alto, CA: Consulting Psychologists Press.

Steketee, G. S. (1993). *Treatment of obsessive compulsive disorder*. New York, NY: Guilford Press.

Stice, E., Ragan, J., & Randall, P. (2004). Prospective relations between social support and depression: Differential direction of effects for parent and peer support? *Journal of Abnormal Psychology, 113*, 155–159.

Strupp, H. H., & Binder, J. L. (1984). *Psychotherapy in a new key: A guide to time limited dynamic therapy*. New York, NY: Basic Books.

Sturmey, P. (1996). *Functional analysis in clinical psychology*. New York, NY: Wiley.

Sturmey, P. (2008). *Behavioral case formulation and intervention: A functional analytic approach*. http://dx.doi.org/10.1002/9780470773192

Sturmey, P. (2009). Behavioral activation is an evidence-based treatment for depression. *Behavior Modification, 33*, 818–829. http://dx.doi.org/10.1177/0145445509350094

Sukhodolsky, D. G., Kassinove, H., & Gorman, B. S. (2004). Cognitive-behavioral therapy for anger in children and adolescents: A meta-analysis. *Aggression and Violent Behavior, 9,* 247–269. http://dx.doi.org/10.1016/j.avb.2003.08.005

Swift, J. K., & Greenberg, R. P. (2012). Premature discontinuation in adult psychotherapy: A meta-analysis. *Journal of Consulting and Clinical Psychology, 80,* 547–559. http://dx.doi.org/10.1037/a0028226

Sylvain, C., Ladouceur, R., & Boisvert, J.-M. (1997). Cognitive and behavioral treatment of pathological gambling: A controlled study. *Journal of Consulting and Clinical Psychology, 65,* 727–732.

Tabakoff, B., & Hoffman, P. L. (1988). A neurobiological theory of alcoholism. In C. D. Chaudron & D. A. Wilkinson (Eds.), *Theories on alcoholism* (pp. 29–72). Toronto, Ontario, Canada: Addiction Research Foundation.

Tafrate, R. C., & Kassinove, H. (1998). Anger control in men: Barb exposure with rational, irrational, and irrelevant self-statements. *Journal of Cognitive Psychotherapy, 12,* 187–211.

Tallis, F., Eysenck, M. W., & Mathews, A. (1992). A questionnaire for the measurement of nonpathological worry. *Personality and Individual Differences, 13,* 161–168. http://dx.doi.org/10.1016/0191-8869(92)90038-Q

Tarrier, N., & Calam, R. (2002). New developments in cognitive-behavioural case formulation. Epidemiological, systemic, and social context: An integrative approach. *Behavioural and Cognitive Psychotherapy, 30,* 311–328. http://dx.doi.org/10.1017/S1352465802003065

Thomaes, K., Dorrepaal, E., Draijer, N., Jansma, E. P., Veltman, D. J., & van Balkom, A. J. (2014). Can pharmacological and psychological treatment change brain structure and function in PTSD? A systematic review. *Journal of Psychiatric Research, 50,* 1–15.

Thorndike, E. L. (1898). Animal intelligence. *Psychological Review Monograph Supplement, 2* (4, Whole No. 8).

Thorpe, G. L., McMillan, E., Owings, L. R., & Dawson, R. (2008). Behavior therapy and termination. In W. O'Donohue & M. A. Cucciare (Eds.), *Terminating psychotherapy: A clinician's guide* (pp. 229–249). New York, NY: Routledge.

Todd, J. T., & Morris, E. K. (1983). Misconception and miseducation: Presentations of radical behaviorism in psychology textbooks. *The Behavior Analyst, 6,* 153–160.

Tolin, D. F. (2010). Is cognitive-behavioral therapy more effective than other therapies? A meta-analytic review. *Clinical Psychology Review, 30,* 710–720. http://dx.doi.org/10.1016/j.cpr.2010.05.003

Tompson, M. C., Pierre, C. B., Boger, K. D., McKowen, J. W., Chan, P. T., & Freed, R. D. (2010). Maternal depression, maternal expressed emotion, and youth psychopathology. *Journal of Abnormal Child Psychology, 38,* 105–117. http://dx.doi.org/10.1007/s10802-009-9349-6

Toro, J., Cervera, M., Feliu, M. H., Garriga, N., Jou, M., Martinez, E., & Toro, E. (2003). Cue exposure in the treatment of resistant bulimia nervosa. *International Journal of Eating Disorders, 34*, 227–234. http://dx.doi.org/10.1002/eat.10186

Treadway, M. T., Bossaller, N. A., Shelton, R. C., & Zald, D. H. (2012). Effort-based decision-making in major depressive disorder: A translational model of motivational anhedonia. *Journal of Abnormal Psychology, 121*, 553–558. http://dx.doi.org/10.1037/a0028813

Trew, J. L. (2011). Exploring the roles of approach and avoidance in depression: An integrative model. *Clinical Psychology Review, 31*, 1156–1168. http://dx.doi.org/10.1016/j.cpr.2011.07.007

Trull, T. J., Solhan, M. B., Tragesser, S. L., Jahng, S., Wood, P. K., Piasecki, T. M., & Watson, D. (2008). Affective instability: Measuring a core feature of borderline personality disorder with ecological momentary assessment. *Journal of Abnormal Psychology, 117*, 647–661. http://dx.doi.org/10.1037/a0012532

Turner, B. J., Chapman, A. L., & Layden, B. K. (2012). Intrapersonal and interpersonal functions of non-suicidal self-injury: Associations with emotional and social functioning. *Suicide and Life-Threatening Behavior, 42*, 36–55. http://dx.doi.org/10.1111/j.1943-278X.2011.00069.x

Twohig, M. P., Masuda, A., Varra, A. A., & Hayes, S. C. (2005). Acceptance and commitment therapy as a treatment for anxiety disorders. In S. M. Orsillo & L. Roemer (Eds.), *Acceptance and mindfulness-based approaches to anxiety: Conceptualization and treatment* (pp. 101–129). http://dx.doi.org/10.1007/0-387-25989-9_4

Uchino, B. N. (2006). Social support and health: A review of physiological processes potentially underlying links to disease outcomes. *Journal of Behavioral Medicine, 29*, 377–387. http://dx.doi.org/10.1007/s10865-006-9056-5

Ullmann, L. P., & Krasner, L. (Eds.). (1965). *Case studies in behavior modification.* New York, NY: Holt, Rinehart, & Winston.

Upper, D., & Cautela, J. R. (1979). *Covert conditioning.* New York, NY: Pergamon Press.

Van Brunt, D. L. (2000). Modular cognitive-behavioral therapy: Dismantling validated treatment programs into self-standing treatment plan objectives. *Cognitive and Behavioral Practice, 7*, 156–165. http://dx.doi.org/10.1016/S1077-7229(00)80026-7

van der Gaag, C., Minderaa, R. B., & Keysers, C. (2007). Facial expressions: What the mirror neuron system can and cannot tell us. *Social Neuroscience, 2*, 179–222. http://dx.doi.org/10.1080/17470910701376878

Vitousek, K., Watson, S., & Wilson, G. T. (1998). Enhancing motivation for change in treatment-resistant eating disorders. *Clinical Psychology Review, 18*, 391–420. http://dx.doi.org/10.1016/S0272-7358(98)00012-9

Vittengl, J. R., Clark, L. A., Dunn, T. W., & Jarrett, R. B. (2007). Reducing relapse and recurrence in unipolar depression: A comparative meta-analysis of cognitive-behavioral therapy's effects. *Journal of Consulting and Clinical Psychology, 75*, 475–488. http://dx.doi.org/10.1037/0022-006X.75.3.475

Vohs, K. D., & Baumeister, R. F. (2004). Understanding self-regulation: An introduction. In R. F. Baumeister & K. D. Vohs (Eds.), *Handbook of self-regulation: Research, theory, and applications* (pp. 1–9). New York, NY: Guilford Press.

Vollmer, T. R., & Wright, C. S. (2003). Noncontingent reinforcement as treatment for problem behavior. In W. O'Donohue, J. E. Fisher, & S. C. Hayes (Eds.), *Cognitive behavior therapy: Applying empirically supported techniques in your practice* (pp. 266–272). Hoboken, NJ: Wiley.

Wagner, A. W., Zatzick, D. F., Ghesquiere, A., & Jurkovich, G. J. (2007). Behavioral activation as an early intervention for posttraumatic stress disorder and depression among physically injured trauma survivors. *Cognitive and Behavioral Practice, 14*, 341–349. http://dx.doi.org/10.1016/j.cbpra.2006.05.002

Wallace, M. D., & Robles, A. C. (2003). Differential reinforcement of other behavior and differential reinforcement of alternative behavior. In W. O'Donohue, J. E. Fisher, & S. C. Hayes (Eds.), *Cognitive behavior therapy: Applying empirically supported techniques in your practice* (pp. 136–143). New York, NY: Wiley.

Watson, D. (2000). *Mood and temperament.* New York, NY: Guilford Press.

Watson, D. (2009). Differentiating the mood and anxiety disorders: A quadripartite model. *Annual Review of Clinical Psychology, 5*, 221–247. http://dx.doi.org/10.1146/annurev.clinpsy.032408.153510

Weiner, I. B. (1975). *Principles of psychotherapy.* New York, NY: Wiley.

Widiger, T. A. (2011). A shaky future for personality disorders. *Personality Disorders: Theory, Research, and Treatment, 2*, 54–67. http://dx.doi.org/10.1037/a0021855

Wilson, G. T., & Davison, G. C. (1971). Processes of fear reduction in systematic desensitization: Animal studies. *Psychological Bulletin, 76*, 1–14. http://dx.doi.org/10.1037/h0031480

Witkiewitz, K., King, K., McMahon, R. J., Wu, J., Luk, J., Bierman, K. L., . . . & Conduct Problems Prevention Research Group. (2013). Evidence for a multi-dimensional latent structural model of externalizing disorders. *Journal of Abnormal Child Psychology, 41*, 223–237. http://dx.doi.org/10.1007/s10802-012-9674-z

Wlazlo, Z., Schroeder-Hartwig, K., Hand, I., Kaiser, G., & Münchau, N. (1990). Exposure in vivo vs. social skills training for social phobia: Long-term outcome and differential effects. *Behaviour Research and Therapy, 28*, 181–193. http://dx.doi.org/10.1016/0005-7967(90)90001-Y

Wolpe, J. (1958). *Psychotherapy by reciprocal inhibition.* Palo Alto, CA: Stanford University Press.

Wolpe, J., & Lazarus, A. A. (1966). *Behavior therapy techniques.* New York, NY: Pergamon Press.

Wolpe, J., & Turkat, I. D. (1985). Behavioral formulation of clinical cases. In I. D. Turkat (Ed.), *Behavioral case formulation* (pp. 5–36). http://dx.doi.org/10.1007/978-1-4899-3644-8_2

World Health Organization. (1991). *International Classification of Diseases (ICD–10)*. Geneva, Switzerland: Author.

Wulfert, E., Greenway, D. E., & Dougher, M. J. (1996). A logical functional analysis of reinforcement-based disorders: Alcoholism and pedophilia. *Journal of Consulting and Clinical Psychology, 64,* 1140–1151. http://dx.doi.org/10.1037/0022-006X.64.6.1140

Yon, A., & Scogin, F. (2008). Behavioral activation as a treatment for geriatric depression. *Clinical Gerontologist: The Journal of Aging and Mental Health, 32,* 91–103. http://dx.doi.org/10.1080/07317110802478016

Young, J. E., Rygh, J. L., Weinberger, A. D., & Beck, A. T. (2014). Cognitive therapy for depression. In D. H. Barlow (Ed.), *Clinical handbook of psychological disorders: A step-by-step treatment manual* (5th ed., pp. 275–331). New York, NY: Guilford Press.

Young, J. F., Mufson, L., & Gallop, R. (2010). Preventing depression: A randomized trial of interpersonal psychotherapy-adolescent skills training. *Depression and Anxiety, 27,* 426–433. http://dx.doi.org/10.1002/da.20664

Younggren, J. N., & Gottlieb, M. C. (2008). Termination and abandonment: History, risk, and risk management. *Professional Psychology: Research and Practice, 39,* 498–504. http://dx.doi.org/10.1037/0735-7028.39.5.498

Zanarini, M. C., Williams, A. A., Lewis, R. E., Reich, R. B., Vera, S. C., Marino, M. F., . . . Frankenburg, F. R. (1997). Reported pathological childhood experiences associated with the development of borderline personality disorder. *The American Journal of Psychiatry, 154,* 1101–1106. http://dx.doi.org/10.1176/ajp.154.8.1101

Zimbardo, P. G., & Gerrig, R. J. (1996). *Psychology and life* (14th ed.). New York, NY: HarperCollins.

Zimmerman, B. J., & Koussa, R. (1979). Social influences on children's toy preferences: Effects of model rewardingness and affect. *Contemporary Educational Psychology, 4,* 55–66. http://dx.doi.org/10.1016/0361-476X(79)90027-4

Zvolensky, M. J., & Smits, J. A. J. (Eds.). (2010). *Anxiety in health behaviors and physical illness*. New York, NY: Springer.

INDEX

Behavioral assessments, 21–51
  behavioral repertoires and skills
      deficits in, 28–29
  client-therapist relationship in,
      24–25
  common features among, 8–11
  core features of, 22–24
  with direct observation, 48–49
  evaluation of coping behaviors in,
      29–30
  in exposure-based interventions,
      280–284
  functional analysis in, 36, 38–47
  of functional impairment, 31–35
  of interpersonal effectiveness,
      200–206
  interviews in, 35–38, 50
  outcomes with, 361
  presenting problems and complaints
      in, 26–27
  and self-monitoring, 48
  and skills training, 178–180
  tools in, 27–28
Behavioral Avoidance Test (BAT), 97
Behavioral case formulation, 53–69. See
      also Treatment planning
  assessing client's needs in, 54–55
  assumptions in, 59–60
  client case example, 87–98
  defined, 26
  general framework for, 60–68
  narrowing client problem areas in,
      55–58
  problem formation with client in,
      68–69
  steps in, 99
Behavioral chains, 223
Behavioral contingency, 102
Behavioral contracting, 130–131, 159
Behavioral deficits, 29, 57, 78–79, 178
Behavioral excesses, 218–234
  and anger management, 218–226
  assessment of, 10, 28–29
  coercive, oppositional, and defiant
      behaviors, 226–232
  covert sensitization for, 127
  dependency-related behaviors,
      232–234
  identification of, 57
  reinforcement of, 41

Behavioral experiments, 137–143, 151,
      257–260, 347
Behavioral inertia, 78
Behavioral inhibition, 79
Behavioral interventions. See also
      specific interventions
  common features among, 11–12
  outcomes with, 361
  overview, 5–12
  selection of, 57–58, 74–80
Behavioral repertoires
  benefits of, 72
  defined, 10
  in depression, 248–249
  identification of, 28–29
Behaviorism, 6. See also Cognitive
      behavior therapy
Behavior modification, 6, 16. See also
      Cognitive behavior therapy
Behavior therapy. See also Cognitive
      behavior therapy
  emergence of, 15–16
  overview, 6
Behaviour Research and Therapy
      (journal), 15–16
Bennett-Levy, J., 138
Benson, L. A., 230
Between-session activities (homework),
      82–83, 192–194
Biglan, A., 235
Binge eating, 39, 41, 109–110, 367. See
      also Eating disorders
Biological origins of problems, 66
Biological therapies, 9
Bipolar disorder, 226, 302
Black-or-white thinking, 148
Body dysmorphic disorder, 140
"Booster sessions" (continuous care),
      356, 366, 367, 374
Borderline personality disorder (BPD),
      44, 174, 248, 310
Borkovec, T. D., 159
Breathing skills, 173
Bulimia nervosa, 44, 367
"Burning bridges" strategy, 108–109

Caffeine intoxications, 34
Capabilities, client, 175–176. See also
      Skills training
Carpenter, K. M., 80, 81

Positive self-expressions, 211
Posttraumatic stress disorder (PTSD)
    anger dysregulation with, 219
    behavioral activation therapy for, 248
    exposure interventions for, 272–273,
        284, 286, 292
    generalization of cues, 112
    skills building interventions for, 173
Premature therapy discontinuation,
    358–359
Presenting problems and complaints,
    26–27
Primary assumptions, 65
Proactive aggression, 220
Problem behaviors. *See also* Behavioral
        case formulation
    and absence of effective behaviors, 60
    exploration of, with clients, 68–69
    generating list of, 62–63
    high-risk, 72–74
    intervention selection for, 74–77
    narrowing down areas of, 55–58
    pointing out, 71
    rule generation for inhibiting,
        158–159
Problem solving, 30, 212–214,
    257–260, 317
Procrastination, 261
Proficiencies. *See* Skills training
Progressive muscle relaxation, 173
Prolonged exposure, 173, 272–273, 284,
    286, 293
Prompting events, 337
Psychodynamic models
    assumptions in, 5
    features of, 8–9
Psychoeducation
    about reinforcement, 107
    in anger management interventions,
        222
    developing new behavior patterns
        with, 371
    on emotions, 311–314
Psychological testing, 67–68
Psychopathology
    diathesis-stress model of, 134
    genetics' role in, 44, 66
    perspectives on, 5–6
PTSD. *See* Posttraumatic stress disorder
Public speaking, 40, 271, 287, 318

Punishment
    in contingency management, 106,
        115, 118
    and depression, 249
    with discriminant stimuli, 38–39
    and emotion regulation, 308
    negative, 42, 128–129
    positive, 42, 127
    rules governing, 40
    of social behaviors, 207
    in therapy, 345

Quality of life, 34, 73
Questionnaires, 28, 56, 64

Radically open dialectical behavior
        therapy (RO-DBT), 310
Random support calls, 113–114
RCPR (response-contingent positive
        reinforcement), 42, 248–249
Reactive aggression, 220
Reciprocal inhibition, 15
Recurrence, 266–267, 363, 367–374
Reflection (communication skills
        building), 210
Reinforcement, 115–129
    of adaptive behaviors, 119–120
    during client crises, 344
    and consequences of behavior,
        40–43
    decreasing and weakening behaviors
        with, 124–129
    for desired behaviors occurring at
        low rates, 122–124
    with discriminant stimuli, 38–39
    effects of, 106
    and externalizing disorders, 226–227
    in four-function model of
        nonsuicidal self-injury, 306
    for interpersonal effectiveness,
        200–201, 241–242
    and positive punishment
        procedures, 127
    prevention of, 117–119
    psychoeducation about, 107
    in regular routines, 267
    and shaping, 120–122
    in skills building, 177
    in skills training, 191–192
    from social environment, 241–242

ABOUT THE AUTHORS

Richard F. Farmer, PhD, is a licensed psychologist and research scientist currently affiliated with the Oregon Research Institute in Eugene, Oregon. After completing an internship at Duke University Medical Center in Durham, North Carolina, he earned a doctorate degree in clinical psychology from the University of North Carolina at Greensboro. Since then, he has served as an associate professor of psychology at Idaho State University and East Carolina University and as a senior lecturer in psychology at the University of Canterbury in Christchurch, New Zealand. Dr. Farmer's main areas of research and clinical interest include behavioral assessment and therapy, emotional and behavioral disorders over the life span, impulsivity, and substance use disorders.

Alexander L. Chapman, PhD, RPsych, is a registered psychologist, an associate professor, and coordinator of the clinical science area in the department of psychology at Simon Fraser University in Burnaby, British Columbia, Canada, and the president of the DBT Centre of Vancouver. Dr. Chapman received his BA from the University of British Columbia in Vancouver, British Columbia, Canada and his MS and PhD in clinical psychology from Idaho

State University in Pocatello after an internship at Duke University Medical Center in Durham, North Carolina. He completed a 2-year postdoctoral fellowship with Dr. Marsha Linehan (founder of dialectical behavior therapy) at the University of Washington in Seattle. Dr. Chapman directs the Personality and Emotion Research Laboratory at Simon Fraser University, where he studies the role of emotion regulation in borderline personality disorder, self-harm, impulsivity, and other behavioral problems. He has coauthored six books and published numerous scientific articles and chapters on these and other topics and has given many scientific conference presentations on his research. He regularly gives local, national, and international workshops and invited talks on dialectical behavior therapy and the treatment of borderline personality disorder; has consulted with and trained clinicians in Canada, the United States, and the United Kingdom; and trains and supervises clinical psychology students. He has received the Young Investigator's Award of the National Education Alliance for Borderline Personality Disorder (2007), the Canadian Psychological Association's (CPA) Early Career Scientist Practitioner Award (2011), and an 8-year Career Investigator Award from the Michael Smith Foundation for Health Research.